Books are to be

WARFARE
IN THE ANCIENT WORLD

WARFARE
IN THE ANCIENT WORLD

Edited and Introduced by General Sir John Hackett

First published in Great Britain in 1989
by Sidgwick & Jackson Limited

Copyright © 1989 by Sidgwick & Jackson Limited
Colour artwork copyright © 1989 by Peter Connolly

Maps and diagrams by Jerry Goldie
Picture research by Charlotte Deane

ISBN 0-283-99591-2

Printed in West Germany

For Sidgwick & Jackson Limited
1 Tavistock Chambers,
Bloomsbury Way, London WC1A 2SG

CONTENTS

INTRODUCTION

GENERAL SIR JOHN HACKETT

Why is reflection on warfare in ancient times generating such interest today? What can Tiglath-pileser III, Alexander the Great, Scipio Africanus, Hannibal, and others of their kind, whose actions did so much to shape the world they lived in, mean to us, living in a world so very different? Fear of war is felt in these times everywhere, fuelled by the conviction that modern technology has brought us to a point where the unlimited use by great powers of the weapons of war now available to them could threaten the survival of humanity. Another notable feature of the world we live in is a great and growing interest in the past. This feeds on a general level of awareness higher today, in an age of advanced communications, than ever before and on the increasing volume of material heard, seen and read, now available to satisfy widespread and increasing curiosity about origins and development in the structure of our societies.

One of the clearest conclusions emerging from a study of the distant past is that human nature, in all the time of which we have record of it, has changed very little, if at all. Given the acceptance of continuity in the pattern of human behaviour, an inevitable result of the convergence of two tendencies, fear of war and interest in the past, has been a thirst for more information about the making of war in earlier times, not only in terms of tools, techniques and methods used in warfare, but also of the people by whom wars are and have been fought and how men have set about the business of preparing for and fighting in them.

Vestigial evidence from the remoter reaches of prehistory, when written records were sparse or non-existent, shows us orderly groups of men, apparently operating under unified command, advancing in column to attack other humans, for which purpose they will deploy from column into line. Spanish rock painting of the late Paleolithic period has clear, though by no means unique, illustration of this practice as also of rudimentary tactical procedures in the engagement itself, such as combining the penetration of a line of enemies with their envelopment. In the actual fighting there was to be, from the Paleolithic period onwards, dependence for a very long time on a combination of crushing weapons (clubs or maces) with slings and hand-thrown javelins (also of some use for thrusting) and a short stabbing weapon like a dagger. The general introduction around the Mediterranean basin and in Africa and the Near East of the bow, of simple wooden or composite construction, would follow, with spears in a variety of forms, a thrusting and slashing sword as soon as the developing use of metals allowed, the growing application of protective armour and the spread of animal mobility.

Patterns of human behaviour remain much the same as they always have been, in war as in peace. Man's cleverness has now, however, brought him into a position of great danger. Since the time of Napoleon, warfare has once again moved towards the totality which was the rule in the remote past. Often in quite recent times great powers have been in a prolonged state of war of which the average person, other than those actually under arms, or their families and close associates, and any not actually fighting but concerned with the management of operations, would be scarcely aware.

From the formation of the Grand Alliance in 1689, and England's declaration of war on France in what has been described as the opening of the second Hundred Years War, through the dynastic and colonial wars of the

opposite
A bronze of a Greek hoplite on horseback, wearing a Corinthian helmet, of the 6th century BC. British Museum, London.

18th century until the Treaty of Paris in 1763 brought the Seven Years War to an end, the great powers in Europe were almost constantly in conflict. Their armies, and consequently their aims, were limited by shortage of materials and, even more, of manpower which could not safely be withdrawn from agriculture. England was almost always at war, usually with France. Yet Laurence Sterne, wishing to travel in France in 1762, towards the end of the Seven Years War, but having no passport, was said to have been given one by the French Foreign Minister himself in Versailles, with the words 'Un homme qui rit ne sera jamais dangereux'. Such were the limited wars of the Enlightenment.

Today major war once more demands total commitment: every member of a nation state at war is in some way and to some degree affected by it. Moreover, the high lethality, huge destructiveness and soaring cost of modern weapon systems, particularly in the non-nuclear field, and the urgent need to find effective means of limiting the damage they can do, now provides one of the most pressing preoccupations of government.

Neither total war between states nor total destruction as the penalty of defeat is new. Sparta's Messenian wars and the early struggle for Rome's survival in the Italian peninsula are only two examples of warfare in which failure would have meant extinction. Carthage failed, and after the last Punic War was totally destroyed. What is new today is the possibility of total destruction not for a few thousand citizens in a city-state but for millions in whole continents. This is a matter of degree, however, not kind. Great wars of antiquity may have involved smaller communities and fewer than would be the case today, but what is probably the most outstanding example of such wars, that between Athens and Sparta and their allies from 431 to 404 BC, the Peloponnesian War, can hardly be described as anything but total. The Athenian decision in 421 to execute all male citizens of rebellious Mytilene, subsequently mitigated to the killing of a thousand of them, or the punishment of Melos for neutrality in 416 by the massacre of all its men and the enslavement of the rest of the population, and the deliberate Spartan destuction of Corcyra, gave something of a foretaste of what could happen in the distant future, in quite different circumstances, in Hamburg, Dresden and Hiroshima. The obliteration of Carthage by the Romans in 146 BC remains one of the best-known and most dramatic of penalties for failure in war. Less dramatic but of more far-reaching consequence was the result of the long drawn-out agony of the great Peloponnesian War itself, in which Sparta's costly victory left her greatly weakened and Athens, the most advanced and civilized and, at the peak of her maritime empire, the most powerful of Greek city-states, reduced to impotence.

The first great military empire of which we have much certain knowledge was that of Assyria. The huge Assyrian army, 100-200,000 strong, dominated the ancient Near East for some 300 years from about 900 BC. It was made up of many different types of units – spearmen, archers, slingers, light infantry, engineers and, above all, horsed troops either individually mounted or riding in chariots – of many different racial origins, gathered into a military organization whose flexibility and efficiency in battle (greatly assisted by the recent introduction of iron technology) had been hitherto unequalled. The Assyrian military empire owed much to outstanding commanders and military innovators in Tiglath-pileser III (745-727 BC) and Sargon II (725-721 BC) but in time outgrew its resources and its command structure and developed weaknesses which allowed it to fall apart. Its successor, the Persian empire, soon to be dominant after the fall of Nineveh to the Medes and Babylonians in 612, deployed an army which was tactically well co-ordinated on the battlefield but retained persistent ethnic and local differences.

A friend and literary collaborator of mine who, as a regular officer in the army of the USSR, commanded a motor rifle company in the invasion of Czechoslovakia in 1968, told me something of his difficulties when ordered to mobilize his command for this operation, and to take in a quota of reservist soldiery. They could come from almost anywhere – Uzbekhs, Azerbaijanis, Kirghiz, Tadzhiks, Turkmen, different sorts of Balts, Armenians, and even possibly a few Ukrainians and Russians. Few actually spoke Russian and most were unable to communicate with one another, let alone with their NCOs and officers. To put these through refresher courses on weapons they had last seen years before, after little more than a brief acquaintance with them even then, had its problems.

The Assyrian army, though with less complex weapon systems, knew such problems well and sought to ease them by the incorporation of local contingents just as they came in, with the weapons, style of fighting and way of life – no less than the languages – they brought with them, all bound together in a huge and flexible organization which could be directed to achieve, with great brutality, its military objectives.

The Persian empire adopted the same methods. Herodotus is certainly wrong in claiming that Cyaxares the Mede was the first to sort out Asiatic troops from a confused mass into units with different weapons. What the Assyrians had known how to do, the Persians showed that they too understood. The account attributed to Herodotus of the different arms, clothing and fighting styles of national and tribal components of the army of Xerxes, massed for his assault on Athens and her associates in 480 BC, is an unsurpassed source of light upon such differences, and the variety in battlefield tactics to which they give rise.

At its widest, the Persian empire stretched from the Aegean to the Indus, from Libya to the Caspian. Its armies were immensely strong in cavalry and missile weapons and other auxiliary support, but its downfall resulted from a lack of heavy infantry capable of defeating Greek hoplites. Owing much to the model of Sparta, hoplite warfare now formed the basis of military practice in mainland Greece.

Greek hoplite infantry offers an excellent example of a war-fighting structure reflecting the pattern of a parent society. The hoplite was the product of the *polis*. The manpower of a hoplite army came from citizenry of sufficient substance to be able to afford costly equipment, men of superior standing in a community accustomed to the resolution of its affairs in orderly discussion. In Athens – though not in Sparta – command of hoplite formations was commonly elective, which is only possible in relatively small forces applying simple war-fighting methods in uncomplicated procedures. Hoplite formations were rigid and inflexible. They could not easily be manoeuvred and made to fight in any direction except that to which they were originally drawn up. On their own ground, which for preference had to be open and level, they were difficult to beat. In the 5th and 4th centuries BC, tactical and structural developments in Greek and Macedonian armies would fashion from warfare initially almost exclusively based on hoplite practice, and then modified to take account of Persian cavalry tactics, a system lasting in important respects until Napoleon. It depended on the substitution of tactics of envelopment for those of massed frontal attack and defence, upon which hoplite practice had hitherto been based, and was to depend still futher upon the integration of other arms with heavy infantry in a co-ordinated whole. The full development of an integral force of all arms was to be the work of Alexander.

It is possible that what happened in the Battle of Marathon in 490 BC, when the Persians broke through the Greek centre but in doing so allowed the Greek flanks to close in on their own rear, in an early example of tactical envelopment, was something of an accident. The same cannot be said of the Battle of Leuctra in 371, when the Theban general Epaminondas set his hoplites, in conjunction with cavalry, to attack a stronger Spartan force, not frontally, but on an echelonned approach which led to a double envelopment and brought about a degree of confusion which even Spartan discipline could not withstand. The result was a total Theban victory.

Someone who learnt from this episode at Leuctra was young Philip of Macedon, already held as a hostage in Thebes for three years. When he succeeded his father as King Philip II of Macedon, in 359, he set about creating a more balanced army, using Persian models as well as Greek, with the hoplite phalanx as a basis but incorporating cavalry, light infantry, archers, slingers and siege artillery, together with logistical support to enhance speed of movement. This was to be the army, developed, improved, trained and led by Alexander the Great, which would march under his leadership from Macedon, on the European mainland, to beyond the Indus deep in the heart of Asia.

Over Alexander the person, his character, his motivation and personal life, there is continual dispute. Over his generalship there can be little. The battle of Gaugamela in 331 remains one of the most outstanding examples in the history of war of double envelopment, though far from being alone in witness to Alexander's tactical genius. His handling of a huge army over immense distances (between Macedon and India it covered some 27,000 km) shows his logistical and operational capacity and his quite extraordinary powers of organization and leadership. For 2,000 more years warfare was to bear the imprint of Alexander the Great.

On his untimely death in 323, no more than 32 years and 8 months old, six years after setting out upon the conquest of the Near East, Alexander's empire crumbled, with warring generals disputing the succession to its parts. Meanwhile a new military power was rising in Rome, which would in its turn dominate the world that lay around the central sea. Once again the military instrument emerging was to be the product of experience, forged in trial and error. The simple phalanx of heavy infantry upon which the republic of Rome first relied, armed primarily with the two-metre throwing and thrusting *pilum* and a broad-bladed cut-and-thrust-sword, but with little, if any, cavalry or missile support, was sufficient for the dominance of the Italian peninsula but was to prove a failure in the wars with Carthage. The disaster of Cannae in 216, when Hannibal's invasion of Italy, and his adroit tactical handling on the battlefield in another double envelopment, was Rome's greatest defeat. This was followed by important steps in creating a military system more suited to the republic's requirements. The patriotic citizen-soldiers of an earlier time had already begun to be replaced by longer-service professionals. Terms of service and unit organizations had been reviewed, and the inclusion of elements of cavalry and light infantry auxiliaries had done much to accommodate Roman military practice to the Republic's current needs.

The Roman army which brought the Second Punic War to a close with the defeat of Hannibal in 202, and was to assert Roman ascendency in Africa, Spain and the Hellenistic East, was something new and different. It was largely the creation of the elder Scipio, surnamed Africanus. A survivor of Cannae, Scipio was given command in Spain at the age of 26 in 210 BC, while Hannibal's army was still in Italy. In four years he achieved complete control of the Iberian peninsula, defeating three Carthaginian armies and training a reorganized Roman army in novel and more flexible tactics (of which more will be said in an important chapter by Peter Connolly) to break out of an already outdated mode and, with new weaponry, adapt to changing circumstances. His bold move into Africa, where Hannibal followed him out of Italy, was to end in a resounding, if somewhat chancy, victory at Zama (202 BC) and the end of the Second Punic War.

Out of Scipio's belief in the need to adapt military structures and practice to changing requirements was born the Roman army which dominated the known world for 500 years. Its principal component would be the legion. The Roman legion that was now coming into being represented the most significant development in military practice since the time of Alexander. It became the instrument of Rome's imperial expansion and survived until the empire's end, with an influence on military organization which endured through the Middle Ages and beyond. It was an outstanding example of a military structure appropriate to, and at its best faithfully reflecting, the pattern of its parent society. Military and civil interests in the empire were later to diverge, which was to prove a great source of weakness in the 4th and 5th centuries AD, while Rome's inability to adapt legionary practice to new requirements would lead to disastrous defeat by barbarian horsemen at Adrianople in 378 AD and a further stage in the empire's steep decline.

The later history of the Western Roman Empire, as it moved towards its final collapse, illustrates a further aspect of the continuity of human experience in the military context. This is the influence of military pressures upon the devolution of civil power. Imperial succession in the Empire's later years, admirably dealt with in the chapter by Roger Tomlin which brings our study to an end, offers uncomfortable parallels to much that has been happening in our own world nearly 2,000 years later.

The influence of the horse on the history of warfare from very early times deserves particular attention. The use of weapons from a horse's back, with all its evident advantages of additional height above the ground for the user, and of increased mobility, has always been beset by problems of stability. The weight and effectiveness of hand-held cutting, thrusting and crushing weapons (axe or sword, for example, spear or mace) was severely limited. The accuracy of missile weapons discharged by a mounted man – usually from a short bow – was gravely impaired unless his mount was stationary and its effective use further reduced by difficulties in manipulation, both of mount and weapons. There is no need for anyone actually to try using a bow while riding a horse, even with a saddle on it, to be sure of this. The requirement for a more stable weapons platform than the back of a horse, in the days before stirrups came into use, was one of the most important influences on the development of the chariot.

The Assyrian army relied heavily on the horse, with a remount service unrivalled until the time of Napoleon and possibly only surpassed (though on a smaller scale) by the British for the purposes of the South African War at the turn of the present century. In the military use of horses it was upon chariots that Assyrian emphasis was chiefly laid. Cavalry, though raised in large numbers, took second place. The chariot was not only useful for the transportation of fighting men around the battlefield, with an implied threat of shock action; it also furnished, when stationary, a stable weapons platform.

Here I come forward as one of the few surviving specimens of a dwindling sub-species soon to become extinct – the genuine British cavalry soldier. When in the early 1930s I came down from Oxford to join my great grandfather's regiment (Light Dragoons in his day, already long designated, after the Napoleonic fashion, Hussars in mine) I was put through the exacting training which made the British cavalry of that time more effective than it had ever been before. An institution or an instrument often only fully flowers when it is already out of date and doomed. The Russo-Japanese war of 1900 demonstrated, what few accepted until the First World War made it painfully clear, that horsed cavalry could play little part on a battlefield now dominated by the machine gun, barbed wire and the spade, to which air power was soon to be added. Cavalry still had indispensable functions, such as reconnaisance, but the shock action with the sword or lance, to which we were so strenuously conditioned, was a fast-receding reality. Offensive action would now be developed dismounted, with rifles and maching guns used on the ground. I did myself once gallop into action with a drawn sword against Arab irregulars in Palestine in 1938, when seconded to the Transjordan Frontier Force. This must make me almost as rare today as a coelocanth, but I take, perhaps perversely, some satisfaction in reflecting that no-one was seriously hurt by anything I did myself that day.

The sword in my hand in 1938 was the 1908 pattern cavalry sword, the best the British army has ever had and the first correctly designed to apply the thrust of a charging horse to a target. Of our exercises in the mounted use of sword, lance and revolver, which were both strenuous and thorough, I recall particularly, in the present context, my own training in missile engagement from a horse's back, in mounted revolver practice. You advanced down the range at the walk, followed by the Sergeant Major on another troop horse, to discharge three shots from a .455 Webley & Scott at three targets, one straight ahead at the level of a mounted man and one on each side on the ground. The first shot, between the troop horse's ears, would startle it so much that it might easily swing round and have you presenting your weapon, ready for the second, at the Sergeant Major. When we were mechanized, some of the problems of missile engagement from a mobile weapons platform would emerge again in tanks. What was evident in tank gunnery from very early on was the extreme difficulty of engagement on the move. Until the tank stabilizer was installed, effective tank gun fire could only be produced at the halt. Even now, with equipment in a high state of technical advance, tank guns are, whenever possible, brought into action from a stationary tank. Assyrian chariots had no springs, let alone stabilizers, and effective missile engagement could hardly be expected from any chariot on the move. We need to know much more about this (and Professor Wiseman's highly informed chapter in this book takes us a good deal further) but it is clear that the use of horses harnessed to chariots, upon which the Assyrians so greatly relied from the 10th century BC onwards, would at some time be largely replaced by their use as mounts for individual men-at-arms. Problems remain. The fire effect of a bow used on the back of a moving horse could hardly have been great, though its psychological impact might have been considerable. The difficulty of furnishing a stable weapons platform for the mounted man persisted. Recent research has suggested the development of a Roman cavalry saddle with four horns so placed as to secure the seat of a rider handling weapons. Though it does not appear on Trajan's Column where it might be expected, there is evidence of its use by the 4th century. A re-creation of it can be seen in some of Peter Connolly's lively and imaginative illustrations to our text, but further evidence on the actual extent of its use would be helpful. The crucial breakthrough in the use of the horse in battle was to come with the stirrup, introduced into the Western world a couple of hundred years or so after the collapse of the Roman Empire.

All commanders in war with similar ends in view – the reduction of a well-defended stronghold, the suppression of an enemy employing guerrilla tactics, the forward defence of an extended frontier or the full defeat and rout in battle of a main army – face problems which have much in common, in spite of the passing of the centuries. Inevitably, this prompts speculation on how the commanders and armies of different eras might fare if pitted against each other in an imaginary encounter. It is, perhaps, the military historian's version of the schoolboy fantasy of selecting a World XI to play football against a team from Mars but it can be of help in sharpening judgement.

If an effort is made to compare the effectiveness of commanders in war, there is no doubt that Scipio, with Hannibal and possibly Tiglath-pileser III, would have been equal to most of the others, even to Gustavus Adolphus, Marlborough or Wellington. Alexander, with little doubt, would have been superior to all of them. Such comparisons should not be pushed far, but speculation also arises about the comparative effectiveness of different organizations and weapon systems. How would the Roman legion of, say, 200 AD have stood up to fully integrated forces like those of Alexander? Poorly, it would seem: they would almost certainly be thrown off balance and prove too inflexible to respond to fast-changing tactical demands. How would a medieval royal army, like Henry V's at Agincourt, have stood up to a Roman legion? Also poorly: better organization and tighter control would have proved superior to the unco-ordinated masses of a medieval array, dominated by the individual action of armoured, mounted, ill-disciplined men-at-arms.

Speculation also arises over the comparative effectiveness of weapons and weapon systems. The slow and clumsy war chariot of the Assyrians was held in an esteem its effectiveness hardly seems to justify, though its psychological effect must have weighed heavily in commanders' minds. The horse archer also seems to have sometimes been overrated, while it is strange to find the longbow so neglected. Little known in antiquity, the longbow did not come into its own, in the hands of English and Welsh archers in England's royal armies, until the 14th and 15th centuries. Like the hoplite, the longbowman was the product of a parent society. A plentiful peasantry conditioned to labour-intensive agriculture in a harsh climate produced the right man-power for bowmen, and long practice at the butts in a demanding skill made them archers. When the Black Death hugely reduced the peasant population and sheep farming greatly lowered the need for manual labour, the longbowman disappeared and the best efforts of Tudor monarchs could not bring him back. Change in the nature and pattern of a parent society is always reflected in the performance of the armed forces it begets. A main cause of Spartan military decline lay in the falling numbers of Spartiates available to bear too great a military burden.

The longbow in 18th-century Europe could have been decisive. The Maréchal de Saxe calculated that in his time it took as many as 200 musket shots to achieve one disabling wound, whereas with the longbow (with twice the musket's rate of fire) one shot in ten disabled. British squares at Waterloo stood firm against relatively ineffective cannon fire and the furious charges of Ney's unsupported cavalry, a tactic which would never have been allowed by Alexander. How would they have fared unarmoured, with their muskets and their bayonets, under a hail of arrows from the sky? Could a hoplite phalanx, even with some armoured protection, have withstood it? The longbow, introduced too late and soon chased out by gunpowder, never saw the success it deserved. The British 1908 pattern cavalry sword embodied a grasp of cavalry shock action which would have devastated medieval Europe but it was already by several centuries too late. In contrast, a weapon which did find its rightful place, and at the right time, was the short, double-edged so-called Spanish sword, in the use of which Scipio trained Roman troops in the 3rd century BC. It would continue to be used to very good effect for another 500 years.

I come now to the book to which this is an introductory note. It is important to indicate what our study sets out to do and perhaps even more important to say what it does not. It was never in the minds of those who put it together to offer a complete and exhaustive account of warfare in the ancient world. The intention was rather to explore in some depth a number of areas of critical interest and importance in the history of ancient warfare, from the earliest times to the fall of the Western Roman Empire. Every one of these areas has been explored before, some several times over, and much has been written on them, attracting abundant scholarly comment upon which the writers of these chapters have been able to draw. As time goes by, further evidence will come to light, under the encouragement of the lively interest now being shown in such matters. Judgements will be modified. What we offer here, however, is believed to be as fair an overview of some of the more important areas of interest in the whole field of ancient warfare as the present state of the art permits.

Our book has Dr Trevor Watkins confidently handling elusive evidence in a first chapter on origins, which is followed by a profoundly informed account of the great Assyrian military empire by Professor D. J. Wiseman. John Lazenby then offers an enlightened review of developments in Greece and Macedonia from 800-360 BC, in which the city-state and hoplite warfare come under scrutiny, after which comes a highly informative chapter from Dr Nick Sekunda on the Achaemenid Persian empire. Dr A. Devine then makes an important addition to what has already been written on Alexander the Great, and Peter Connolly follows him, investigating in his own erudite and lively fashion the early Roman army and the struggle for the Mediterranean. Dr Lawrence Keppie has then much of interest to offer in a chapter on Roman military institutions in the late Republic and the Civil War, followed by an important chapter from Dr Brian Dobson on the Empire. Dr Roger Tomlin winds up with an illuminating and thought-provoking essay on military aspects of an empire in decline.

Much thought has been given to the supporting illustrations, and when they are original, as with Peter Connolly's reconstructions, to their execution. They do much to enrich the written text.

There has been no attempt at symmetry. In the military part of my own life I have seen more than one triumph of tidiness over commonsense. In the academic part of it I have known outstanding work compromised by an obsessive urge to make the evidence fit the conclusions. It is hoped that this collection of essays on ancient warfare, supported by the illustrations, will avoid both errors. If they suggest any conclusion at all, it is that human nature, consistent and unchanging, will continue to seek ends in warfare along the same lines as have been followed in the past, since as far back in time as we can see.

Epaminondas put down in command at Waterloo, Alexander the Great at Alamein or Julius Caesar invading Gaul from the other side of the Channel in World War II, would all have found irritating alterations in the battle-fighting scene to which they had become accustomed. Artillery, airpower, rocket propulsion, armoured mobile weapons platforms for missile discharge more effective than horse-drawn chariots, and many other changes in material and method, would require absorption and adjustment of approach. The essential problem for the commander, however, would continue to be what it always had been. It would be to seek, in spite of what would be done by an enemy to prevent it, to establish his own control over the situation he found before him and impose upon it, in whatever state of disorder he might find it, an order of his own choosing.

It is probably no paradox that as the study of the Latin and classical Greek languages has declined in the schools of the Western world, interest in classical antiquity has greatly increased. Beautiful and desirable as the study of these languages may be, and however regrettable any reduction in attention to them in our schools, it is no longer held to be the case that such studies afford the only useful point of entry into the ancient world. There has never been a greater volume of vernacular publication than there is now upon life in ancient Greece and Rome, in all its high variety, with its lively response to external stimuli and its own impact upon the world around it. Thus while we may mourn the diminution of emphasis on Greek and Latin studies in our schools (and particularly Latin, essential to the writing of good English, which has never been more important than in this communications age) we should rejoice that it seems to have done nothing whatever to diminish interest in the way the ancient Greeks and Romans behaved, and the perpetual rediscovery that these too were people like us, and that humanity, in all essentials, has not changed.

There can be few better points of entry into a study of continuity in human behaviour than consideration of man's conduct of war, and few better sources of illumination for it than an examination of warfare in the ancient world. It is in this conviction, and the confidence that the content of these chapters will in other important respects be found of high interest, that this book is offered.

THE BEGINNINGS OF WARFARE

DR TREVOR WATKINS

The origins of warfare are hidden in the mists of human prehistory, but by 1200 BC there was a long tradition of armies, campaigns, pitched battles and siege warfare. This chapter surveys a vast geographical perspective – the whole of Europe and western Asia – and an equally formidable time-scale, from the earliest human times down to 1200 BC. However, it is only as we approach the end of our period, and only in certain parts of the Near East, that we find information which is sufficiently concentrated and historically detailed for us to draw concrete conclusions. Here is the springboard for an examination of an evolving tradition of arms and armour, the fighting of pitched battles and the development of extended strategies of war.

For much of the period under review the information we have is shadowy, tantalizing and ambiguous. As we peer back into the most distant periods of human history, we must temper our enthusiasm to interpret what we think we see with two general caveats. The first is that written records, the stuff of history, cover only approximately the last thousand years of the long period covered in this chapter, and that only in those limited parts of the Near East where writing was early in use. In most of Europe away from the Mediterranean we have to wait for the classical authors to record their observations of their barbarian neighbours before we have any written information; up to that time in the last centuries BC, we must rely on the evidence of archaeology alone – the surviving weapons and the eroded and decayed remains of fortifications. Where only such survive, it is necessary to recognize that we cannot reconstruct with any degree of certainty how battles were fought, how the opposing forces were composed, how they were led or why, or even who they were.

Even when writing is first used – just before 3000 BC in some parts of the Near East – we have to be aware of the second caveat. People choose what to record in writing (or in sculpture or painted record) and it is not until many centuries after hieroglyphic writing appears in Egypt, or the cuneiform script in southern Mesopotamia, that detailed and dispassionate information begins to be set down. Only in the concluding centuries covered in this prelude do kings feel it appropriate to record the course of events in battle. Several centuries were to pass before the first Greek historians began to write analytical accounts of affairs. From as early as 2500 BC in southern Mesopotamia, and even earlier in Egypt, kings commemorated military victories, but only in the most general (and usually the most generous) terms, and with little indication as to how those victories were achieved. As we approach the end of our period, we find the first detailed Egyptian accounts of deeds in battle, but written in such a suspiciously self-congratulatory style that one suspects hieroglyphic hyperbole.

Aggression, personal conflict and fighting have always been part of the human condition, but the evidence for institutionalized conflict – warfare – makes a relatively late appearance in human history. The earliest signs are doubly ambiguous. Among the stone tools of the Upper Palaeolithic period, the last part of the Old Stone age in Late Glacial times, are what appear to

The late hunter-gatherers of south-eastern Spain not only engaged in hunting but on occasion used their bows and arrows against each other. Rock-painting from Morella la Villa, Castellon.

be spearheads and small sharp points. However, it is difficult for us, who are unfamiliar with the making and use of chipped stone tools, to be sure that we can identify correctly their precise functions. If we can identify them as spears and arrowheads, there is still a second problem of interpretation. We know that the Stone Age people of the last stages of the Ice Age period, about 20,000 years ago, were hunters specializing in the larger game animals in which Europe and the Near East abounded – reindeer, red deer, the great wild cattle, gazelle, wild sheep and goat and wild horses. The difficulty lies in recognizing whether a heavy arrowhead or a large spearhead, superbly and skilfully chipped from flint, was used for the hunt or as a weapon in fighting among humans. Only in one or two rare examples of later rock-art from south-east Spain are there pictorial references to the use of bows and arrows in conflicts between groups of people. Even then one is entitled to ask if what we are shown is a skirmish between rival bands or serious, organized warfare. Similar pictorial references to fighting between groups of archers can also be found in the rock-art of other people of other times in such areas as the central Sahara and southern Africa.

Tiny flint arrowheads from the earliest known settlement on the Mesopotamian plain in Iraq, Qermez Dere, about 8000 BC. The broken tip of one of the arrowheads shows the fluting typical of an impact fracture. Iraq Museum, Baghdad.

Just before 8000 BC in the Near East there began to appear sophisticated and refined projectile points made of flint, and later often of obsidian, a rare black volcanic glass. What is striking is that projectile points became increasingly common and more elaborate in design at the moment when hunting was becoming less important, for it was at this period that many people in the Near East were herding the first domesticated animals. At about the same time these people were also beginning first to harvest and then cultivate wheat and barley, peas and lentils. They had exchanged the fluid and mobile life of the nomadic hunter-gatherer for that of the permanent village-community, dependent on the resources of a much more·clearly defined territory around their villages. They had homes, herds and harvests to defend. The growing interest in well-made projectile points is therefore more likely to be a symptom of new attitudes to territory and ownership, and related to increased competition and conflict, and with it the greater social importance of possessing weapons for communal defence which were in all respects up to date.

Fortified Settlements

Beside the evidence of an interest in weapons we can place the unequivocal indication of the first fortified settlements. Around the precocious township of Jericho, which had begun to grow up before 8000 BC around a permanent spring in the Jordan valley, a circuit wall was built of stone; outside the wall a deep, V-bottomed ditch was cut to protect the wall-face. In one of the archaeologists' trenches was found a circular bastion of stone attached to the face of the wall. The tower was a solid construction, with a staircase leading up through its core.

Over the succeeding millennia settlements in different parts of the Near East reveal similar traces of a serious concern with communal defence. The overall arrangement of the large town at Çatal Hüyük in central Turkey, which was already well-established by 6500 BC, may be interpreted as defensive. The square, flat-roofed houses were built side by side like a pile of children's building blocks pushed together. Access to each house was by means of a door at roof level, from which a steep ladder led down into the living area. Circulation around the settlement was across the flat roofs. The edge of such a settlement would have presented a solid, blank wall to any intruder or attacker. Once the ladders which gave access from the ground to the outermost roofs were drawn up, the settlement would have been impregnable. In north Mesopotamia settlement sites of the 6th and 5th millennia BC have produced stockpiles of baked clay sling bullets. In Cyprus, at the site of Khirokitia, what was first thought to be a stone-paved causeway has now been re-interpreted as a massive perimeter wall, which was superseded and overrun by a spreading

The huge circular tower at Jericho was built about 10,000 years ago, attached to the circuit wall which surrounded the settlement.

Massive multiple ramparts around hilltop sites like Maiden Castle, near Dorchester in southern England, were the climax of a long history of warfare and fortification which stretched back almost 3,000 years before this site, which was finally overcome by one of the Roman Emperor Claudius' invading legions.

settlement. At least for part of the settlement's life, the times were sufficiently insecure to warrant heavy investment in self-defence.

An early concern for the defence of the settlement at the heart of the community's territory was not confined to the Near East. The Neolithic enclosures of north-west Europe, which were previously thought to have been intended either to ward off or to keep in animals, or to provide ritual enclosures for seasonal tribal gatherings and ceremonies, are now seen as serious attempts at self-defence whose construction involved enormous communal effort. Several sites in southern Britain provide dramatic evidence of successful attacks launched against heavily defended enclosures almost 5,000 years ago.

One of these sites is at Hambledon Hill on the chalk downlands of Dorset. Part of the hilltop is crowned by a prominent and well-known multi-vallate hillfort of the last centuries of the first millennium BC, but there are also much more extensive, though much less obvious, traces of earlier enclosures. Recent excavations have revealed two and probably three successive hilltop enclosures dating back to the early centuries of the third millennium BC, the traditionally peaceable Neolithic period of the first farming population of Britain. The last stage in the sequence was the ambitious construction of a contour-fortification which enclosed all three of the previous enclosures.

The rampart was timber-fronted; in front of the rampart a linear quarry-ditch was excavated and the material thus obtained deposited in a bank behind the timber face. The effort was justified, for there is evidence of a major attack. However, the precautions proved ineffective, for there is also gruesome evidence of the failure of the defences and their destruction at the hands of the attackers. Somehow the defences were overtaken, and a great length of the timber frontage set on fire. As the facade went up in flames, the rampart collapsed into the ditch, a scorched and discoloured mass of chalk rubble. Buried beneath the collapse were some of the bodies of the fallen defenders. Among them was the skeleton of a young man, shot by a stone-tipped arrow as he tried to escape, carrying a baby in his arms. Other sites of similar date have shown evidence, only slightly less direct and vivid, of their destruction. In at least two cases dense scatters of leaf-shaped arrowheads of flint have been found around the ramparts, with particular concentrations at the gateways. These fortified settlements were built only a few centuries after the appearance of farming populations, and they tell us something of the long-term consequences of an expanding population with a limited farming technology. An important detail has been noted among the remains of the dead at Hambledon Hill; there were surprising signs of poor nutrition, evidence for the theory that agricultural land and resources were already seriously over-stretched.

In the succeeding prehistoric period there are fewer traces of inhabited settlements, but the tombs of the dead provide testimony to the need to bear arms. In the Neolithic period in Britain, as in much of northern and western Europe, the dead were buried in large communal tombs, often characterized by megalithic construction. At the beginning of the Bronze Age, around 2000 BC, there were two developments in the burial tradition: communal burial gave way to essentially single burial, emphasizing the significance of the individual rather than submergence of the dead in the community of the ancestors; and some of the deceased were honoured in the grave by the inclusion of prestige objects. In male graves we find battle-axes of polished stone and daggers made in the novel and mysterious material of copper, signifying the importance of warrior status.

The Earliest Armies

In the Near East metals had been used experimentally over many centuries before weapons of war were manufactured from the new material. The major change in the use of metals, and in weaponry and warfare, sprang from the establishment of urban centres and centralized kingdoms in Egypt and western Asia. In the third millennium BC these earliest states mobilized substantial armies, and built sophisticated defensive walls to protect their cities and administrative centres. The armies required large amounts of what thus became the most important strategic raw materials, copper and tin to make bronze, and the organized and skilled industries for the large-scale manufacture of high-quality armaments.

With the advent of urban, civilized states the nature of the information available to us changes. In Sumer, the earliest urban civilization of southern Mesopotamia, kings used writing to record and commemorate significant military victories. Occasionally the same events were recorded in pictorial form. Unfortunately we do not have the sober, descriptive and analytical historical accounts of the kind pioneered by early Greek historians 2,000 years later. Nevertheless, the pictorial representations are rewarding to study in detail.

From the Sumerian city-states of southern Mesopotamia we have the earliest evidence for the development in pitched battle of trained formations of heavy infantry, the ancestors of the phalanx. Around the middle of the third millennium BC the wars of which we hear are those between the neighbouring city-states of Sumer. In the second half of the third millennium we encounter evidence for the use of armies on far-ranging military campaigns in what can be interpreted as the beginnings of the ambition for empire. Once a king had subjected the other city-states of southern Mesopotamia, he could turn his attention to the extension of his political power by military means. Kings of the dynasty of Agade, for example, who ruled between about 2350 and 2200 BC from a capital not far from modern Baghdad, left the remains of their military garrisons as far away as north-east Syria, and monuments to the passage of their armies are carved on rock-faces in the mountains of western Iran and eastern Turkey. Their own inscriptions also refer to campaigns which reduced the city-states of western Syria and reached the shores of the Mediterranean Sea.

The armies of the Sumerian city-states were the first to employ wheeled vehicles as mobile firing-platforms. They were clumsy, solid-wheeled wagons drawn by four onager-like animals. The most impressive illustration of a Sumerian army in action is provided by the so-called Vulture Stele of the king of a city-state called Lagash. His name was *Eannatum*, and he ruled a middle-ranking city-state in about 2500 or 2400 BC. He is depicted both in the upper and the lower registers of one side of the stone slab. The stele takes its name from the gory depiction on another broken fragment of the consequences of victory for the defeated enemy, whose abandoned bodies are shown being picked by vultures.

The battle-scene shows the army at the moment of victory, marching over the bodies of their defeated and slain enemies. In the upper register a troop of heavy infantry is led by the king himself; in the lower register the king is shown riding in his battle-wagon in the van of a troop of light infantry. The light infantry wear no protective armour and carry no shields; each holds a long spear in the left hand and a battle-axe in the right. The heavy infantry is depicted schematically and with artistic licence, but the sculptor has clearly carved massed ranks of helmeted spearmen behind a front rank of men bearing shields. It is fruitless to count the heads above the great rectangular shields or the bare marching feet below; they have been carved to fill the space available. What is significant is the number of spears projecting between the shields. The artist emphasizes the solidity of the formation, protected from chin to ankle by the almost interlocking shields. The implied battle tactics anticipate those of the Macedonian phalanx and the Roman legion, but at a date in the middle of the third millennium BC. It also suggests that the armies of those city-states contained a hard core of trained professional soldiery. No seasonal levy of yeomanry could have managed such precision and solidarity: and these soldiers were trained, uniformed and equipped to fight as a corps.

More detail of the battle-wagons is seen on the inlaid sound-box of a lyre from the royal cemetery of the ancient city of Ur, which the excavator, Sir

A small plaque of engraved shell from the ancient city of Mari on the Euphrates shows a warrior of about 2500 BC with metal helmet, battle-axe and sickle-sword. Musée National de Louvre, Paris.

19

Leonard Woolley, nicknamed 'The Standard of Ur'. One side of the box shows a three-register scene in which processions of people carry agricultural produce and lead animals, while at the top a banquet is in full swing, perhaps celebrating the victory in battle seen on the other face of the box. Again the scene is in three registers: battle-wagons roll over the bodies of the slain, prisoners of war are led from the field, and the king dismounts from his battle-wagon to inspect prisoners, who have been stripped and their arms tied behind their backs. It is victory and the fruits of victory which are celebrated, and we learn nothing of how the opposing armies drew up against each other, and how the battle-wagons were deployed.

The four draft-animals for each wagon are shown in detail, but are difficult to identify. They are larger than donkeys, but otherwise closely resemble that species. It has been suggested that they are onagers, a species larger than the wild ass; but the onager enjoys a reputation for not being domesticable. Perhaps they belong to some more amenable but now extinct species related to the ass and the onager; or perhaps they were mule-like hybrids. It is even possible that they were part-horse hybrids, for the horse is known to have been in use at this date from Iran to western Turkey, and the Sumerians had a word for this foreign animal – the mountain-ass. The draft-animals are yoked to a draft-pole and controlled by reins, which are run through a rein-ring mounted on the draft-pole. The vehicle is a platform with a basket-woven breastwork. It seems to be mounted directly on the axles, and the four solid disc-wheels are each composed of three pieces. Two men ride in each wagon, and the armament consists of a large quiver of various lances. At least one of the soldiers is equipped with a battle-axe, a weapon suited to close combat. The problem in reconstructing the use of these vehicles in battle is that there is no indication that the front axle was capable of pivoting; even if it could pivot, the degree of turn would be slight, since the front wheels could not have swung under the wagon's body. Their turning circle must have been immense and their manoeuvrability minimal. Their four-abreast draft animals would have presented a large and vulnerable target, and it is difficult to imagine that they could have moved with any impressive speed. Their representation in pictures shows that they were considered highly prestigious, and indeed fit for kings. But perhaps their true function lay in providing a chauffeur service for top persons rather than in surging around the field of battle.

There were also two-wheeled chariots, although we have evidence of them only in small clay models; and there was a strange two-wheeled vehicle which modern historians have named the straddle-car. The straddle-car consisted of an axle with two wheels, and a saddle on a vertical post set into the draft-pole directly above the axle. We have no evidence to tell us of the use of these lighter and potentially more manoeuvrable vehicles. But they are symptomatic of a constant factor in man's organization for war, even at this early date: the quest for new and more powerful weapons, and the willingness to invest great resources in experimentation and deployment.

Weaponry

From the burials of the period, like the famous Royal Cemetery at Ur, we have examples of many of the weapons which are to be seen in the pictorial representations. However, there is a curious disparity between the uniformed troops and the elaborate, craftsman-fashioned weapons, often made in precious metals, which are found in the graves. Presumably the dead who were buried in the rich tombs, and provided with such superbly made weapons, belonged to an aristocracy whose officer or warrior status was signified by weapons which were more suited to display than to simple functionalism in battle. Bronze was also used widely throughout the Near East, and indeed in many parts of still-prehistoric Europe, for the manufacture of handsome and distinctive high-status weapons. The importance of bronze, in addition to its superior qualities both in the manufacturing process and in the hardness of the metal, is that nowhere in the Near East was there a substantial source of tin,

opposite
The upper and lower scenes on a stone slab (known as the Vulture Stele) from the middle-ranking city-state of Lagash in southern Mesopotamia commemorate in pictures and words a military victory of the king Eannatum around 2500 BC. In the broken lower scene the king rides ahead in his battle-wagon (see also illustration on page 22) and wears a helmet which models his hairstyle and ears (see illustration on page 26). Musée National du Louvre, Paris.

21

On the soundbow of a lyre from the Royal Cemetery at Ur in southern Mesopotamia, a craftsman portrayed, in delicate inlay of lapis lazuli and shell, scenes from a battle of the middle of the 3rd millennium BC. The actions of the heavy battle-wagons (bottom row) and the infantry in their studded leather cloaks (middle row) lead to a victory, in which the king dismounts to inspect the captives. British Museum, London.

the metal commonly blended with copper to produce the superior alloy. In Europe major tin sources are also few and far between. All the tin necessary for the armaments industry had to be obtained from distant sources, which inflated its price in the Near Eastern military market to that of a precious metal.

Many of these weapons, some of them made from gold or silver, were ultimately removed from circulation through burial with their owners in death, and introduced to our awareness through the excavation of the burials. To the high value of the materials from which they were made we should add the rare and highly developed skills invested in their manufacture. These objects were extremely precious, and their presence in burials is therefore token of the great importance attributed to the warrior status of their owners, whether in Bronze Age Europe, or in the literate, urban civilizations of the contemporary Near East. In a few of the largest and most sumptuous tombs of the Royal Cemetery at Ur there are many other bodies buried with that of the central personage. Among these attendants, who must have submitted to ritual murder or suicide, were superbly bejewelled serving-women and armed bodyguards. The simple standardized equipment of the bodyguards – a copper helmet and a spear – gives us a more accurate picture of the quality of arms and armour supplied to the ordinary infantryman.

The personal arms of the early Near Eastern soldier, whether poor regular infantryman or elegantly accoutred aristocratic warrior, show a remarkable degree of continuity over a huge geographical area and over more than 1,000 years. Within this overall continuity we can detect fascinating changes, some the result of advances in technology, others apparently the result of evolving fashion or styles of combat. The standard weapons were the heavy spear, the battle-axe and the dagger. The early spearheads had long tangs, which were thrust into the spearshaft. One technique for creating a firm link between the two parts was to form a hook on the end of the tang, ensuring that the spearhead stayed in place as the spear was thrust into an enemy, or when it was withdrawn. The technical advance with the spearhead was the production of a socket type, which could be more firmly attached to the shaft.

When battle-axes were first produced in southern Mesopotamia early in the third millennium BC, they demanded the highest level of skill from the smith. They were relatively complicated castings which included a cylindrical shaft-hole for the wooden handle. Unlike a wood-cutting axe, the blade of a Mesopotamian battle-axe was round, its function to pierce helmets and skulls and slash gaping flesh-wounds. In the countries of the Levant a quite different form of battle-axe was evolved. It had a curved cutting edge and three flanges for attachment to the axe-shaft, and has been called the *epsilon-axe* because of its resemblance to the Greek letter 'e'. As casting techniques became more sophisticated, smiths learned to make more complicated shapes in vertical, two-piece moulds, where previously they had been confined to flat castings in a horizontal, single-element mould. Bivalve moulds allowed the smith to make a more elegant and much stronger form of curved blade for the battle-axe. Because it retained the windows of the earlier axe, archaeologists call this type the fenestrated axe. Their use was widespread, from central Turkey, down the lands of the east Mediterranean coast and into Egypt, dating from the last centuries of the third millennium BC. The fenestrated axe was best suited to hacking and slashing at an enemy's head and body. Perhaps because of the increasing use of metal helmets, a new tactic was devised and a sharply pointed battle-axe began to appear in the Levant. Between the two types there was also an adaptation of the fenestrated battle-axe, in which the chord of the arc is reduced and the blade is pulled out into a much more penetrative shape. It is not difficult to see why archaeologists have nicknamed this variety the duck-bill axe.

The third common weapon was the dagger. Usually all that has survived is the metal part of the dagger, but occasionally we find the hilt and pommel. Early examples of the dagger are simple, but with the regular use of bivalve moulds it became possible to cast elaborate and delicate detail on the blade. The blade was usually hidden inside the sheath, and the hilt, pommel and sheath could serve as the vehicle of sumptuous display, as in the case of the several daggers buried about 2600 BC with a man called *Mes-kalam-dug* in an extraordinarily rich grave at Ur.

Mes-kalam-dug also possessed a superb helmet, although it is unlikely that he ever wore it in combat for it is made not of sheet metal but solid gold. The surface of the helmet models the wearer's long hair, tied in a bun on the back of his head, and the detail of the ears. The king *Eannatum* of Lagash is shown on the Vulture Stele wearing a similar helmet. Ordinary soldiers also wore metal helmets, even those from the cities of the alluvial plains of southern Mesopotamia, where all metal had to be imported. Some soldiers are shown wearing heavy (possibly leather), metal-studded cloaks as a form of body-protection. Metal body-armour in the form of mail coats appears only later, in the second half of the second millennium BC. In the early periods there is also a

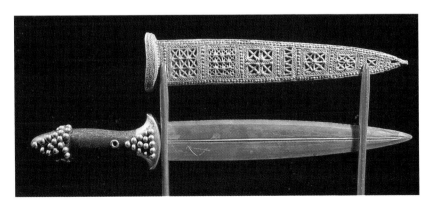

A superb gold dagger with gold-studded hilt and openwork gold scabbard from the tomb of Mes-kalam-dug *in the Royal Cemetery at Ur was surely more for display than use on the battlefield. Iraq Museum, Baghdad.*

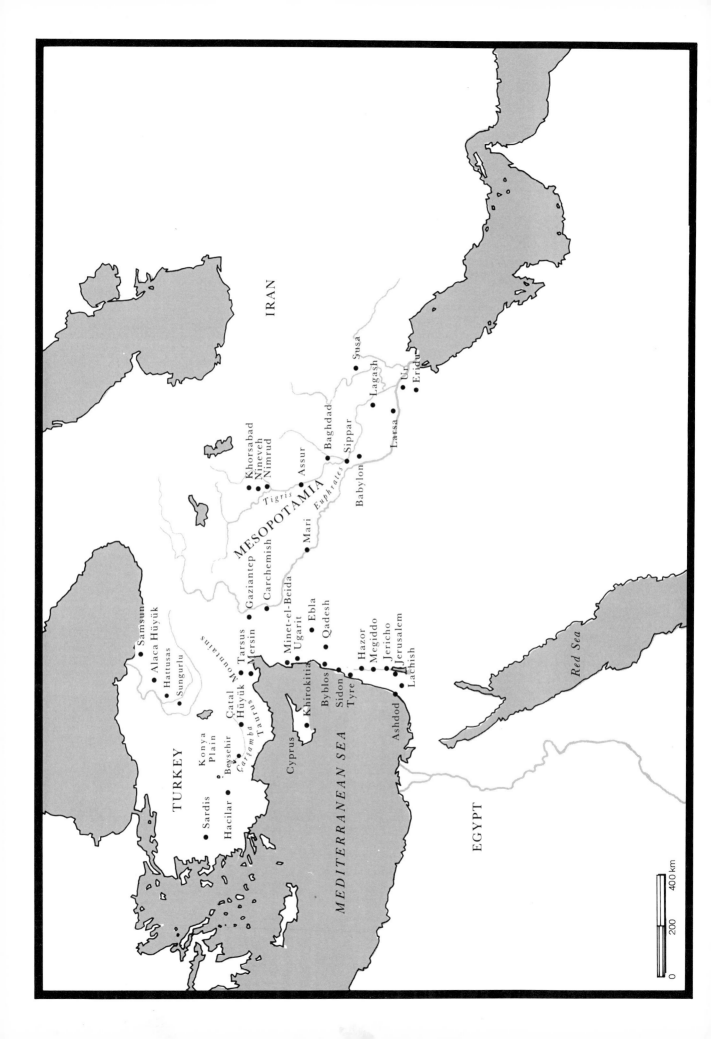

scarcity of evidence for shields. We have noted the solid front rank of huge, heavy, rectangular shields protecting the Sumerian phalanx illustrated on the Vulture Stele, but other examples are hard to find. One reason for their scarcity may be that the carrying of a shield restricted the warrior to the bearing of a single weapon. Warriors are seen carrying a spear for thrusting and a battle-axe in the other hand for slashing; they may have had a dagger at their belt as a precaution against the loss of one of their main weapons, but they could not have carried a shield.

When using a shield the warrior must have a single offensive weapon. Here we should note some of the gaps in the early Near Eastern record, the most significant of which is the sword, a weapon which allows the wielder a long thrust as well a slashing blows at close quarters. The long stabbing and slashing sword seems to have been developed by European metalsmiths. It reached the world of Mycenaean Greece in the last centuries of the second millennium BC, and was exported from the Aegean to Cyprus. It appears on the mainland of Asia about 1200 BC in the hands of the hordes who threatened the gates of Egypt and whom the Egyptians called the 'peoples of the Sea'. For all their skills, the Asiatic armourers and smiths could not make a sword which was sufficiently long and strong; sword-making has always since been a supreme skill of the metalsmith.

There are other puzzling gaps in the record. Weapons like the sling, the bow and arrow, and the mace, are rarely seen in commemorative sculptures or pictures, although we know of their existence. Perhaps the mace and the sling were peripheral and their effectiveness limited in the pitched battles fought by massed ranks of trained heavy infantry. The virtual absence of the bow and arrow, however, is much more difficult to explain, not least because all major settlements were enclosed by walls from which defenders could fire missiles down on attackers. The composite bow was known from ages past, but its full effectiveness was not grasped until the second millennium BC. One of the most ambitious and most successful kings and would-be emperors of southern Mesopotamia, Naram-Sin, who ruled about 2250 BC, depicted himself and his army armed with composite bows on a victory stele. However, the stele shows that the fighting took place in mountainous terrain, and it may indicate that Naram-Sin's success in this campaign, beyond the plains of his Mesopotamian homeland, was secured by his intelligent adaptation of campaign tactics. In the normal circumstances of early Near Eastern warfare, archers were support troops, and the pictures we see concentrate on the central action of the infantry and the heroic completion of the victory by the senior officers riding in their clumsy battle-wagons. It was not until the latter half of the second millennium BC that archery became an appropriate skill for the high-born, like the kings and pharaohs of Egypt, who are depicted wielding bows on national monuments.

Siege Warfare

The victory stelae and the terse inscriptions tell a story of campaigns based on pitched battles. It is only later, in the first millennium BC, that we have clear illustrations and descriptions of siege warfare from the Assyrian kings whose names resound from the Old Testament. However, the lack of direct evidence does not demonstrate that siege warfare was not practised until late Assyrian times. From a very early date towns and cities in many parts of the Near East were protected by massive fortifications. These walls were not designed simply to keep out casual nocturnal marauders, for they were enormous civil engineering investments which were clearly designed to counter major military attack. The early city fortifications consisted of curtain walls with projecting towers and carefully planned and strongly defended gateways. Although we do not find signs of archery in the grave-goods of the dead (perhaps because archery did not possess the necessary status overtones), the city defences seem designed for defence by archers.

From the tomb of Meskalam-dug *again came a heavy gold helmet, exquisitely engraved to reproduce the curls of his hair and the bun at the back of his head. Royal Cemetery of Ur, about 2500 BC. Iraq Museum, Baghdad.*

Although fortifications around settlements of the historic and protohistoric periods were common from Turkey to Egypt, that part of the Near East which provides us with the bulk of our knowledge of the nature of the early city defences covered modern Israel and Jordan. Towns like ancient Jericho were heavily fortified with circuit walls protected by deeply dug ditches. Such settlements of densely packed mud-brick architecture, which may have been occupied for millennia, had grown into tall mounds (usually known by the arabic term *tell*), as succeeding generations rebuilt their houses on the debris of earlier buildings. At such sites the defences could take advantage of the resulting artificial hill, and the walls could be set into the top of the slopes of the tell. In some cases it is possible to gauge the ingenuity and effort which was put into the design and construction of urban defences. The gateways at many sites were massively built to provide strength in depth. At intervals along the line of the walls were projecting towers, which gave the defenders extra height for their archers, and the ability to fire at the flanks of any attackers who approached the base of the wall. In front of the main wall there might be an additional curtain wall punctuated with gaps. From postern gates the defenders could move unseen behind the curtain wall to sally forth unexpectedly against attackers.

Early in the second millennium BC city defences underwent a change, notably in the Levant. Huge dump ramparts were thrown around entire cities, faced with a steep glacis of smooth plaster. On the top of the rampart was a vertical wall with a walkway. Additional obstacles were incorporated, such as a near-vertical masonry wall-face at the base of the glacis and intermediate walls in the slope of the glacis. These were measures against siege warfare. The defenders stand further removed from the attackers' archers, but can still fire down on them from their elevated platform; the huge base of the rampart, which may be as much as 20m thick and 9m tall, effectively nullifies attempts at mining or breaching.

The evidence of the surviving city walls and gates, and the finely made weapons found in the tombs, is augmented by texts of the early second millennium BC, which illustrate the central importance of the organization of defence. The 18th century BC was a period of competing imperial ambitions in Mesopotamia. Hammurabi the Great, as later generations recalled him, the

26

king who raised the name of the city of Babylon to world significance, was the ultimate victor, combining ruthless diplomacy with force majeure. His principal rival was Shamshi-Adad, the first internationally significant king of Assyria, whose capital at that time was at Assur on the Tigris in north Mesopotamia. The rich city-kingdom of Mari on the middle Euphrates, close to the modern frontier of Syria with Iraq, was one of the disputed prizes. First Shamshi-Adad took control of Mari, ousting the local dynasty, but later Hammurabi succeeded in out manoeuvring the Assyrians. Excavations in the extensive palace-complex at Mari have located the royal archives, and tens of thousands of clay tablets illustrate vividly details of many aspects of a kaleidoscopic 'life at the top'.

Among the documents relating to the reign of the last native king of Mari before the interlude of Assyrian domination are several which tell of the difficulties of obtaining census information. The land around Mari was inhabited by inconveniently mobile tribes of semi-nomads, who were reluctant to submit to a census which they knew implied not only taxation but also military service. Even promises of free meals and maintenance while attending census stations, and offers of fields to farm, often failed to persuade the tribesmen to turn up and give their names to the royal officers. One senior official of the kingdom of Mari wrote to the king, Zimri-Lim, proposing drastic measures *pour encourager les autres*:

> If my lord will agree, let me execute a criminal in the prison, cut off his head and parade it all around the town . . . to make the men afraid so that they will assemble quickly.

The palace administration was also responsible for the provision of arms, munitions, and siege equipment. King Zimri-Lim wrote while on a military campaign to order further supplies of arrowheads:

> To Mukannishum [his official in the palace] say this,
> Thus speaks your lord.
> When you hear this letter read, have made:
> 50 arrowheads of 5 shekels [40 grams] weight in bronze
> 50 arrowheads of 3 shekels
> 100 arrowheads of 2 shekels
> 200 arrowheads of 1 shekels.
> Give orders to have this done at once. Then have them put in store to await my further instructions. I suspect that the siege of Andariq will be prolonged. I shall write to you again about these arrowheads. When I do write, have them brought to me as quickly as possible.

Another letter from the king to the same official orders him:

> When you hear my letter read to you, have made 1,000 bronze arrowheads at ¼ shekels [2 grams] each. Have them made from the red bronze at your disposal, and have them sent to me at once.

Later, when Shamshi-Adad's son Yasmah-Addu was installed as vice-regent at Mari, it is clear that the palace armourers were still in business, and that the palace workshops at Mari were important to Assyria. In a letter to his son, Shamshi-Adad ordered 10,000 arrowheads to be made, requiring almost five tons of bronze. Some of the bronze for the job had to be transported from Assur since the Mari palace armourers did not have enough stock. The accounts were kept straight by the repayment from Mari to Assur of an equivalent amount of silver.

New Technology

In the early centuries of the second millennium BC, three different innovations appear in significant conjunction: the widespread use of the domestic horse; the effective development of the composite bow; and the new technology of lightweight, bent-wood construction. Although the horse was known in

The Egyptian pharaohs of the 19th century BC garrisoned massive forts like this one at Buhen, beside the Nile close to the modern frontier with Sudan, in order to maintain the peace necessary for the regular transit of trade in vital supplies.

eastern Europe and central Asia at much earlier dates, it was in the early second millennium BC that the domesticated species was quicky spread throughout much of Europe and the ancient Near East. In the Near East we can see from the reliefs and paintings that the horse was not ridden, but was harnessed to chariots. The development of bent-wood techniques allowed the construction of the spoked wheel with a rim made of curved felloes, and the manufacture of lightweight chariot bodies. The lightweight chariot with spoked wheels drawn by teams of horses provided a fast, manoeuvrable firing-platform which at last was effective in battle.

The effective development of the practical composite bow introduced a rapid-fire missile delivery system necessary for mounting on the fast new chariots. The composite bow, which had been known for thousands of years, requires much more skill in manufacture than the simple bow. We do not know the breakthrough which made the composite bow so much more effective in the early second millennium, but the technology of manufacture is formidable. To the ogivally curved wooden bow it is necessary to glue gut on the outer side and long slivers of bone on the inner. As the bow is drawn the gut is stretched and the bone is compressed. The composite bow gives a higher velocity than the simple longbow, is much shorter (and therefore much easier to use, for example, in a chariot), and is capable of being kept strung for long periods without distortion or loss of power.

Such combinations of a chariot and a team of four highly-trained horses were extremely expensive to establish and to maintain, and required a skilled team of driver and warrior. Their presence in the field was underwritten by the complex logistics of horse-breeding and training, a small army of wheelwrights and chariot-builders, composite bow makers, metal smiths and armourers, and the support teams on campaign who managed the spare horses and repaired damaged vehicles. Thus chariotry became a means of displaying the highest level of military investment together with the most challenging of martial skills, a suitably heroic mode for the display of the bravery of kings such as the Egyptian pharaohs or the kings of Mycenaean Greece, the role-models for the heroes in Homer's epics. The employment of chariotry in warfare was the prerogative of rich and powerful kingdoms, and corps of 'independent' charioteers could hire their services dearly.

In the last four centuries of our period, from 1600 to 1200 BC, the world of the Near East emerges into a clearer historical light. It was a period in which the great powers of the day, Egypt in its militarily most vigorous and expansionist age, the Hittite Empire in central Turkey, the Assyrian kingdom in one of its several appearances on the world stage, and a still mysterious and transient kingdom called Mitanni, based in north-west Mesopotamia, sought to conquer and hold great empires. Below this super-power level there was a kaleidoscope of kingdoms and city-states of all sizes, jostling for position by both political and military means.

Egyptian Expansion

The period is most readily viewed from the Egyptian standpoint, since his record of military achievements formed the basis of a pharaoh's claim to fame and honour before his gods, and was the subject of long inscriptions and vivid reliefs carved on temple walls. From about 1600 BC, adopting the powerful new combination of horse, lightweight chariot and composite bow, the kingdom of Egypt began a long haul back from a period of political weakness and internal division. The pharaohs of Egypt's 18th dynasty adopted a new, personally militaristic role and welded the Egyptian state into a potent war-machine. Egypt's old enemies, the tribes and petty kingdoms at the southern frontier in the Sudan, and to the west of the Nile Delta in Libya, were subdued by punitive military campaigns; the pacified southern frontier was subjected to control from military garrisons at key points.

Egypt's north-east frontier with Sinai, the passageway from the lands of the southern Levant, had been leaking badly. Asiatic immigrants had infiltrated Egypt in large numbers during the period of internal difficulties, and parts of the country were now under the control of interloper groups and their chiefs. The main thrust of the resurgent 18th dynasty was directed against these Asiatic peoples, who were first expelled from the eastern Delta and then pursued across Sinai. As Egyptian armies found themselves campaigning further and further north among the little kingdoms of the southern Levant, the policy of expulsion and the establishment a safe buffer-zone beyond the frontier evolved into one of military expansion and conquest. Once Egypt was politically reunified and stable, its massive manpower, material resources and monolithic centralized power system allowed it to assemble an army numbering tens of thousands, which could campaign for long periods far from home. Yearly campaigning abroad gave it unrivalled experience. The pharaohs of Egypt had always had a warrior aspect, but at this period they were the commanders-in-chief of a mighty standing army, organized under a well-defined hierarchy of officers into 'divisions', 'brigades' and smaller units. According to their inscriptions, the pharaohs themselves led their armies on long seasons of campaign to the limits of empire, and even in the thick of battle. Further north in the Levant there were tempting pickings, the rich merchant-cities of the coast and the larger and wealthier kingdoms of inland Syria.

Early in the 15th century BC the reigning pharaoh, Tuthmosis III, the most active and successful in a long series of warrior-kings, found his way northwards blocked by the powerful city of Megiddo, which commanded the key route passing round the inland flank of the mountains of the Lebanon and into southern Syria. Around the king of Megiddo was gathered a federation of other rulers from as far north as Qadesh, intent on frustrating the Egyptian advance.

The Egyptian account of the struggle at Megiddo does not provide a detailed account of the battle or of the successful siege which followed it, but it is nevertheless full of fascinating detail. Tuthmosis halted his army some way short of Megiddo, having intelligence that the anti-Egyptian coalition was preparing to make a stand there. There was a choice of routes by which the Egyptian army could approach, but the pharaoh's generals were concerned that the huge Egyptian army would be caught at a disadvantage as it emerged in column from either of the narrow valley roads to confront the waiting enemy

THE BATTLE OF MEGIDDO

The Egyptian chariotry arrive at the crucial moment and charge to break up the wrong-footed forces of the opposing federation of local forces at the battle of Megiddo. The appearance of the Egyptian chariot, its horses and crew is known with accuracy and confidence because Tuthmosis, the Egyptian pharaoh who fought the battle of Megiddo in about 1485 BC, proudly erected monumental and detailed reliefs showing himself and his army in the thick of the battle. We also have the actual chariots, perfectly preserved, from the slightly later tomb of the young pharaoh Tutankhamun.

The essentials of chariotry were superbly crafted equipment and trained horses, together with remarkably skilled and highly trained teams of men. The Egyptian army of the New Kingdom took advantage of three important innovations, bent-wood construction technology, the horse and the composite bow, and raised chariot warfare to its greatest achievements.

The chariot itself was built for speed and manoeuvrability, without protective screens for its two-man crew. The driver controlled his team of horses and at the same time managed a light shield on his left arm. His partner likewise needed both hands for his task of archery. The chariots were armed with a variety of arrows held in a series of quivers, which were shot from a small but easily-handled and powerful composite bow. The specially bred horses were harnessed to a yoke attached to the single, long, curving shaft.

Chariotry was a highly prestigious, hugely expensive and very vulnerable part of any army. It would not be used in battle until the critical moment had arrived; then its task was to launch a drive which would induce a breaking of ranks in the opposing infantry lines. Once the tide of a battle had been turned the chariotry might then also harry and hunt down the dispersed enemy, preventing an orderly retreat, maximizing losses of men and equipment, and turning defeat to rout.

forces. Tuthmosis decided to embark on a daring gambit of bluff and double bluff. His advisers urged that at all costs the Egyptian army should avoid the narrower of the two approach roads, so Tuthmosis calculated that the enemy would expect him to come by the broader route. He therefore chose the narrower road, and emerged in view of the enemy from an unexpected direction. While the enemy took counsel and rerranged its confederate army, the Egyptians had time to deploy their entire army out of the defile and into battle array. When the pitched battle took place next day, the Egyptian army shattered the opposition in a single decisive blow. Tuthmosis played a leading role in the centre of the battle and the enemy forces had to abandon expensive chariots, arms, and other rich booty which fell into Egyptian hands. Diverted by the prospect of booty, the Egyptians allowed many of the enemy to escape into the fortified city of Megiddo. The reduction of the city by siege took the Egyptian army a further seven months, but, as Tuthmosis' inscriptions explain, the effort was justified: 'All the princes of all the northern countries are cooped up within it, so the capture of Megiddo was the capture of a thousand towns'. With the elimination of the federation which had made its stand at Megiddo, the way was open for the Egyptians to move north into what is now southern Syria and ultimately right up to the Euphrates, though the task took many more years of campaigning.

In central Turkey the war-like Hittite kings reflected the national concern with military might in their portrayal of their deities. Here is a sculpture of a god in a horned helmet (the prerogative of divinity) with a fine dagger tucked into his belt and a battle-axe in his right hand from the Hittite capital of Hattusas. Anadolu Medeniyetleri Müzesi, Ankara.

above right
The Hittite capital city of Hattusas in the heart of the Anatolian plateau was a citadel within a massively defended city. The Lion Gate with its huge monoliths was designed to impress as well as to defend.

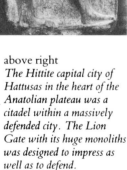

With the passage of time the Hittite empire based in central Turkey grew in power, and its ambitions expanded to take western Syria under its control. The most famous and most detailed account of a major battle of this period relates to the climax of the long-running confrontation between Egypt and the Hittite empire, whose capital Hattusas lay in the heart of Anatolia to the east of modern Ankara. Early in his reign at the beginning of the 13th century BC, Ramses II of Egypt led his army north via Gaza and then inland past Damascus and on towards the strategically situated city of Qadesh on the river Orontes in western Syria. His objective was to reduce to subjection the hostile city of Qadesh, which blocked the Egyptian advance to direct confrontation with the Hittite army. Ramses' intelligence reports, neatly laced with false information from Hittite agents, were that the Hittite king and his army were far away at Aleppo in northern Syria. In fact the Hittite army lay in concealment on the far bank of the Orontes river and on the 'wrong side' of the city of Qadesh, awaiting Ramses' arrival.

The first division of the Egyptian army, led by the pharaoh, had halted near Qadesh and begun making camp, when the Hittite king launched his chariot forces across the river ford against the following Egyptian division,

QADESH

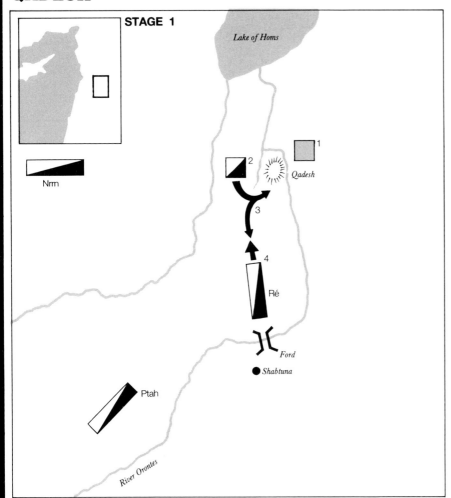

STAGE 1

Lake of Homs

Qadesh

Nrm

Ré

Ford

● *Shabtuna*

Ptah

River Orontes

STAGE 1

1 Muwatallish, the Hittite king, waits in camp while –

2 – Ramses, the Egyptian pharaoh, arrives and makes camp with the Division of Amun

3 Ramses' scouts spot the Hittite camp and a message is sent to –

4 – the following Division of Ré, which is ordered to hurry

STAGE 2

5 As the Division of Ré reaches the Egyptian camp –

6 – 2,500 Hittite heavy chariots pounce, driving the Egyptians into a disorderly rush for safety in their camp

STAGE 3

7 The Egyptian camp becomes the scene of a melée as the Hittite chariots follow the Division of Ré

8 The third Egyptian Division, Ptah, arrives from the south

9 Ramses rallies the Division of Amun and personally leads the counter-attack.

10 In the nick of time an additional detachment of Egyptian chariotry arrives from the west and its charge proves decisive

11 The Hittite chariotry retreats. The Hittite army withdraws within the walls of the city of Qadesh

STAGE 2

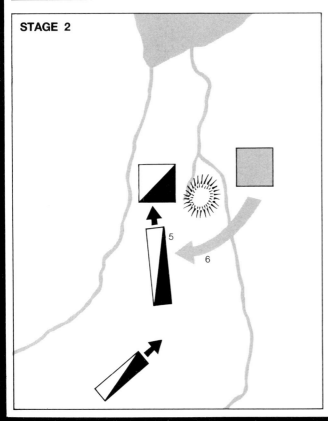

STAGE 3

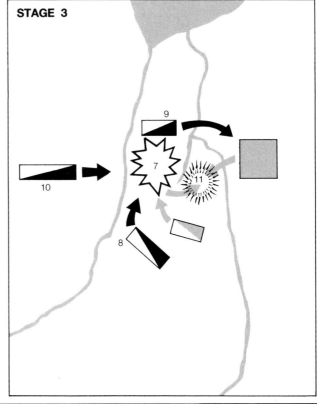

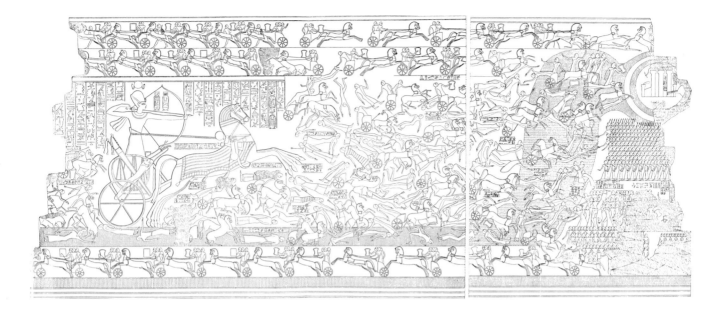

The Egyptian pharaoh Ramses II had himself portrayed in the thick of the battle near the city of Qadesh. The city is at the top right, with its walls, towers and moats; the main Hittite army is at the bottom right. Ramses rides fearlessly to the attack, alone in his chariot, the reins of his horses looped round his waist. Relief on the second pylon of the Ramesseum, Western Thebes.

which was caught on the march and thrown into disarray. They fled to the Egyptian camp – which had already been established by the leading division – pursued by the Hittite chariotry, which surged through the Egyptian defences. According to the Egyptian accounts, Ramses personally rallied his confused forces and led the counter-attack with acts of extraordinary personal bravery. The Egyptian forces held out until the balance of the battle was dramatically tilted by the arrival, late in the day, of a second Egyptian force which was approaching by another route to rendezvous with the main army at Qadesh. Ramses' inscriptions proclaim the scale of his victory (although they remain silent on whether the pharaoh was calculating on the arrival reinforcements out of the setting sun). The Hittite king was equally inclined to claim success. In fact both armies seem to have been severely mauled. The two commanders suffered from faulty intelligence, the Egyptians were caught unprepared, but the Hittites failed to commit their infantry, which was on the wrong side of the river, and were in turn apparently unaware of the approach of another Egyptian division from the west. The battle resulted in a non-aggression pact between the two great powers, which recognized their respective spheres of influence and saved them from further costly, head-on conflict.

Around 1200 BC, much of the ancient Near Eastern world underwent a cataclysmic transformation. Great powers like the Mycenaean kingdoms of Greece collapsed, echoes of their heroic golden age forming the basis of the Homeric epics of the Trojan War. In Anatolia the Hittite kingdom collapsed. The rich merchant cities and kingdoms of Syria likewise came to an end amid anxious pleas for help and panic-stricken messages of the approach of huge hostile armies and fleets of pirate ships.

The pharaoh's empire was pushed back to Egypt's modern frontiers. Nevertheless the pharaoh, another Ramses, maintained the tradition of the exercise of military might and its extravagent record in inscriptions and painted reliefs on the walls of the temples at Medinet Habu. These densely populated illustrations provide us with our clearest insight into the cataclysmic events of this period. To the Egyptian scribes these threatening hordes approaching Egypt by land and sea down the Mediterranean coast were a welter of various displaced peoples from vaguely distant parts, 'the people from the islands in the midst of the sea', as they wrote, presumably indicating an Aegean origin. The sculptors show an interestingly close acquaintance with their appearance, for some of the vanguard of these peoples had been taken into Egyptian employment as mercenaries to fight against the main wave of advance. They are shown, some with plumed and some with horned helmets, coats of mail, round shields and their novel and most effective weapons, long slashing swords.

At the gates of Egypt in a series of breathtakingly dangerous encounters by land and sea (if we are to believe the rhetoric of Ramses III) the Egyptian army broke the wave of advance. Some elements of the Sea Peoples, notably the militaristic Philistines, were allowed to settle as a buffer in Palestine, to which they gave their name. Other groups were dissipated further afield. The political landscape which emerged from this disruption on an almost continental scale was entirely different from the Bronze Age world which had lasted for 2,000 years. The military picture of the new age is also quite different. The great empires were replaced by smaller kingdoms, such as the Phrygians in Turkey, the kingdom of Solomon and David and all the other kingdoms familiar to us from the Old Testament, and the coastal city-states of the Phoenicians, who planted colonies at places such as Carthage and carried Near Eastern culture throughout the Mediterranean world. Egypt would never again lay serious claim to empire in the Levant. East of the Mediterranean coastlands of the Levant, in the fertile plains of north Iraq, the Assyrian kingdom was unaffected by the Sea People disasters. The Assyrians were to become the single, major, military and imperial power of the centuries to come, dedicated heirs to a long history of military technology and tradition.

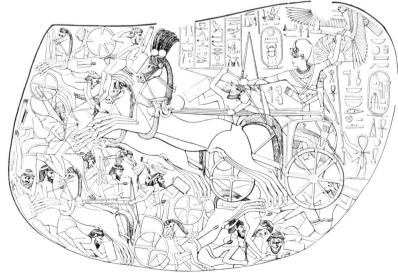

The decorated side-panels of the chariot of Tuthmosis IV repeat the motif of the pharaoh at the heart of the action, the creator of his army's victory. On one side he fires his bow, and on the other he swings a battle-axe. In both depictions he is accompanied by royal protective deities, including the vulture and the falcon Horus. Egyptian Museum, Cairo.

THE ASSYRIANS

PROFESSOR D.J. WISEMAN

The Tide of Assyrian Conquest

Throughout the second millennium BC the rulers of Assyria, ancient north Iraq, fought to defend their fertile land from the hill tribes to the north and east, and from the marauding semi-nomads of the western deserts which stretched from the River Tigris to the River Euphrates and beyond the steppe lands watered by the Rivers Habur and Balih and across into the north Syria.

Through this region passed the busy trade routes which brought metal ores and precious stones, gold, copper and tin-bronze from Iran which was traded by the Old Assyrians for the silver and lead or tin-alloys (*anakum*) of Anatolia. Thus the people of the area, who had already benefited from the development of bronze, possessed an alloy for their weapons which was harder than copper; by the first millennium they had exploited the carbonized hardening of iron for similar purposes. Early in their history they had become the heirs of the technological developments which had enabled the Sumerian and Old Babylonian civilizations to master and influence the whole of the so-called Fertile Crescent. The Sumerians had already developed urban centres with manufacturing capability and used the cuneiform script for communication. The fruits of their science had brought them mathematics, the division of the circle into 360 degrees and the day into 24 hours, observational astronomy, cartography and a technology which had given them the wheel and metallurgical skills which were employed at an early stage in warfare between city-states.

These developments enabled the Assyrians, in 1100 BC, to initiate measures to protect their largely agricultural heartland – roughly the triangle between their major cult centres of Nineveh, Kalhu (Nimrud) and Ashur – from the incursions of the Aramaean tribes. Tiglath-pileser I led his well-armed troops no fewer than 28 times across the Euphrates to attack the Aramaean bases. Nevertheless, a century later they still threatened Nineveh. Adad-nērāri II (911-891 BC) dislodged this enemy from the Kashiari Mountains (modern Tur-Abdin) and pushed rebel hill folk deeper into the mountains of Kurdistan to the east. Assyria's southern rivals, the Babylonians, were defeated and held at the River Diyala. A decade later Adad-nērāri's grandson fought to defend an Assyria which stretched from the River Habur to the Zagros Mountains and south to Tekrīt. The aim was to protect the state by calling up men each springtime, after the crops had been sown, to patrol the border and move out to harass intruders. Assyrian methods were harsh, designed to inflict a lesson of 'frightfulness' upon the peoples who transgressed the bounds set by their god. Those who failed to flee were killed, their villages sacked and their crops fired. Gradually the new areas overrun were forced to pay an initial tribute followed by annual payments to ensure good behaviour. In this way great quantities of booty were taken, with the emphasis on rare materials and potential war weapons, including horses and other animals. The Assyrians came to rely on this as a source of luxuries which supplemented their economy.

The ruler of the raided area was forced to agree terms of a loyalty-treaty enforceable under oath which invoked the wrath of the Assyrian gods on any infringement. This provided the religious and legal sanction for any subsequent Assyrian intervention as well as a strong incentive to the vassal not to repeat any misdemeanour. In this way Ashur-nasir-apli II (883-859) collected spoil from five neighbouring countries and nine major capital cities. Henceforward the threat of Assyrian invasion was to be no mere 'propaganda' move but often sufficient in itself to bring leading officials to sue for peace. As one means of control the Assyrians left behind a local official, backed by a small garrison or guard to report on the local situation and on any subversive activity. These intelligence reports were sent in by messengers and often alerted the Assyrians in time to take remedial action in concert with loyal vassals.

The success of this policy, and increasing dependence on trade and tribute, gradually led to the desire for a more permanent extension of territory. When communications were interrupted by rebels, swift retaliatory action was invariably set in motion. Even in mid-summer the Assyrian army found itself marching as far west as the Habur at a rate of 32 kilometres a day. Ashur-nasir-apli soon faced simultaneous threats from more than one direction and had to march east to Zamua (Suleimaniah) and north to Nisibin and Urartu (ancient Armenia). Resistance from the Aramaeans in the Upper Euphrates valley brought the need to move heavy siege equipment out against the fortified centres at Bīt-Adini and other Syrian city-states. The Assyrians reached Carchemish by 877 BC, then the Amanus range and eventually the Mediterranean Sea.

Each area was systematically brought under Assyrian control before the process was extended to its neighbours. Initially a native ruler was appointed as governor, but when the loyalty of the new client kingdom was questioned it was added to Assyria proper under a provincial governor. Because of distance from the capital, certain places were designated as 'store-cities' for the collection of taxes in kind and of materials ready for the provisioning of any returning Assyrian force passing through these border areas on a subsequent campaign. The vassal rulers were obliged to supply auxiliary troops and many Aramaeans have been identified as mercenaries within the Assyrian army. Communication between these centres and the headquarters was maintained by a network of élite royal troops (*qurbūti*) while mounted messengers provided both a postal service and escort for important persons back to the royal court. Many written texts attest the crucial role played by the army in this close-knit administrative arrangement. Typical of such communications is a letter

'To the king my lord, your servant Tab-šar-Aššur (writes); a cohort commander of the Chief Eunuch delivered me the king's sealed message in the town of Anisu on the 27th. The messenger of the commander of the fort came to

The caption in the cuneiform script panel reads: 'I besieged and conquered Hamanu, a royal city of Elam. I carried off spoil, wrecked and broke it up and then burnt it with fire.' This records Ashurbanipal's campaign against Elam. From North Palace of Ashurbanipal (Room S), Nineveh. British Museum, London.

Assyrian cavalry, infantry and chariots attacking fleeing Arabs. For defence, the latter use pairs of riders on their camels. From North Palace (Room L) of Ashurbanipal, Nineveh. Middle 6th century BC. British Museum, London.

Tiglath-pileser III, King of Assyria, in his royal command chariot after the capture of Astartu in Gilead. The ornamental dress and trappings imply a celebration of victory or similar occasion. British Museum, London.

see me, so I asked him about the news and he told me: 'The city of Birate and the whole land of Habha are well. Everybody is doing his work . . . '

In the reign of Shalmaneser III (859-824) these increasingly far-flung responsibilities began to place a strain on the Assyrian militia, which he called out 31 times in his 35-year reign to fight as far afield as Cilicia, Palestine, the Zagros and even the Gulf. Major alliances formed against his coming, so that stiffer resistance was met in Urartu (modern north-west Iran) and the campaigns of 843-841 were inconclusive. This constant activity forced the king to devolve power to his commander-in-chief, who sometimes acted independently. Moreover, Assyria was drawn into successive accretions of territory, as native rulers were easily corrupted. Til-Barsip in Bît-Adini had to be retaken in 856 and another Assyrian garrison-fort established nearby called 'Depot of Shalmaneser'.

The Aramaean states of Syria were now in the path of his advance, and at the Battle of Qarqar in 853 BC, Hadadezer of Damascus added to his own force of 1,200 chariots, 1,200 cavalry and 20,000 infantry those of Irhuleni of Hamath (700 chariots and 20,000 infantry), Ahab of Israel (2,000 chariots, 10,000 infantry), contingents from north Syria (Que and Musri), north Palestine (Arvad, Usanate and Shiani), Ammon and some Arabs (1,000 camels) – in all a force of 4,000 chariots, 1,200 cavalry and more than 65,000 infantry. These figures are probably no exaggeration for the Assyrians, as others, used 20,000 to denote an army group and 10,000 an army. Thus it was a formidable force, though with few cavalry for an encounter in open terrain. The Assyrians were unable to capture Damascus until a century later. Despite Assyrian claims, the outcome of the battle was severe check on their advance, precipitating internal conflict within Assyria which enabled the western city-states, including Israel and Judah, to take the initiative to expand their control into the neighbouring regions of Palestine and Syria.

The Assyrian recovery was led by Tiglath-pileser III (745-727 BC) who initiated extensive administrative and military reforms. He subdivided the provinces, reducing the power of individual governors to take independent action. The smaller regions of command also increased the overall amount of intelligence reaching the king. Another layer of officials enforced a higher rate of regular tribute payment and increased efficiency in the procuring of supplies of men and material at strategic locations. In turn, this facilitated swifter punitive action against rebels. Now the provinces contributed on a regular basis to raise local contingents for a centrally controlled standing army.

Tiglath-pileser's first move was to launch a series of systematic operations

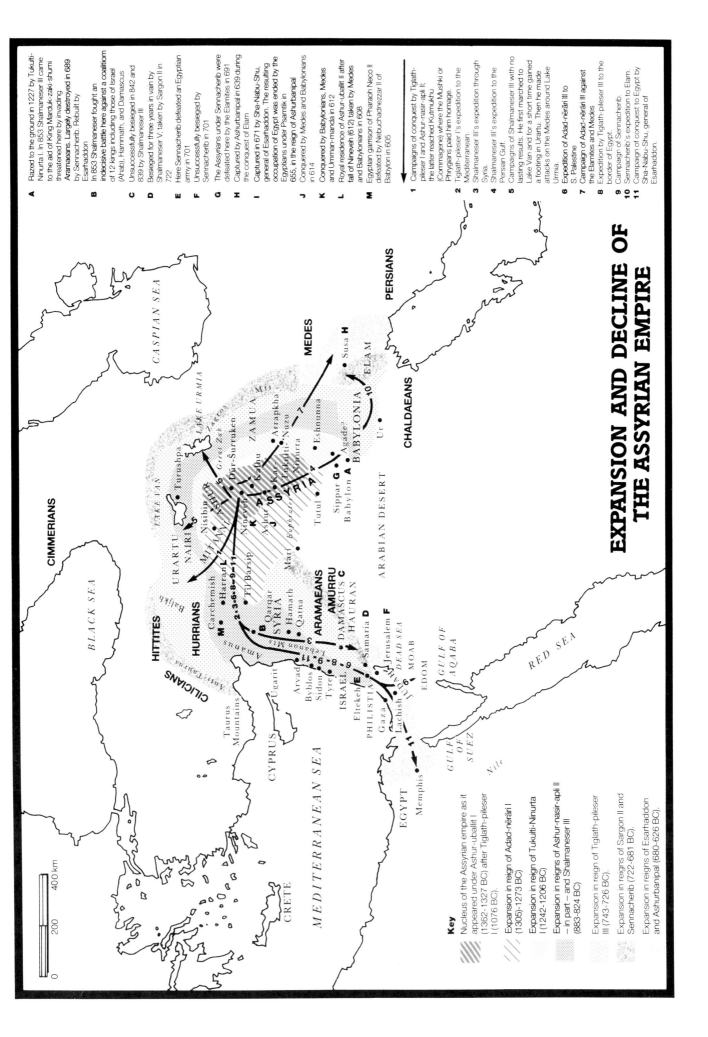

EXPANSION AND DECLINE OF THE ASSYRIAN EMPIRE

A Razed to the ground in 1227 by Tukulti-Ninurta I. In 853 Shalmaneser III came to the aid of King Marduk-zaki-shumi threatened here by invading Aramaeans. Largely destroyed in 689 by Sennacherib. Rebuilt by Esarhaddon

B In 853 Shalmaneser fought an indecisive battle here against a coalition of 12 kings including those of Israel (Ahab), Hammath, and Damascus

C Unsuccessfully besieged in 842 and 839 by Shalmaneser III

D Besieged for three years in vain by Shalmaneser V, taken by Sargon II in 722

E Here Sennacherib defeated an Egyptian army in 701

F Unsuccessfully besieged by Sennacherib in 701

G The Assyrians under Sennacherib were defeated here by the Elamites in 691

H Captured by Ashurbanipal in 639 during the conquest of Elam

I Captured in 671 by Sha-Nabu-Shu, general of Esarhaddon. The resulting occupation of Egypt was ended by the Egyptians under Psamtik in 655, in the reign of Ashurbanipal

J Conquered by Medes and Babylonians in 614

K Conquered by Babylonians, Medes and Umman-manda 612

L Royal residence of Ashur-uballit II after fall of Nineveh (612) taken by Medes and Babylonians in 608

M Egyptian garrison of Pharaoh Neco II defeated by Nebuchadnezzar II of Babylon in 605

1 Campaigns of conquest by Tiglath-pileser I and Ashur-nasir-apli II; the latter reached Kutmukhu (Commagene) where the Mushki or Phrygians paid him homage.

2 Tiglath-pileser I's expedition to the Mediterranean.

3 Shalmaneser III's expedition through Syria.

4 Shalmaneser III's expedition to the Persian Gulf.

5 Campaigns of Shalmaneser III with no lasting results. He first marched to Lake Van and for a short time gained a footing in Urartu. Then he made attacks on the Medes around Lake Urmia.

6 Expedition of Adad-nērāri III to S. Palestine

7 Campaign of Adad-nērāri III against the Elamites and Medes

8 Expedition by Tiglath-pileser III to the border of Egypt.

9 Campaign of Sennacherib.

10 Sennacherib's expedition to Elam.

11 Campaign of conquest to Egypt by Sha-Nabu-Shu, general of Esarhaddon.

Key

- Nucleus of the Assyrian empire as it appeared under Ashur-uballit I (1362-1327 BC) after Tiglath-pileser I (1076 BC).

- Expansion in reign of Adad-nērāri I (1305)-1273 BC)

- Expansion in reign of Tukulti-Ninurta I (1242-1206 BC)

- Expansion in reigns of Ashur-nasir-apli II – in part – and Shalmaneser III (883-824 BC)

- Expansion in reign of Tiglath-pileser III (743-726 BC).

- Expansion in reigns of Sargon II and Sennacherib (722-681 BC).

- Expansion in reigns of Esarhaddon and Ashurbanipal (680-626 BC).

0   200   400 km

against the vassals of Sardur of Urartu, whom he defeated, although the latter's capital by Lake Van repulsed an Assyrian attack. Nevertheless, Sardur was now isolated from the neo-Hittite and Aramaean states he had ranged against Syria. The stronghold of Arpad, capital of an independent Aramaean state north-west of Aleppo, was reduced to vassal status after a three-year siege in 741, and this was followed by the conquest of Sama'al, north and west Syria and finally Damascus. These operations were later put to propaganda use as examples of Assyria's irresistible military might.

An anti-Assyrian defensive coalition backed by Tyre, Sidon and Egypt was crushed and part of Israel, governed by the native appointee Hoshea, was absorbed into the extended Assyrian domains. When Hoshea rebelled, his capital at Samaria was taken after a siege in 722. The new Assyrian policy was to avoid the infliction of excessive casualties, enabling them to transport large numbers of nobles, trained military personnel and skilled craftsmen to their homelands to offset manpower shortages. Some were incorporated into the Assyrian army. The populations deported by the Assyrians during this period, numbering up to 250,000, were in part replaced by groups of dissidents from other provinces. The latter, isolated far from home among strangers, were bound in allegiance to Assyria. In Babylonia, Tiglath-pileser initiated a programme of direct rule through his nominee. This raised fresh opposition, and Elamites from the hills to the east came to Babylonia's aid, as did the Egyptians to the Palestinian cities. Henceforth the Assyrian army was employed to counter the subversive influence of these two great powers in the new territories for which Assyria had taken direct responsibility.

Sargon II (721-705 BC) was forced to fight open battles against Elam and the southern Babylonian tribes at Dēr, and at Qarqar against the Egyptian-backed Palestinians. He sent a raid in force against Ursâ (Rusas I) who stirred up the Mannai and adjacent hill-tribes (see below for an account of this campaign). Ursâ had also roused Que (Cilicia) and Carchemish to act in alliance with Mita (Midas, King of the Phrygians) to interrupt the main trade routes to the west. It is to Sargon's credit that within ten years his revitalized armies had won back the whole of Syria-Palestine and held sway from the Mediterranean to the Arabian Gulf. Urartu was dormant following its defeat; Phrygia and Elam maintained peaceful relations out of respect for Assyrian power; and kings from distant places, such as Cyprus and Arabia, paid tribute.

Within a few years of this high point of peace in the ancient Near East the Assyrian king fell in battle while quelling a minor revolt in Tabal. Sargon had wisely trained his crown-prince Sennacherib in military and intelligence roles on the northern front, where Cimmerian incursions were a new threat. Sennacherib reported to him: 'The troops of the Urartian king have been utterly defeated on his expedition against the Cimmerians. Eleven of his governors have been eliminated with their troops; his commander-in-chief and two of his chief officials have been taken prisoner . . . They have suffered a terrible defeat. Now the country is quiet again and each of his officials has gone to his own region. All the guards at the forts along the border have sent me similar reports'.

Though his expertise, to judge from his letters, lay on this front, Sennacherib (705-681 BC) was to spend a large part of his career countering Egyptian intrigues in Palestine. Like most Assyrian kings, he recorded details of his military activities in historical annals updated after each campaign, with his major victories illustrated on bas-reliefs on the walls of his palaces to impress both his own citizens and foreign visitors. These sources tell us that the restoration of control in Palestine by the siege of Jerusalem, the capture of Lachish and the defeat of the Egyptians at the battle of Eltekeh in 701 were Sennacherib's crowning achievements.

Esarhaddon (681-699) renewed the loyalty-treaty obligations imposed on all his vassals and made them swear to the agreed division of the kingdom on his death between his sons Ashurbanipal (668-627) in Assyria and Shamash-shum-ukin in Babylon. These terms included the vassals' obligation 'to fight and even die for the king [of Assyria]', never to rebel, and always to report any governor or officer who should revolt.

Under Esarhaddon the army had been constantly employed on the periphery of the empire. While preparing to march against Egypt, Esarhaddon was taken ill and died at Harran. It was left to Ashurbanipal's commander-in-chief to collect auxiliary troops from 22 kings along the Phoenician and Philistine coast to support the Assyrian standing army in the defeat of Taharqa and to march on the capital at Thebes. There he appointed 20 local governors to rule Egypt, watched over by Assyrian officials and an army of occupation. The sensitive Assyrian intelligence antennae picked up plans for an insurrection led by Taharqa's son-in-law Tanutamun, who occupied Thebes. The Assyrians had sufficient warning to call up reinforcements. Thebes was ransacked 'like a floodstorm' and the Palestinian princes who threatend their lines of communication brought to heel. Controlling restive territory 2,000 kilometres from their main base proved impossible to sustain, for increasingly the bulk of Assyria's forces were committed to the campaign against Elam and the capture of Susa. By 655 Psamtik in Egypt was able to regain its independence with the help of Ionian and Carian mercenaries and the support of distant Lydia. At the same time uprisings in Babylonia had to be suppressed. Although the Assyrian empire was now at its furthest geographical extent, and still immensely strong on paper, it had reached a critical stage of vulnerability. With its army fragmented and overstretched by operations on every frontier, it soon disintegrated and came to a swift end soon after Nineveh fell to the combined force of the Babylonians, Medes and northern tribes (Umman-manda) in 612 BC.

Army Organization

With the exception of the royal bodyguard, with its contingent of foreigners, the Assyrian kings relied principally on the mass call-up or levy of native Assyrians. These were mainly agricultural workers but also included groups of hard hillmen and semi-nomads prepared to forego their independence to maintain a defence force for times of crisis.

A permanent branch of the civil service was responsible for a census which enabled whole villages to be mobilized for such communal work as major building projects, canal clearing or military and policing operations. As these mobilizations became more frequent, and the need for specialist skills became apparent, a more permanent force was drafted to supplement the royal bodyguard (kiṣir šarrūti). This enabled the army to remain in the field without disrupting agricultural work and the economy. Some tribes, such as the Itu's and Gurra living near Babylonia and the eastern hills, were used as police and semi-military frontier guards. From the second millennium some foreign mercenaries and captives were included in the forces. Recruits were required to swear loyalty to the deity and to the king and his household by ritually saying 'Amen' to the terms of their loyalty oath. As greater stress was placed on offensive action, a highly trained group of charioteers and mounted men or 'cavalry' (pēthallu, a term used to distinguish them from non-military mounted messengers, kāllapu) was raised and classified as 'well-equipped' (heavy) or 'lightly armed', according to the weapons carried.

At an early stage foreigners were employed in peacetime on guard duties in urban centres, but by the time of Sargon II Aramaeans, Philistines and Greeks increasingly appear among infantry units. In Esarhaddon's day some prisoners-of-war were grouped into distinct units according to their skills. He records that '50 charioteers, 200 horsemen and 500 infantry were added to my royal corps'. After the fall of Samaria in 722, Sargon incorporated equestrian officers, who were among his 27,290 prisoners, into his royal army. This group of 13 named commanders of chariot teams, probably professionals, was kept together as an élite Samarian unit.

While the king is specifically recorded and depicted leading his army in major field operations, a 'field marshal' (tartānu) was responsible for detailed control. Dayyān-Aššur, under Shalmaneser III at the battle of Qarqar, and Shamshi-ilu (780-752) were noteworthy both as commanders-in-chief and as powerful provincial governors. In some large-scale operations with cavalry, separate commanders for the right and left wings are mentioned.

The strength of the forces raised may be stated in general terms, as in an Old Babylonian text from Mari on the Euphrates dating from the early second millennium BC and listing an army of 100,000 men with 20,000 archers and 1,500 cavalry. Enemy forces are rarely enumerated in detail, the opponents of Shalmaneser at the battle of Qarqar in 853 being an exception. Numbers of enemy casualties killed are stated to enhance the record of victory: 22,000 killed by Tiglath-pileser I *c.* 1105; 14,000 by Shalmaneser III. With Tiglath-pileser the emphasis shifts to the prisoners taken (103,000 against 20,000 killed), underscoring the policy of re-employing skilled personnel in civil and military roles following mass deportations. Though foreigners were not commonly named in the texts, their presence can be deduced from Assyrian sculptures and their nationality identified by dress. Philistines are depicted with their characteristic 'feathered' headdress; others, such as Egyptians, Nubians or Elamites, can be identified by their features, dress or the inscribed captions to their sculptured figures.

There are hints that, while not stating their own losses in battle, the Assyrians maintained lists of them by arm (see below on Sargon's Eighth Campaign). Assyrian letters refer to the casualties in individual skirmishes, and one calls on the recipient to 'enquire, investigate, write down and despatch to me the names of the soldiers killed . . . Perhaps there is a son who has gone into conscription in place of his father . . . be sure to enquire and find out all the widows, write them down, define their status and send them to me'.

There was a well-defined military chain of command. Large units were distinguished by the standard borne on the march, with its divine emblem – the gods Ashur, Shamash (the sun) and Nergal (the god of destruction). Some units may have been named after their commanding officer (e.g. Sîn-ahu-usur). The commander was also marked by his official position (the governor and chief cupbearer Rab-shaketh of 2 Kings 18:17), or by the size of his command of 1,000 or 200 men (possibly a battalion, *kiṣru*), 'chief of 100' (a company) or captain of 50 (*rab hanše*, of 2 Kings 1), and down to ten men under a section commander. This series of groupings seems to have been common to all the ancient Near Eastern armies. Chariots were formed into squadrons of 50.

Chariots

The principal strength of the Assyrian army lay in its chariotry. This mobile weapons-platform was in use in the area of the northern plains during the 13th-12th centuries BC and then developed by the Hurrian and Mittian infiltrators into the region to combine the skilled employment of horses with a specially

Assyrians ride amid the slaughter of fallen enemies at the battle of Tuba. From South-West Palace of Ashurbanipal, Nineveh. British Museum, London.

Assyrian archer protected by a full-length shield held by his escort and followed by a pair or rank of slingers. Other soldiers are shown kneeling to fire from behind similar shields. From South-West Palace of Sennacherib, Nineveh. British Museum, London.

constructed vehicle. Chariots of the 9th century were sometimes drawn by a team of four horses but their clumsiness and vulnerability led to their abandonment as war vehicles. Changes in technology enabled ironsmiths to design a light vehicle with a wooden frame set on a metal undercarriage with the wheel axis moved back from the centre to the rear. The result was a highly manoeuvrable vehicle which required less traction effort. There is, however, no evidence to suggest incontrovertibly that the Assyrians enjoyed a technical superiority over their enemies in chariotry or in the breeding of the animals which pulled them.

The chariot's driver was held steady against the front screen while the rigid shaft, originally elliptical but later straight, made control of the two yoked horses easier. The car became increasingly rectangular in shape to accommodate more armour and crew. The wheel was strengthened by the addition of up to eight spokes and fitted with a studded metal rim or tyre to increase wear and grip in turning. On the approach to battle an additional or spare horse was hitched to the rear. The light chariot was usually manned by a crew of two, the driver and an archer or lancer, but after the 9th century a third man was added to strengthen rear defence with one or more shields. In the time of Sargon two shield-bearers was the norm.

Chariotry was employed either in shock action in the centre of the attack, a tactic which greatly reduced the value of massed infantry in open battle, or on the wings in encircling manoeuvres in concert with the cavalry. Movement on campaign was swift. There is a record of a chariot squadron taking only two days to reach the Lower Zab River from its base at Kalhu (Nimrud), a distance of some 100km. The heavy royal ceremonial chariot was replaced in some field situations by a lighter version for a single occupant and one which could be partly dismantled and carried where there was no easy passage.

Horses

Increasing military demands in the 8th century meant that more horses had to be found for use with chariots and horsemen. They were especially used over rough terrain, but were a less stable firing platform and more vulnerable than chariots. Horses were ridden bareback for the stirrup was not introduced into the area until the 6th century AD as part of Sassanian or Byzantine influence on the Arabs. They were often used in pairs with one rider, or squire, holding the reins of both horses while the other, shield on his back, fired the bow. The second rider was armed with a lance or shield. Horsemen, or cavalry, were regularly used en masse, with Sargon employing up to 1,000 at a time. As many as 900 lightly armed horsemen were used in Assyrian raiding parties.

There were few horses in common use in Assyrian agriculture and their presence is noted in census returns. It was therefore necessary for the central administration to organize a constant supply of suitable animals. Fine horses, particularly good breeding stock, were noted when received as tribute from Egypt, Anatolia and foreign courts and then added to the royal stables. Tiglath-pileser specifically portrays black, white, 'pink', greys and piebalds among such mounts on the coloured frescoes which adorned his palace at Tīl Barsip (Tell Ahmar). Esarhaddon overcame the shortage by undertaking several expeditions or raids into Media and the Iranian plateau mainly as a means of rounding up the horses he needed. He encouraged his local officials there to do the same. However, the primary means of recruitment was the appointment of one or more 'remount officers' (mušarkisu) to each province. These issued 'horse reports' detailing the numbers and places they were held, and their condition, with other comments such as whether the horses were suitable for, or already trained to the yoke. The horses are listed by type; Kusean (some think Nubian, by import via Palestine) were treasured as particularly fine stud horses, and those from Mēsu, east of Assyria, were frequently noted, as were also other riding-horses and mules. These mounts were stated to be from, or in, most of the provinces, their capitals or in the possession of senior officials. Daily reports survive of those animals brought in to the major collection points (pirri). Thus Nabû-šūm-iddin reports to the king: 'Twenty-five teams (of horses) from the reserve stocks have just arrived at the three delivery centres of Kalhu, Nineveh and Dūr-Šarrukēn. Shall I inspect them tomorrow? I will do whatever the king says'. The same official gives details of other entries, for example: 'Sixteen yoke-trained horses, 13 Kusean, 14 riding horses, 9 mules from Qarnae; 9 trained horses, 6 Kuseans, 14 riding horses, 5 mules from Dana; 19 trained horses, 38 riding horses from Kullania; 25 riding horses, 6 mules from Arpad; 13 horses, 10 mules from Isana on the second day of the month Siwan'. Then, dated two days later: '24 (Kusean) trained horses, 16 mules from Damascus; 10 Kusean horses with riders'. The next day he records: 'One hundred and twenty-two horses from the commander-in-chief; 5 from the provincial governor of Kalhu'.

These were the sites of the central military barracks and arsenals (ekal mašarti) at which excavations show extensive ranges of barracks and storerooms with adjacent parade grounds, review stands and training facilities. The various manoeuvres taught included advancing, charging, turning and retreating, according to an early document (The Kikkuli Horse Training Manual) known to the Hittites, Mitanni and then the Assyrians. Since the remount returns are mostly dated in the early months of the year (March-May) they may indicate preparation for an early summer campaigning season. Chariots were also stationed at some provincial sites with horses left in the charge of charioteers or riders. It is possible that in the winter, or between campaigns, these were responsible for feeding and caring for their mounts as part of their taxation responsibilities (iškaru). In much earlier censuses leading individuals were noted as 'possesses chariot or horse' which could thus be drawn upon in time of public need. This also furnished reinforcements which did not have to march great distances from base before beginning a campaign beyond Assyria's borders.

Bowmen

The principal offensive weapon of the Assyrian infantry was the bow (qaštu) used by men in groups or individually when covered by a companion who defended the archer with a shield. The bow was used in all aspects of warfare, in open and close battle, in rugged terrain and in siege warfare. Bows of many types, some developed by native groups, are mentioned (Assyrian, Akkadian, Babylonian, Cimmerian etc.) with the simple type in use as much as the composite. The bow was effective over 250-650 metres. The wood or reed shafts carried arrowheads of metal, some mass produced by smiths, or more rarely of bone or flint with tail feathers taken from eagles or vultures. Some arrows – 'the messenger of death' – were set with flaming tow for attacks on habitations or crops. Since a quiver could hold up to 50 arrows, the firepower before or during a charge, or from massed kneeling or standing archers, was formidable. However, bowmen were vulnerable and were normally protected by a large shield, greater than the height of a man standing, with a top curved inwards above head level to ward off missiles. Some infantrymen, armed only with the ubiquitous short belt dagger for personal defence, acted as shield-bearers, holding these large rectangular shields by an inner handle with their base on the ground or large ('heavy') or light round shields. These shields were made of, or covered with, metal or oiled skins over dense matted reeds. In the time of Shalmaneser III, a captain commanded 100 shield-bearers.

Lancers

Lancers were used in large numbers in Tiglath-pileser's reformed army, both chariot-borne and on foot, just as Sargon had used as many as a thousand lancers and slingers together. The iron-tipped lance was not normally thrown but Ashurbanipal claimed he could throw a medium-weight unwieldy lance as if it were a dart. Pikes and javelins, the throw-spear or thrusting weapon (*yakītu*) are, like the earlier throw-stick (possibly a type of hooked stick) or spiked mace, rarely mentioned or depicted. Slingers using a variety of pointed pear-shaped stones with long leather slings are shown working in pairs or grouped line abreast.

This array of weapons led to an increase in personal defence in addition to the use of shields. Individual armour or protective clothing consisted of large or small metal links sewn on leather. Reliefs and finds indicate a remarkable continuity from the 14th century at Nuzi to the first millennium at Nimrud. This armour was worn by Assyrian cavalry, some charioteers and even a few infantry down to knee level. The earlier pointed or conical helmet with neck protection seems to have been largely replaced in the latter part of the 7th century by the crested helmet curving forward from the top. Crests, tassels or ribbons on helmets seem to designate special units of Assyrian slingers, just as maces or short sticks identified officers and officials. Long daggers or swords (*namṣaru*), some with sheaths, are less common than the common short dagger (*paṭru*) carried in the belt either singly or in pairs. Seals show that they were the essential weapon for close-quarter fighting. Assyrian soldiers wore high laced boots with upturned toes reminiscent of earlier Hittite hillmen, but by the 7th century BC these were commonly replaced by a shorter straight-toed style.

The army was fed on the march from 'travel rations' or from stores held at the provincial centres. In enemy territory it normally lived off the land. Sargon reported that the vanquished Ullusunu of Mannā 'poured out oil and wine and fed my army just as my officials and provincial governors did in Assyria itself'. Most campaign reports tell of the grain and wine stores looted.

Communication between units was by messengers and runners, while mounted military riders attached to each provincial or army headquarters maintained essential contact with the king. Fire and smoke signals, used commonly in the Old Babylonian period, were still employed to transmit warnings or pre-arranged messages over long distances. Piles of brushwood set about half a kilometre apart sent news of an impending attack, defeat, or change of ruler or government. In this way a message was passed swiftly from Ashur in the north to Babylon in the south. Similarly watch-towers encircling the cities of Jerusalem and Lachish signalled an impending Babylonian advance in 588-7 BC.

THE SIEGE OF LACHISH

This artist's impression of the siege of Lachish by the Assyrian army under Sennacherib in 701 BC is derived from the bas-reliefs on the walls of the royal palace in Nineveh and from details in the royal annals. Lachish, a stronghold in Judah, guarded the south-west approaches to Jerusalem which was also beseiged at this time. Well tried military techniques were used. After the city had been surrounded to prevent any escape, negotiators tried propaganda addressed at the citizens and their representatives on the walls, inviting surrender through fear of the proven Assyrian military might and conquests, and promising leniency to those renouncing rebellion.

An earth ramp topped with stone or wood enabled siege-engines to be brought up close to the walls which stood atop a high mound. Mobile battering-rams on wheels and propelled by manpower aimed to make a breach in the thinner upper part of the gate defences which could then be exploited. Where such a contraption could be floated into

place, the Assyrians also used high wooden siege-towers as a platform from which to fire down on the defenders. The defenders reinforced their protective towers, which provided enfilade fire, with raised wooden barricades and shields.

The ram itself was armoured with a heavy oiled leather canopy and carried a water reservoir and flexible arm for dowsing torches or flaming arrows directed upon it. The attacking infantry, including those undermining the walls or mounting scaling-ladders, were covered by shield-bearers and archers. As shown these shields were sometimes of full body-length. Like the cavalry, many attackers wore body armour made of metal links or platelets and protective helmets. At Lachish there is evidence of diversionary attacks made at other points in the walls and of a massive counter-ramp built by the defenders within the lower walls. Casualties were heavy and a mass grave for 1500 has been found. Lachish was later besieged by the Babylonians in 588-87 BC using similar methods.

The assault on the heavily defended royal city of Hamanu in Elam by the Assyrians in 655 BC. Sappers, beneath shields, undermine the outer wall, perhaps as a diversion from an attack by scaling-ladder. From North Palace of Ashurbanipal (Room F), Nineveh. British Museum, London.

Siege Warfare

The Assyrian policy of expansion inevitably led to the need to besiege rebel cities which impeded the advance. In the Near East ancient cities commonly stood on the high mounds made by earlier occupation, though many were sited near rivers which afforded defence on that side and with double or triple encircling defence walls. Siege techniques as first developed in the mid-second millennium were brought into operation. A ramp or causeway of piled up earth, rubble or wood enabled the attacker to gain closer access to the upper, more penetrable and fragile walls. A battering-ram was brought up by animal traction and then manhandled into position. This formidable weapon was a ram of metal-tipped wood housed in a wooden framework shielded by a covering. It was propelled on wheels or foot to dislodge the upper brickwork or smash down gateways or weak places. Attempts by defenders to set fire to these machines and the ramp by pouring burning oil or torches down on them usually failed, for the Assyrians devised contraptions to dowse the canopy with water. The design of the defences with protruding crenellated wall-towers and balconies, ensuring a wide field of fire, proved more successful against infantry scaling the walls by ladder. Where the objective lay by a river, the Assyrians used a siege tower. Constructed upstream and floated into position, this gave a field of fire down on the defenders within the walls. City-gateways were constructed for defence in depth and to enable enfilade fire to bear in all directions. Meanwhile sappers, covered by bowmen and shields, attempted to tunnel and undermine the walls, leaving wooden poles to support the holes and then be fired to weaken the superstructure.

Faced with a formidable array of defences, the besiegers often resorted to throwing up earth walls around the city and bombarding the besieged with propaganda, threats and demands for surrender. Anyone who emerged was turned back to his fate. The texts report long sieges 'When the army had besieged the city and there was such a hard famine that for one shekel of silver only three sutu (c.20 litres) of barley could be bought in secret'. In these circumstances texts occur in which mothers sought to sell their very small children for a stated small sum. While ostensibily this was a desperate measure to help them survive, there is a possibility that cases of cannibalism might have occurred.

A primary concern of the defence was the provision of water-supplies, and for this most Palestinian cities dug underground cisterns, like those at Megiddo and Gibeon, to which access was gained by steps and through tunnels. At Jerusalem Hezekiah of Judah, forseeing the inevitable Assyrian retribution by siege, enlarged a long tunnel from the Gihon spring to reach below the walls to a point under the enemy camp.

While a siege was in progress the Assyrians devastated the surrounding countryside to cut off forays for food. At Jerusalem in 701 the siege lasted less than a year (see below) compared with the two years needed by Nebuchadnezzar to take the same city in 588-7 BC. Some sieges lasted only a few weeks, but Arpad held out against Tiglath-pileser for three years; Samaria resisted Shalmaneser V and Sargon II for a similar length of time in 725-2 BC. The 13 years required by Nebuchadnezzar II at Tyre may indicate that the principal aim of the operation was to contain that offshore city and guard the Babylonian army's flank while it moved southwards against Judah and Egypt.

Siege of a city using assault ladders, while sappers breach the walls. From North-West Palace of Ashurnasir-apli, Nimrud. 9th century BC. British Museum, London.

Sargon's Eighth Campaign to Urartu, 714 BC

Detailed historical texts record most Assyrian rulers' military claims, in the process illustrating the strategy, tactics and methods employed. One such contemporary war report describes the eighth campaign of Sargon II in 714 BC. The large inscribed clay tablet is dated to the same year as the operation and was compiled from the first reports made by eye-witnesses in the field. These included military scribes and war artists, for such were known to inscribe and carve victory stelae at suitable places to mark the passage of Assyrian arms. The result is a travelogue noting the landscape, fauna and flora, weather conditions and local customs of the peoples encountered. The text is written up from notes and lists by a senior royal scribe in the form of a letter addressed to the national god, all the gods, the city of Ashur and its people. It was probably read out at a victory ceremony after the army's return to base, for it included oratorical passages and renders events not always in strict chronological and geographical order. Its main purpose was to describe the outstanding defeat of Ursâ, ruler of the hill-state of Urartu, east of Lake Van and of Mittati of Zikirtu, who had fomented rebellion among their neighbours.

The route taken, the hardships endured by the Assyrian force, and the damage they inflicted, is given in dramatic detail. The campaign was taken to all seven sub-provinces of Ursâ's kingdom, with 430 named towns and villages sacked. In an appendix the precise booty taken from Urzana of Muṣaṣir is listed. The letter ends with a note of the Assyrian dead as charioteers – one; cavalrymen – two; sappers – three. This is an indication of the order or columns of names or numbers given on a separate tablet rather than a complete casualty list, for it is to be noted that similar numbers occur on a text of Esarhaddon.

The Assyrian army was called up by royal command and then a full muster made in an assembly before the gods. The latter were consulted by taking the omens three times to ensure a favourable outcome of the expedition. The army was then inspected and given its orders before it moved off, with the group designated by the god Adad taking the lead. As the advance was through hilly and wooded country not favourable to chariots, progress was slow and pioneers had sometimes to cut a track with metal axes and sledgehammers. When entering more open terrain and passing though valleys, the king led in his command chariot followed by chariots, cavalry, specialist combat infantry and then support services with a light military detachment serving as the rearguard. In unknown territory one group (Ashur) was sent ahead to reconnoitre the route and outriders guarded the flanks. Camp-sites

Members of the royal bodyguard of Ashurbanipal stand watch during a campaign in southern Iraq. From South-West Palace of Ashurbanipal, Nineveh. c. 640 BC. British Museum, London.

were set out like a fortress with tents set within a guarded rampart. The approach of the army was sufficient to strike fear and panic ahead of its path, bringing out delegations of minor chiefs to offer submission and tribute. Dread of the Assyrian army and the havoc it could wreak led even major opponents sometimes to submit. Their vassal status was solemnly confirmed in an initial or renewed loyalty-treaty and by a feast at which the invaders were given bread and wine. The first tribute now collected included large horses already trained to the yoke. Ursâ's ally Ullusuŋu of Mannā was pardoned on the renewal of his treaty terms; future tribute payments were considerably increased and Assyrian officials appointed to ensure loyalty and report failures.

Sargon then changed tactics. Using a lighter mobile force, he made a sudden bound forward over 320 km against the rebellious Mittati of Zikirtu. The lightning advance caught Mittati by surprise, and he withdrew the troops defending his capital, together with its inhabitants, to the safety of the adjacent hills. Sargon outflanked him and, taking him in the rear, inflicted a defeat on one of his outposts before destroying 12 walled towns and villages around the capital by fire, reducing them to rubble. Meanwhile Ursâ continued to spread confusion and distrust among outlying tribes and attempted to gain time by delaying tactics against the advancing Assyrians, with whom he eventually expected a direct encounter. Sargon decided to take a direct line to his objective, which involved scaling a high snow- and ice-covered mountain ridge. Sargon himself had to walk and his chariot was carried over by bearers. The entire march is described in detail, not least because of its unusual plan and the effort required for its execution. At last the exhausted force descended into a valley between two steep mountains, where the Urartian had hastily drawn up a battle line. Ursâ sent messengers to the Assyrians with a challenge to do battle.

Here the report is interrupted by a laudatory account of Sargon's attributes as a good and just king and a prayer for divine help offered up before crossing the border to meet Ursâ. The Assyrians claim that their forced march meant that they had not stopped even to drink or camp for the night. Sargon, nevertheless, chose to attack immediately, leading his army in his chariot with a large detachment of cavalry, who inflicted heavy initial casualties on the enemy. They were followed by waves of the elite infantry supported by archers and spearmen. Tactical surprise was complete and the ground ran red with blood. Captives recorded include 230 members of the royal family, state officials, district governors and many Urartian cavalry and troops. Ursâ escaped on a mare and the Assyrians pursued the retreating Urartians for another 64 km. Heavy rain and massive hailstones inflicted further losses and was interpreted as divine judgment by the enemy, who laid down their arms. Ursâ abandoned his capital Turushpa by Lake Van 'threw himself on his bed, refused to drink and inflicted on himself an incurable disease'. Sargon took no further action but spared the people so that they would serve as witnesses to the power of the Assyrian armed forces, to their liberation from a tyrant and, above all, to the great victory won. Mopping-up operations continued in the areas held by Ursâ's former allies; Zikirtu was ravaged, as was the bordering district of Mannā. The operations were planned to cut off any district from its support systems. Towns and villages were set ablaze and their stores plundered for loot and food. A careful record was kept with names of each zone attacked with any relevant detail added. In one, Sangibuti, the fortress of Hundar was the main objective as it housed some of Ursâ's family and the temple of the local god Haldia. Everything was destroyed and the fertile region, with its crops, plantations and forests, fired to prevent support for humans or cattle and preclude renewed rebellion.

A separate expedition against Urzana of Muṣaṣir was undertaken with 1,000 horsemen under the king's command. Again the dismantled royal chariot was carried on men's backs over very rough terrain. The aim was once more to 'show the flag' in a powerful punitive demonstration. The treasures of the main temple of Haldia and his goddess Bagbartu were carried off and listed before the campaign drew to an end in a triumphant return south via Nineveh to Ashur. There the captured treasures were dedicated to the god Ashur, but the text makes no mention of the customary victory triumph with the army leading captive kings, nobles and officials in their train.

Sennacherib's Campaign in Palestine 701 BC

In 701 BC, Sennacherib of Assyria marched west to help his vassal Padi of Ekron, whose citizens had handed him over to Hezekiah, king of Judah, leader of the resistance to Assyrian control. The details are recorded both in Assyrian annals and in the Bible (2 Kings 18:13-19; Isaiah 36-39) and minor discrepancies between the accounts can be reconciled.

Hezekiah had encouraged a mission to Jerusalem by envoys from Merodach-baladan. Here they were shown the Judean preparedness for withstanding the expected invasion which would follow the break in treaty relations with Assyria. Hezekiah ensured water supplies for his capital (the Siloam tunnel), strengthened the walls, rebuilt stables, implying that his chariotry was alerted, filled his storehouses and held a census indicating a new mobilization. His expansionist policy towards Gaza and the Negeb at the expense of Philistia would have been known to the intelligence service watching for anti-Assyrian activity through their agents ('men of the tongue', the later 'eyes of the lord').

The Assyrians first received the renewed allegiance of the Amorite and Syrian coastal rulers, thus safeguarding their lines of communication, before moving south to capture Beth-Dagan and Joppa and its hinterland and confining Sidqa of Ashkelon. Sennacherib lists the fortified towns taken as he moved down the Phoenician coast from Sidon to Acco and received tribute from Sidon, Byblos and as far afield as Transjordan (Ammon, Moab and Edom). Then an advance was made on Eltekeh, dominating the coastal route, to isolate Philistia from Judah. Timnah was taken after the valley of Sorek had been blocked and Ekron cut off by the Assyrian control of the valley of Elah. Meanwhile Lachish was besieged in its turn. The Assyrian commander-in-chief negotiated with Jerusalem through interpreters who knew the local dialect and could address their propaganda to the citizens crowding the walls of the besieged capital. He stressed the victories already won in the north and the benefits of Assyrian overlordship. Sennacherib had 'shut up Hezekiah, the Judean in his capital Jerusalem like a bird in a cage' and claimed the capture of 46 strong walled towns and countless villages 'by building earthworks then bringing up siege engines and taking them with the help of assault troops, making breaches in the walls, by mines under the ramparts and onslaughts with the battering-ram'. He deported 200,150 persons and took unnumbered spoil from the region.

Judean towns were handed over to the new vassals set up in Ashdod, Ekron and Gaza and Judah was therefore diminished. Archaeological evidence confirms the massive destruction of sites around the capital but Jerusalem itelf was not captured. In part this may be due to the intervention of Tirhakah (Taharqa) who led out the Egyptian army in this same year to cut off any Assyrian retreat northwards. The armies clashed in a major battle at Eltekeh in which Sennacherib claimed victory, although this may disguise the scale of his own losses. According to Herodotus the Assyrians were defeated when mice (or possibly rats) gnawed through their bowstrings and leather accoutrements. The Bible claims that the Assyrians lost 185(000) dead in one night. Though this is often interpreted as an instance of bubonic plague, it could equally be taken as an outbreak of a tropical form of bacillary dysentery, for infectious diseases or plagues are recorded accompanying large scale army movements in the ancient Near East. Other examples of such epidemics include possible typhus among Hittite troops, schistosomiasis among the inhabitants of Jericho after its destruction, and plague among the Philistines at Ashdod following the battle nearby.

It is interesting to compare these field operations with those of the Babylonian Nebuchadnezzar II (605-562 BC), who fought in Syria against the Egyptian garrisons on their supply lines through Megiddo, Qadesh, Hamath and Carchemish. On taking over the empire once held by the Assyrians, he first set up his own garrisons or outposts on both banks of the River Euphrates below Carchemish and so checked the Egyptian thrusts southwards. Then he took a mobile force across to the west bank in an attempt to cut off the Egyptians by encircling Carchemish and attacking it from the north. According to the Babylonian Chronicle, the city fell in 605 and though many of the garrison broke out, the Egyptians were pursued as far as Hamath and 'not a single man escaped'. The Babylonians claim that they rapidly recovered control of all the land as far as the Gaza border. Indeed, the Egyptians did not re-emerge as a major power in Asia until more than a thousand years later. Nebuchadnezzar consolidated his hold by the annual call-up of his now largely mercenary army and marched through Syro-Palestine ('Hatti-land') to collect tribute and reinforce his garrisons. It was now possible to keep the army in the field for long periods at a time and Greek mercenaries are attested in both Egyptian and Babylonian armies. In 601 BC both super-powers clashed in a great open battle near the border. The Babylonians claim that they 'fought and inflicted a major defeat on each other'. Indeed the effect was such that, according to the same reliable and usually objective Babylonian Chronicle, Nebuchadnezzar had to spend the whole of the next year re-equipping his forces, which were unable to venture abroad.

In his seventh year Nebuchadnezzar 'marched out and beseiged Jerusalem, capturing it on the second of Adar [16 March 597] and took its king [Jehoiachin] prisoner. He appointed a king there of his own choice [Zedekiah] and sent the heavy tribute he received back to Babylon'. Thus the Jewish exile began and ten years later, when Judah plotted its independence, Jersualem, was sacked. This freed Babylon for another advance and in 570 she attacked pharaoh Amasis in the Delta. Like the Assyrians before them, the Babylonians discovered that it was impossible to hold a far-ranging empire by military garrison and army operations alone. The need to counter constant military incursions by foes on the borders and to police restless subordinates on every frontier proved too great. Babylon itself was to fall to Cyrus, king of the Medes and Persians, when his general Gobryas took the city in October 539 BC. He used the stratagem of diverting the course of the River Euphrates near Opis, rendering the water defences of the great city to the south useless. The Persian troops marched down the dried-up river bed and so gained surprise access into the city. Little did they realize that they – just as Alexander the Great, who sought to revivify Babylon – would have to fight over the same ground to hold the Near East together as part of their empire.

PRINCIPAL SOURCES

Assyrian Annals

Scribes at the Assyrian capital cities wrote on tablets, prisms and clay cylinders concise accounts of major military campaigns. While for most kings, from Ashur-nasir-apli to Ashurbanipal, these aimed to glorify the king, the military details are generally reliable and taken from contemporary sources. These annals follow a geographical or chronological order, and notes from an Assyrian Kings List or the Eponym Canon enable the events to be dated precisely.

Assyrian and Babylonian Chronicles (8th-5th centuries BC)

These are objective, accurate and brief statements of the main military, political and religious events in each regnal year. They can be compared with other texts, also written in the cuneiform script, which provide additional military intelligence, such as letters, administrative lists and reports. The report of *The Eighth Campaign of Sargon II* (701 BC) is one example.

Assyrian Sculptures (*c.* 747-627 BC)

The stone bas-reliefs on the walls of palaces at Nineveh (Sennacherib and Ashurbanipal); Kalhu (Tiglath-pileser and Esarhaddon); Khorsabad (Sargon) and the bronze gate panels from Balawat (Shalmaneser III) are a rich source of illustration of the military forces, men, mounts and arms. These are displayed in The British Museum, The Louvre, The Iraq Museums, etc.

The Bible

The Old Testament includes in its history of Israel and Judah battle reports, stories and accounts of the capture of Samaria (722 BC) and the unsuccessful Assyrian siege of Jerusalem in 701. These, and the subsequent capture and sack of Jerusalem (597, 587), supplement, and generally agree with, the Assyrian and Babylonian sources (2 *Kings* 17-18; 24-25).

HOPLITE WARFARE

JOHN LAZENBY

What little evidence we have from archaeology and the Homeric poems suggests that 8th-century Greek warfare was fluid and disorganized, and the battlefield dominated by a few, comparatively well-armed, aristocratic 'heroes'. The main weapon seems to have been the throwing-spear, and such a weapon perhaps limits the extent to which tactics can begin to be refined, and leads to the glorification of individual exploits we find in Homer. The dominance of the heroes was probably never as complete as Homer suggests – in real life, an aristocratic champion is always likely to be killed by a nonentity. Centuries later, for example, Pyrrhus of Epirus, rated by Hannibal as a general second only to Alexander, was brought down by a tile flung by a woman, and such a death for a hero was poetically impossible. Nevertheless, although some aspects of Homeric warfare may be unreal, there is no reason to doubt that the heroic attitude was real enough. Essentially a hero fought for himself and his own personal glory, and one who could declare, as Hector does in the *Iliad*, that 'one omen is best – to fight for one's country', was a rarity. Even in classical times, when Athenian aristocrats sang of the deaths of their ancestors at the hands of the 'tyrant' Hippias, they praised them not for dying for the freedom of Athens, but for not having shamed their forefathers, as we can see in a drinking-song, quoted in the Aristotelian *Constitution of the Athenians*.

The Emergence of the Soldier

By about the middle of the 7th century, however, a new style of warfare had appeared in Greece, and in the poetry of the Spartan Tyrtaeus, we meet a different kind of ideal. In his verses a warrior's duty is to stand shoulder-to-shoulder with his comrades and not to engage in individual acts of bravery. On Tyrtaeus' battlefields it would have been an Achilles who would have been out of place – the hero has become a soldier.

How and when the change came about is a matter of controversy, but it seems likely that the opening up of new and old trade-routes, and the beginnings of the colonial movement, led to the spread of wealth in the homeland. Archaeological evidence suggests that greater numbers of men were now able to afford helmet, armour, greaves and shield, and thus take their places in the battle-line. The increasing number of armoured infantry was probably the major factor in the decline in the importance of individual prowess and the move towards organization, but there may also have been a psychological reason for the change of attitude. Perhaps the new breed of warriors lacked the desire for personal glory which aristocratic birth engendered, for one cannot shame ancestors one has not got.

Technical innovation also reinforced the growing willingness to co-operate. The Homeric poems and contemporary vase paintings suggest that by the end of the 8th century, at latest, warriors were armed much like those of Tyrtaeus' time, with one important difference: the shield appears to have been suspended by a shoulder-strap, and, judging by a hero's ability to hold it out in front of him, held by a single, central handgrip. At some point, however, this method of carrying the shield was abandoned. The shoulder-strap was discarded, and the single, central handgrip replaced by a double-grip,

consisting of an armband in the centre of the shield, through which the arm was thrust to the elbow, and a grip for the hand near the rim.

The essential difference between the new shield and the old was that although the old shield could have been allowed to hang by its strap from time to time, to rest the arm, in combat it would have to be held, and its full weight would then have depended on the wrist. In contrast, the new shield was locked on the fore-arm and its weight thus borne by the left shoulder, enabling both the shield itself to be more substantial, and its owner to carry it more easily in protracted combat. One potential drawback, however, was that since the new shield was gripped by the left hand near its rim, it protected only the left side of its owner's body, if held comfortably, while half of it projected to his left. But if warriors stood shoulder-to-shoulder, each of them could rely on the shield of the man on his right to protect the right side of his body. Thus Thucydides explains the tendency of these soldiers to edge to their right as the result of 'each man, in their anxiety, getting his unprotected side as close as possible to the shield of the man standing on his right, and thinking that the more closely the shields were locked, the better the protection'. Another consequence was that the throwing-spear had, sooner or later, to be abandoned in favour of a thrusting-spear. Although throwing-spears still seem, oddly, to be depicted on the Chigi Vase, for example, close-packed infantry can really have had little use for them – even swords were henceforth only used in emergencies.

Thus was born the characteristic infantry formation of archaic and

The duel between Achilles (left) and Hector from an Attic red figure volute crater by the Berlin Painter (c. 490 BC), found at Cerveteri in Italy. Note the typical hoplite shields, and the unusual under-arm thrust used by Achilles; Hector, in contrast, continues to grip his sagging spear for an over-arm thrust. British Museum, London.

One of the earliest vase-paintings showing hoplites in battle (c. 650 BC or later), from a Protocorinthian olpe (the 'Chigi Vase'). Note the metallic corslets, individualized blazons, and what look like extra spears, carried 'at the slope'. These are puzzling because the carrying of two spears is usually thought to imply throwing-spears, and yet these soldiers are obviously using the typical over-arm thrust. Perhaps the spears 'at the slope' are to be thought of as the spears of soldiers not yet engaged. Note also the piper, presumably giving the step, as Thucydides says was still done in the Spartan army at First Mantinea in 418 BC. Museo Nazionale di Villa Giulia, Rome.

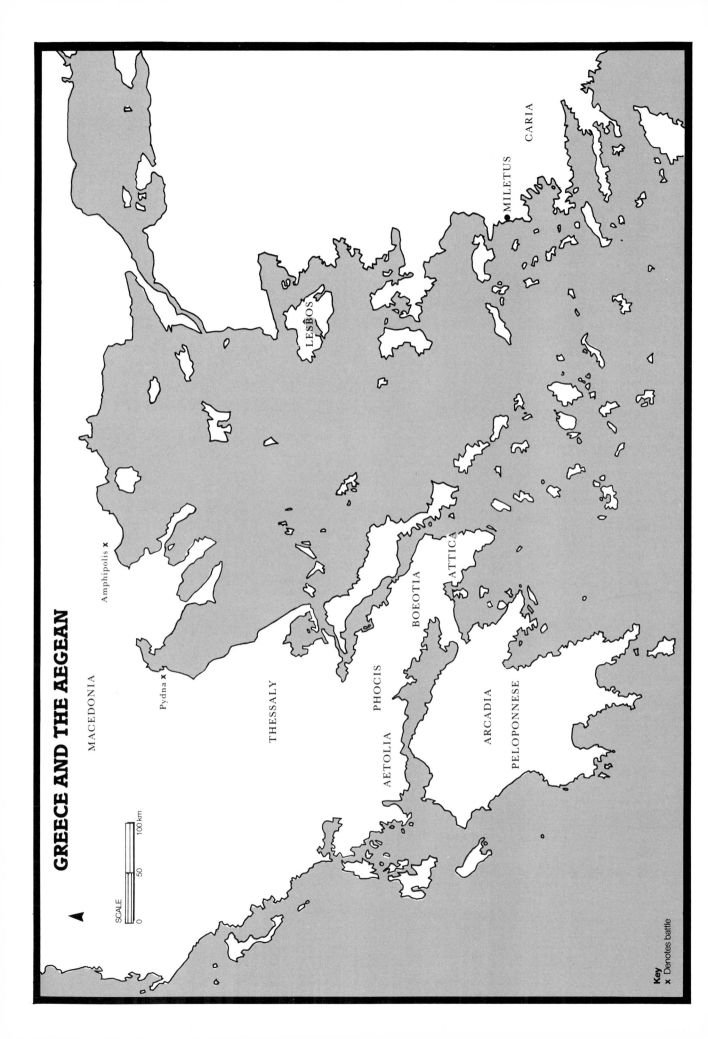

GREECE AND THE AEGEAN

SCALE

0   50   100 km

MACEDONIA

Amphipolis **x**

Pydna **x**

THESSALY

AETOLIA

PHOCIS

BOEOTIA

ATTICA

ARCADIA

PELOPONNESE

LESBOS

MILETUS

CARIA

Key
x Denotes battle

classical Greece, the phalanx, consisting of files of men, eight deep or more, standing as close as possible to each other, with shields touching or even overlapping. From now on a man depended on his 'mates' in a very real sense: as a character in one of Euripides' plays observes, however brave a man was, he could be killed by the cowardice of those standing next to him. Even acts of individual courage came to be frowned upon if they involved leaving the line. At the battle of Plataea, in 479, for example, the bravest man on the field, in Herodotus' view, was Aristodemus, the sole survivor of Thermopylae. But the Spartans thought another man braver, he says, because Aristodemus had been 'behaving like a lunatic and leaving the line' – he had been in disgrace since Thermopylae for not accompanying his fellow-sufferer from ophthalmia, Eurytus, to his death, and had been determined to prove his courage. The supreme disgrace for a soldier came to be the loss of his shield; as one of Plutarch's *Sayings of the Spartans* puts it, unlike helmet or corslet, a man carried a shield 'for the sake of the whole line' – hence the injunction of Spartan mothers to their sons to come back either with their shields or on them. It is even possible that the term used for the new-style soldiers – 'hoplites' (*hoplitai*) – came from the word *hoplon*, which could mean 'shield', though the normal word for the hoplite shield was *aspis*.

The Hoplite

In trying to determine when and where hoplites first appeared on the battlefield, we must be careful to distinguish between the first appearance of the equipment which became characteristic at least of early hoplites, and the first grouping of men armed in this fashion into a phalanx. The equipment began to appear before 700, judging by the depiction of what look like metallic corslets on Attic vases of about 720, and by an actual bronze panoply found in an Argive grave of about 710; the typical 'Corinthian' helmet – covering the head and leaving only the eyes and mouth clear – had appeared by about 685. By this time there are representations of the inside of shields showing the double grip, and it is possible that it is indicated earlier by vase-paintings showing shields with asymmetrical blazons. This implies a shield that was not likely to be held upside-down, since to have gone into battle with one's blazon inverted would have been a truly awful omen. The first certain representations of hoplites in a phalanx, however, occur a little later, on proto-Corinthian vases of about 670; the best known, the Chigi Vase, dates from about 650 or later. In literature, the early 7th-century poet Archilochus' joke about the loss of his shield hints at its new importance, and by about 650, in the poems of Tyrtaeus, we are clearly dealing with hoplites.

As to where hoplites first appeared, Argos has as good a claim as any. The panoply mentioned above is suggestive, and the Argives may have been the first mainland Greeks to use the double-grip shield. Herodotus appears to attribute its invention to the Carians, a non-Greek people of south-west Asia Minor. This is not implausible, as they were famous as mercenaries at this time; some of them, for example, helped the Egyptian nationalist hero, Psamtik I, to throw off the Assyrian yoke in about 650. But the Carians had close ties with the neighbouring Greek city of Miletus, and Miletus in turn with Argos; the fact that the shield was sometimes later called the 'Argive' shield suggests that it was there that it first came into use in mainland Greece. There is no proof that the Argives were the first Greeks to mass men armed with the new shield in a phalanx, but there is an interesting anonymous poem, preserved in the Palatine Anthology, which in listing the best things in Greece, mentions Sparta only for its women, but celebrates as best of all, 'the linen-corsleted Argives, the goads of war'. The first battle in which hoplites took part may thus have been the battle of Hysiae in 669, where the Argives defeated the Spartans – for the last time.

Thus the earliest hoplites were infantry of the line, equipped with helmet, corslet, greaves and round double-grip shield, and armed with thrusting-spear

Bronze panoply from a Late Geometric grave at Argos (c. 710 BC). The corslet is obviously the product of a sophisticated workshop, but the helmet seems designed more for show than for safety, although it is reminiscent of helmets shown on Assyrian reliefs of the reign of Tiglath-pileser III (745-727 BC). The warrior to whom this panoply belonged would probably have fought in a pre-hoplite style, but it is part of the evidence which suggests that it was the Argives who introduced hoplite warfare to Greece. Archaeological Museum, Argos.

and sword. As time went on, the typical 'Corinthian' helmet was modified in various ways, and some Greeks possibly discarded the metallic helmet altogether. By 425, for example, Spartan hoplites are described by Thucydides as wearing *piloi*, which strictly speaking were felt caps, although it is possible that these were made of bronze but called *piloi* because they resembled the conical shape of such caps. Some of the earliest hoplites, as indicated by the poem quoted above, wore some kind of linen corslet, and later on many hoplites appear to have discarded their bronze 'bell' corslets, consisting of back and front plates, in favour of one probably made out of strips of linen glued together. It is possible that some eventually discarded body-armour altogether, and fought in just a tunic, short cloak, or even, perhaps, in the nude. But the double-grip shield remained the essential piece of hoplite equipment to the end: Greek writers often refer to a phalanx as 'so many shields deep', and when, for example, the Spartans abandoned this kind of shield in the 220s, they effectively ceased to be hoplites, and became instead 'phalangites' on the Macedonian model. Surviving hoplite shields average 80 cm in diameter, and are made of wood or stiff leather, with a bronze facing and rim. Vase-paintings show an immense variety of blazons, but by the end of the 5th century the soldiers of some states carried shields with a blazon consisting either of the initial letter of their nationality, or of a national symbol. Spartan shields, for example, bore a *lambda* (L) for *Lakedaimonioi*, the name by which they were usually known, Theban shields a club.

Battle

We know that such troops were deployed for battle in close-knit formation, normally eight deep, though Thucydides says the Thebans were 25 deep at the battle of Delium in 424, and the Syracusans 16 deep at a battle against the Athenians just outside Syracuse, nine years later; in the 4th century we hear of phalanxes 12 and 16 deep, and at Leuctra, in 371, the Thebans are said by Xenophon to have been 50 deep. We know, too, that opposing phalanxes closed to within spear-thrust either at the double, as the Athenians did at Marathon and Delium, and the Thebans at Second Coronea, or more slowly, keeping step to the sound of the pipe, as the Spartans did at First Mantinea in 418, according to Thucydides. But what happened next is unclear, and very difficult for anyone who has not taken part in hand-to-hand combat to visualize.

One theory is that there was an opening stage in which the hoplites fought in loose order, man to man, in a series of individual duels, before they closed up and what the Greeks called 'the shoving' (*othismos*) took place. But although there are one or two accounts which appear to imply that fighting went on for some time before the *othismos*, in these the term may be used for the final 'heave'

Arming scene from an Attic red figure cup signed by Douris (c. 500-460 BC) from Cerveteri. Note the undergarments worn by the third man from the left, to prevent chafing, the complex corslet being put on by the man in the centre, the hollow, basin-like quality of the shields, with their sharply off-set rims, and the man on the right doing up his hair before donning his helmet – Spartan troops often let their long hair fall below their helmets. Kunsthistorisches Museum, Vienna.

with which one side bore the other down, for there are other accounts which suggest that the opposing front ranks literally crashed together, shield to shield, and that the *othismos* began there and then. Xenophon, for example, says of Second Coronea in 394, of which he was an eyewitness, that the Spartans and Thebans 'smashing their shields together, shoved, fought, slew and died'. Delium, according to Thucydides, saw 'tough fighting and shoving of shields', and later he describes the Thebans as 'shoving the Athenians back little by little'. Plato, moreover, in his dialogue *Laches*, has the Athenian general, Nicias, declare that skill-at-arms was relatively unimportant until the lines broke and individuals found themselves compelled to fight other individuals either in flight or pursuit.

Obviously at least the men in the front ranks tried to stab each other: vase-paintings suggest that the typical thrust was overarm, aiming for the throat or shoulders, over the rim of the shield. Men were certainly killed by spear thrusts – Epaminondas, for example, perhaps the greatest of all hoplite generals, was mortally wounded by a spear thrust at Second Mantinea, in 362. But what Thucydides says about the desirability of standing as close as possible to the man on one's right, and the importance attached to the depth of the phalanx from Marathon to Leuctra, demonstrates that its weight and cohesion as a whole was what mattered, not the prowess of the hoplites as individuals. A hoplite phalanx was not quite like an armoured rugger-scrum – for one thing, the rear ranks did not 'bind' on the first. The men in the second rank, at least, may have been able to use their spears – they were 2-2.5 m long – and it was presumably their duty to take the place of anyone in the front rank who fell. But it is difficult to see what the men in the rear ranks did – in a phalanx 'fifty shields deep' the men right at the back would have been a long way from the action. There is no evidence that they were ever deployed to left and right of the men to their front, to outflank the enemy while the front ranks pinned them, as has been suggested, so we can only suppose that they added 'weight' to the attack – at the very least they would have stopped the front ranks fleeing unless and until they did the same. Traditions such as the one recorded by Polyaenus that at the crucial moment in the battle of Leuctra, Epaminondas cried to his men, 'give me one more step and we'll win', suggest that something like the 'shove' of a scrum took place. Many battles were decided more or less immediately by one side or the other giving way – morale is even more important in hand-to-hand combat than in other forms – but there is some reason to believe that if both sides stood to fight it out, the losers may almost literally have been bowled over by the winners. It may not be just a coincidence, for example, that at Leuctra the Spartans lost about a 1,000 men altogether, according to Xenophon, for the Theban frontage was probably about 80 shields, and the Spartans were 12 shields deep. The 50-deep Thebans may virtually have annihilated the part of the Spartan line directly opposed to them.

Bronze helmet of 'Corinthian' type from Olympia. An inscription on it says that it was dedicated to Zeus by the Argives as spoil taken from the Corinthians. The letter-forms suggest a date of c. 460 BC, and although nothing is known of a particular war between Argos and Corinth at that time, Argos is known to have been involved in war with Sparta and her allies – of whom Corinth was one – in both the 460s and the early 450s. Note how much better the protection afforded by this helmet would have been, compared with the one depicted on page 57. British Museum, London.

The Persian Wars

The supreme test of the hoplites against different troops came in the Persian wars and it is fairly clear, even from the meagre information we possess, that it was the mass tactics of the Greeks which won the day, not their individual superiority. Indeed, at first the Persians had it all their own way. They brought the Greeks of Asia Minor, Thrace and the off-shore islands under their control, without much apparent difficulty, in the last half of the 6th century. Then, early in the 5th century, when these Greeks rebelled in alliance with the Carians and Cypriots, but with minimal help from the mainland, the Persians won all but one of the land battles of which we have any knowledge. The one exception – which proves the rule – was when a Persian army was ambushed at night. Unfortunately our sources do not give any details, but Herodotus tells us that in one battle – fought at Malene, near Atarneus, on the mainland east of Lesbos – the Persian cavalry arrived late and tipped the balance. It is possible

Part of the north frieze of the Siphnian Treasury at Delphi (c.525 BC). The scene is a battle between gods and giants, and real hoplites would not normally have expected to meet chariots in battle – though Xenophon and his comrades did at Cunaxa – let alone ones driven by goddesses and pulled by lions. However, the details of the warriors' equipment are authentic. Note how closely those to right and left are packed, and how they all use the over-arm thrust.

that the Asiatic Greeks had lost their aptitude for hoplite fighting during a generation of subjection, or that they had never really developed it, though this is belied by the Carians' reputation as, in a sense, the inventors of hoplite warfare; possibly confronted by overwhelming numbers, they allowed themselves to be shot to pieces by Persian archers, mounted and on foot, without ever being able to close. What happened at Plataea, in 479, suggests the fate of other hoplites perhaps less resolutely handled or even just less lucky.

When the Persians invaded mainland Greece it was a different story. At Marathon in 490, the Athenians and their Plataean allies closed at the double – the first Greeks known to Herodotus to have done so – putting the Persian archers off their shot and cutting down the time they had for their volleys. The stronger Greek wings apparently overcame the Persian wings with some ease, and then, instead of pursuing, they probably wheeled to take the Persian centre, which had broken through the weaker Athenian centre, in both flanks. These appear to be relatively sophisticated tactics, and it is possible that they had been worked out in advance. However, it is equally possible and perhaps more likely, that what happened was pure coincidence. In the first place, the thinning of the Greek centre is said by Herodotus to have been purely defensive and designed simply to make their line as long as that of the Persians. Secondly, although the action of the wings, which had probably been left at normal depth, looks as though it was planned, it should be borne in mind that the hoplites forming them may not have been capable of pursuing their more lightly-equipped foes, especially if they had just doubled 1,500m, as Herodotus implies. The converging of the Greek wings – if that *is* what happened (Herodotus' Greek is unclear) – could have been an almost automatic response to what happened to their centre. The files nearest to the point where the centre gave way would inevitably have ground to a halt, and the wings would then have tended to hinge on them as the Persian wings broke and fled. Nevertheless it was a famous victory, although Herodotus is less than fair to his own fellow-countrymen in Asia Minor when he claims that the Athenians were the first Greeks even to face the sight of Persian dress and the men clad in it.

Ten years later, at Thermopylae, Greek hoplites again showed their prowess, although ultimately they were outmanoeuvred. In spite of standing strategically on the defensive, their tactics seem to have been offensive, perhaps to deny the enemy's missile-troops a static target. Herodotus says that the Spartans at least feigned a series of retreats, which induced the enemy to close with them, but possibly what really lay behind this tradition were the tactics the Spartans certainly later developed for dealing with a similar enemy – ordering the younger men, in the front ranks, to charge out from the phalanx and then fall back after driving the enemy away. 'Shoving' was also in evidence, at least on the final day, round the body of the fallen Leonidas, and the formidable fighting qualities of even a small body of hoplites – by then

MARATHON

STAGE 1

The Athenians thin their centre to make their line as long as the Persians', and advance at the double.

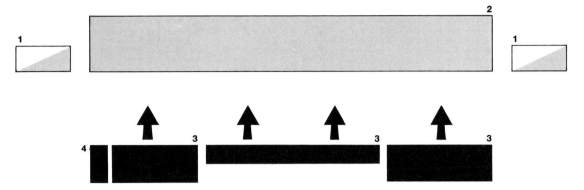

STAGE 2

The Athenian and Plataean wings smash into the Persian wings, and the latter flee, taking the cavalry with them, but the Persian centre pushes the weaker Athenian centre back.

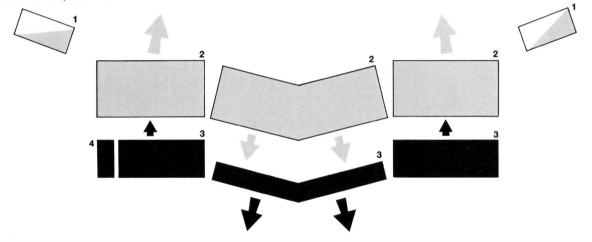

STAGE 3

The Persian centre breaks through the Athenian centre, but the Athenian and Plataean wings, hingeing on the points where their centre has given way, swing inwards to take the Persian centre in both flanks.

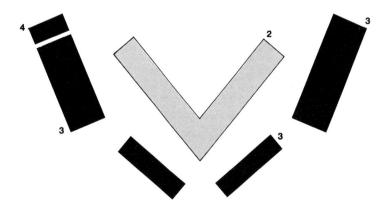

Key
1. Persian Cavalry.
2. Persian Infantry.
3. Athenians.
4. Plataeans.

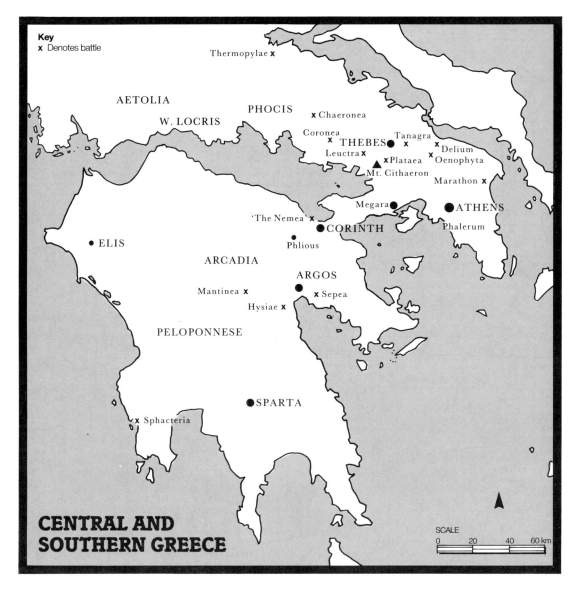

Key
x Denotes battle

Thermopylae x

AETOLIA

W. LOCRIS

PHOCIS

x Chaeronea

Coronea
x   THEBES●   Tanagra x
Leuctra x   x Delium
        x Plataea   x Oenophyta
Mt. Cithaeron
                    Marathon x

Megara ●   ●ATHENS

'The Nemea' x   Phalerum

●CORINTH

● ELIS

Phlious ●

ARCADIA

ARGOS
●
Mantinea x   x Sepea

Hysiae x

PELOPONNESE

●SPARTA

x Sphacteria

**CENTRAL AND
SOUTHERN GREECE**

SCALE
0   20   40   60 km

there can hardly have been more than about 1,000 left – were repeatedly shown if it is true, as Herodotus claims, that they flung the enemy back four times. But when they heard that the Persian flanking force was in their rear, and retreated to the hillock which was their final position, they presumably at last presented a static target, and it is significant that Herodotus seems to suggest that they were overwhelmed by missile fire.

The decisive clash came in 479, at Plataea (see map, page 74). After days of harassing the Greeks at a distance with missile-troops, the Persians were tempted by the apparent break-up of the Greek army into closing with its isolated right wing. Some scholars have again seen sophisticated tactics behind all this, but Herodotus clearly thought that the Greeks had almost blundered to defeat, and we should believe him. It was the Persians' ill fortune that the Greek right consisted of 5,000 Spartan troops and a further 6,500 of the best of their allies, and the result was fatal. Herodotus emphasizes that the Persians were not inferior in spirit or strength, but that they lacked armour and experience, and were not their opponents' equal in skill. When he goes on to remark that 'rushing out singly or in groups of ten, more or less, they fell upon the Spartans and were destroyed', he seems to imply that their lack of experience and skill lay precisely in their failure to combine. Their lack of protective clothing he sums up by saying that they were 'unarmoured troops [*gumnetes* – literally 'naked'] trying to make a fight of it against hoplites.'

The verdict of Plataea was finally hammered home at Cunaxa, somewhere west of Baghdad, in 401. Greek mercenaries – one of whom was Xenophon – fighting for the rebel Persian prince Cyrus against his brother Artaxerxes, King of Persia, swept the field of their immediate opponents, even though the death of Cyrus himself, elsewhere on the battlefield, cost their side the victory. Xenophon's eyewitness description of their charge in his *Anabasis (Persian Expedition)*, howling their warcry and some clattering their spears against their shields, is marvellously evocative. Earlier in the campaign even a mock advance by the Greeks, at a review, had alarmed Cyrus' native troops and terrified his Cilician mistress.

Spartan Military Organization

As Herodotus' accounts of Thermopylae and Plataea imply, it was the Spartans who were the past-masters of hoplite fighting. By the middle of the 6th century they controlled the greater part of the Peloponnese, and by about 494 their reputation was so formidable that the Argives confronting them at the battle of Sepea are said by Herodotus to have been afraid of being 'caught out by some trick' (i.e. of being outmanoeuvred). Their way of trying to avoid this was to conform to all orders given to the Spartans, whereupon the Spartan king Cleomenes I instructed his men to attack when next orders were issued to fall out for the morning meal! For nearly two centuries, down to the battle of Leuctra in 371, Spartan hoplites effectively dominated the battlefields of Greece, and by the time of the Peloponnesian War their opponents are often said to have been afraid to face them. Even in 368, after Leuctra, a whole army of Argives and Arcadians is said by Xenophon to have broken and run at what became known as the'Tearless Battle', because allegedly not a single Spartan was killed.

The reason for this dominance is often thought to have been the rigorous training to which young Spartans were subjected, possibly from the age of seven and certainly from the age of 14. But although this regime would undoubtedly have had the effect of making Spartans tough, and of instilling in them habits of obedience, discipline and courage, we have seen that individual qualities were not what mattered in a hoplite battle. The crucial factor was the ability to combine, and it was probably here that the Spartans had the edge over their opponents. As their ex-king Demaratus told Xerxes when challenged to fight ten Persians, 'fighting singly the Spartans are no worse than other men, but together are the best of all mankind'.

Remarkable as it may seem, for a long time the Spartans appear to have been the only Greeks to have broken their army down into manageable tactical units. There is no evidence that the Athenian and Theban armies, for example, contained units smaller than a *lochos*, which, though the number varied from army to army, almost always contained at least several hundred men; the Theban *hieros lochos* ('Sacred Band'), the crack unit in their army, was 300 strong. But at First Mantinea, in 418, the Spartan *lochoi* each contained four *pentekostyes*, and each *pentekostys* four *enomotiai*, the latter having an average strength of only 32 men. The implication of Thucydides' description is that this was something unusual, as was the chain of command from king to polemarchs (*polemarchoi*), and thence to *lochagoi*, *pentekonteres* and enomotarchs (*enomotarchoi*). How early such an organization existed is controversial, but Herodotus says that *enomotiai* were instituted by the semi-mythical lawgiver, Lycurgus, which should at least mean that they came into existence before his own time, and he mentions a Spartan *lochos* in his account of Plataea. It is even possible that what were later the largest units, the *morai*, first mentioned by Xenophon in connection with events in 403, already existed in 418, despite Thucydides' failure to mention them. In his chain of command polemarchs come between the king and the *lochagoi*, and the polemarchs were certainly the

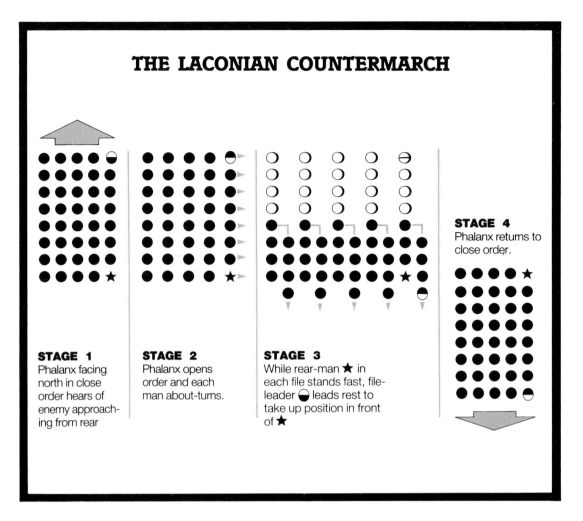

THE LACONIAN COUNTERMARCH

STAGE 1
Phalanx facing north in close order hears of enemy approaching from rear

STAGE 2
Phalanx opens order and each man about-turns.

STAGE 3
While rear-man ★ in each file stands fast, file-leader ◖ leads rest to take up position in front of ★

STAGE 4
Phalanx returns to close order.

Note how this manoeuvre has the effect of making it appear that the phalanx is *advancing* on an enemy appearing from the rear.

commanders of *morai* in Xenophon's time. In this case, it may be significant that the first Spartan polemarch mentioned in the sources is Euainetus, the man whom Herodotus identifies as the commander of their contingent at the Tempe Pass in 480.

Even if the *morai* did not exist before the end of the 5th century, as many scholars believe, it would appear that the Spartan army already had a complex organization which in all probability enabled it to manoeuvre in a way that was beyond other Greek armies. In the 4th century, each full-strength *enomotia* seems to have contained 40 men, five from each of the eight groups of age-classes into which men were divided from their 21st to their 60th years. Normally the oldest group, comprising men in their 56th to 60th years, were not required for front-line duties, so that the campaign-strength of an *enomotia* will usually have been 35 men. There were probably 32 *enomotiai* in a *mora* – though this, too, is controversial – divided into eight *pentekostyes* and two *lochoi*. Thus the full strength of a *mora* will have been 1,280 men, of a *lochos* 640 men, and of a *pentekostys* 160 men. The call-up system obviously enabled the Spartan government to mobilize a force of any size, by varying the number of *morai* – there were six in all – and the number of age-classes represented. At Leuctra, for which 35 age-classes had been called up, according to Xenophon, each of the four *morai* present will have contained 1,120 men. In addition, when a king

THE *ANASTROPHE*

In order to double the depth of the right wing of a phalanx, men in the required number of right-hand files about-turn, march to the rear, and wheel to come up behind the new right wing.

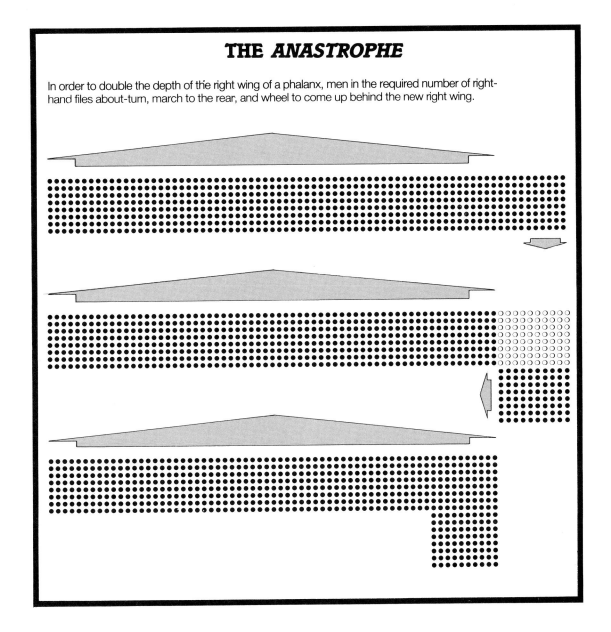

was in the field, a Spartan army usually included the 300 *Hippeis* ('Knights'), who acted as a Royal Guard, and, in spite of their name, fought on foot.

An essay on *The Constitution of the Lacedaimonians*, attributed to Xenophon in antiquity, but possibly written by another hand, tells us something of the basic drills used by the Spartans: for example, for deploying from line-of-march into line-of-battle, or for facing to meet an enemy approaching from different directions. Xenophon's accounts of warfare in the *Hellenika (History of Greece)* sometimes give us a glimpse of the operational employment of such drills. He observes, for example, that at Second Coronea, King Agesilaus 'countermarched the phalanx' to face the Thebans, who had broken through his left and were now in his rear. Presumably he used what was later known as the 'Laconian (i.e. Spartan) countermarch', in which each file about-turned and while the original rear-man stood fast, the file-leader led the rest of the file to take up their positions in front of him. Another manoeuvre, employed by Agesilaus in Arcadia in 370 to extricate his army from a defile, was the so-called 'wheeling-back' (*anastrophe*). This seems to have involved files on one or

SECOND CORONEA

'Smashing their shields together, they shoved, fought, slew and died' is how Xenophon describes the final encounter between the Spartans and the Thebans at Second Coronea in 394 BC, of which he was probably an eyewitness. Unfortunately, after the Chigi Vase and a few other vases of the 7th century, Greek artists tended to depict individual combat, rather than the confrontation between phalanxes. This, therefore, is an imaginative attempt to show what a hoplite battle would have been like.

The viewpoint is that of someone overlooking the battle from the north, with the Thebans to the right and the Spartans – note the 'lambdas' on their shields – to the left. It is not certain how much armour, or what kind of helmets would have been worn by such troops at this date, but the Spartans at least probably wore the conical helmet *(pilos)* shown, and all hoplites still carried the typical, double-grip shield, and were armed with a thrusting-spear as their main offensive weapon.

FIRST MANTINEA

STAGE 1

The two armies advance obliquely to the right, as each man seeks the protection of the shield of the man on his right.

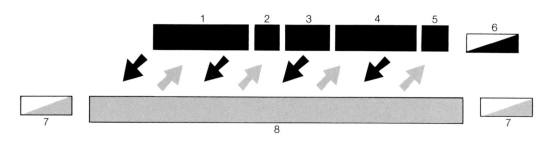

STAGE 2

The Spartan king orders the units on his left to shift to their left, but when the two units from the right, ordered to plug the gap, fail to do so, the enemy right routs the Spartan left, and charges through the gap. But the enemy left takes to flight on contact with the Spartan right.

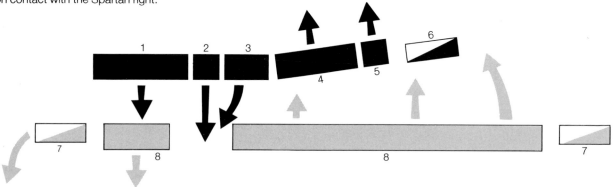

STAGE 3

The Spartans allow the enemy left to retire, protected by its cavalry, and, wheeling right, take the victorious enemy right in its shieldless flank as it streams back across the field.

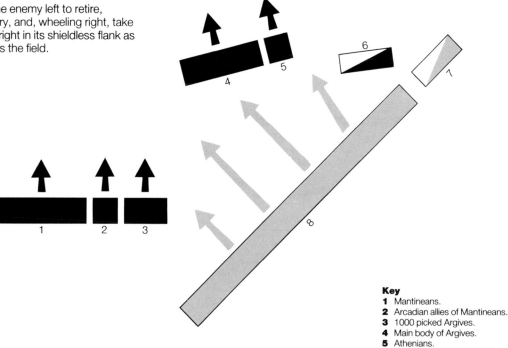

Key
1 Mantineans.
2 Arcadian allies of Mantineans.
3 1000 picked Argives.
4 Main body of Argives.
5 Athenians.
6 Athenian cavalry.
7 Spartan cavalry.
8 Spartan army.

other flank about-turning, marching to the rear, and then wheeling to take position behind the files to their left or right, thus doubling the depth of the phalanx at that point. Modern ceremonial drills, such as 'Trooping the Colour', give a good idea of what can be accomplished along these lines by highly trained troops, and one should not forget that these now archaic-looking rituals once had a real significance on the battlefield. In a hoplite battle, manoeuvring to fall on an enemy's shieldless flank could be decisive.

The author of *The Constitution of the Lacedaimonians* makes the point that many people thought the drills he describes difficult, which implies that they were not widely practised, and this seems to be confirmed by other remarks in our sources. Pericles, in the Funeral Speech, glories in the contrast between the natural courage of the Athenians and the 'laborious training' of the Spartans, and it is possible that there was no formal military training in Athens in his day. Thucydides states that at First Mantinea only 1,000 of the hoplites from Argos had been trained at the state's expense, and Xenophon seems to imply that the Boeotians only developed a taste for training after Leuctra. *The Constitution of the Lacedaimonians* also tells us that there was one thing which *was* difficult for all except those trained under 'the laws of Lycurgus' – the ability to reform and fight alongside anyone if the phalanx was thrown into confusion. Thus the Spartans would not only appear to have had an advantage if all went well, but could still be formidable if things started to go wrong – a point Plutarch stresses in his life of Pelopidas when describing Leuctra. Here the Spartans were caught in confusion, but still managed to fight off a Theban phalanx 50 deep long enough to get their mortally wounded king to the rear.

The Set-Piece

Spartan skills were often demonstrated in the set-piece battles of which any kind of detailed accounts survive. At First Mantinea, for example, the Spartan king, apprehensive about the threat to his left as the two armies edged to their right in what Thucydides says was the customary way, ordered the two units on his extreme left to shift to their left, to cover the enemy's right, and two units from his right to march behind his advancing phalanx to plug the gap. In the event, the commanders of the two units on the right refused to obey orders, and the resulting gap in the Spartan left wing led to it being routed. But the mere fact that the king could even contemplate such a manoeuvre in the face of the enemy illustrates the supreme confidence Spartan commanders had in their men. Moreover, since the enemy centre and left gave way almost immediately on this occasion, the king was able to wheel his right round to take the troops of the victorious enemy in their shieldless flank as they streamed back cross the battlefield after plundering the Spartan baggage-train. The contrast between the enemy's apparent inability to exploit their success on their right, and the

Battle scene on a 'Chalcidian' hydria of c. 540 BC, copying Attic black figure style, but using the script of Chalcis and her colonies, and possibly produced in Rhegium. The scene is apparently, as usual, mythological, though the names – from left to right, Antaios, Antiochos, Polydoros, Fachys and Medon – are obscure. It vividly conveys something of the violent movement of a real fight between hoplites. British Museum, London.

'THE NEMEA'

STAGE 1

The opposing armies march to the right in column until they partially overlap the enemy left, then wheel left into line-of-battle.

STAGE 2

Most of Sparta's allies flee on contact, as do the Athenian regiments facing the Spartans.

STAGE 3

The Spartans wheel left and smash into the shieldless side of the enemy right as it attempts to withdraw across the battlefield, rolling it up.

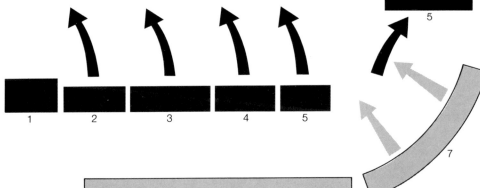

Key
1 Boeotians.
2 Corinthians.
3 Argives.
4 Euboeans.
5 Athenians.
6 Sparta's allies.
7 Spartans.

way the Spartans manoeuvred their way out of difficulty, could not be more striking.

At a battle fought 24 years later just west of Corinth, and usually known as 'the Battle of the Nemea', the Spartans appear to have deliberately exploited the tendency of hoplites to edge to their right. Xenophon's account suggests that they faced right and marched for some distance to the right in column to create an overlap on their right. In effect, they had sacrificed the left, which this time consisted of allied soldiers, but the Spartan right was able to wheel to a position at right angles to the enemy's line of retreat, once more catching the victorious enemy on its shieldless side as it attempted to withdraw, and 'rolling it up' contingent by contingent.

At Second Coronea some months later, Agesilaus tried different tactics. Again both armies won on their right, but instead of wheeling his right to take the victorious Thebans in flank, Agesilaus countermarched his phalanx, as we have seen, and met the Thebans head on, possibly hoping to annihilate them. In the event, the Thebans were able to break through, perhaps because their phalanx was too deep to hold. But the ability of the Spartans to manoeuvre on the battlefield is again remarkable. Moreover, the result was another defeat for the Thebans and their allies since they sustained heavy losses and were unable to achieve the strategic objective of preventing Agesilaus from marching home.

In the end, perhaps, the Spartans paid the price for the over-confidence bred of too many victories. At Leuctra the Theban general Epaminondas introduced new tactics, massing his best troops on his left in a great block 50 deep and possibly 80 long, and 'refusing' his right. The Spartans responded by attempting to change their formation in the face of the enemy, as they had done before, but what precisely they tried to do is unclear. The best account, in Plutarch's life of Epaminondas' friend Pelopidas, suggests that they were trying to extend their line to the right, as usual, as a preliminary to taking the Thebans in flank, and possibly trying to deepen it at the same time – they started the battle only 12 deep. However, they were thrown into confusion by their own cavalry which, like their Theban counterparts, had unusually been positioned in front of the phalanx, perhaps to screen the hoplites' movements. Thus, when the cavalry was defeated by the Theban horse, it reeled back into its own advancing infantry. The latter, unable either to complete their manoeuvre or resume their original formation, and thrown into confusion from the collision with their cavalry, were then charged head-on by the 'Sacred Band', which formed either the whole front of the Theban phalanx or its left front. The result was a catastrophic defeat for the Spartans, but although they had at last clearly met their match in Epaminondas' tactical brilliance, it is worth noting that it was still they, and not their opponents, who were trying to manoeuvre: once set in motion all the Thebans had to do was to advance, with the possible exception of the 'Sacred Band', whereas the Spartans were evidently up to something more complicated.

Cavalry

Leuctra was still primarily a hoplite battle, and the limited role of the cavalry on both sides was typical. Only once, perhaps, in three centuries of hoplite warfare, did cavalry play a decisive part in a pitched battle, and that in a negative way. At Tanagra in about 457, Thucydides says the Thessalian cavalry which had come to the aid of the Athenians, 'deserted to the Spartans during the action', and it may have been this defection which cost the Athenians the victory. Herodotus tells us that over half a century earlier, Thessalian cavalry serving Hippias, 'tyrant' of Athens, had ridden down a Spartan force in terrain specially cleared of trees, between Phaleron and Athens. But we hear nothing of any cavalry at Oenophyta, two months after Tanagra, or at First Coronea ten years later. At Delium, in 424, both sides fielded cavalry, but it apparently played little part in the fighting until the sudden appearance of two squadrons of Boeotian cavalry from behind a hill

LEUCTRA

STAGE 1

Epaminondas 'refuses' his right, and leads the Theban phalanx obliquely towards the Spartan right, screened by his cavalry, which defeats the Spartan cavalry screen.

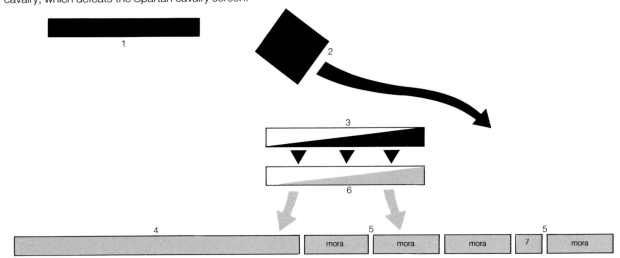

STAGE 2

The Spartan cavalry is driven into their advancing phalanx, which is shifting to the right, and, possibly, also trying to increase depth; in the confusion, the 'Sacred Band' crashes, at the double, into the Spartan line, at the point where the King and *Hippeis* are stationed.

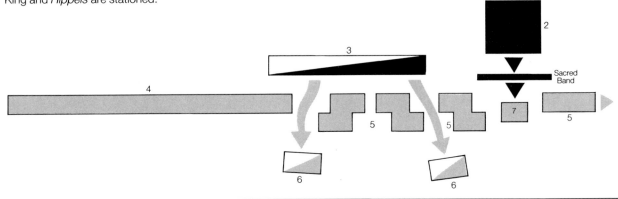

STAGE 3

The Thebans annihilate the *Hippeis* and the Spartans to either side, and burst through the line; the rest of the Spartan army flees.

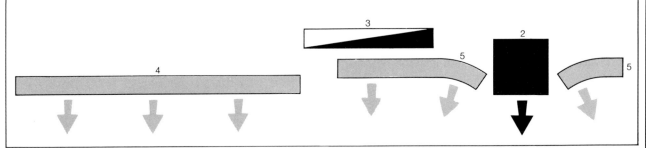

Key
1 Boeotians.
2 Thebans.
3 Theban cavalry screen.
4 Sparta's allies, etc.
5 Spartan army.
6 Spartan cavalry screen.
7 *Hippeis*

caused a panic in the victorious Athenian right and led to the flight of their whole army. At First Mantinea, Thucydides notes that the Spartans had cavalry on both wings, but it seems to have played no part in the fighting, and the role of the Athenian cavalry, on the enemy left, was limited to protecting their infantry when they started to retreat. At the Nemea and at Second Coronea cavalry seems to have played no part at all, though shortly before the latter, Xenophon tells us, Agesilaus' cavalry had won a notable victory over Thessalian cavalry near Mount Narthacium.

Herodotus implies that during the Persian Wars the Persian cavalry was particularly feared by the Greeks, but only once does it play a decisive part in his narrative – at Malene during the revolt in Asia Minor. He suggests that the Persians chose to land at Marathon in 490 because the terrain favoured their cavalry. Nevertheless, it does not figure in his account of the battle, and surely not because it was not present. Many modern scholars have chosen to believe a story, told in a Byzantine lexicon compiled at least 1,500 years later, that the cavalry was absent, by implication because it had been re-embarked in preparation for a move on Athens by sea. But Herodotus clearly assumed that it was present, since he remarks that the Persians considered the Athenians mad and doomed to destruction for attacking *without* cavalry and archers. We should believe a man who could have talked to survivors of the battle rather than a source which – as has been pointed out – is actually nearer our own time. Possibly the speed of the Greek advance denied the Persian cavalry an opportunity to engage in the ensuing mêlée.

Support for this view is provided by what happened at Plataea. The Persian cavalry was relatively successful during the first stage of the campaign, when it attacked the Greek army at the foot of Cithaeron in successive waves, discharging its missiles and then wheeling away, as Herodotus describes. It was only finally driven off when its capable commander Masistius was unhorsed after his mount had been hit by an Athenian archer, and then stabbed in the eye as he lay on the ground. In the second stage, after the Greek army had moved down to the vicinity of the River Asopus, the Persian cavalry was even more successful, cutting to pieces at least one supply-train in the Greek rear, and harassing their watering-parties along the river – as Herodotus remarks, 'being horse-archers, they were very difficult to get at'. But although it was also the Persian cavalry which initially brought the retreating Greek right wing to a halt at the beginning of the final stage, and which protected the fleeing Persian infantry when the rout began, it seems to have played no decisive part in the battle itself.

On the other hand, the Theban cavalry fighting on the Persian side routed a force of Megarian and Phliasian hoplites, hurrying in disorder across the plain to the aid of their right wing, and left 600 of them dead on the field. This incident, and the destruction of the Spartan force by Hippias' Thessalian cavalry, indicate that hoplites could be vulnerable to cavalry if caught isolated in flat terrain or if not properly organized. But cavalry has rarely, if ever, been able to ride down unbroken infantry, and cavalry such as the Persians and most of the Greeks employed, riding without stirrups, was certainly not capable of a successful head-on charge against a properly formed and deployed phalanx of hoplites. Only towards the end of the hoplite era did cavalry play a decisive part in a set-piece battle. At Second Mantinea in 362, Epaminondas used cavalry, 'hamippoi' (if this *is* what Xenophon wrote: they were perhaps infantry trained to run behind cavalry into battle, holding onto the horses' tails) and peltasts (see below), to defeat the enemy cavalry and thus bring about a general rout. In many respects this combination of hoplites with other arms foreshadows the changes in warfare which were introduced by Philip II of Macedon, father of Alexander the Great, and it is interesting that he was for a time a hostage in Thebes, when the Thebans, under Epaminondas' inspired leadership, were carrying all before them. It is possible that Philip learned in Thebes lessons which he proceeded to put into practice when he ascended the throne of Macedon a few years later.

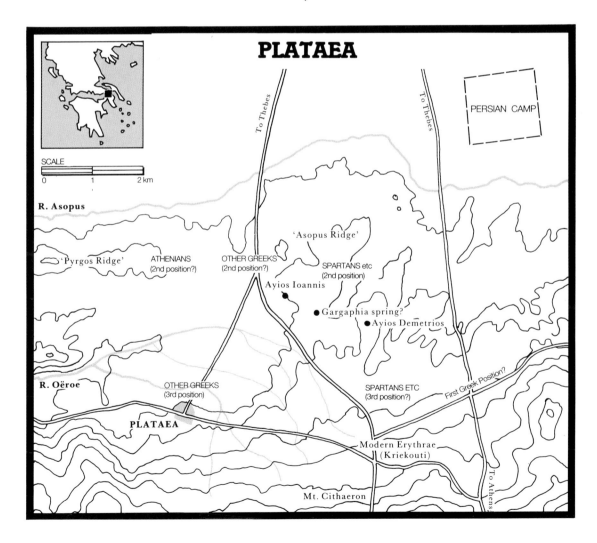

Miniature frieze depicting a battle-scene on an Attic exaleiptron *(unguent vase) of c.570-65 BC. Although the scene is split into individual duels, it perhaps conveys some idea of the kind of fighting hoplites would have faced when one side gave way and the phalanxes broke up in flight or pursuit. Musée National de Louvre, Paris.*

Light Troops

Light troops armed with missile-weapons – archers, javelineers, slingers, even mere stone-throwers – also seem to have played a minor role in the decisive engagements of archaic and classical Greek warfare, although, if our sources are to be believed, they were used from the earliest times, and often in considerable numbers. Herodotus, for example, claims that there were 69,500 light troops in the Greek army at Plataea, and although it is barely credible that there were really 35,000 helots there – seven for each Spartan hoplite – it is possible that each of the 38,700 hoplites eventually present was accompanied by a soldier-servant, and that these were in some fashion 'armed for war', as Herodotus says was the case with the helots. There was certainly a force of Athenian archers present, perhaps 800 strong, but only these play any part in Herodotus' account of the fighting.

Similarly at Delium, Thucydides says, the Boeotians had more than 10,500 light troops, and it is difficult to believe that they were all prevented from playing any part in the fighting simply by the terrain, which seems to be what he implies. At the Nemea, according to Xenophon, the Spartans had 300 Cretan bowmen and not less than 400 slingers from the borders of Elis, while the enemy fielded a considerable number of light troops, but none of these elements figure in his account of the battle. At Second Coronea, too, he says that Agesilaus had more peltasts than his opponents, but these did not help his victory, though if Xenophon used the term 'peltasts' in its strict sense, he would be referring to specialized troops: they originated in Thrace and were usually armed with javelins, although their name derived from the light shield (*pelta*) they carried.

The term 'light troops' is perhaps an unfortunate one, though now hallowed by tradition and convenient to use, for the essential difference between such troops and hoplites was not the 'lightness' of their equipment, but the weapons they used and the way they used them. In the early days of

opposite
The Plataea Campaign: for convenience, only the Greek positions are shown. Persian cavalry attacked the Greeks in their first position, and the Persian army probably moved out to confront the Greek army in its second positions, using cavalry to harass watering-parties along the river Asopus, to choke up the Gargaphia spring and, by riding round the Greek right, to cut off supply-trains coming over Mt Cithaeron. When the Greeks retreated to their third positions, the main encounter took place with the Spartans, while the Boeotians, who were fighting for the Persians, confronted the Athenians, and the Theban cavalry rode down the Megarians and Phliasians somewhere between the 'other Greeks' and the 'Spartans, etc.'

hoplite warfare, hoplites probably did wear armour of considerable 'weight' –
bronze helmet, bronze armour and bronze greaves – but as time went on many
of them seem to have discarded pieces of this equipment, until in many cases
perhaps the only items left were the typical hoplite shield and spear. But
hoplites normally fought in line, in a close-packed phalanx, and it was the unit
which mattered, not the individual. 'Light' troops might also wear protective
clothing and helmets, and carry shields, but were usually armed with missile-
weapons which required space for effective use. Hence they were not
accustomed to fight in line or file, but as individuals. If they could keep their
distance, they could hurt hoplites without being hurt themselves; but if they
allowed hoplites to close with them, they became terribly vulnerable. The
evidence of the sources is clear: there was really no place for light troops in a
hoplite battle.

Light troops only seem to have been able to defeat hoplites in
circumstances which were favourable – if, for example, the terrain suited them,
or if they enjoyed overwhelming numerical superiority, or if they were also
supported by hoplites. Thucydides describes an incident in about 459, when a
force of Corinthian hoplites, retreating from a defeat at the hands of the
Athenians in the Megarid, blundered into a private estate surrounded by a
ditch and were stoned to death by Athenian light troops, who took up a
position along the ditch, while hoplites closed off the entrance. In the
Peloponnesian War, the Athenian general Demosthenes ventured into the
Aetolian hills with a force of hoplites, and lost over a third of his number at the
hands of Aetolian javelineers in the high country commanding his line-of-
march. Significantly, he had not waited for a force of similarly armed troops
from Athens' allies in western Locris, and even then, Thucydides says, he was
able to hold the Aetolians off so long as his archers still had arrows, since they
outranged the enemy. But Demosthenes at least appears to have learned his
lesson. In the following year, according to Thucydides, he used light troops –
archers, javelineers (including Thracian peltasts) and stone-throwers – to
eliminate a force of 420 Spartan hoplites, trapped on the island of Sphacteria,
off the south-west Peloponnese; 128 were killed and the remaining 292
surrendered. But it is also significant that he had exactly twice as many
hoplites alone – 800 Athenian and 40 Messenian – as well as 800 archers, 800
peltasts and over 8000 armed sailors! It says something for the reputation of
Spartan hoplites that even then the Athenians and their allies went ashore
'obsessed by the thought that they were going against Spartans'.

Light troops also played a significant part in the final defeat of the
Athenian expeditionary force to Sicily in 413. After vainly besieging Syracuse
for some two years, the Athenians tried to break out by sea, and when this
failed, to retreat by land to a friendly city. The Syracusans harried their retreat
with missile troops, being unwilling, as Thucydides says, to fight hand-to-
hand with desperate men, and it is surprising that the Athenians apparently
did not at least try to protect their hoplites with the archers, slingers and
javelineers they are said to have had in some numbers at various stages of the
siege. Demosthenes, in particular, who was one of the commanders, should
have remembered what had happened in Aetolia.

Perhaps the most sensational example of a defeat inflicted on hoplites by
light troops is described by Xenophon in his *History of Greece*. It occurred near
Corinth in 390, when a Spartan *mora* was badly beaten by peltasts commanded
by Iphicrates, one of the best Athenian commanders of the day. As was the
case on Sphacteria, it appears that it was partly the combination of peltasts
with hoplites which secured victory. The polemarch in command of the *mora*
tried the tactics of ordering his front ranks to charge and disperse the peltasts;
he also used cavalry when it came up to aid him. But these charges proved
useless, possibly because the close proximity of Athenian hoplites inhibited the
young Spartans from pressing home their attacks. Eventually the *mora* broke
when the Athenian hoplites also began to close, and in all lost 250 of its original
600 men. Although the reverse was clearly a serious blow to Spartan prestige,

it was an isolated incident, precipitated perhaps by Spartan over-confidence. The ability of the Spartan soldier-servants to get the first of the wounded away to safety suggests that if the polemarch had simply ordered his *mora* to form a square and beat a fighting retreat, he might have got away with it.

These incidents show that hoplites were vulnerable in certain circumstances, even if they were the obvious battle-winners in set-piece engagements. It is surprising that more attention was not paid to the possibilities of combining hoplites with other arms to produce an integrated army ready for any eventuality. One would have thought that the experiences of Xenophon and his fellow-mercenaries, on their long retreat from Cunaxa in Irak to Trapezus (Trabzon) on the Black Sea, would have suggested to the Greeks the value of such a combination.

It is true that the Spartans began to appreciate the value of cavalry and light troops during the Peloponnesian War. According to Thucydides, they first raised a force of cavalry and archers in 424, to counteract Athenian raids, and during the 4th century they had a regular force of cavalry divided into six *morai* like the infantry, and made frequent use of light-armed forces. It was their enterprising commander Brasidas who first seems to have realized the potential of such troops. In 424, according to Thucydides, he was sent to Thrace in command of a force of 1,700 hoplites, including 700 helots. Once in Thrace he was joined by allies, including several towns which had risen against Athens, and was soon using peltasts both to attack and to defend fortified places in the area. In the battle outside Amphipolis, in which he lost his life, he had more cavalry and light troops than hoplites, and it was the former who surrounded and cut up the Athenian right wing when it made a stand on a hill.

However, on an earlier campaign, when forced to retreat by the betrayal of his Macedonian allies, even Brasidas drew up his hoplites in a square, with the light troops in the centre, when one might have expected the light troops to protect the hoplites. Instead, Thucydides says, he ordered his younger men, who normally formed the front ranks, to charge out if the phalanx was attacked, and this is the first unequivocal example of this Spartan techinique for dealing with such an attack. It was regularly used by Spartan hoplites in the 4th century – for example in the fight with Iphikrates' peltasts near Corinth – and on at least one occasion we hear from Xenophon of their catching peltasts who were 'not less than a javelin's-throw away'. It is also striking that a Spartan army, in a somewhat similar situation to the one which had confronted Demosthenes in Aetolia, was, according to Xenophon, able to drive Acarnanian light troops from a hill top by using younger hoplites supported by cavalry.

Nonetheless it is clear that hoplites remained the decisive force in Greek warfare down to the time of Philip II, and this requires explanation. One reason why cavalry was not more important, at least in southern Greece, was that horses were rare and expensive. In Sparta in the 4th century, the wealthiest citizens are said by Xenophon to have provided the horses, although they did not serve in the cavalry themselves. The further north one went, the commoner horses became, and thus the Boeotians had good cavalry and the Thessalians and Macedonians even better. But the southern states could produce light troops in considerable numbers, as the sources indicate, and one might have thought that geography favoured guerrilla warfare, as more recent conflicts have shown.

One reason for the continued dominance of hoplites may be that the defence of the plains, where most of the food was grown, was literally vital, for although such troops could not defend all the farmland, they could, in the ultimate resort, virtually force a set-piece confrontation, and it was in such engagements that they excelled. This hypothesis is supported by what happened in the early years of the Peloponnesian War, for the Peloponnesian invasions of Attica were clearly made in the expectation that the Athenians would come out and fight, and although the latter refused to be drawn, it took

The funeral stele of Lisas the Tegeate, found on the old royal estates near Tatoï, north of Athens. Tatoï is the ancient Decelea, and the stele perhaps commemorates the death of one of Sparta's allies, serving in the garrison of the Spartan fort (the ruins of which lie on the Palaiokastro hill above the modern village) during the latter part of the Peloponnesian War. National Archaeological Museum, Athens.

Part of the frieze from the 'Nereid Monument', dating to c.400 BC; the tomb from which it came is at Xanthos in Lycia. The scene shows two hoplites confronting each other, shield to shield, and both using the over-arm thrust, though the spears are not shown – they would possibly have been painted in – but the presence of the archer to the left shows that this is not a typical hoplite battle. British Museum, London.

all Pericles' eloquence to hold them back. Pericles' strategy was only made possible by Athenian seapower, and because the single fortress-complex formed by Athens and its seaport, the Piraeus, linked by the 'Long Walls', both provided the population of Attica with a refuge and ensured that it could be fed. Herodotus quotes the dry observation of the Persian general Mardonius that, in normal circumstances, when the Greeks declared war on each other, they looked out the best and flattest piece of ground and had their battle on that.

Class Warfare

There was also a social and political dimension to hoplite warfare. Even though the very development of hoplites marked a break with the aristocratic past, they remained an élite. Except perhaps in Athens, in the years just before the Peloponnesian War, they probably always formed a minority of the free, adult male population, mainly because their equipment was expensive, and, in the early days at least, provided by themselves. By the time of the Peloponnesian War, Spartan hoplites may have been equipped by the state – Brasidas' helot-soldiers, at all events, could presumably not have found their own equipment – and by the second half of the 4th century, at the latest, young Athenian hoplites beginning their two years' military training were issued with shield and spear by the state. In the 4th century, we hear of poor Athenian hoplites, for example in Demosthenes' speech *Against Meidias*, and Xenophon refers to Arcadians who could not serve in their standing-army unpaid. But in general hoplites seem to have continued to be well-off, and in many states those not qualified to serve were not even accorded full citizen-rights. Thus the defeat of a state's hoplites was a blow to its whole social and political fabric, out of all proportion to the losses incurred. This is why a single battle often decided the outcome of a war. Oenophyta (457), for example, led to the whole of Boeotia, Phocis and Locris passing under Athenian control. Ten years later First Coronea put an end to it. First Mantinea led rapidly to the collapse of the anti-Spartan coalition, though not before the Spartans had been brought to fight for their all, on a single day, as the Athenian Alcibiades was later said by Thycydides to have claimed. Leuctra, above all, was the 'one blow' Aristotle says Sparta was unable to sustain, probably because her losses included 400 of her dwindling number of full citizens – there were probably only about 1,000 of

military age left at the time – even though the majority of her soldiers were no longer full citizens.

There could even be an element of ritual to the decisive clash between hoplites, as exemplified by the so-called 'Battle of the Champions', in about 546, described by Herodotus, where 300 men each of Argos and Sparta were picked to fight for the disputed territory of Thyrea. Admittedly, the effect was spoiled when, at the end of the day, the two Argive survivors decamped, claiming the victory, leaving the sole Spartan survivor to stake a rival claim as being left in possession of the field. (The dispute was resolved by a full-scale battle which the Spartans won.) But as late as 420, Thucydides tells us, the Argives insisted on the inclusion of a clause in a treaty, allowing for disputes about the territory to be settled by another 'Battle of the Champions', though by then the Spartans are said to have thought the idea 'silly'.

This may hint at a growing 'professionalism', at least among the Spartans, but although hoplite warfare was capable of some refinement in the hands of experts like them, or geniuses like Epaminondas, it remained essentially limited in scope and amateurish, and most hoplites evidently saw little reason to change it. Service in the hoplite ranks was expected of all adult male citizens of a certain class, but with the exception of Sparta, this was not their only or even their main occupation. A story told by Plutarch in his life of King Agesilaus of Sparta illustrates the point. When some of Sparta's allies complained that she was not fielding as many soldiers as she should, Agesilaus bade his whole army sit down, and then the men who practised various trades to stand up, occupation by occupation, until almost all the allied soldiers were on their feet, but not a single Spartan.

The 'Lion of Chaeronea'. Discovered in 1818 in the fields east of the ancient city of Chaeronea by a party of English tourists, it was smashed by the brigand patriot Odysseus Androutsos, looking for treasure, during the War of Independence, and restored early in this century by the Greek Archaeological Service. It marks the resting-place of 254 men, possibly members of the Theban 'Sacred Band', killed in the battle. The battlefield itself is about 2 kilometres to the east.

There is, as we have seen, very little evidence that other Greeks received any kind of military training, at least until the 4th century, and the implication of the constant references to the unusual nature of the Spartan way of life is that it was virtually unique. But even the Spartans only seem to have trained at the level we call 'square bashing', although their battle tactics made it far more important then than it is now. There is no evidence that there was any training in tactics or strategy for officers or generals: Plato's dialogue, *Laches*, is not about whether young men of the upper classes should study military science, but whether they should learn weapons-drill. The earliest studies of warfare to survive are no earlier than the first half of the 4th century: Xenophon's semi-fictional account of the upbringing and subsequent training-methods of Cyrus, King of Persia; his essays on horsemanship and the duties of a cavalry commander; and the sections on siege-warfare from a military treatise by one Aeneas, who may or may not be the Stymphalian general of that name, mentioned in Xenophon's *History of Greece*. It is thus extremely doubtful whether even Spartan officers were trained in any proper sense, and they were probably picked for their social standing rather than any ability. There is no evidence that there was any system whereby a man could rise through the ranks. The top commands were normally reserved for kings or other members of the two royal families, who, if they were or had been heirs to one of Sparta's two thrones, were even exempt from the youth-training to which other Spartans were subjected.

In these circumstances it is not surprising that there was little incentive to change, and that we constantly find ancient Greek armies behaving in a totally 'unprofessional' way. At Thermopylae, for example, the Phocians were given the task of the guarding the Anopaea path, a mountain track which could be used by the Persians to outflank the Greek force blocking the coastal route south. Although the Phocians came from mountain country, they neglected to post pickets, and the first they heard of the approach of the Persian flanking force was the sound of feet trampling last year's oak leaves strewn across the path. Forgetting their mission and assuming that they were the Persians' main target, the Phocians withdrew to the top of the nearest hill, leaving the path wide open, whereupon the grateful Persians ignored them and pushed on over the mountain. As we have seen the Athenian general Demosthenes blithely led hoplites into Aetolia without sufficient support from missile-armed troops, and in 422 the right wing of the Athenian army retreating from Amphipolis committed the classic blunder of wheeling to expose its shieldless side to the enemy who, Thucydides says, could be seen within the gates of the town. Even the Spartans, who could claim to be the only 'professional' soldiers in Greece, were frequently caught by surprise. According to Thucydides, the men manning their guard-post on Sphacteria were killed while still asleep or donning their arms. Before First Mantinea, he declares, their army was astonished to find the enemy, drawn up in battle-array, only a short distance away, even though the advance had been across a flat plain, and Xenophon records an incident in 369 when Spartan troops guarding prepared defences east of Corinth were caught in their beds when Epaminondas launched a dawn attack.

Philip of Macedon

Thus we can understand why the Athenian orator Demosthenes viewed the advent of Philip of Macedon with such alarm. Nothing had lately been so revolutionized as warfare, he declared in his *Third Philippic* of 341: Philip made no use of a hoplite phalanx, but fielded light troops, cavalry, archers, mercenaries and siege-artillery, and made no distinction between summer and winter. One reason for the revolution was undoubtedly that, in Philip's part of the world, there never had been a substantial hoplite class. Macedonia was a land where the nobility, the king's 'Companions' (*hetairoi*), provided magnificent cavalry, but the peasantry had hitherto been of little account.

There was some kind of Macedonian infantry at least as early as the reign of Archelaus (413-399), if Thucydides is to be believed, but it was almost certainly Philip who first realized their potential, and created what were known as the 'foot-companions' (*pezhetairoi*), who were to form the backbone of the Macedonian army, and who certainly existed by 349, when they were mentioned by Demosthenes in his *Second Olynthiac*.

But although armed with a 5.5 m pike, the *sarissa*, and formidable enough, according to the contemporary Polybius, to cause the Roman general Aemilius Paullus considerable disquiet nearly 200 years later when confronted with them at Pydna, these Macedonian 'phalangites' were not the ultimate battle-winners, as the hoplites had always been. The job of the 'phalangites' was to pin the enemy infantry and bring about a situation in which the cavalry could win the battle – a style of warfare altogether different from the hoplite warfare which had been seen in Greece for three centuries.

The new warfare was demonstrated in Philip's first victory, over the Illyrians, at the beginning of his reign, if we can trust Diodorus' account, and again at Chaeronea, on 2 August 338. Here for the first time, a Macedonian army encountered a traditional hoplite army, composed largely of Athenians and Boeotians – sadly the Spartans were not there. The details of the battle are not known, but it is possible that Philip, by apparently withdrawing on the right, induced the Athenians on the allied left to pursue, and so stretched the enemy line until a gap opened up on their right, into which the young Alexander, commanding the Macedonian cavalry on their left, charged with devastating results. At the end of the day half the Athenians were either dead or prisoners, and the Boeotians had probably lost even more heavily; the day of the battle of annihilation had arrived.

Although hoplites continued to fight for a century or more, Chaeronea marked the end of the hoplite era. The grim, stone lion which today glares out over the battlefield from its grove of cypress trees, marks the resting-place of 254 men, whose skeletons repose in seven rows beneath it. No-one knows who put the lion up or who the dead men were, but it is difficult to believe that they have nothing to do with the battle. Possibly the dead are those of the Theban 'Sacred Band', whose desperate courage, according to Plutarch's life of Pelopidas, Philip so much admired. Whoever they are, the lion may surely stand as a fitting monument to all hoplites.

PRINCIPAL SOURCES

Herodotus (c. 484-c.424)

Born at Halicarnassus (Bodrum), in south-west Asia Minor; wrote an account of wars between Greeks and Persians, largely based on oral evidence, often, probably, that of eyewitnesses. He is probably more reliable on military matters – as far as he goes – than sometimes thought.

Thucydides (c.471-c.399)

Athenian general; failed to save Amphipolis from Brasidas and was exiled for 20 years; wrote a history of the Peloponnesian War (431-404), between Athens and Sparta. He is generally thought to be a model of reliability.

Xenophon (c.425-c.355)

Athenian soldier; spent much of adult life in exile, in Spartan territory; wrote an account of experiences during younger Cyrus' rebellion, and of retreat of Greek mercenaries (the *Anabasis*), as well as other works, including a *History of Greece (Hellenika)*, from 411 to 362. He is generally reliable on military matters, though less so on others.

Plutarch (c.50-c.120 AD)

Biographer and philosopher from Chaeronea in Boeotia wrote a series of 'parallel lives' of famous Greeks and Romans, and large number of essays on various topics *(Moralia)*, in general, he is probably as reliable as his sources.

THE PERSIANS

DR NICK SEKUNDA

The Rise of the Empire

For half a century after the fall of Assyria a 'balance of power' existed in the Near East between the kingdoms of Egypt, Lydia, Babylon and Media. The King of the Medes ruled both his own people, and even more so the other nations under his power, with great cruelty. The prince of the Persians, who was later to become Cyrus the Great, was able to exploit the internal dissensions engendered by this cruelty to seize power from Astyages, the last king of the Medes, in 550, following which the rest of the empire came within his grasp. A series of campaigns in the West, resulting in the conquest of Lydia and Babylon, followed.

The Persians continued to use many of the military traditions and tactics found in the Assyrian army. During this early period the mainstay of the Persian army was its infantry. Persia, a land-locked country lying in the mountainous valleys of south-west Iran, was poor and rugged. The ancient Persians were hardy, and trained in the use of bow and sling, which kept away the local wolves and worse from their flocks, and so made good infantry. But horses, which had no function in their economy, and which were extremely expensive to maintain, were virtually unknown to them. The mainstay of the Persian army throughout this early period were the *sparabara*.

Two Achaemenid sparabara *are shown on this broken Attic vase. It may depict the battle of Marathon. The contrasting leather and osiers are clearly shown in the shield held by the warrior on the right, who may be a Mede. Note also the artist's detailed observation of the oriental cuirass and shoes. Ashmolean Museum, Oxford.*

The Sparabara

Present in virtually all military scenes in the Assyrian reliefs is the 'archer-pair': an archer firing from behind the cover of a large body-shield. The 'archer-pair' had been a tactical feature of Near Eastern warfare for a long time, and the use of this combination had also spread to Greece via Cyprus, for it appears on Greek vase-paintings and in the *Iliad* in a number of passages; most famously those where Paris shoots from behind the cover of Hector's shield, or where Telamon shoots from behind Ajax's shield. These passages reveal the intrusion of Near Eastern military practices into Greek warfare during the 8th century. The impact of shielded archery upon Greece, however, was not sufficient to displace the opposite and conflicting trend in warfare in the East Mediterranean lands – that of the heavily armoured spearman. In the case of Greece, these developments led to the evolution of the hoplite phalanx. In Mesopotamia, however, the dominance of archery in warfare was too firmly rooted to surrender paramount place.

Assyrian monumental sculpture began to flower fully in the 7th century BC. Only now are battle scenes shown in three-dimensional representation, which enables the military archaeologist to discern how the different types of troops are drawn up for battle. The archer-pair has previously been found operating alone, usually at sieges. Now we find scenes depicting a long line of archers drawn up behind a line of spearmen armed with body-shields. The student of warfare is strongly reminded of similar developments in medieval warfare, which culminated in formations of crossbowmen defended by a 'shield-wall' of pavises: large body-shields either carried by the archers themselves, or by attached formations of spearmen called *pavisarii*.

In medieval times the pavise was usually made of heavy wooden planking, but the Persians used shields formed from a large rectangle of thick

Polychrome brick-faced wall from the royal palace at Susa, from a painting of the last century by Saint-Elme Gauthier. Two regiments of Amrtaka are shown. Both have the same equipment of spear and bow (and probably a dagger too, if any of these guardsmen were shown frontally), but the two regiments are distinguished from each other by different coloured robes. The appliqué badges sewn on to the two different tunics represent the regimental standards, which would have been carried as plaques on the top of a pole. One standard shows the solar disc, borrowed from Assyria, but now sacred to the supreme Persian deity Ahuramazda. The second standard seems to show a triple fire-altar, and this is also of religious significance. Musée National du Louvre, Paris.

leather, into which osiers would be inserted when still supple and uncured; when the leather hardened, the combined virtues of the two materials employed resulted in a shield of great lightness, yet of great resilience and rigidity. These pavises were called *spara* in Old Persian, and the troops who carried them were called *sparabara* or 'pavise-bearers'.

The Assyrian pavise-walls seem to be composed of two different units of troops of equal strength, brigaded together in a tactical formation comprising only a single line of archers behind a single line of shield-men. However when we find such formations in the Persian army, both types of troops are operating in the same unit. This enabled the ratio of archers to shield-men to be altered so as to give a heavier concentration of shot.

Organization

The Persian army was organized into regiments of a thousand men. The Old Persian term for one of these regiments, or 'Thousands', was *hazarabam*, a word formed from *hazara-*, meaning 'thousand' with a suffix of *-bam* to turn it into a numeral-noun. Each regiment was commanded by a *hazarapatiš*, or 'commander of a thousand', and was divided into ten *sataba* of a hundred. Each *satabam* was commanded by a *satapatiš* and was, in turn, divided into ten *dathaba* of ten men. The *dathabam* of ten formed the basic tactical sub-unit in the infantry, and was drawn up on the battlefield in file. The *dathapatiš* was stationed in the front rank, carrying the *spara*. Behind him the rest of the *dathabam* would be drawn up in nine ranks, each man armed with a bow and falchion*. Normally the *dathapatiš* carried a short fighting-spear six feet long, and was expected to protect the rest of the *dathabam* should the enemy reach the line. Sometimes, however, the whole of the *dathabam* were armed with bows, and the *spara* were propped up as a 'wall' at the front, allowing the entire the *dathabam* to discharge projectiles.

Xenophon mentions all these ranks in his *Cyropaedia*, though he gives them in their Greek equivalents. He also mentions Persian commanders of 5 and of 50. Of these only one has an equivalent in the Persepolis ration documents, which mention a *pasčadathapatiš*; literally an 'after' or 'rear' *dathapatiš*. These men seem to have operated as deputies to the *dathapatiš*, and in battle would have been stationed in the rear rank of the *dathabam*. There is no indication in our sources, however, that the *satabam* was physically divided in two. Perhaps the *pasčasatapatiš* simply functioned as second-in-command of the *satabam*.

Above the regiment the decimal system was maintained, and regiments were formed into divisions of 10,000 men. We hear of Persian 'myriads' (i.e. 10,000 in the Greek sources), but unfortunately no Near Eastern document has survived from which the Old Persian equivalent of this term can be worked out. Avestan, a language closely related to Old Persian, preserves *baivar-* for myriad, so the Old Persian for a unit of ten thousand was probably *baivarabam*. This is, however, purely speculative.

The Immortals

The most important 'myriad' was the King's famous personal division of 10,000 'Immortals', or *Amrtaka* in Old Persian. Herodotus tells us that these troops were called 'Immortals' because the division was unfailingly kept up to strength. The myriad of the *Amrtaka* comprised chosen Persians, and within the myriad the élite regiment, which was known as the King's 'Spearbearers', or *Arštibara*, was composed of Persians of the highest rank, selected from the rest of the *Amrtaka*. It seems, then, that the *Arštibara* were formed from the Persian nobility, known as 'the equals', while the other regiments were formed from Persian commoners.

Military service was compulsory for all Persians, and it is probable that the *Amrtaka* comprised the pick of the conscripts. Before the age of five a Persian boy was not admitted into the presence of his father but lived entirely with the women; then from the age of five to 20 he would be taught 'to ride, to use the bow, and to speak the truth'. The young man next performed military service till the age of 24, and was liable to serve up to the age of 50.

The Formation of Cavalry

Thus far the victories in the West had largely been secured by the military ability and political astuteness of Cyrus, but the Persian army itself contained considerable deficiencies. It was almost entirely an infantry army. The Lydians, on the other hand, maintained a large and efficient corps of cavalry. In the battle of 'The Plain of Cyrus' fought in 546 to the east of Sardis, Cyrus was only able to overcome the Lydian cavalry by sending the camels of the baggage train against them. The Lydian horses, which had never met camels

---

* A broad sword more or less curved with the edge on the convex side.

before, were terrified by their strange appearance and scent, and the entire Lydian cavalry force bolted. Such tactics could not be used against the Bactrians.

The core of the army was a levy of the Persians fighting as infantry. This Persian force was supplemented by, it seems, other myriads of infantry levied from the subject, or 'allied' peoples, and smaller forces of cavalry contributed by nations possessing troops of that arm. Foremost among these cavalry contingents was that of the Medes, who were the finest horsemen in the ancient East. Their loyalty could never be trusted completely, however, and thus Cyrus was compelled to raise a purely Persian force of cavalry. The need became especially critical in 539, when the campaigns in the West culminated in the fall of Babylon, and Cyrus began to look eastwards. The possibilities for Median conspiracy with eastern Iranian tribes must have increased, as must the need for cavalry. It may be at this period, therefore, that Cyrus resolved to raise a force of Persian cavalry.

Both horses and the wealth necessary to maintain them, which had been raised in the recent campaigns of conquest in the West, were distributed among the Persian 'equals', and Cyrus ordained that henceforth they should ride everywhere, and that it should be considered a disgrace for a Persian nobleman to be seen on foot. At the top of the Persian social hierarchy were the 15,000 noblemen given the honorific title of the 'Kinsmen', or *Huvaka*. The élite cavalry regiment of the Persian army consisted of a thousand men drawn from the King's *Huvaka*. This regiment constituted an élite within an élite, for other references, including Herodotus, mention a myriad of Persian cavalry.

The traditional Persian calf-length tunic was unsuitable for riding, and before long Persian noblemen and cavalry adopted Median dress, though this does not seem to have happened immediately. Median dress consisted of trousers, a long-sleeved tunic reaching down to the knee, and a sleeved cloak worn on the shoulders leaving the arms free, rather like a hussar's pelisse, which was called a *kandys*. Later representations show élite cavalrymen wearing cloth of gold tunics and silver embroidered trousers. These cavalrymen may belong to the *Huvaka* regiment. The purple *kandys* with a leopard skin lining could also be a badge of the *Huvaka*. Other regiments of cavalry were more simply attired in cloaks of purple, nightshade, crimson or sanguine, which Xenophon tells us Cyrus distributed to the various regiments.

Magnificent military attire did not compensate for inexperience in horsemanship and cavalry tactics, and Persian cavalry did not perform well against the Saka and Bactrian tribes in the later campaigns of Cyrus. Following the conquest of Bactria, in 530, Cyrus was wounded in an insignificant cavalry skirmish fought against the Derbices, a rebel Bactrian tribe. The wound festered and Cyrus, conqueror of half the known world, died. Cyrus was succeeded by his son Cambyses. Most of Cambyses' reign was taken up with the conquest of Egypt.

The First Persian Fleet

The Egyptian pharaoh Amasis relied on his absolute mastery of the sea to keep Cambyses out of Egypt. An invading army could only move along the desert coast road into Egypt if it had a fleet to support and supply it. In these circumstances Cambyses decided to build a fleet, which enabled the Persians to conquer Egypt, and later to attack Europe.

Details concerning these early Persian fleets are scarce. The Persians themselves, most of whom could not swim, provided the marines, but the oarsmen were recruited from the coastal cities of Phoenicia. Persian fleets seem to have been organized into squadrons of 300, for this figure recurs constantly in the ancient sources.

Curiously enough Aeschylus tells us that the Greek fleet at Salamis was divided into ten *triakades* of 30, and a *dekas* of ten ships besides. At that time Corinth possessed the largest fleet in Greece, and it is reasonable to suppose that the Greek fleet was organized along Corinthian lines. Originally the *triakas* was a Spartan military sub-unit of 30 men, introduced about 750, which was copied by many states, including Corinth. It seems that the Corinthians transferred their organizational structure based on 30 to their fleet, and this then became the standard for all fleets, including the Persian, operating in the Mediterranean. The number 30 lent itself well to naval operations, for a squadron of 30 ships could conveniently be divided into three units of ten ships each, which would constitute two wings and a centre in battle.

Darius the Great

Upon the premature death of Cambyses in 522 the Empire was temporarily thrown into confusion, as are the historical sources. It was said that Cambyses had murdered his brother during his reign, but now this 'brother', probably an imposter, came forward to take the throne. This impostor, one Smerdis, was deposed by a conspiracy of seven noblemen, one of whom, Darius, ascended the throne. After a year in which he fought 19 battles and seized nine rebel kings, Darius embarked on a new period of imperial expansion. Under his rule the Persian empire was to reach its furthest extent.

Having surpressed dissent within the empire, Darius launched his first war in 519 against the Saka tribes of central Asia, some of whom were now incorporated into the empire. The principal military significance of this campaign was that it made resources of Saka manpower available for mercenary service. Even under Cyrus the levied army was being replaced with a mercenary army. Henceforward increasing use was made of mercenaries. The eastern Iranian tribes and the Saka of central Asia seem to have played a very important role in supplying contingents of mercenary troops to the army, at the same time introducing new tactics and equipment.

In 515 Darius completed the eastward expansion of the empire with a campaign in India. The border was fixed on the River Indus, and a new satrapy was established with its capital at Taxila. India, too, introduced mercenaries and new military ideas to the army. In turn the Persian conquest of the north-western corner of India had a tremendous impact on the rest of the subcontinent. The Persian imperial system, even down to its architecture, was copied by the Mauryas. Military influence is a little harder to detect other than in the field of organization.

Early Indian armies, as described in the *Mahabharata*, seem to be organized along lines similar to many medieval armies. The medieval 'lance' consisted of a knight accompanied by a specific number of horsemen, bowmen, etc. These troops would then be drawn up in separate tactical formations on the battlefield after the army had come together. The Indian equivalent of the 'lance' consisted of one war-elephant, one chariot, three horsemen and five infantry. Thus a *gulma* or 'thicket' consisted of nine elephants, nine chariots, 27 horse and 45 infantry; and a *gana*, a 'flock' or 'troop', comprised three *gulmas*. So it went on, in multiples of three or nine.

Texts dating from after the Persian conquest, however, mention ranks such as that of *satapati*, which has clearly been introduced under Achaemenid influence.

War in the West

Now that firm borders had been secured in the East, Darius turned westward. The campaign waged against the European Scythians in 513 ended in disaster. The strength of the Scythian army lay in its horse-archers who withdrew before the Persians pursuing a 'scorched earth' policy. The Persians advanced deep into Europe, but could not bring the Scyths to close quarters, and so the King was forced to beat a painful retreat, losing most of the army in the process. Fortunately the bridge of boats which Darius had thrown over the Danube was still intact, as Histiaeus the tyrant of Miletus had managed to persuade his fellow Ionian Greeks not to desert the King. Little had been lost during the campagin, for a mercenary army could soon be reconstituted, and in any case the Persians had never had a reputation for invincibility, but the King was grateful to Histiaeus for his loyalty, and he took him to live at Court.

Histiaeus, tired of life at Court and despairing of returning to his native land concocted a hare-brained scheme to incite the Ionians to revolt so he could be sent down to deal with them. The Ionians managed to take over the Persian fleet by treachery, following which a widespread revolt broke out. The Ionians failed to exploit the initial advantage conferred by their command of the sea, and by their dilatoriness frittered away the initiative. The revolt was put down. During the revolt the Athenians, together with the Eretrians, had sent forces to help the Ionians. These had participated in the burning of the satrapal capital of Sardis. Furthermore in 507 the Athenian democrats had rendered Darius earth and water, the traditional symbols of submission, but were now fighting the empire. Such activities could not go without punishment.

The Battle of Marathon

In 490 an expeditionary force was sent through the islands to Euboea, and the city of Eretria was razed. A detachment, which seems to have consisted of a Median myriad commanded by one Datis, stiffened by some Persian and Saka infantry regiments, plus attached cavalry, was shipped over to Athenian territory on the mainland opposite, and camped in the Plain of Marathon. There it was opposed by the Athenian army numbering 9,000, assisted by 1,000 Plataeans. Thus the two sides were roughly evenly matched. The Athenians were afraid to attack as they had no cavalry, and the Persians decided to wait for reinforcements. A stalemate followed which lasted for several days. Then the Persian detachment was ordered to re-embark and join the rest of the fleet as it sailed to Athens where, it was hoped, the city would be

Three types of 'guardsmen' are shown in the Persepolis reliefs. All guardsmen, it seems, carried spears as well as bows. Centre: the fluted cap may well have been the badge of a nobleman at this early period, and so these guardsmen may belong to the Arštibara regiment. Only these troops carry the distinct oval shield with circular segments cut out of the sides. Other regiments of Amrtaka, not shown here, wear turbans, the normal headgear of the Persian commoner. Right and left: the Amrtaka were exclusively Persian, and so these guardsmen in Median dress presumably belong to the corps of Median guardsmen who were normally stationed in the royal palace at Ekbatana, as we are told in one Persian inscription mentioning 'the Median army which was in the palace' which revolted and went over to Phraortes in 522. Note the distinctive battlements surmounting this relief.

betrayed to them. On the first day the cavalry re-embarked, and Miltiades persuaded the other Athenian generals to attack now that they held the advantage. This took some persuasion as few of the Athenians had ever faced a Persian army before, and no Greeks had ever defeated one. In order that the Athenians should not leave any flank of the opposing line uncovered during their advance and risk encirclement, for the Athenian line might edge to one side or other during the advance, the tribal regiments in the Athenian centre were only drawn up in shallow files, but the regiments on the two flanks were drawn up in deeper files. This made the Athenian line somewhat longer than the Persian.

The Athenians charged and drove back their opponents on both flanks, where they were evenly matched in number. In the centre, however, the Athenian advance was slowed down and disrupted by some scrub growing in the plain in between the two lines. When the Athenians reached the deep enemy centre, the élite Persian and Saka regiments, they were driven back. Meanwhile, some of the Athenian regiments which had been successful on the flanks managed to halt their advance, reform, and attack the Persian troops who remained in the centre. From the Persian point of view the Battle of Marathon was an uncomfortable setback suffered in a minor divisional action, but for the Greeks it was of tremendous psychological importance to discover, for the first time, that they could confront a Persian army and win.

The Persian fleet arrived at Athens, but they failed to take the city by treachery, and sailed away rather than face a long siege. The real test of Greek arms was to come ten years later when not just Athens, but all of Greece was faced by a Persian invasion. Darius died in 486 at the age of 64, and was succeeded by his son Xerxes.

The Greek Expedition

The Persians returned in 480 with a massive fleet and army. The precise number is not known. Herodotus, in a passage known as his 'Catalogue of Forces' purports to give us a complete list of all the nations which marched on the continent and were counted in a military review at Doriskos in Thrace. This entire section of Herodotus is a complete fabrication by the author, designed to exaggerate and inflate the forces sent against Greece. Herodotus himself tells us that the historian and geographer Hecataeus tried to persuade the Ionians not to revolt, by enumerating all the nations in the empire they would have to face. It seems that Herodotus, impressed with the catalogue as a literary device in Hecataeus, has copied the passage, expanded it, and transposed it chronologically to the later invasion of 480. In this passage he tells us that the army numbered 1,700,000. Ctesias, who used Persian sources, tells us that the army numbered 800,000.

The army marched on to the pass at Thermopylae which led into central Greece. There it was briefly held up by a small force of Spartans and others, which was soon outflanked and totally destroyed. The army pushed on to Athens, which was razed to the ground. Meanwhile, the fleet had suffered a minor reverse at Artemisium. The Greek fleet had been stationed in the straits between the Greek mainland and the island of Euboea in order to back up its force at Thermopylae. The Persian plan had been to bottle the Greek fleet up in these straits by sealing off their southern end. A Phoenician squadron was sent to accomplish this task, but it was completely scattered, with heavy loss, by a freak storm. This storm cost the Persians the whole campaign for, although the Greek fleet had been savagely mauled in the fighting at Artemisium, it was able to slip away south to fight again another day. In the meantime it hid from the superior Persian fleet between the Greek mainland and the island of Salamis. Again the Persians attempted to trap the Greek fleet in the straits, but, weakened by the loss of the Phoenician squadron, it could no longer divide its forces and still retain sufficient strength to guarantee the victory of either half. The battle was lost, and with the battle all chance of using the fleet to outflank the Greek forces defending the isthmus which led to the Peloponnese.

The Battle of Plataea

Xerxes withdrew to Asia, leaving a portion of the army, some 300,000 strong, in winter quarters in Boeotia under the command of Mardonius. In the new year, by a skilful manoeuvre which involved a second thrust at Athens, the Greek confederate army was coaxed out of its impregnable hiding-place on the isthmus. It advanced to the border of Boeotia, and took up a position in the Plataean plain. This was just what Mardonius had been waiting for. He resolved to use the advantage the plain gave his cavalry.

The Greek forces were severely harried by incessant cavalry attack. If any unit attempted to move, the Persian cavalrymen would move in to isolate it from any protecting forces, and would then javelin them down. Persian cavalry was still not a 'shock' weapon which was used in a direct charge. We also hear of the Persians using horse-archers, which had played such a central role in their defeat at the hands of the Scythians in 513. The cavalry were backed up by units of *sparabara*, who would loose their arrows on any section of the Greek line which started to retreat before the harrying attacks of the cavalry. One presumes that the Persians had combined the mobility of their cavalry with the missile-power of their *sparabara* in their earlier battles during the 6th century.

The Greeks endured these tactics until they were cut off from their water-supply, following which they decided to retreat into the hills at the back of the plain. The retreat began on the following night, but due to the indiscipline of one of the Spartan regimental commanders, who refused to quit the field, the whole of the retreat was held up. Dawn found the Greek army strung out between the plain and the mountains. Seeing this, the Persian forces moved out of their camp and ran, in some disorder, after the Greeks, who now fell under an intense arrow barrage. Sensing that his men could no longer take any more of this punishment, the commander of the Tegeans decided that the only recourse was an attack on the Persian line. The Spartans, their fighting spirit severely shaken by their military impotence over the last few days, were shamed into agreeing. Fortunately for the Greeks, their charge was a success. In all justice it should not have been, for the Persian cavalry should have taken the Greek hoplites in flank when they were on the move. Some days beforehand, however, the Persian cavalry commander Masistius had been killed in a cavalry attack. Not only was the cavalry now leaderless, but Masistius had been adored by his men, and the whole army had been severely depressed by his loss.

Against all the odds the Greeks reached the Persian infantry line and tore down the wall of *spara*. The Persian infantrymen were now placed at a terrible disadvantage. Those in the first rank who had spears attempted to fight off the Greeks, but even these lucky few were at a disadvantage as their spears were shorter than the hoplite spears. The others laid their bows to one side and rushed courageously on the Greeks both singly or, where the *dathapatiš* took a local initiative, in groups of ten. When all else failed, they attempted to lay hold of the Greek spears with their bare hands and break them. The desperate struggle of the Persians could only postpone defeat. Mardonius was struck down and the Persians began to falter and give ground. Then their line broke and rushed headlong for their camp on the other side of the River Asopus. Only the Boeotians stood their ground. The 300 'First and bravest' of the Thebans – possible ancestors of their Sacred Band – perished to a man. The Persian retreat was covered by the cavalry, a testimony to its training and discipline. However, they could do little to prevent the massacre of the Persians in their camp by the vengeful Greeks. Persian losses were huge, although exaggerated by the sources. Herodotus claims that only 3,000 of those who took refuge in the camp survived. He also mentions some 40,000 men who were extricated from the debacle by Artabazus. Total Greek losses

This Athenian vase belongs to 'The Group of the Negro Alabastra', a group of over 30 vases showing black soldiers in Persian dress. Herodotus tells us that a contingent of Aethiopian marines were disembarked after Salamis and attached to the land army. These troops fought at Plataea and inspired this group of paintings. Note the cloak wrapped round the left arm. British Museum, London.

THE TRIREME

The Greek trireme of the 5th century BC had a crew of about 200 of whom 170 were oarsmen, the rest being deck hands and marines. Although a trireme might sail before the wind on the open sea, masts, sails and rigging were stowed before going into battle. The main tactic of galley warfare was to try to ram the enemy vessels, using the metal plated 'beak' at the front of the ships, as galleys had reinforced bows. A common ploy, but one which required superior skill, was to charge the enemy as if intending a head-on collision and at the last moment veer slightly to one side or the other, shipping the oars on the side closest the enemy with the aim of smashing the enemy's oars as the two galleys passed close

alongside each other. This is shown on the left side of the illustration. Emerging behind the enemy line, the victorious galley turned sharply, reversing the stroke of the oars on the inside of the turning circle to bring the ship round more quickly, and rammed and crippled enemy ship in its unprotected stern. The enemy ship, with oars operational on only one side, could do little more than row in circles. This situation is shown on the right side of the illustration. The only chance for the crew of the stricken ship was to board the enemy vessel before it could reverse to withdraw its ram.

are given as 1,360 men. The courage of the Persians had not been found wanting but serious question marks had been raised over their equipment and tactics. They had outmanoeuvred and outgeneralled the Greeks throughout the campaign but had stumbled fatally during the crucial encounter.

Shielded Archers

Plataea was not the last battle of the war, and the same dismal picture of Persian forces defending themselves valiantly though woefully ill-equipped for the job, repeated itself at Mykale the next year. The Persians made an attempt to entrench the *spara*, so as to provide a more secure barrier from behind which to fight. Even so Herodotus tells us that 'so long as the *spara* of the Persians remained standing, they defended themselves strenuously, and had not the worst of the battle'; but the Greeks, 'having broken through the *spara* fell in a body on the Persians; and they, having sustained their attack and defended themselves for a considerable time, at last fled . . . All except the Persians took to flight; they, in small detachments, fought with the Greeks who were continually rushing within'.

What the *sparabara* lacked, even more than adequate offensive weapons, was a means of protecting themselves once the *spara*-wall had been breached and it came to hand-to-hand fighting. Some of the troops wore cuirasses, but by no means all, and what was desperately needed was some kind of shield which could be used to ward off the Greek spear-thrusts.

It is interesting to note that a number of Greek vase-paintings show Persians fighting with a fringed cloak wrapped around their left arm as a makeshift shield. An extremely interesting gemstone shows a Persian hunting with a spear and with the same makeshift shield wrapped around his arm. So it may be that the local initiative taken by Achaemenid troops campaigning in the West was inspired by hunting practices.

However, this was only a temporary expedient until a more permanent solution could be found. From about 460 onwards Greek vases begin to show archers equipped with effective shields. These shields were made of wood or leather, reinforced with a metal rim. A segment was cut out of the top of the shield to give the archer good vision, and so they are crescentic in shape, similar to the crescentic *pelté* familiar to the Greeks, but considerably larger. The Old Persian for these shields seems to have been *taka*. The *spara* was retained by these units, and still used to construct a *spara*-wall in front of the regiment.

Sealing from an Achaemenid gem showing a Persian spearman hunting a boar. Note the cloak wrapped round the left arm as a makeshift shield. Athens Numismatic Museum.

The Peace of Kallias

The war in the West between Athens and Persia continued for several more years. The Athenians and their allies were able to seize the strategic initiative with their large efficient fleet. Athenian support brought succour to rebel groups in the Nile Delta, Cyprus, and elsewhere. The Persians successfully contained these threats, and eventually, around 449, peace was made with Athens. The peace was known as The Peace of Kallias. In return for Athenian agreement that they would no longer send expeditions into Persian territory, the King agreed not to send his army west of the River Halys, nor his fleet west of Lycia. Henceforward the western satraps would be responsible for their own defence, and a royal army would only march westwards if the terms of the treaty were broken.

Satrapal Defences

Xenophon tells us that when Cyrus the Great first established the satrapies he commanded those who had been appointed satrap to do exactly as he had done. Thus we find that each satrap seems to have a regiment of *arštibara* at his personal disposal. In the 6th and 5th centuries these troops would frequently be Persians, but regiments of Medians or Egyptians are also found. In the 5th and 4th centuries they came to be replaced by regiments of native troops raised locally. The *arštibara* were commanded by a *hazarapatiš*, who would perform the same military functions as those of his counterpart at court and was responsible for the military security of the satrapy. The satrap would also be assisted in his administrative functions by a Royal Secretary. Citadels and forts of strategic importance were placed under commanders (*didapatiš*) directly responsible to the King, and were garrisoned by regiments of fortress guards drawn directly from the Royal Army. This division of powers within the satrapy made rebellion more difficult.

The satrap supplemented his defences by raising a regiment of heavy cavalry from the Persian nobility settled on estates within his satrapy. These forces were stiffened by regiments of mercenaries raised locally by the satrap. Following the Peace of Kallias the responsibilities of the satrap to provide local defence had greatly increased, and so certain categories of tribute, previously paid directly to the King, were allocated to provide him with sufficient resources to maintain these forces.

Regiments of 'King's mercenaries' tended to be raised from among the warlike tribes of eastern Iran, such as the Bactrians or Hyrcanians. Sometimes they can be regarded simply as oddities, but in some cases these eastern troops brought new techniques of fighting or equipment which would eventually be adopted by the rest of the army.

Shielded Cavalry

A new type of troop encountered from the middle of the 5th century onwards is the shielded cavalryman. Previously cavalry did not generally use shields. The new practice seems to have been introduced by Saka cavalrymen, who carried a smaller elongated version of the *spara* for cavalry use. The wicker and leather shield was presumably favoured over others because of its lightness, which would interfere less with riding. The Persians had been clashing with the Saka for the best part of a century already, but it seems that the shield was introduced only in the middle of the 5th century, by regiments of Saka cavalry employed to serve as mercenaries throughout the empire.

From about 450 onwards Greek vase paintings start to show shielded cavalrymen. Though the figures are usually of mythological Amazons, in many cases their dress is heavily influenced by Persian clothing. It is safe to presume that the shield suddenly appears in paintings of mounted Amazons at about this time because it simultaneously appeared in Persian cavalry regiments which the Athenians began to encounter around the middle of the 5th century.

Before long the shield had been adopted by the rest of the cavalry. An interesting document dated early 421 tells us that one Gadal-Iama, a Jew, was obliged to furnish the following items to equip a cavalryman: a horse with groom, harness, and an iron caparison, and a helmet, leather cuirass, shield, 120 arrows, an iron attachment for the shield, two spears and ration money.

Persian Heavy Cavalry

Eventually the shield was adopted by the Persian heavy cavalry regiments. An interesting sculpture, now lost, depicting three shielded cavalrymen was discovered and photographed early this century at Yenice Köy near Daskyleion, the capital of the satrapy of Hellespontine Phrygia.

In the second half of the 5th century the wars fought by the Persians were mainly internal. The wars of expansion had long since finished, but for nearly 50 years the external borders were reasonably safe and unthreatened. The nobility of the empire, accustomed to war and possessed of a formidable code of self-esteem, fell to fighting among themselves. Rebellion and attempts to seize the throne abounded. These rebellions would culminate in a pitched

This Persian shield, dating from the Parthian period, was recovered during American excavations at Dura-Europos. Its size indicates that it would have been used by cavalry rather than infantry. Originally the leather and osiers would have been dyed or painted in contrasting colours, giving a highly decorative contrast between the osiers and the reserved V- or W-shaped areas of leather. Yale University Art Gallery, New Haven, Connecticut.

THE DEATH OF CYRUS THE YOUNGER

At the Battle of Cunaxa, Cyrus the Younger took personal command of his regiment of 600 cuirassiers, recruited from the Persian noble families settled in Lydia. This regiment was armed with cuirasses, thigh-protectors attached to the saddle, horse-armour for the forehead and chest, and Greek swords. Cyrus himself fought bareheaded, but his cuirassiers wore helmets, possibly with white plumes. All wore crimson surcoats. King Artaxerxes Mnemon ('The Mindful', or *Abiataka* in Old Persian) was a devotee of the goddess Anahita 'The Pure One', consequently his troops wore white, the colour of ritual purity normally worn by priests.

Following Cyrus' charge, Artaxerxes withdrew to a hill behind the battlefield, rallying his forces round the royal standard, which Xenophon describes as a kind of golden eagle on a shield *(pelte)*. Cyrus' troops had become scattered as night came on, and the young prince was carried away on his spirited horse Parsakas, accompanied only by a few of his 'table-companions'. At this point the precise story of Cyrus' death becomes confused. The most verbose account comes from Ctesias, the Carian court physician, who claimed to be at Artaxerxes' side on the hill. Cyrus gallops on and his princely headgear falls off. One Mithridates unwittingly wounds him in the temple near his eye with a lance. Cyrus swoons and falls from his horse, then he and his companions fall in with some Caunian baggage-carriers from the King's army. Cyrus is speared in the leg, and in falling dashes his wounded temple against a rock and dies. 'Such', says Plutarch, 'is the account of Ctesias, in which, as with a blunt sword, he is long in killing Cyrus, but kills him at last.'

battle. The forces of the rebel could be defeated, but unless the rebel himself was captured and either killed or brought to terms, the rebellion would not end. These rebellions often ended in personal duels between the rebel and the King or his representative. Descriptions of these duels have survived in the *Persika* of Ctesias of Cnidus, a doctor working at the Persian court. Time after time the protagonists are wounded in some unprotected part of the body such as the thigh.

It was warfare in these conditions which encouraged the growth of Persian heavy cavalry and the development of shock tactics. In effect the heavily-armoured regiments of Persian cuirassiers (as they are termed by Xenophon) were used as a kind of armoured 'battering-ram' which smashed into the centre of the enemy line. The cuirassiers were not formed up in line, but in column to add momentum to the charge. The sculpture from Daskyleion demonstrates how heavy Persian cavalry armour had become. As well as the helmets and cuirasses worn by these cavalrymen, we can also see a peculiar piece of armour attached to the saddle and curving round the leg, covering it from waist to toe.

Mercenaries

Most regiments of mercenaries stationed in the western satrapies were not exotic units of Iranian cavalry in the King's service. More frequently they tended to be regiments of mercenary infantry raised locally, often by the satrap rather than the King. The pool of manpower from which these mercenaries could be raised was not great. Most of the nations of the empire had long since ceased to administer any form of military training to their young men. Indeed, this was Persian policy. Upon the conquest of Lydia, for example, military training was discontinued, and within a very short time the Lydians lost any thought of revolt. Even if the Lydians had wanted to resist the empire, they would no longer have known how to. Thus most mercenaries tended to be recruited from nations which were still 'free'. In the ancient world this word can be used almost as a synonym for any society which administered some form of organized military training to their youth.

In the West the greatest source of mercenaries was Greece. Within Greece the most productive regions were the mountain areas which had a pastoral economy based on sheep or goat herding. Later historical examples of similar

96

military catchment-areas are provided by Switzerland, Andalucia and Catalonia. Such economies could release large numbers of men for lengthy periods of time, as animal husbandry could continue without them. Half the 'Ten Thousand' Greek mercenaries who served in the *Anabasis* of Cyrus the Younger came from Arcadia and Achaea. The first Arcadian mercenaries are found in Persian service in 480, when they had deserted from the Arcadian contingent in the Greek army 'in want of sustenance'.

In time Persian armies came to rely heavily on Arcadian or Achaean mercenaries, but the importance of Greeks should not be over-emphasized. Our sources are practically confined to Greek historical accounts of events in the west of the empire, and we know practically nothing of what is happening elsewhere. There is little doubt that Greek mercenaries were of crucial importance to Persian policy in the West, but elsewhere different sources of mercenaries were to hand. In the satrapies of the Caucasus mercenaries were recruited from the Chalybian and Taochian tribes which lay outside the empire. The pools of mercenary manpower available in the Saka tribes lying to the north of the empire have already been mentioned. To the east high-quality manpower could be raised from among the free warrior-republics of northern India. The Hydrakai are one people known to have been a principal source of mercenaries for the Persians in India.

The Takabara

Not all mercenaries came from tribes lying outside the empire. Regiments of Hyrcanians and Bactrians have already been mentioned. A surprising feature of Persian history is that we learn of a number of minor hill peoples, such as the Kurds, the Mysians, or the Pisidians, who seem to be continually in revolt against the authority of the King. The Persians were discomfited when from time to time the brigandage of these tribesmen erupted, but rarely were massive punitive expeditions mounted against them. On the contrary, the Persians were reluctant to destroy the freedom of these peoples entirely, lest they also destroy a principal source of mercenaries employed to keep the rest of the empire down.

These troops were rarely equipped as *sparabara*. First they preferred to fight with their native weapons. Secondly, because they were employed in a wide variety of garrison and patrolling tasks, it would have been undesirable to equip them in the same manner as troops who fought in the main battle line. Most of these troops fought with spears and the *taka*, or leather shield, and so came to be called *takabara*, or '*taka*-bearers'. In Greek sources they are either called peltasts, or more correctly *peltophoroi* or '*pelté*-bearers'. The *takabara* differed from the Greek peltasts, however, for whereas peltasts are used exclusively as missile troops (i.e. javelin-men), the *takabara*, whose shields and spears were much larger, were also used as troops of the line in hand-to-hand fighting. These troops now assume an increasing importance as they are more and more used in satrapal defence, and it is only in the last decades of the 5th century that they appear in Greek vase-paintings. The *sparabara* continued to be used, however, as the main infantry of the line.

The Cuirassiers

Two events occurred in the last decade of the 5th century which shattered the tranquillity of the empire. First the Egyptians staged a successful revolt in 405. Henceforward until just before the Macedonian conquest the main aim of the empire was to reconquer Egypt. The second event was the rebellion in 401 of Cyrus the Younger against his elder brother Artaxerxes II. The revolt was unsuccessful. Clearchus refused to lead his 'Ten Thousand' Greek mercenaries against Artaxerxes in the centre of the enemy line, where the main blow of the army should have fallen. Instead of using the Greeks to break the centre of the enemy line, then using his cuirassier regiment to hunt the King down, Cyrus was forced to use the cuirassiers to guard the Greek troops from encirclement. Thus, although Clearchus' forces won the battle, they lost Cyrus the war, for the prince was unable to kill Artaxerxes and so conclude the revolt successfully. In the confusion surrounding the end of the battle Cyrus himself was killed and the Greeks had to march home unpaid.

The revolt of Cyrus had received Spartan support, and Artaxerxes was now drawn into a war with Sparta. Once again the Persian royal army marched west across the Halys to fight the Greeks. Fear worked on the Persian side, for the Greeks, particularly those who had lived under the Persians in Asia, were reduced to a state of terror. Nevertheless, once they had learned to stand up to the Persians, their ranks stiffened by mercenaries drawn from those who had fought in the 'Ten Thousand' and by levies drawn from Greeks who had fought in the Peloponnesian War, they found that the *sparabara*, and even the *takabara* who by now made up the bulk of the Persian infantry, were no match for the Greek hoplite.

The Persians had to rely on their excellent regiments of cuirassiers to keep the enemy at bay by lightning harassing charges against the Greek cavalry. In one such encounter in 396 Pharnabazus' Persian cavalry regiment surprised the Spartan King Agesilaus on the march near Daskyleion. Xenophon, who was serving in the Greek cavalry, witnessed the charge of the Persian cuirassier column, which was executed with devastating effect against the hastily formed Greek cavalry line. When Xenophon released his two books *On Horsemanship* and *The Cavalry Commander* between 367 and 365, in the hope of encouraging reform in the Athenian cavalry, he recommended the adoption of heavy armour (including Persian armoured saddles) and column formations.

Pharnabazus also experimented with combinations of cuirassiers and scythed chariots. On one occasion a Greek force was caught in the open while foraging. The chariots, an excellent 'weapon of terror' – not least to the driver – tore into these troops, supported by the cuirassiers, and cut the Greeks up. About a hundred of the enemy were killed.

Scythed chariots are also known in the 5th century, but we are not sure how far back their use stretched. Xenophon tells us that they were introduced into the Persian army by Cyrus the Great, while Ctesias mentions their use even further back. This need not to be taken too seriously, for no scythed chariots appear on Assyrian reliefs, and so Xenophon may be quite correct. Indian sources mention scythed chariots, together with stone-throwers, being used in the campaigns waged by the Mauryas against the Vriji confederacy during the reign of Ajatashastru (494-467), Unfortunately, it is impossible to

Relief from the Temple of Athena Nike on the Athenian Acropolis, executed around 425 BC. It has been suggested that this relief represents the Battle of Marathon, but we know that the Persian cavalry were not present at that battle, so the relief more probably records some incident during the battle of Plataea. A Persian cavalryman and a Greek hoplite are disputing the body of a dead Persian. The dead Persian could be Masistius, the Persian cavalry commander, who was killed by the Athenians after being thrown from his wounded horse. The Persian cavalry desperately tried to recover the body, but without success. The armour of Masistius was later displayed in the Temple of Athena Palias on the Acropolis. British Museum, London.

say whether scythed chariots were an Indian invention adopted by the Persians or a Persian invention adopted by the Indians.

The Infantry in Decline

Notwithstanding the local and temporary successes of the Persian cavalry, the Spartan army in Asia wrought terrible damage, eventually forcing its way into Phrygia. The tables were finally turned by the Persian fleet, which had been built during the winter of 397-6. The Spartan fleet was defeated at Cnidus in 394, and the Persians established a fort at Kythera, off the Peloponnesian coast, from which they harried Spartan territory. Meanwhile, those Greek states hostile to Sparta had been persuaded to band together into a league which declared war on Sparta. Agesilaus was recalled to Europe with his army in 394. The Persian King had managed to bring the league into existence by the skilful bribery of selected Greek politicians. Persian gold coins (which were traditionally stamped with the device of the King carrying a bow) flooded into Greece, and Agesilaus was heard to declare that he had been driven out of Asia by the King's 10,000 Persian 'archers'. In 387 a common peace was agreed upon. Henceforward Persian diplomacy and bribery encouraged peace in Greece as a means of preserving a balance of power there, and also in order to release mercenaries to serve in the many expeditions mounted to reconquer Egypt.

The war had once again highlighted the poor equipment of the Persian infantry. Xenophon mentions an imaginitive Persian order of battle, which he attributes to Cyrus the Great. The various regiments of a myriad are to be drawn up in this way: in front two ranks of cuirassed infantry, presumably *sparabara;* then two lines of troops variously called 'javelin-men' or 'peltasts', by which he presumably means *takabara;* then behind these two ranks of archers (it is more probable that there were four ranks of archers, to bring the total strength of the line up to ten); finally, at the rear, there were two ranks of 'file-closers' of unspecified armament. Such a formation was designed to combine the traditional virtues of heavy missile power with the new supremacy of heavy infantry on the battlefield. We do not know whether this 'composite phalanx' is a pure invention of Xenophon's, or whether it reflects contemporary experimentation, or at least contemporary debate, as to how the Persian battle line was to be reformed. Curiously enough, Alexander the Great, who read Xenophon and introduced some of his recommendations, notably the Boeotian cavalry helmet, into the Macedonian army in 336, attempted to weld his Macedonian and Persian forces into a 'combined phalanx' in 324. He died before the experiment could be put into effect, but there can be little doubt that he was influenced by Xenophon and, possibly, by Persian experiments carried out in the first 30 years of the 4th century.

The Reforms of Iphicrates

The Peace of 387 once again released large numbers of Greek mercenaries for service with the King. First Cyprus, which had revolted, was reconquered. Then in 379 Pharnabazus started to assemble an expeditionary force against Egypt. It was envisaged that Greek mercenaries, who were expendable, would be used as the spearhead in this risky undertaking. Pharnabazus asked the Athenians to send him their general Iphicrates. Iphicrates had first distinguished himself at the age of 18 while serving in the Persian fleet at Cnidus under the command of Pharnabazus. He now served as commander to the King's mercenaries. Unfortunately there were just not enough mercenaries to be had in Greece at that time, for war had broken out there once again. King Artaxerxes tried to make peace among the Greeks again in 375, in order to free sufficient mercenaries for service with him, but the attempt was unsuccessful. Some 20,000 Greek mercenaries had already been assembled, but it seems that of these perhaps only 8,000 were hoplites. The increasing pauperization of

Coin of Datames, struck c.370-368 BC to pay the army at Ake. The general is shown seated, testing an arrow for straightness, and wearing the new arm-guards and trousers covered in iron scales. These armoured trousers are found earlier on in the 5th century BC, but they had been displaced by the armoured saddle; now they return to displace the armoured saddle.

Greece during the 4th century had reduced the number of citizens who could afford to supply themselves with hoplite equipment. It is probable, moreover, that few of these Greeks had received military training in hoplite warfare.

To remedy these deficiencies, Iphicrates conceived the idea of creating a peltast who could fight in the front line and stand up to hoplites. Essentially he was converting the 12,000 non-hoplite Greek mercenaries into *takabara*, but further strengthening their equipment. His troops were given a *taka*, or *pelté* as our Greek sources describe it, which Diodorus mentions as being equal in size to the hoplite shield. The fighting spear was lengthened by half, from the normal 2.5m spear used by hoplites and *takabara* alike, to a 3.5m pike. These 12,000 troops were known as 'Iphicrateans' after their general and creator.

The invasion fleet finally set sail for Egypt in 373, but the invasion was a disaster. Pharnabazus, now an old man, refused to take decisions without referring them to the King for approval, and the initiative was lost. Iphicrates' enemies in the army started plotting against him again, and so the wily Athenian slipped back to Athens in the hold of a ship, and his army of mercenaries disintegrated. The 'Iphicrateans', however, had proved themselves on the field of battle, and the 'Iphicratean peltast' now became a feature of warfare on the Greek mainland, most spectacularly when Philip of Macedon used the concept to reform the Macedonian army in 359. The Macedonian word used for the 3.5m pike was *sarissa*. It is curious to think that the Persian *takabara* inspired the Iphicratean peltast, which in turn inspired the Macedonian phalangite.

The Reforms of Datames

In 372 Datames replaced Pharnabazus as commander-in-chief of the Egyptian expeditionary force, and Timotheus replaced Iphicrates as commander of the Greek mercenaries. The supply of mercenaries from Greece now became even more constrained. Following her decisive defeat at Leuctra in 371 the power of Sparta in the Peloponnese was broken. Arcadian and Achaean Leagues sprang up, which began to maintain standing armies of picked citizen troops (*epilektoi*). Thus the supply of mercenaries from Greece's two principal recruiting grounds dried up almost entirely. A solution had to be found to the chronic shortage of Greek mercenary hoplites.

The answer was the *Kardaka*. The Greeks were not the only group of mercenaries present in the expeditionary force; there were also some 120,000 barbarians. Datames promptly started to train and equip these troops to fight as hoplites, aided by Timotheus, who had a reputation as a 'military intellectual'. These barbarian hoplites were called *Kardaka*.

Reforms in cavalry equipment were also introduced. The Persian cuirassier was rapidly developing into the fully armoured 'cataphract' we find in later armies. While the army was preparing for the Egyptian expedition in its quarters at Ake, the process advanced one step further with the introduction of arm-guards. Xenophon in *On Horsemanship*, whilst recommending the armoured saddle, also urges the adoption of 'that weapon which has just been invented' called the 'arm'.

The Satrapal Revolts

Datames never marched against Egypt. His enemies at court, jealous of his success, poisoned the mind of the King against him. Informed of these intrigues by a friend at Court, Datames deserted Ake for his own satrapy of Cappadocia in 368. The next year Autophradates, his successor at Ake, was sent against him with an army largely composed of his own *Kardaka*.

The next ten years were a sorry time for the empire, a catalogue of palace intrigue and rebellion. Even the quality of the famous Persian cavalry began to cause considerable alarm. The ranks of the Persian landholders in the western satrapies, from whom the satrapal regiments were recruited, had been thinned out by constant war and devastation. Xenophon talks of times past when the Persian land-holders had supplied men for service in the cuirassier regiments from their own households, and had undertaken military service themselves in times of necessity, with only garrison troops having to be paid for their service. Now the rulers made cavalrymen out of 'their door-keepers, and their cake-bakers, and their cooks, and wine-waiters, and bath-pourers, and serving-men, and waiters, and chamberlains, and valets, and even their beauticians, who eye-pencil and rouge them and in other ways order their looks'; and even these had to be paid to serve.

Artaxerxes II died in 358. The new King, Artaxerxes III 'Ochus', an extremely capable monarch, perceived that the satrapal armies could no longer guarantee the peace of the western borders, and merely provided the western satraps with the means to carry out their treachery. Consequently he ordered that they be disbanded. A further satrapal revolt, that of Artabazus, ensued.

Greek Epilektoi

Over the preceeding 20 years a new military and political system had arisen in Greece. The old type of city-state was gradually giving way to larger federal units. These new federal states, such as the Arcadian and Achaean Leagues founded around 370, maintained forces of permanently embodied 'picked troops' (epilektoi) raised from their own citizens. These troops, frequently peltasts of the 'Iphicratean' type rather than hoplites, had to be paid on a regular basis, but fiscal reform had not kept pace with military reform. Thus the states of Greece found themselves in command of fairly large bodies of efficient citizen troops which they could not afford to pay, while on the other side of the Aegean the rebel satrap Artabazus, who had plenty of money, was desperately in need of a body of efficient soldiery. A mutually beneficial solution to this double problem was rapidly achieved. Henceforward contingents of Greek mercenaries in Persian service tended not to be paid on an individual basis; rather, the Greek state itself was paid a specific sum for loaning out its army in times of peace.

Artabazus was first supported by an Athenian army under Chares, which penetrated deep into Phrygia and won a significant victory, which the Athenian general somewhat immodestly referred to as a 'second Marathon'. Chares was replaced by the Theban Pammenes, who was also victorious. Artaxerxes eventually came to terms with Artabazus, however, and after Pammenes had been kidnapped and killed, the Theban army was signed over to the King.

Following the settlement of the revolt in the West, Artaxerxes dealt with a succession of provincial revolts before turning his full attention to the reconquest of Egypt. Greek military contingents were hired from Thebes, Argos, and from the Greek cities of Asia. These troops were backed up with some Kardaka, but it was intended that the brunt of the fighting should be borne by the expendable Greek contingents. By 343 the reconquest of Egypt was complete. Artaxerxes now turned his attention to reforming the institutions of the empire to achieve tranquillity on a reasonably permanent basis.

Military Settlements

Many of the Kardaka, who had been raised and trained from young men in their early 20s in the years 372-368, were now ready for discharge. The system of settling retired mercenaries on allotments within the empire was not new, but under Artaxerxes it was not only revived but also transformed. The new allotments were not placed randomly in the empire where land might be available. Rather, whole communitites of retired veterans were sited in a number of strategic locations throughout the empire with the aim of maintaining the peace in the area. Thus, while our picture of where these communitites were sited is far from complete, we regularly seem to encounter them in areas either recently conquered, or perennially restless. A 'Village of the *Kardaka*' in Lycia is mentioned in later inscriptions, as is a community called the 'Maibozanoi' in Lydia Katakekaumene, possibly centred around Gölde in 'The Plain of Castolus'. In Egypt in Hellenistic times we come across a group of military settlers called 'The Persians', who may be the remnants of a community of *Kardaka*. Another community of Iranian military settlers is attested in Avroman in the Parthian period. All these settlements could well be remnants of a once extensive system of military settlements of retired *Kardaka* established in the 350s and 340s to impose peace on the empire. The system was resuscitated by Alexander the Great, who retrained the *Kardaka* in Macedonian tactics and equipment.

Thus the *Kardaka* system survived long after the death of Alexander. It seems that the settlers and their descendants incurred a liability for military service upon receipt of the allotment, and the Hellenistic rulers who followed Alexander were eager to make use of any available source of military manpower. Polybius mentions a regiment of 1,000 *Kardaka* fighting in the Seleucid army at Raphia in 217. Furthermore the *Kardaka* provided the inspiration for further developments in the system of military settlement. Now discharged Greek and Macedonian soldiers were settled on allotments in return for a liability for military service which fell upon them and their descendants. In this way the East was Hellenized.

In some cases it was not only the idea that was taken from the *Kardaka*, but even the very allotments. Polyaenus tells us that some 3,000 Persians who had been attempting a rebellion against Seleucus I were massacred in an ambush by the same number of hoplites. Henceforward we regularly find that the Seleucids raise a force of 3,000 settlers from Persis. History was to repay this act of treachery, for Polyaenus goes on to tell us that little more than a century later Oborzes, a Persian dynast who had shaken free from Seleucid domination, massacred 3,000 Greek military colonists settled in Persis on hearing that they were conspiring against him.

The Fall of Empire

Tragically Artaxerxes III Ochus died in 338. Had this capable and energetic monarch lived but a few years longer Alexander may not have succeeded in conquering the empire. His successor, Darius III Codomannus, was brave but lacked the ability to save the empire. In fairness it must be said that against an Alexander only a general of supreme ability could prevail. The successes of Alexander have, however, tended to obscure the military successes of the Persians during that period.

Following the defeat of Issus (333), major attempts were made both to seize the strategic initiative and to prepare forces to replace those lost in the battle. An army was sent into Anatolia to make contact with the Persian fleet operating in the Aegean while Alexander was marching south to Egypt. It made considerable headway, but failed to reach the coast. Meanwhile in Babylonia new forces of infantry were raised and issued with shields and new swords longer than those in use before. Thus we may conclude that the losses suffered by the *Kardaka* at Issus were now made good. Cavalry spears much longer than those in use before were also produced and issued. The development of the 'cataphract', the forerunner of the medieval knight, was now complete, for the Persian cuirassiers had finally discarded their fighting javelins (*palta*) in favour of the two-handed lance (*kontos*).

The main hope still rested on the cavalry, and a large force of scythed chariots was created to operate with them. It seems that the Persians hoped that the chariots, either through fear or through contact, would open up gaps in the Macedonian line which the cavalry could then exploit. Unfortunately the Macedonian battle line was constructed so compactly that the chariots caused no dislocation, and outflanking cavalry could find no target for attack. The sad story of the fall of the empire need not be repeated in full here, but one is consoled that, to some extent, the Persian army lived on through its military institutions, which were borrowed and modified by the Greek and Macedonian conquerors.

PRINCIPAL SOURCES

Herodotus (484 BC – ?)

Born in Halicarnassus in Caria within the Persian empire. *Histories* describe the events of the wars between the Greeks and Persians, and enquire into the origins of the conflict. His enquiries led him to travel extensively in the empire. He drew on oral tradition as well as earlier written sources, but would also resort to invention if his enquiries drew a blank. Consequently, though he contains much valuable information on Persian warfare, he must be treated with some circumspection.

Xenophon (c.425 BC – post 355 BC)

Born into noble Athenian family, he joined the Greek mercenary force led upland by Cyrus the Younger in 401 as a gentleman volunteer. His close contact with Persians during this period gave him a detailed knowledge of the Empire and considerable sympathy for the Persians. A pupil of Socrates and joint general of an army of 10,000 men before his 30th birthday, Xenophon was a 'Renaissance man' of considerable breadth of understanding, writing on matters as diverse as estate management, hunting, reform of the Athenian silver-mining industry, and Socratic dialogue. Most interesting to the military historian are his two pamphlets, *On Horsemanship* and *The Cavalry Commander*, published between 367 and 365 in an attempt to reform the Athenian cavalry, to some extent along Persian lines. His *Cyropaedia*, published between 363 and 358, is a curious multi-layered work, containing valuable information on Persian history and military organization, interspersed with general recommendations on how an army should be run.

The Persepolis Tablets

Two deposits of administrative clay documents, called the 'Treasury' and 'Fortfication' tablets after their findspots, were recovered during excavation at Persepolis. They are administrative documents, largely concerned with the issue of rations. References to units and ranks, appearing as Old Persian loan-words in the scribal Elamite of the tablets, both support the detailed account of military organization given in Xenophon's *Cyropaedia* and in other sources, and provide us with the Old Persian terms.

Diodorus Siculus (1st century BC)

Though a late source, the Sicilian historian Diodorus draws on a large number of earlier sources now lost. Through Diodorus much valuable information is preserved. His *Bibliotheca Historica*, which once ran to 40 volumes, now largely lost itself, was organized according to a strict chronogical order. Unfortunately Diodorus was occasionally unable to resolve chronological problems in his sources, and this poses problems for the modern historian. Diodorus is the only source dealing with many principal events of Persian history during the 4th century in anything like adequate detail.

ALEXANDER THE GREAT

DR ALBERT DEVINE

The greatest and most spectacular military leader of the ancient world was born in 356 BC, the son of Philip II of Macedon. Philip was then engaged in turning a weak feudal state into the greatest power in the Balkans. Subjugating the Illyrians, who for generations had raided Macedonia, Philip turned his attention southward to where Thebes had established a hegemony over Greece as the result of Epaminondas' victories over Sparta at Leuctra in 371 and Mantinea in 362. Philip had been a hostage at Thebes from 368 to 365 and had there absorbed the tactical and organizational lessons which underlay his reform of the Macedonian army. Philip's intrusion into Athens' sphere of influence led to war, in which a worried Thebes sided with Athens. The result was Philip's great victory at Chaeronea in 338 in which the eighteen-year-old Alexander led the Macedonian left which crushed the spearhead of the Theban army, the legendary Sacred Band. Having formed the Greeks into a loose confederation, the League of Corinth, under his own leadership, Philip was establishing a bridgehead in Asia Minor for a war of Greek national revenge against Persia when he was assassinated in 336. Alexander's accession occasioned a strengthening of Macedonian control, as the twenty-year-old king crushed in turn the restive Illyrians and Thebans, destroying outright the city of Thebes in 335. By spring 334 Alexander was ready to invade the Persian empire at the head of a veteran army.

THE MACEDONIAN ARMY: ITS UNITS, EQUIPMENT, AND TACTICS

The Companion Cavalry

The Macedonian aristocracy had traditionally provided the army's cavalry and fought under the King's personal leadership, hence their honorific title 'Companions'. Under Philip the Companions were expanded from a feudal chivalry into a formidable cavalry arm of 3,300, including some Greek settlers attracted to the Macedonian court.

The 1,800 Companions who crossed to Asia Minor were organized in a Royal *ile* (squadron) and seven other *ilai* on a territorial basis. The Royal *ile* probably had an establishment strength of 300 horsemen, while the others each mustered at least 200. In 331 each of the *ilai* was divided into two *lochoi* (companies). The Companion cavalry were increased in number, to make up for the demobilization of the Thessalian cavalry in 329, and reorganized in 328 into seven or eight hipparchies of 500 horsemen each. The Royal *ile*, however, was retained as the *Agema*, 300 strong.

The Companions fought with each of their *ilai* in an *embolos*, the delta-shaped wedge-formation, invented by the Scythians and adopted by Philip II. This formation permitted rapid wheeling and withdrawal and was ideal for penetrating other cavalry formations. Armed with the sarissa, a spear at least

4.5m in length, the Companions were also able to penetrate formations of infantry armed with the normal 2-2.5m hoplite spear.

The Phalanx: The Hypaspists and the Pezhetairoi

The iron core of the Macedonian army was the phalanx. The ordinary Macedonian served as an infantryman, and the successes of Philip and Alexander derived to a large extent from the steadiness and reliability of the *Pezhetairoi*, the 'Foot Companions,' so called to stress their relationship to the King as a tactical and political counterpoise to the aristocratic Companions. In 334 the Macedonian infantry numbered 24,000, of which 12,000 were left behind in Macedonia (together with 1,500 Companion cavalry) under Alexander's Regent, Antipater. Of the 12,000 who formed part of Alexander's expeditionary force, 9,000 were organized, on a territorial basis, in six *taxeis* (brigades) of *Pezhetairoi*, while the remaining 3,000 constituted an élite Guard, the Hypaspists, 'Shield-bearers'. Later, beginning after the Battle of Issus (333), three *taxeis* of *Pezhetairoi* were honoured with the title *Asthetairoi*, 'Best Companions'. In 330 a seventh *taxis* was added.

Although the *taxis*, with a strength of at least 1,500, was the basic tactical unit of the *Pezhetairoi*, it was subdivided into smaller units of which the most fundamental was the *dekad*, originally of 10 men as the name implies, but by 333 of 16 men. The *dekad* corresponded to a file of the *taxis* drawn up in deep battle-order or a double file in the eight-deep battle-order which Alexander preferred. Although we have detailed information about the internal organization of the phalanx in the century or two after Alexander's death in the surviving Hellenistic tactical manuals of Asclepiodotus, Aelian and Arrian, the only unit intermediate between the *dekad* and the *taxis* we know of in Alexander's own time is the *lochos*. Since their commanders were of high enough status to attend Alexander's staff briefings, the *lochoi* must have been much larger than their Hellenistic namesakes which, like the old *dekad*, contained only 16 men. The Alexandrine *lochos* probably corresponded to the Hellenistic *xenagia* or *syntagma* with a theoretical strength of 256 men; thus six such *lochoi* per *taxis*.

The Hypaspists were organized in three chiliarchies of 1,000 men (of which one was the élite *Agema*, parallelling the Royal *ile* among the Companions), each of which was further subdivided into two pentakosiarchies nominally of 500. It is probable that from this level down the organization of the *Pezhetairoi taxeis* and the chiliarchies of the Hypaspists paralleled each other, so that both types of unit were subdivided into *lochoi* of 256, hekatontarchies of 128, tetrarchies of 64, and double files of 32 men.

The Hypaspists and *Pezhetairoi* invariably occupied the centre of the Macedonian order-of-battle, flanked by the Companion and Thessalian cavalry, with which they were trained to co-operate in large-scale movements in oblique order. The Companions punched a hole in the enemy battle-line and the phalanx exploited it, rolling up their opponents like a carpet, while covering their cavalry's flank and rear. Their repertoire included the formation of grand tactical wedges, beginning with the simple lambda-shaped formation used by Epaminondas against the Spartans in the decisive breakthrough at Leuctra in 371. This Alexander himself utilized against the Illyrians at Pelion in 335, while also developing the more complex mixed wedge of cavalry and infantry which Epaminondas had used in his last battle at Mantinea in 362, carrying it into spectacular operation at Gaugamela.

The Sarissa and its Use: Related Equipment

The sarissa, the characteristic weapon of Macedonian cavalry and infantry alike, consisted of a long shaft made from cornel wood, an iron point attached to the upper end by a socket, and either a second iron weapon head (in the case of the cavalry version of the sarissa) or a conical butt-spike (in the infantry

Scene from Boscoreale. Alexander the Great's posthumous son, Alexander IV (reigned nominally 323-310 BC), with his mother, the Bactrian princess Roxane. Both are in Bactrian dress, but the boy has a sarissa and shield of the type carried by the Companion Cavalry and Pezhetairoi. The shield was originally bronze, but later sometimes plated with silver or (as here) gold, with a pattern of seven triple crescents (or moons), each enclosing an eight-pointed sun, around the rim of the shield. The central star or sun represents the person of the Macedonian King, while the crescents and smaller suns represent the days of the week, symbolizing the Companions' motto, 'Seven days and night (a week) around the King'. Museo Archeologico Nazionale, Naples.

variant) fastened similarly to the lower end. The cavalry sarissa's second weapon head could be used for fighting if the forward point was broken off in battle, while the butt-spike served as a means to plant the sarissa in the ground so that a charging horseman or horse could be impaled on the point. The two halves of the wooden shaft were joined by an iron coupling-sleeve, so that the sarissa could be dismantled for carrying on the march. Sarissas varied considerably in length, up to 6.5m and even 7.3m, though in Alexander's time most would have been in the range of 4.5-5.5m. The sarissa heads with their sockets seem to have averaged around 0.51m in length; the butt-spikes were a little shorter, around 0.445m. Modern reconstructions have shown that a 4.5m sarissa would have weighed only 5.5kg, while an 5.5m sarissa weighed 6.5kg, which indicates that they required considerable training to use effectively.

The phalangite wielded his sarissa with both hands, keeping it carefully aligned with the weapons of his comrades. Phalanx drill called for the sarissas of the first five ranks to project beyond the front-rank men in the compact formation used for attack. The phalangite was allowed one-third of sarissa length to balance and hold his weapon, so that a 6m sarissa, when levelled at the enemy, projected 4m ahead of the man holding it. The men in the second rank, 1m behind the file leaders, extended their weapons 3m beyond the front rank, but raised them somewhat; the third rank 2m, raising them higher; the fourth rank 1m, raising them still higher; while the sarissa-points of the fifth rank were held above the heads of the file-leaders. The result was a towering hedge of sarissas, impenetrable to enemy infantry, cavalry, and even, as at the Hydaspes, elephants.

While the cavalryman would normally have charged with his sarissa held underarm, ready to strike upwards rather than down, the sarissa could also be used overarm for a downward stroke against a dismounted opponent or an infantryman. As the stirrup was unknown to ancient cavalry, the sarissa could not be used to impale opposing horsemen like the medieval knight's lance.

106

Instead, Macedonian cavalry drill was to aim for the enemy horseman's face or his horse's head, a procedure which was more likely to dismount than to kill an opponent. *Hamippoi*, light infantry, like the Agrianian javelin-men, who ran alongside (or even in between) the heavy cavalry, dealt with dismounted enemy horsemen.

As the phalangite used both hands to wield his sarissa, he could carry only a small bronze shield, 60cm in diameter, suspended from his neck to cover his left shoulder. The Hypaspists' shields were decorated with silver plates in 327 and the corps acquired the name Argyraspids, 'Silver Shields', which stuck until they were disbanded by Antigonus Monophthalmus in 317. Encumbered with their sarissas, the phalangites dispensed with heavy body armour and contented themselves with leather corslets (in lieu of breastplates), helmets, and greaves, and used knives as their secondary weapons.

The Thessalian Cavalry

The 1,800 Thessalians followed Alexander as Archon of the Thessalian League. Alexander had secured this elective position in succession to Philip II, who had acquired it by a combination of force and diplomacy in 352. The Thessalians, coming from the best horse-breeding region in Greece, were arguably the finest cavalry unit in the army. Their interventions at Issus and Gaugamela turned near defeat on Alexander's left, their normal battle position, into spectacular successes. Organized in 8 *ilai* like the Companions, their *ilai* fought in the *rhombos*, the diamond-shaped formation invented by Jason of Pherae, Archon of Thessaly, 374-370.

The Prodromoi

The four *ilai* of Macedonian *Prodromoi* (Scouts) – alternatively called, as they too were armed with the sarissa, *Sarissophoroi* (Lancers) – made up a brigade of light cavalry with two units of Alexander's subject allies, the Paeonians and the Thracians. The 600-strong *Prodromoi* fought in small *ilai* of 150 horsemen.

The Paeonian and Thracian (Odrysian) Cavalry

The Paeonians and the Odrysian Thracians were initially one-squadron units, each 150 strong. As light cavalry, they were ideal for use as flank guards for larger and more valuable units. The Paeonians were normally brigaded with

Painting in tempera on Etruscan sarcophagus from Tarquinii (late 4th century BC). Battle with Amazons, showing (centre) hoplite (heavy infantry) arms and equipment used by Alexander's allies of the League of Corinth and the Greek mercenaries in his service and that of Darius. The Amazon (right) is equipped as a Scythian archer. Museo Archeologico Nazionale, Naples.

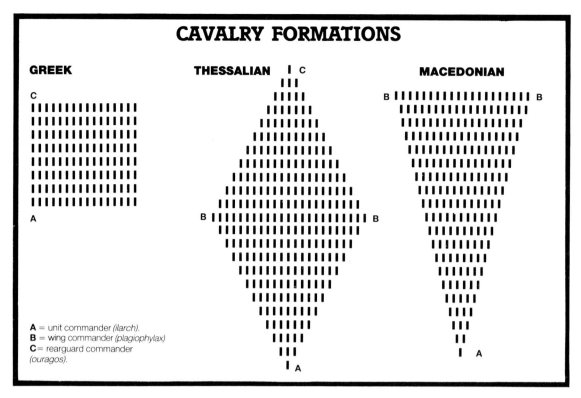

CAVALRY FORMATIONS

GREEK **THESSALIAN** **MACEDONIAN**

A = unit commander *(ilarch)*.
B = wing commander *(plagiophylax)*
C = rearguard commander
(ouragos).

the *Prodromoi* and the two units assigned to protect the Companions' flank. The Odrysians, however, were regularly assigned to the left wing as flank guards for the Thessalian cavalry. By the time of Gaugamela (331), the Odrysians had been built up to a four-squadron unit of 600. Thracian cavalry had used the delta-shaped wedge before the Macedonians, and the Odrysians continued to use this formation in Alexander's service.

Greek and Balkan Allied Troops

The minor kings of the Balkans were under obligation to supply their overlord with troops when required. In 334 the Odrysians and other Thracians fielded about 3,000 infantry, the Illyrians another 3,000, and the Triballians, subjugated by Alexander in 335, 1,000 infantry. Paeonia also provided 500 Agrianian javelin-men at first, but reinforcements before Issus brought this up to 1,000. Together with the Macedonian and Cretan archers, they were regularly used to screen the Companions before they engaged and to act as *hamippoi* for them in their attacks. A similar unit, the Thracian javelin-men, led by the Odrysian prince Sitalces, performed the same duty for the Thessalians at the Granicus (334) and Gaugamela. The Greek allies of the League of Corinth provided 7,000 infantry and 600 cavalry. Alexander's 5,000 mercenary infantry normally appeared, with the 7,000 Greek allied infantry, in the order-of-battle as a second-line phalanx.

Alexander's expeditionary force in 334 mustered 32,000 infantry and 5,100 cavalry. By the time of Gaugamela, in October 331, this had been brought up to 40,000 infantry and 7,000 cavalry. As Alexander subjugated the warlike peoples of the Persian empire, he was able to build up his forces to 120,000 men by 326, though the core army was kept small, totalling only 23,000 foot and 8,800 cavalry at the Hydaspes (326). Many new specialist units, like the Dahae horse-archers, were incorporated into the field army. Alexander's last great innovation, the training of 30,000 young Persians in the use of Macedonian equipment and tactics and their incorporation into pre-existing Macedonian units, set the model for the armies of the Hellenistic Age.

ALEXANDER'S CAMPAIGNS

The Battle of the Granicus

At the beginning of spring 334, Alexander crossed to Asia Minor via the Hellespont, where he was confronted at the River Granicus by a combined army commanded collectively by the satraps (governors) Arsites, Spithridates, and Arsames, and the Greek mercenary commander Memnon of Rhodes. Memnon had urged a 'scorched earth' strategy on the Persian satraps, but this had been rejected through the intervention of Arsites, who refused to lay waste his own satrapy to hold up the Macedonian advance. The Persians had drawn up 10,000 cavalry along the bank of the Granicus, with 4-5,000 Greek mercenary infantry in their rear on higher ground.

Rejecting Parmenion's advice to delay offering battle until the following day, Alexander deployed immediately, posting on his right seven of the eight *ilai* of the Companion cavalry, which with the detached *ile* mustered 1,800 horsemen, along with the archers and the Agrianian javelin-men, together 1,000 strong. Next to these units he posted the detached Companion *ile* of Socrates, the Paeonian cavalry, and the *Prodromoi*. Next he stationed the phalanx, 12,000 strong, with the Hypaspists first on the right, then the *taxeis* of Perdiccas, Coenus, Craterus, Amyntas, son of Andromenes, Philip, and Meleager. Adjacent to them were the Thracian cavalry, which with the *Prodromoi* and Paeonians made up a brigade of 900 light horse. Next were the 600 allied Greek cavalry and, on the extreme left, the Thessalian cavalry, 1,800 strong. Doubtful about the reliability of his Greek allied and mercenary infantry, Alexander had advanced without them, and his available forces amounted to a modest 18,100 men – 12,000 heavy infantry, 1,000 light infantry, and 5,100 cavalry.

This advantage in numbers (18,100 to 14-15,000) explains why Alexander was content to risk a frontal assault on the Persian positions, instead of manoeuvring around either of the enemy's flanks. His intention was not merely to circumvent the immediate Persian opposition, but to destroy the

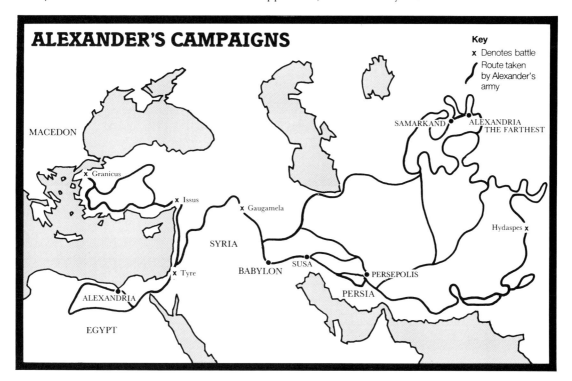

ALEXANDER'S CAMPAIGNS

Key
x Denotes battle
Route taken by Alexander's army

MACEDON

SAMARKAND • ALEXANDRIA THE FARTHEST

x Granicus

x Issus

x Gaugamela

Hydaspes x

SYRIA

x Tyre

BABYLON SUSA PERSEPOLIS

ALEXANDRIA

PERSIA

EGYPT

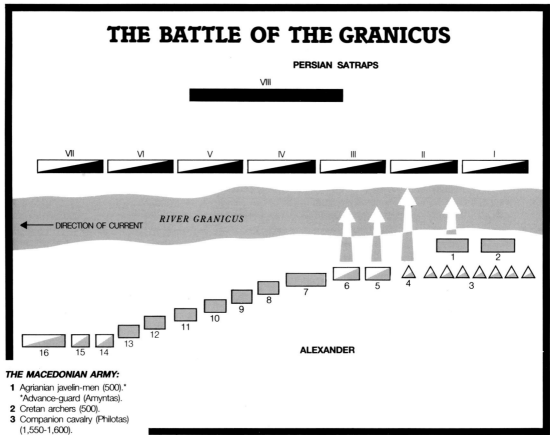

THE BATTLE OF THE GRANICUS

PERSIAN SATRAPS

RIVER GRANICUS

DIRECTION OF CURRENT

ALEXANDER

THE MACEDONIAN ARMY:

 1 Agrianian javelin-men (500).*
   *Advance-guard (Amyntas).
 2 Cretan archers (500).
 3 Companion cavalry (Philotas)
   (1,550-1,600).
 4 The *ile* of Socrates (200-250).*
 5 Paeonian cavalry (150*).
 6 *Prodromoi* (600).
 7 Hypaspists (Nicanor) (3,000).
 8 *Pezhetairoi* – *Taxis* of Perdiccas
   (1,500).
 9 *Pezhetairoi* – *Taxis* of Coenus
   (1,500).
10 *Pezhetairoi* – *Taxis* of Craterus
   (1,500).
11 *Pezhetairoi* – *Taxis* of Amyntas
   (1,500).
12 *Pezhetairoi* – *Taxis* of Philip
   (1,500).
13 *Pezhetairoi* – *Taxis* of Meleager
   (1,500).
14 Thracian Odrysian cavalry
   (Agathon) (150).
15 Allied Greek cavalry (Philip, son
   of Menelaus) (600).
16 Thessalian cavalry (Calas)
   (1,800).

THE PERSIAN ARMY:

  I Cavalry of unspecified
    nationality (Memnon and
    Arsames).
 II Paphlagonian cavalry (Arsiteş).
III Hyrcanian cavalry (Spithridates)
 IV Cavalry of unspecified
    nationality (?Mithridates and
    Rheosaces).
  V Bactrian cavalry (2,000).
 VI Cavalry of unspecified
    nationality (Rheomithres)
    (2,000).
VII Median cavalry (1,000).
VIII Greek mercenary infantry
    (?Omares *vice* Memnon) (4-
    5,000).

only Persian field force in Asia Minor then and there. To march several miles upstream (or downstream) and then ford a stream only 4-5m wide would have been no great hardship, but the Persian army could make good its escape once it saw its flank turned.

Alexander opened the battle by sending forward Socrates' Companion *ile*, and then the Paeonians, *Prodromoi*, and Agrianian javelin-men, under the overall command of Amyntas, son of Arrhabaeus. The Macedonians advanced, with Socrates' *ile* in the van to give the impression that a full-scale attack, involving Alexander himself and the Companion cavalry, was under way. Their role was to draw the Persian left-wing cavalry out of their formations and down into the riverbed in disorderly pursuit. Once this was achieved, Alexander could launch his main attack and deal with them piecemeal, their advantage of position neutralized. The Persians took the bait and counter-charged and the Macedonians were driven back in disorder.

With the Persian left-wing cavalry pouring chaotically into the river bed in pursuit of the retreating advance-guard, Alexander, leading the Macedonian right, advanced with his army in oblique order. The advantage of thrust afforded the Macedonians by the length of their sarissas, together with their drill in the most effective use of these weapons (i.e., against the faces of the enemy's horses and horsemen), enabled them to break through the disorganized Persians. The collapse of the Persian horse, who were also exposed to the attentions of the Agrianians and Alexander's archers, was not long delayed and, with their flight, the Greek mercenaries stood alone.

At first, they did not realize the gravity of their situation and made no attempt to retreat. The hope of a successful transfer to a new employer (i.e., Alexander) may have exerted more influence than consternation at the rapidity of Alexander's victory over the cavalry. The mercenaries were surrounded by the Macedonian cavalry and the phalanx brought up against

Detail of Roman mosaic from Pompeii, showing Alexander and his favourite horse Bucephalus attacking Darius III at Issus. Alexander is shown wearing a Macedonian breastplate and wielding his sarissa under-arm, while the Companion cavalryman behind him wields his over-arm. Museo Archaeologico Nazionale, Naples.

Another detail of the Roman mosaic from Pompeii, showing Darius III in his chariot fleeing before Alexander at Issus. Behind him are visible Macedonian sarissas (and a Macedonian helmet and shield). Museo Archeologico Nazionale, Naples.

them. Their request for terms was refused, and the work of butchery began. The mercenaries fell before the sarissas of the phalanx and Companion cavalry without being able to reply in kind, owing to the limited thrust of their own shorter spears. When the massacre ended, only 2,000 of the mercenaries remained alive, and these had surrendered unconditionally.

The Macedonians lost 85 cavalry (including the 25 Companions who fell in the preliminary encounter) and 30 infantry killed. The Persian losses totalled about 5-6,000, with 1,000 cavalry and 2-3,000 Greek mercenaries killed, and a further 2,000 Greek mercenaries taken prisoner.

The battle highlights Alexander's ability to size up a situation quickly and his readiness to deliver a direct *coup de main* when nothing more subtle was required. It was an inspired stroke of strategic opportunism.

Having destroyed the only Persian field force in Asia Minor, Alexander was able to take Sardis without a fight and move down the coast of Ionia, liberating its Greek cities. Only at Miletus and Halicarnassus did he encounter resistance from the Persian garrisons. At Miletus, Alexander demobilized his fleet which, in view of Persian naval superiority (400 ships to 160), was more of a liability than an asset. Turning north, Alexander subjugated central Asia Minor, cutting the famous Gordian Knot on his way and thus acquiring prophetic endorsement for his conquests. Alexander's anxiety about his line of

THE BATTLE OF ISSUS

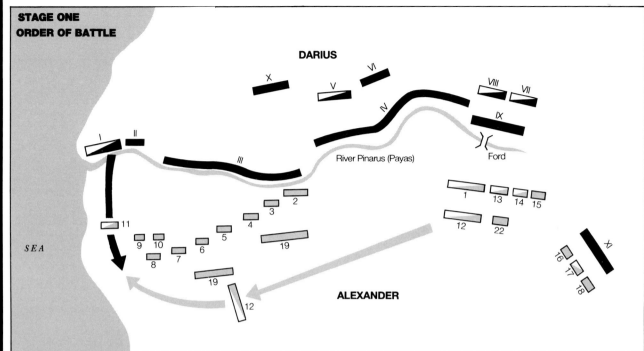

**STAGE ONE
ORDER OF BATTLE**

DARIUS

X   VI

V

VIII   VII

IX

IV

Ford

I   II

III

River Pinarus (Payas)

11

1   13   14   15

12   22

SEA

9   10

5

6

19

8   7

X/

16

17

18

19

12

ALEXANDER

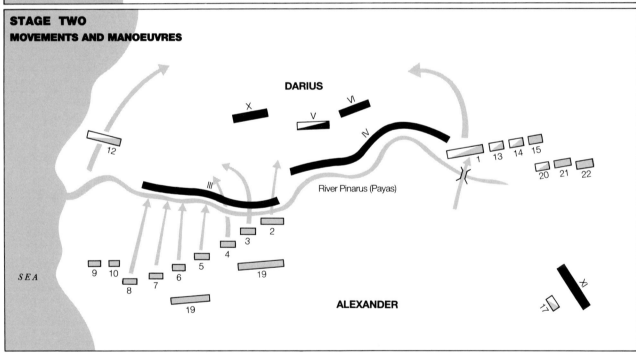

**STAGE TWO
MOVEMENTS AND MANOEUVRES**

DARIUS

X   VI

V

IV

12

III

River Pinarus (Payas)

1   13   14   15

20   21   22

2

3

4

9   10   5

8   7   6

19

19

SEA

ALEXANDER

X/

17

Key

THE MACEDONIAN ARMY:

1 Companion cavalry (Philotas).
2 Hypaspists (Nicanor).
3 *Pezhetairoi* – *Taxis* of Coenus.
4   *Taxis* of Perdiccas.
5   *Taxis* of Meleager.
6   *Taxis* of Ptolemy.
7   *Taxis* of Amyntas.
8   *Taxis* of Craterus.
9 Cretan archers.
10 Thracian javelin-men (Sitalces).
11 Allied Greek cavalry.
12 Thessalian cavalry.
13 *Prodromoi* (Protomachus).
14 Paeonian cavalry (Ariston).
15 Macedonian archers (Antiochus).
16 Agrianian javelin-men (Attalus).
17 300 cavalry.

18 Some of the Macedonian archers (*ex* 15).
19 Greek mercenary infantry.
20 Two *ilai* of Companion cavalry (Peroedas and Pantordanus (*ex* 1).
21 Some of the Agrianians (*ex* 16).
22 Some Greek mercenary infantry (*ex* 19).

THE PERSIAN ARMY:

I Persian cataphracts (Nabarzanes).
II   Slingers and archers.
III Greek mercenary infantry (Thymondas).
IV Persian infantry (= ? Cardaces) (Aristomedes).
V Persian Guard cavalry (with Darius).
VI Persian Guard infantry.
VII Hyrcanian and Median cavalry.
VIII Persian cavalry.
IX Javelin-men and slingers.
X Infantry levies.
XI Detached infantry.

communications was relieved by the death, while operating in the Aegean in the spring of 333, of Memnon, whom the Persian king Darius III regarded as his only competent commander. Turning south-east from Gordium, Alexander forced the western Taurus and occupied Cilicia.

Cilicia is closed in on three sides by high mountain ranges. To the north and west Cilicia is cut off by the Taurus. The region is even less accessible from the east, where the narrow coastal plain around the Gulf of Iskenderon is hemmed in by the Amanus, which is pierced by only a handful of passes. Alexander decided to hold this vast natural fortress and stand on the defensive until Darius himself advanced against him. Darius finally encamped at Sochoi near the entrance to the Beilan Pass at the southern end of the Amanus in early October 333. Alexander, however, declined to accept battle on the Syrian plain around Sochoi, where the terrain favoured the numerically superior Persians. Confident that the onset of winter would force Darius to move against him via the Beilan Pass, Alexander continued on the defensive behind the Amanus, though he did move his army to Myriandrus, south of the point at which the Beilan Pass debouches on to the coastal plain. His intention seems to have been to take the Persians in the flank if and when they came through the pass. However, he reckoned without Persian knowledge of the existence of two other passes over the northern Amanus. When, at the beginning of November, Alexander still had not come to meet him on the Syrian plain, Darius broke away under cover of bad weather and marched north, crossed the Amanus and descended on to the coastal plain in Alexander's rear and across his line of communications. For the first and last time in his military career, Alexander was taken by surprise. But he recovered quickly and marched rapidly north to try conclusions with Darius in a battle with reversed fronts.

The Battle of Issus

At both Issus and Gaugamela Alexander was confronted by a Persian army whose main strength lay in its cavalry and whose natural grand tactics were those of double envelopment. In contrast, the main strength of the Macedonian army lay in its heavy infantry and its natural grand tactics were those of central penetration. Persian and Macedonian practice thus tended to cancel each other out and victory would go to the side which maintained its specific tactical advantage while nullifying that of the enemy.

About 5.5km from the Persian positions on the Pinarus, Alexander deployed his heavy infantry, the Hypaspists and the *Pezhetairoi*, 32 ranks deep. Behind this massive block of phalangites, the rest of the infantry could deploy without fear of harassment by the cavalry of the Persian advance-guard, while its own cavalry brought up the rear. As they neared the Pinarus, Alexander reduced the depth of the phalanx, first to 16 ranks and then to the customary battle-order of eight ranks.

The line of contact between the armies was the River Pinarus (Payas), which rises in the Amanus Range and crosses the plain, more or less at right angles to the Gulf of Iskendron. For about 500m upstream the river runs between low banks that permit crossings by cavalry. From the 500m point to 1,600m from the mouth, the river bed is only 5-15m wide, but with steep banks. A crossing here is possible only for infantry. From 1.6km to about 3.5km upstream, the banks are consistently steep and difficult even for infantry. At the 3.5km point there is a space of about 30m with a narrow ford. Above this point up to the foot of the Amanus, a further 1.5km upstream, the riverbed is shut in by sheer rock walls 3-20m high. No crossing, even by infantry, is possible here.

Alexander's 12,000 Hypaspists and *Pezhetairoi* were kept up against the shore. Ranked eight deep, they would present a front of 1,500 files and occupy less than 1,500m of the river-line, and could thus cross below the 1.6km point. The Companion cavalry, however, would have to cross almost 2km further upstream at the ford.

Darius countered Alexander's strength in heavy infantry with the Greek mercenaries, which he stationed between the 500m and the 1.6km points, where they would block the advance of Alexander's phalanx, and strengthened their positions with abatis. Spread out between the 1.6 and 3.5km points on the river-line, covering the mercenaries' left flank, were the light-armed Cardaces. Nabarzanes' cataphracts constituted the extreme right of the Persian line and were screened by slingers and archers. In centre rear were posted 3,000 of Darius' Guard cavalry, supported by Persian infantry. The extreme left was held by Hyrcanian and Median cavalry, backed up by a further body of horse. Javelin-men and slingers were deployed in front of the main battle-line, while the rear was brought up by Asiatic infantry levies.

Darius' battle-plan was a double envelopment of the Macedonian army. The ideal setting for these traditional Persian grand tactics was an open plain like Gaugamela, and the unfavourable topography of the Pinarus constrained modifications. The first was the strong defensive along the river-bank. The second concerned the flanking moves. The advance-guard was to substitute a threat to Alexander's flank and rear for the full-scale envelopment precluded by the broken ground on the Persian left. Its infantry was therefore withdrawn to the foothills of the Amanus, there to await the opportunity that the Macedonian advance past them would present.

Alexander's problem was how to achieve a central penetration without exposing his flanks to envelopment. On his left the solution was straightforward. The phalanx was gradually deploying as it advanced with its flank against the seashore. Drawn up from right to left were, first, the Hypaspists, then the *taxeis* of Coenus, Perdiccas, Meleager, Ptolemy, Amyntas, and Craterus.

As the ground opened out near the Pinarus, Alexander brought forward the cavalry to protect his flanks. Assuming that any attempt to envelop his right would come from Darius' heavy cavalry, he made ready to counter-attack with an overwhelming force of cavalry. To this end he initially massed almost all of his own cavalry on this wing: the two largest and most formidable units, the Companions and the Thessalians, together with two light cavalry units, the *Prodromoi* and the Paeomians – altogether 4,350 horsemen. The cavalry component of the left wing, however, was a mere 600 allied Greek cavalry.

However, neither side had taken full account of the terrain. Having deployed his left-wing cavalry, Darius realized that the ford at the 3.5km point would so constrict the manoeuvres of his horsemen as to make them tactically useless. He therefore transferred the bulk of his cavalry to his right, where it was by now clear the battle would be decided, and himself took up a position in the centre. A relatively small force of cavalry might suffice to hold the ford against Alexander, while a flank attack by the light infantry in the foothills might seriously embarrass the Macedonians on that side. On Darius' own right, the Greek mercenaries would contain the advance of the phalanx, while Nabarzanes' cavalry would turn its left flank and fall on its rear. This was an admirable plan and reflects favourably on Darius' tactical skill. Its failure was due to the rapidity with which Alexander reacted to the changing tactical situation and the morale and battle discipline of the Macedonians.

Realizing that the heavy cavalry on the Persian right would overwhelm his own left-wing cavalry, Alexander ordered the Thessalians to transfer at speed to the left, taking care to conceal their movement from the enemy by keeping behind the phalanx all the way. Alexander now reorganized his right, bringing forward the *Prodromoi,* the Paeonians, and the Macedonian archers, and posting them to the right of the Companions. In response to the threat to his right flank rear, Alexander formed the Agrianians, some cavalry, and a detachment of archers, into a flank-guard, drawn back at an angle to the army's main front, the prototype of the formidable flank-guards at Gaugamela.

On the left, light infantry – the Cretan archers and the Thracian javelin-men – had been brought forward to cover the left flank of the phalanx as it moved to the right to engage Darius' Greek mercenaries, thus edging away from the security of the seashore. The intervening ground was now precariously held by the allied Greek cavalry, a puny force likely to be swept away by the massive formations of cataphracts which faced them across the Pinarus.

As this threat grew more immediate, and while the Thessalians were being transferred to the left to counter it, Alexander strove to complete his deployment. Alexander's own Greek mercenary infantry were posted along the rear of the army. As a last-minute precaution against envelopment, Alexander extended his right by moving up, to the right of the *Prodromoi* and Paeonians, two *ilai* of Companion cavalry, screening them with the Macedonian archers, some of the Agrianians, and a detachment of Greek mercenary infantry. Since a raid by the Agrianians and the archers of the flank-guard had driven the Persian detachment on the edge of the plain up into the Amanus, Alexander, now in the process of creating a new flanking force – the *Prodromoi*, the Paeonians, the two detached *ilai* of the Companions, the Macedonian archers, Agrianians, and Greek mercenary infantry – broke up the old flank-guard, telling off 300 cavalry to watch the slopes.

Alexander had started out with the expectation of having to fight cavalry battles on both flanks. Approaching the battlefield, he had realized that the ground towards the Amanus would rule out any large-scale cavalry manoeuvre. Observing that Darius had arrived at the same conclusion and was transferring the bulk of the Persian cavalry to his seaward wing, Alexander countered by moving across the Thessalian cavalry. The order for the Thessalians to keep behind the phalanx all the way, so as not to betray the movement to the enemy, shows that Alexander was intent on more than just the reinforcement of a threatened point. Rather, he aimed to achieve a major tactical surprise. Assigning the weak allied horse to the left wing as its only cavalry support was no mistake. If Darius declined to attack in force, this unit would be adequate to hold the space between the phalanx and the sea. If, however, the Persians moved to envelop his seaward flank, the allied cavalry would serve as the bait in the trap that Alexander proposed to spring. Once Alexander's allied cavalry were driven from the field, Nabarzanes' cataphracts could be expected to turn and fall on the rear of the phalanx. The Thracian javelin-men and the Cretan archers might be able to keep the Persians away from the phalanx's flank, but could scarcely prevent them attacking the rear. In the event, as the cataphracts swept the allied Greek cavalry from their path and advanced into the open space behind the phalanx, their pursuit became disorderly; and when the Thessalians struck them in the flank, they were unable to reform fast enough. The superior mobility of the Thessalians proved decisive. Wheeling about in their accustomed rhomboid formations, they put Nabarzanes' horse to flight and pursued them back across the Pinarus.

In contrast, the cavalry action on Alexander's right was a relatively tame affair. The Persians were driven back from the ford by the *Prodromoi*, Paeonians, Macedonian archers, and Agrianians. Once across the Pinarus, Alexander deployed his Companions into their 'wedges', while the light cavalry and infantry kept the enemy at bay. Then, with Alexander at their head, the Companions charged and broke into the depleted ranks of the Persian left-wing cavalry, despite the fire of their archers. The weak Persian left was broken through and isolated, and Alexander wheeled his Companions inward towards the Persian centre. The cavalry attack from Alexander's right, enveloping Darius' internal flank, in concert with the advance of the rightmost *taxeis* of the phalanx across the Pinarus, sealed the fate of the Persian centre, and Darius himself fled the field.

The fighting between the phalanx and Darius' Greek mercenaries was bitter, especially where the development of a gap in the phalanx exposed it to counter-attack. The appearance of this gap was due to the precipitous nature of the riverbanks and the phalanx's own movement towards the right.

Boeotian-style helmet (late Classical and Hellenistic), used by Alexander's Thessalian cavalry and occasionally by the Companion Cavalry, and later the standard helmet of the Greek kingdom of Bactria (Afghanistan). Ashmolean Museum, Oxford.

Conical helmet or pilos (late Hellenistic), the preferred helmet of Macedonian phalangites. Ashmolean Museum, Oxford.

Thracian helmet (late Classical and Hellenistic), favoured by the light-armed infantry from the Balkans serving in the Macedonian army. British Museum, London.

Considerations of space and the need to link up with Alexander obliged the phalanx to advance *en echelon*, with the rightmost *taxis* leading. This oblique order attack permitted the phalanx to make a breakthrough without having to engage the mercenaries along the full length of their abatis-protected position. The Hypaspists and the *taxeis* of Coenus and Perdiccas, striking at the vulnerable hinge between the Persian left and centre, broke through without much difficulty and enveloped the interior right flank of the Persian centre. The leftward *taxeis* of the phalanx, however, ran up against the solid front of the mercenaries and were unable to follow their comrades through the breach. Darius' mercenaries exploited the resulting gap and inflicted a severe check, killing the taxiarch Ptolemy and 120 *Pezhetairoi*. At this, since the Persian centre was already collapsing, the two rightward *taxeis* wheeled round and enveloped the left flank of the Greek mercenaries.

Meanwhile Alexander, with only 1,000 horsemen but intent on finishing the war at a single blow, pursued Darius from the field. The phalanx rallied and drove the Greek mercenaries back from the Pinarus, but suffered so severely that it was unable to maintain a sustained pursuit of the enemy, who retired in good order. Instead, the Macedonian infantry turned their attention to the sack of Darius' camp, and the battle ended in an orgy of looting and rape. The Macedonian casualty figures were probably 302 infantry (including 120-130 phalangites) and 150 cavalry killed with 4,500 of both arms wounded, a total of 4,952. The Persian losses must therefore have been around 15,000 killed, wounded, and prisoner.

Not only was the battle bloody, but it was also a near defeat for Alexander. Darius made full use of the excellent defensive position afforded by the Pinarus. His grand tactics, moreover, show a clear understanding of the value of concerted operations by cavalry and infantry. The fault, however, lay in their complexity and in the fact that the Persian cavalry were unused to co-operating tactically with heavy infantry. Nabarzanes' cataphracts, for example, allowed themselves to be lured away from the Greek mercenaries and thus had no secure position on which to retire when counter-attacked by Alexander's Thessalians. The device of posting a detached force in the foothills to threaten Alexander's flank was frustrated by the imperturbability of the Macedonian veterans and the rapidity with which Alexander formed a flank-guard to keep the Persians at bay. Thus, while Darius' plan was sound, his formations were lacking in battle discipline and experience of large-scale tactical manoeuvres, and so were unable to translate his projects into effective action.

In contrast, Alexander's manoeuvres were executed by a veteran army, accustomed to its leader's methods and possessed of a battle discipline which ensured co-operation, even where rapid movements and changes of battle-order were required. However, the main credit belongs to Alexander's own genius for tactical improvization. His creation of highly mobile flank-guards effectively excluded the Persian left from the battle; the phalanx's oblique order attack sidestepped the obstruction presented by Darius' Greek mercenaries; the double envelopment of the interior flanks of the Persian centre made short work of what should have been a virtually unassailable section of the enemy line; and his apparent undermanning of his extreme left cast the allied Greek cavalry in the role of a Judas-goat to lure the cataphracts of the Persian right to their destruction by the suddenly unmasked Thessalians. Most striking, however, is the prominence of the 'offensive-defensive' idea in Alexander's tactics. Despite his 'heroic' pretensions and posturing, Alexander shows a distinct preference for luring his enemy into a false position before delivering his attack.

The Siege of Tyre

While Darius retraced his steps to Babylon, where he began to raise another army, Alexander marched south into Phoenicia, the home base of the bulk of

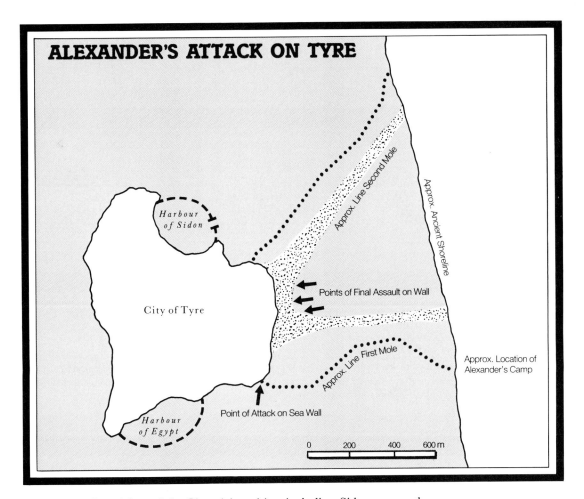

ALEXANDER'S ATTACK ON TYRE

Harbour of Sidon

Approx. Line Second Mole

Approx. Ancient Shoreline

City of Tyre

Points of Final Assault on Wall

Approx. Line First Mole

Approx. Location of Alexander's Camp

Harbour of Egypt

Point of Attack on Sea Wall

0   200   400   600 m

the Persian fleet. Most of the Phoenician cities, including Sidon, promptly surrendered to him. However, the greatest of the Phoenician cities, Tyre, out of rivalry with Sidon, offered resistance. Anxious to gain complete control of the Levantine coast, Alexander settled down to besiege the city.

Situated on an island half a mile offshore, Tyre was easily defensible and it was six months before Alexander finally took it. In February 332, Alexander began the construction of a 60m wide mole from the mainland to the island. The channel was shallow for most of the distance, but near the island the depth was about 5.5m. As the mole neared the city, the Tyrians attacked the Macedonians with showers of missiles from their ships and catapults. But Alexander constructed two high siege-towers at the end of the mole, armed with catapults to return fire against the city and the Tyrian triremes, which numbered 80. The Tyrians, however, made a fire-ship attack on the towers and succeeded in burning them. Almost immediately afterwards, heavy seas submerged most of the mole.

At this point Alexander's grand strategy of defeating the Persian fleet by depriving it of its bases began to bear fruit. The Phoenician contingents, 80 ships strong, of the Persian navy which belonged to the cities that had gone over to Alexander arrived at Sidon and placed themselves at his disposal. With the arrival soon afterwards of the Cypriote kings and their fleets, also anxious to transfer their allegiance to the conqueror, Alexander had over 200 ships in hand.

With this fleet Alexander defeated the Tyrians in a naval battle. He then assigned the 120 Cypriote ships to blockade the Harbour of Sidon at the northern end of the island and the Phoenician squadrons to blockade the Egyptian Harbour on the southern side. A second mole was begun and rapidly

THE MACEDONIAN PHALANX

The phalanx consisted of the Hypaspists, the King's
infantry guard 3,000 strong, and the *taxeis* of the *Pezhetairoi*,
'Foot-Companions', the line infantry recruited on a
regional basis from the Macedonian peasantry.
Alexander's expeditionary army contained at first six, then
seven, such *taxeis*, each 1,500 men strong. Normally drawn
up for battle eight-deep, the phalangites fought with the
sarissa, a pike 6-7m long. In the compact order mandatory
for the attack, each man occupied a space less than 1m in
width, but when receiving an enemy attack the phalanx
closed up still further into *synaspismos* or 'locked-shield order',
in which each phalangite presented a front of less than 0.5m.
The first five ranks extended their sarissas beyond the bodies
of the men in the front rank, holding their weapons
progressively higher in each rank, thus presenting an
impenetrable hedge of sarissas to the enemy. This alone
usually served to intimidate their opponents, who rarely
closed with the phalanx in hand-to-hand fighting. Darius'
Greek mercenaries at Issus, sheltering behind abatis on a
high river-bank, and Porus' elephants at the Hydaspes,
were among the few exceptions – and neither force proved
able to withstand the direct onslaught of the phalanx.

pushed towards Tyre. Alexander discovered that by lashing some of his ships together he could use them as platforms for battering rams. To prevent the Macedonians from anchoring these in position, Tyrian divers using snorkeling devices cut their cables, until Alexander switched to chains. As the siege progressed, the Macedonians had to endure all the defensive devices the ingenious Tyrians could bring to bear, including multi-spoked wheels which rotated mechanically, and destroyed, deflected or broke the force of the bolts from the Macedonian catapults; they also placed padding on the walls to soften the effect of the stones.

Around the beginning of August, Alexander's wall-breaking ships brought down part of the city walls between the Egyptian Harbour and the mole. Alexander now ordered a general assault on the breach and from the end of the mole, while the Phoenician fleet broke into the Egyptian Harbour and the Cypriote squadrons took the Harbour of Sidon. The storming of the city ended in bitter street-fighting, in which the Macedonians gave little quarter. Tyre was burnt and 2,000 surviving Tyrians were crucified to satisfy Alexander's anger. The Carthaginian envoys who had encouraged Tyrian resistance were sent back to Carthage with a declaration of war whose implementation Alexander postponed indefinitely.

Alexander again encountered resistance at Gaza, where the garrison commander was the eunuch Batis. After a siege of two months (September-October), during which the Macedonians threw up vast earthen ramps against its high walls, the city was taken by storm. Alexander celebrated by dragging Batis around the walls behind his chariot in imitation of Achilles' treatment of Hector's body at Troy.

Egypt welcomed Alexander as a liberator, and he was crowned Pharaoh at Memphis. A visit to the oracle of Zeus Ammon at Siwah in Libya produced a propaganda coup. The god, through his priest, declared Alexander his son and promised him world conquest.

The Battle of Gaugamela

In the spring of 331, Alexander marched north to deal with Darius. Crossing the Euphrates at Thapsacus in August, he struck eastward across north-western Mesopotamia. For logistical reasons, Alexander intended to move on Babylon down the Tigris. Darius meanwhile, anticipating his choice of route, had moved 300 miles north-west to take up a position on a plain north-east of the middle Tigris. The terrain here would facilitate the Persian grand tactics of double envelopment with cavalry, and Darius tried to improve it still further by levelling most of the ground in the vicinity, though an area on his extreme left remained unlevelled.

Alexander arrived at the end of September and, after a thorough reconnaissance of the ground, moved to attack the Persians on 1 October, 331. Because the terrain was so favourable for a double envelopment, Alexander deployed his army in a kind of 'tactical square', with a flank-guard drawn back at an angle of 45 degrees at either end of the main front.

The right-wing flank-guard was an arrangement of units drawn up *en echelon* in three potential lines that could, when the need arose, be formed into three actual lines facing outward from the centre. Adjacent to the Royal *ile* of the Companion cavalry, on the extreme right of the main front, in the rearmost of these lines, stationed from left to right, and from front to rearward, were one half of the Agrianians, the Macedonians archers, and, right flank rear of the entire army, Cleander's veteran mercenary infantry. In front of the Agrianians and archers were the *Prodromoi* and the Paeonian cavalry, and in front of them Menidas' mercenary cavalry, who were ordered, if the Persians attempted to envelop the wing, to charge them in the flank.

The left-wing flank-guard was similarly deployed, with Andromachus' mercenary horse in front, and behind them some allied Greek and Odrysian cavalry, with the Thracian javelin-men, the Cretan archers, and the Achaean mercenary infantry in the rearmost line.

In the centre, from right to left were, first, the Hypaspists, then the *taxeis* of Coenus, Perdiccas, Meleager, Polyperchon, Simmias, and Craterus. Flanking them were the army's strongest cavalry units: on the left, the 1,800 Thessalians, supported by Erigyius' 600 allied Greek cavalry; and on the right the 1,800 Companions, led in battle by Alexander himself. The remaining halves of the Agrianian contingent and the Macedonian archers, together with Balacrus' javelin-men, were posted in front of the Companions. Though the army mustered 7,000 cavalry and 40,000 infantry, the front line numbered only about 12,000 heavy infantry, 4,200 cavalry, and 1,000 light-armed troops.

Alexander drew up a second line of allied Greek infantry and mercenaries, which were, in the event of a Persian attempt to envelop the rear, to wheel about and deal with the attackers. The baggage-park, guarded by Thracian infantry, was some distance in their rear.

The Persian left, commanded by Bessus, was held by 8,000 Bactrian cavalry. Stationed next to them were 1,000 Dahae and 2,000 Arachosian cavalry, a mixed unit of Persian cavalry and infantry, and 2,000 Susian and 2,000 Cadusian horse, with an advance-guard of 2,000 Scythian and 1,000 Bactrian cavalry, and 100 scythe-chariots.

The centre was commanded by Darius himself, attended by his Household brigade, the 'Kinsmen' cavalry and the *Melophoroi* infantry. 2,000 Greek mercenary infantry were deployed on either side of them. The remainder of the centre's front line was occupied by units of Indians, resettled Carians, and Mardian archers. Behind the centre were the Uxians, Babylonians, Red Sea tribesmen, and Sitacenians. Fifteen elephants and 50 scythe-chariots were posted in front of the Kinsmen cavalry.

The Persian right, under Mazaeus, was made up of Syrians, Mesopotamians, Medes, Parthian and Saca mounted archers, Tapurian and Hyrcanian cavalry, Albanians and Sacesinians. An advance-guard of Armenian and Cappadocian cavalry, with 50 scythe-chariots, was stationed in front of the wing.

The battle was precipitated by Alexander's movement towards the right, which alarmed Darius, who was afraid that if the Macedonians reached the unlevelled ground, his (supposed) advantage in weaponry, the scythe-chariots, would be nullified. He therefore ordered the advance-guard of his left wing – the 1,000 Bactrian cavalry and 2,000 Scythians – to ride around the Macedonian right wing and halt its march. Menidas charged the enveloping Persians, but was thrown back in disorder. Alexander now ordered a charge by the *Prodromoi* and Paeonians, supported by Cleander's veteran mercenary infantry. As this second counter-attack met with more success, Bessus threw in the remaining Bactrians. These were themselves repulsed after a prolonged fight. Meanwhile the scythe-chariots were demonstrating their ineffectiveness in a charge against the Macedonian right centre, where they were swiftly routed by Balacrus' javelin-men and Agrianians.

The crisis came as Alexander swung into a direct advance against the Persian front. The movement of some cavalry, which Darius had sent to support the horsemen attempting the envelopment of the Macedonian right, had left a gap in the Persian left centre. Alexander wheeled towards this gap and, making a wedge of the Companion cavalry and part of the phalanx, rode directly against Darius, who fled the field.

Alexander's wedge was a complex of units arranged *en echelon*, in two oblique lines, slanting in opposite directions but meeting in a broad point. The left-hand side of this massive wedge was made up of the Hypaspists and the *taxeis* of the *Pezhetairoi* from as far left as (and including) that of Polyperchon, while the *ilai* of the Companion cavalry made up both the much shorter right-hand limb and the broad apex.

In the centre the pace of Alexander's advance and the forming of the wedge had opened up a gap in the Macedonian front. While all the units from Polyperchon's *taxis* rightward surged forward in the rupture of the Persian

THE BATTLE OF GAUGAMELA

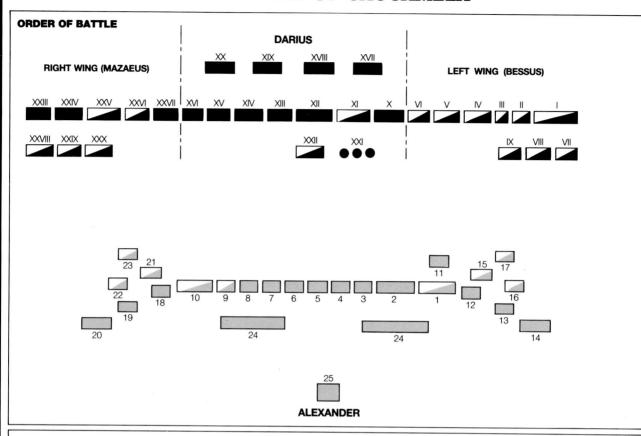

ORDER OF BATTLE

DARIUS

RIGHT WING (MAZAEUS)

LEFT WING (BESSUS)

ALEXANDER

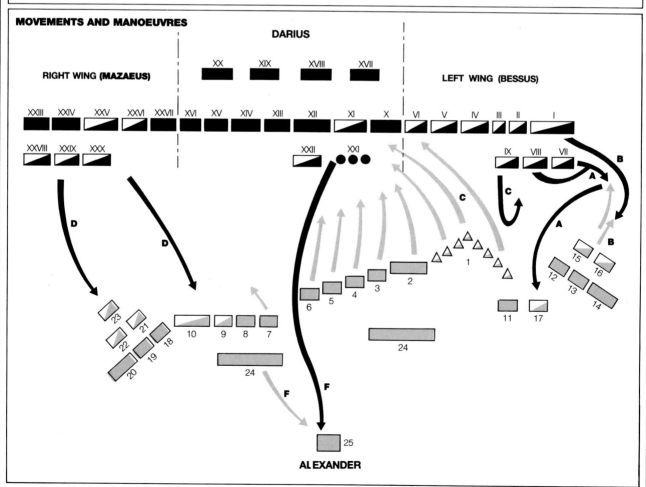

MOVEMENTS AND MANOEUVRES

DARIUS

RIGHT WING (MAZAEUS)

LEFT WING (BESSUS)

ALEXANDER

centre, Simmias, unable to push forward as rapidly and learning that the left was in difficulties, halted his own *taxis* to aid it. Through the resulting gap penetrated a force of Indian and Persian cavalry from the disintegrating enemy centre. Reaching the Macedonian baggage-park, they overwhelmed its defenders and freed the prisoners they found there before being repelled by the Macedonian second-line infantry.

Parmenion, meanwhile, hard pressed by Mazaeus' attempt to envelop his wing, despatched riders to Alexander, asking for assistance. But when Parmenion's messengers reached the Macedonian right, they found Alexander already far gone in his all-out pursuit of Darius and returned without delivering their message. Parmenion nonetheless succeeded in checking the Persian attack with the Thessalian cavalry. Then, as news of Darius' flight filtered through to the faltering Persian right, the repulse rapidly became a rout.

Eventually nightfall, and the loss of Darius' trail at the Great Zab, forced Alexander to turn back. During this rearward ride, Alexander was involved in a short but bloody clash with a large body of retreating Persian cavalry, who broke through his squadrons, killing 60 of the Companions, and made good their escape.

When he had assured himself that victory had been secured, Alexander renewed his pursuit. Parmenion meanwhile advanced and took the Persian camp, along with the enemy's baggage-train and elephants. Alexander bivouacked on the far side of the Great Zab and rested his cavalry until around midnight, when he rode on to Arbela, 64 kilometres away, where he found the Persian field-treasury but no Darius. The Great King had ridden on to meet an ignominious end at the hands of his own subjects. The battle cost Alexander at least 500 men killed, while 1,000 of the Macedonian horses had died of wounds or had been ridden to death in the pursuit.

Alexander's order for Menidas' small force to open the battle on their own is controversial. As Bessus' cavalry were moving around his flank in a disciplined manner, Alexander had to open up their formations for a decisive attack. He could do this by sending in a small unit to attack and be driven back in disorder, which could be expected to extend to their pursuers. The enemy's disorganization could then be exploited with a counter-attack by stronger Macedonian units. That this ploy failed can be ascribed to the Persians recalling Issus and anticipating it, while Alexander underestimated the enemy forces available to counter his opening move. Nevertheless, the initial failure was quickly retrieved. Alexander, like Napoleon, always had 'a plan with branches'. When his original plan became bogged down in a hard-fought cavalry action on the right, Alexander activated its main branch, the central penetration in wedge-formation. This was a major advance in tactics, for though the grand tactical wedge had been introduced by Epaminondas at Leuctra, Alexander was the first to develop it significantly.

Alexander's tactical masterpiece was marred by his unrestrained pursuit of Darius, which endangered his left. There was never much chance of catching Darius, to whom the open terrain afforded an easy retreat, and a return to the battlefield proper once the rout of the Persian centre was complete would have been tactically more sound. Nonetheless, Alexander's evident confidence in the ability of Parmenion and the Thessalians to withstand the Persian right's onslaught was justified by the outcome of a similar situation at Issus.

Darius fled north into Media, while Alexander moved on to Babylon to gather the fruits of victory. Mazaeus, as satrap of Babylonia, surrendered the ancient capital. During the winter of 331-330, Alexander occupied the Persian homeland, burning the capital Persepolis as the concluding act of Greek national revenge against Persia. In June he set off after Darius, who continued his flight towards Bactria, whose satrap Bessus was the most powerful of his surviving vassals. The Persian satraps had by now lost all confidence in Darius and murdered him in July. Bessus was proclaimed king as Artaxerxes IV, but

Key

THE MACEDONIAN ARMY:

 1 Companion cavalry (Philotas).
 2 Hypaspists (Nicanor).
 3 *Pezhetairoi and Asthetairoi –*
      Taxis of Coenus.
 4 *Taxis* of Perdiccas.
 5 *Taxis* of Meleager.
 6 *Taxis* of Polyperchon.
 7 *Taxis* of Amyntas (Simmias).
 8 *Taxis* of Craterus.
 9 Allied Greek cavalry (Erigyius).
10 Thessalian cavalry (Philip).
11 Agrianians, Archers, and Javelin-men (Balacrus).
12 Agrianians (Attalus).
13 Macedonian archers (Brison).
14 Old mercenary infantry (Cleander).
15 *Prodromoi* (Aretes).
16 Paeonian cavalry (Ariston).
17 Mercenary cavalry (Menidas).
18 Thracian javelin-men (Sitalces).
19 Cretan archers.
20 Achaean mercenary infantry.
21 Allied Greek cavalry (Coeranus).
22 Odrysian cavalry (Agathon).
23 Mercenary cavalry (Andromachus).
24 Greek infantry.
25 Thracian infantry, guarding the baggage-park.

THE PERSIAN ARMY:

A. Left Wing (Bessus):

I   Bactrian cavalry
         (Bessus in person): ?8,000.
II   Dahae cavalry: 1,000.
III   Arachosian cavalry
         (?Barsaentes): ?2,000.
IV   Persian cavalry and infantry.
V   Susian cavalry: ?2,000.
VI   Cadusian cavalry: ?2,000.
VII   Scythian cavalry: 2,000.
VIII Bactrian cavalry: 1,000.
IX   Scythe-chariots: 100.

B. Centre (Darius in person):

X   Greek mercenary infantry (?Paron): ?1,000.
XI   Kinsmen cavalry (with Darius): 1,000.
XII   *Melophoroi:* ?1,000.
XIII   Greek mercenary infantry
         (?Glaucus): ?1,000.
XIV   Indians.
XV   Resettled Carians
         (?Bupares).
XVI   Mardian archers.
XVII Uxians (?Oxathres).
XVIII Babylonians (?Bupares).
XIX   "Red Sea" Tribesmen (?Ocondobates,
         Ariobarzanes, and Orxines).
XX   Sitacenians (?Bupares).
XXI   Elephants: 15.
XXII Scythe-chariots: 50.

C. Right Wing (Mazaeus):

XXIII   Syrians and Mesopotamians
           (Mazaeus in person).
XXIV   Medes (?Atropates).
XXV   Parthian and Sacae horse-archers
           (?Mauaces).
XXVI   Tapurian and
           Hyrcanian cavalry
           (?Phrataphernes).
XXVII Albanians and Sacesinians.
XXVIII Armenian cavalry (?Orontes).
XXIX   Cappadocian cavalry (Ariaces).
XXX   Scythe-chariots: 50.

he too fell victim to the disloyalty of the satraps, who handed him over to Alexander in mid-329.

In 329-327 the Macedonians overran the eastern satrapies of the Persian empire in successive campaigns of tough guerilla warfare. During the winter of 327-326 Alexander crossed the Hindu Kush into India. As there was little unity among the Indian rajahs, resistance was chaotic, and only the attempt of the Indian king Porus to stop the Macedonian advance, at the River Hydaspes in June 326, is memorable.

The Battle of the Hydaspes

When Alexander reached the Hydaspes, he found Porus waiting on the far bank to prevent his crossing. Alexander, however, managed to lull him into a false sense of security, and then made the following dispositions: Craterus was left behind in the base camp with his own hipparchy of Companion cavalry, two phalanx *taxeis*, and 5,000 allied Indians. Craterus was ordered not to cross the Hydaspes until Porus had moved off to engage Alexander's turning force. This Alexander arranged in two divisions:

(1) The Forward Division, which was to cross with him. This consisted of the 300 strong *Agema* of the Companion cavalry; the hipparchies of Hephaestion, Perdiccas, Coenus, and Demetrius (each 500 strong); 2,000 Bactrian, Sogdian, and Scythian cavalry; 1,000 Dahae horse-archers; the 3,000 Hypaspists; the phalanx *taxeis* of Cleitus and Coenus, each 1,500 strong; 2,000 archers, 1,000 Agrianians, and 1,000 javelin-men – in all, 5,300 cavalry and 10,000 infantry.

(2) The Rear Division, consisting of the *taxeis* of Meleager, Attalus, and Gorgias, together with 500 mercenary cavalry and 500 mercenary infantry, was strung out between Alexander's base camp and the island where the forward division crossed. These troops were to cross by sections when they saw the Indians fully engaged.

Alexander's base camp was near Haranpur on the Jhelum (Hydaspes). From there he marched 28km upstream to Jalalpur, where there was a headland projecting from the west bank. Opposite it was the large island of Adana, separated from the east bank by a shallow channel. Here Alexander crossed under the cover of a thunderstorm, but mistakenly landed on the island and had to ford the nullah.

Turning southwards to face Porus, Alexander had time to deploy before the enemy appeared. He posted the *Agema* of the Companions on his extreme right, with the Companion hipparchies on its left, and the horse-archers along their front. Next to the cavalry were the Hypaspists and the phalanx *taxeis*. On either flank were detachments of archers, Agrianians, and javelin-men.

Ordering the phalanx to follow in formation, Alexander took the cavalry and archers and advanced at speed. Porus, however, stood his ground opposite the Macedonian base camp, and sent against Alexander only a small detachment of 1,000 cavalry and 60 chariots under his son. This force was quickly destroyed by the Macedonian cavalry. Porus' son and 400 of his cavalry fell in the action. Alarmed by the news that Craterus was showing signs of attempting the crossing, Porus decided that his only hope lay in attacking Alexander before all the Macedonian forces could be concentrated. Like Napoleon at Waterloo, Porus tried to stave off disaster by detaching part of his army to keep the fresh enemy force from intervening in the main battle. Allocating a few elephants to this holding force in the hope of preventing Craterus from landing any cavalry, Porus marched north to confront Alexander. Reaching a place which was level and firm enough for the movement of cavalry, he drew up his army.

Porus stationed his 85 elephants along the front of his infantry at 15m intervals. His infantry, about 20,000 strong, thus occupied a front of at least 1.3km. The infantry line extended beyond that of the elephants and was in turn flanked on either wing by cavalry, in front of which were stationed chariots. Porus himself took post on the extreme left of the line of elephants, atop the

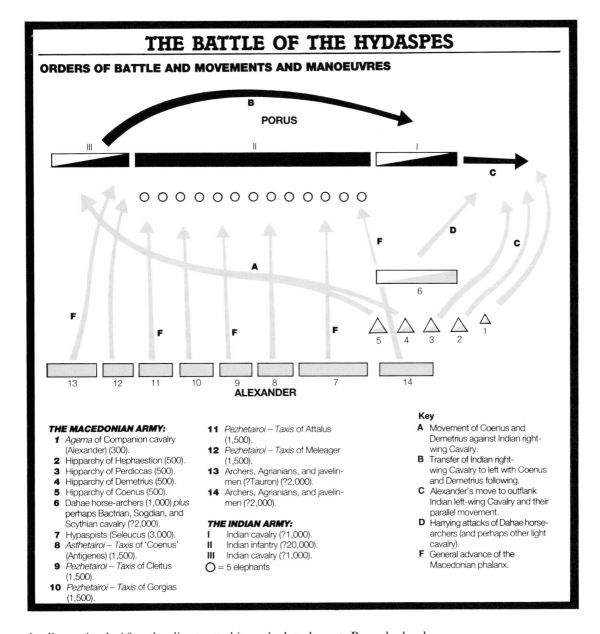

THE BATTLE OF THE HYDASPES

ORDERS OF BATTLE AND MOVEMENTS AND MANOEUVRES

THE MACEDONIAN ARMY:

1 *Agema* of Companion cavalry (Alexander) (300).
2 Hipparchy of Hephaestion (500).
3 Hipparchy of Perdiccas (500).
4 Hipparchy of Demetrius (500).
5 Hipparchy of Coenus (500).
6 Dahae horse-archers (1,000) *plus* perhaps Bactrian, Sogdian, and Scythian cavalry (?2,000).
7 Hypaspists (Seleucus (3,000).
8 *Asthetairoi – Taxis* of 'Coenus' (Antigenes) (1,500).
9 *Pezhetairoi – Taxis* of Cleitus (1,500).
10 *Pezhetairoi – Taxis* of Gorgias (1,500).
11 *Pezhetairoi – Taxis* of Attalus (1,500).
12 *Pezhetairoi – Taxis* of Meleager (1,500).
13 Archers, Agrianians, and javelin-men (?Tauron) (?2,000).
14 Archers, Agrianians, and javelin-men (?2,000).

THE INDIAN ARMY:

I Indian cavalry (?1,000).
II Indian infantry (?20,000).
III Indian cavalry (?1,000).
○ = 5 elephants

Key

A Movement of Coenus and Demetrius against Indian right-wing Cavalry.
B Transfer of Indian right-wing Cavalry to left with Coenus and Demetrius following.
C Alexander's move to outflank Indian left-wing Cavalry and their parallel movement.
D Harrying attacks of Dahae horse-archers (and perhaps other light cavalry).
F General advance of the Macedonian phalanx.

leading animal. After the disaster to his son's detachment, Porus had only 2,000 cavalry and 240 chariots.

Porus' tactical plan amounted to frightening off the Macedonian cavalry with his elephants, and then pinning the Macedonian infantry with his own infantry, while the elephants were wheeled into any gap which appeared in the phalanx. His cavalry were accustomed to tactical co-operation with elephants and could thus cover the flanks of their own infantry or fall upon those of the Macedonian phalanx advancing to engage their centre.

Alexander divined Porus' plan and, deciding to eliminate the Indian cavalry first, advanced against the Indian left with all four of the Companion hipparchies. However, as he approached the enemy wing, he detached Coenus with two of the hipparchies – his own and that of Demetrius – and sent him towards the Indian right. After detaching Coenus, Alexander still had in hand at least 3,000 cavalry, giving him a superiority of up to 3:1 over the Indian left-wing cavalry. To stand any chance of successful resistance on either flank, Porus would have to concentrate all his cavalry. Thanks to the elephants, his infantry was immune from attack by the Macedonian cavalry and would not need a cavalry flank-guard on both wings. Once he knew, from the presence there of Alexander himself, that his left would be the object of the enemy's main attack, Porus ordered his right-wing cavalry to transfer to his left. To reach the left, the Indian right-wing cavalry moved across their infantry's rear. As the untrained Macedonian cavalry horses could not be brought to approach the elephants deployed along the Indian front, Coenus' two hipparchies were obliged to follow the enemy's right-wing cavalry along the rear of the main Indian battle line.

As his cavalry came within range, Alexander sent his 1,000 horse-archers against the Indian left to throw the enemy horse into disorder with their fire. Accompanied by the two right-wing hipparchies of Companion cavalry, Alexander rode towards his right and, by means of an oblique march flankward, compelled the Indians to keep extending to their own left. This manoeuvre obliged the Indian horse to change from line to column-of-march. Alexander now wheeled his own cavalry into formation and fell upon the Indians before they themselves could get back into line.

While Alexander was thus drawing the Indian left-wing cavalry, now reinforced by their comrades from the right, into his tactical trap, Coenus' cavalry began to appear in rear of the Indian horse. Seeing this, the Indians tried to throw their cavalry into a double-fronted formation, the stronger division facing Alexander, the other wheeling round to confront Coenus. But Alexander's attack caught them still in disorder, and the Indians on his front did not even await his charge, but fell back upon the elephants.

It was now the turn of the Macedonian phalanx to advance to the attack. Confronted by 10,500 heavy infantry (3,000 Hypaspists, and 7,500 phalangites in five *taxeis*) and 4,000 light infantry, the elephants crowded together, inflicting as much damage on their own side as on the Macedonians. The Indian cavalry, sheltering around the elephants, sustained particularly heavy losses. The Agrianians and the Thracian javelin-men harassed the animals, retiring before them as they charged and pressing after them when they withdrew. The discipline and tactical co-operation of the Macedonian

below
Silver phalera of 2nd century BC, denoting military rank, from Bactria, showing a war-elephant carrying a castle with two men, one with Boeotian cavalry helmet (worn because elephant corps were classed as mounted troops in Hellenistic armies). State Hermitage Museum, Leningrad.

right
Campanian plate (3rd century BC), showing war-elephant and calf. Indian elephants were bred on an elephant-farm at Apamea on the Euphrates in Syria by the kings of the Seleucid dynasty. Large numbers of elephants (180 at Paraitacene and Gabiene; 475 at Ipsus in 301 BC) were used in the wars of Alexander's successors. Museo Nazionale di Villa Giulia, Rome.

phalanx and light infantry proved decisive. While the light infantry strove to confuse and incapacitate the elephants, the phalanx provided a refuge for their light-armed comrades, at the same time gradually pushing the animals back into the lines of their own infantry by continually constricting the available space as they advanced their hedge of sarissas, which not even the elephants could penetrate. With the elephants disabled, the Indian infantry were unable to stand their ground. The Indian collapse was hastened by the inability of their archers to keep the Macedonians at bay with their fire, and the presence of Alexander's cordon of cavalry across their rear completed the demoralization of the Indian infantry and turned the inevitable retreat into a rout. As the Indians gave way on all sides, Craterus' troops made their appearance and, still fresh, took over the pursuit. Porus himself was taken prisoner, and the last resistance collapsed.

·The battle had been hard fought and cost Alexander about 230 cavalry (including 20 of the Companions, 10 horse-archers, and 200 of the remaining cavalry) and 700 infantry (including 80 phalangites). The Indian army was virtually annihilated, with 12,000 killed and 9,000 prisoners, while 80 elephants fell into Macedonian hands.

Porus' personal courage had made an impression on Alexander, who reinstated him as king under Macedonian overlordship. Intent on reaching the Ganges, Alexander continued his march eastward, brushing aside local opposition in hard fighting around Sangala. At the River Beas, the eastern frontier of the Persian empire at its greatest extent, the Macedonians, having marched 27,350 km since leaving Europe, refused to go any further. After a campaign down the Indus to round off his Indian conquests, Alexander turned back. The march across the Gedrosian Desert (325) was a logistical disaster and casualties were heavy. Resting his army at Susa in Persia in early 324, Alexander was joined by 30,000 young Persians who had been trained and equipped to fight as Macedonians. The integration of these troops into the Macedonian army and the demoblization of 10,000 veterans provoked a mutiny at Opis, which was suppressed with a blend of brutality and diplomacy. Alexander was preparing for a new series of conquests (involving a march along the North African coast to annex Carthage and a return to Greece via Spain and Italy) when he died suddenly, probably of malaria, at Babylon on 10 June 323.

ALEXANDER'S MILITARY LEGACY

Alexander's death precipitated a lengthy series of civil wars in which his generals tested their skills against each other, demonstrating the efficacy of the lessons they had learnt from him. Three early Hellenistic battles illustrate this.

Antigonus Monophthalmus' tactical plan at Paraitacene (317) was based on Alexander's at the Granicus and Gaugamela. Antigonus made his battle line oblique by pushing forward his stronger right wing, but his left-wing commander took it upon himself to engage first, relying on his cavalry's superiority over Eumenes of Cardia's right wing. A frontal assault was ruled out by the elephants lining Eumenes' front, but Antigonus' horse-archers were able to attack his flank. Eumenes counter-attacked with light infantry and cavalry from his left, which routed Antigonus' left wing. The infantry battle in the centre was severe, but the Argyraspids drove Antigonus' phalanx back to the nearby foothills, 5.6km from the battlefield. Noting the enemy left's isolation after the advance of the centre and right, Antigonus, like Alexander at Gaugamela, drove through the gap in the enemy's front with his cavalry and charged Eumenes' exposed internal flank and routed him. This gave Antigonus the opportunity to rally his own centre and left along the foothills. The defeat of his left had forced Eumenes to halt his infantry's victorious advance and, as darkness fell, both sides settled down to reorganizing their battle lines. Eumenes' victory was spoiled by the self-interest of his troops who, concerned for their property, forced him to march back to camp rather than renew the attempt to crush Antigonus.

The rematch at Gabiene at the end of 317 ended even more paradoxically. As the battle was fought, like Gaugamela, on an open plain, Eumenes, following Alexander, made use of a flank-guard (of elephants) drawn back at an angle to his left wing. Antigonus also imitated events at Gaugamela by having some of his cavalry ride around Eumenes' flank and seize his baggage-park. Antigonus' attack was again in oblique order. His right-wing cavalry broke through the cavalry of Eumenes' left, obliging Eumenes himself to transfer to his right wing. Eumenes' infantry, spearheaded by the Argyraspids under Antigenes, advanced in a wedge-formation reminiscent of Alexander's wedge at Gaugamela. Antigonus' infantry was rolled up by the Argyraspids. Meanwhile, Antigonus' raiders had captured Eumenes' baggage, news of which demoralized his surviving cavalry wing, which likewise retired, leaving the victorious infantry isolated. In response to harassment by Antigonus' cavalry, Eumenes' infantry formed a tactical square and fell back on their cavalry. Eumenes urged his army to renew the battle. But the Argyraspids, concerned with recovering their baggage and families lost with the baggage-park, entered into secret negotiations with Antigonus and treacherously handed Eumenes over to him in exchange. Antigonus ended the campaign by executing both Eumenes and Antigenes.

The battle of Gaza (312) illustrates the tactical methods of Ptolemy I of Egypt against Demetrius Poliorcetes, son of Antigonus Monophthalmus, a second-generation imitator of Alexander. Ptolemy's use of a 'minefield' of elephant-traps in the centre, covered by archers and javelin-men, against Demetrius' main attack with war-elephants led to the capture of many animals. Likewise, Ptolemy's concentration and aggressive cavalry tactics on his right forced Demetrius on to a defensive he was able to reverse. This demoralized his cavalry and the infantry in the centre, which broke and fled after the defeat of the elephants.

Alexander's posthumous influence on warfare was greater than that of any other leader in history, with the possible exception of Napoleon, and the military system he established prevailed until the 2nd century BC. In his short career Alexander completely changed the face of war. More than any of his predecessors he demonstrated the fundamental tactical principles of concentration of force, co-operation between different arms, and a sustained offensive arising from a circumspect defence. His army defied conventional logistics by living off the land whatever the local conditions. Campaigning in unknown lands, Alexander broadened world horizons and provided a model for unlimited conquest that continued to inspire military leaders down to the 20th century.

PRINCIPAL SOURCES

Arrian (c. AD 90 – c. 165)

Lucius Flavius Arrianus, a Greek-speaking Roman citizen born at Nicomedia in northern Asia Minor between AD 85 and 90, served in the Roman army during the eastern wars of the emperor Trajan, and was governor of Baetica (c. 125), before becoming consul in 129 or 130. Thereafter he served as governor of the frontier province of Cappadocia in eastern Asia Minor, repulsing an invasion by the nomadic Alani and driving them north through the Caucasus in 135, an event described by Arrian himself in his *Ectaxis*. He retired to Athens, where he was eponymous Archon (titular head of state) in 145-6, and died probably in the 160s. Arrian's main surviving work, the

Anabasis Alexandri (Alexander's March Up-Country) is our fullest and most reliable source for the campaigns of Alexander, beginning with those of 335 BC. It is based on the Alexander-histories of Ptolemy, one of Alexander's most prominent generals and later King of Egypt, and Aristobulus, a Greek technical expert in Alexander's entourage. Also relevant are Arrian's *Indica*, giving details of Alexander's invasion of India, and his *Tactica*, Arrian's own revision and adaptation of a Hellenistic tactical manual.

Curtius (*c.* 10 BC – *c.* AD 53)

Quintus Curtius Rufus, a professional rhetorician of humble origins, who entered the senate as a candidate of the emperor Tiberius but fell from favour through his association with Tiberius' disgraced favourite Sejanus. He wrote his *History of Alexander the Great* during his period of enforced retirement from politics between AD 31 and 41, using his portrayal of Alexander as a veiled attack on Tiberius. Restored to favour on the accession of Claudius in 41, Curtius became consul in 43, then held the military governorship of Upper Germany in 46-67, and ended his career as governor of the province of Africa, where he died in office, probably in 53. Curtius' work was based on a variety of sources, among which the Greek sensationalist historian Cleitarchus was the most prominent. Curtius takes a less favourable view of Alexander than Arrian, but retains much material of value neglected by Arrian.

Diodorus Siculus (died after 21 BC)

A Sicilian Greek, born at Agyrium, who wrote a *Universal History* in the third quarter of the 1st century BC. His Book 17 is a fairly comprehensive, though sensationalist, account of Alexander's reign. Based on the same range of sources as Curtius, Diodorus often mixes authentic military detail with a lurid presentation. His Books 18-20, based on the work of Hieronymus of Cardia, a protégé of Eumenes of Cardia, show Diodorus at his best and provide our fullest account of the wars of Alexander's immediate successors down to 302 BC.

Plutarch (*c.* AD 46 – *c.* 120)

A Greek philosopher and biographer, who produced a series of 22 paired biographies of famous Greeks and Romans. Plutarch's *Life of Alexander* is paired with his *Life of Caesar*. As a biographer Plutarch was not interested in providing a full-scale history of Alexander, and his selection of material (intended to illustrate the personality of his subject) appears very arbitrary to the modern mind. His biography of Alexander nonetheless contains much of interest, especially in relation to the battle of the Hydaspes.

Aelian (latter half of 1st century AD to early 2nd century AD).

The author or, more accurately, the editor of the most important surviving Hellenistic tactical manual, which he dedicated to the emperor Trajan *c.* AD 106. Aelian's *Tactica* provides details of Macedonian military organization, equipment, drill, and tactics.

HELLENISTIC WARFARE

DR NICK SEKUNDA

Equestrian statue, depicted on a coin of Demetrius Poliorcetes, showing Demetrius in the uniform of a cavalryman of the xystophoroi. These light-horsemen were much favoured by Demetrius, especially for his mobile raid on Babylon in 311 BC, which this statue may commemorate. Notice the Macedonian beret, or kausia. Munzkabinett, Staatliche Museen zu Berlin.

Tombstone of a Ptolemaic soldier from Sidon, dating to the invasion of Syria by Ptolemy VI Philometor (147-5 BC). The deceased, an Anatolian mercenary, is equipped 'after the Roman fashion' with a thureos, bronze helmet, and scale armour, and belongs to one of the regiments of the Ptolemaic army reformed along Roman lines by Ptolemy VI. Istanbul Arkeoloji Müzeleri.

The death of Alexander was followed by a generation of wars fought over the empire by his generals. Countries were won and lost almost overnight. Seleucus recaptured Babylon with only 800 foot and 400 horse following his ally Ptolemy's victory over Demetrius Poliorcetes at Gaza in 312. When Seleucus marched east to conquer further lands, Demetrius overran and devastated Babylonia. In 319 Demetrius' father Antigonus Monophthalmus ('The One-Eyed') covered 2,500 stades (462 kilometres) with an army of more than 40,000 foot, 7,000 horse, plus elephants, in a forced march of seven days and nights through the Tauric mountains, to destroy the army of his rival Alcetas. Cavalry performed an essential role as scouts and skirmishers ahead of the main army. Heavy cavalry, such as various guard or 'Companion' regiments, remained important as shock troops, and so retained their armour and short fighting spears. Possible Italian or Galatian influence led to the adoption, *c.*280, of large round Celtic cavalry shields. Even so, there are increasing references to regiments of *xystophoroi*, light unarmoured mercenary cavalry, carrying a long lance (*xyston*) to compensate for their lack of armour, and enabling them to fulfil a battlefield role in addition to reconnaissance.

Military Settlement

By the early 3rd century the disintegration of the empire was complete. The Ptolemies held Egypt, the Seleucids Syria and the lands to the east, the Antigonids Macedon, and the Attalids the kingdom of Pergamon. The development of powerful torsion catapults, between 353 and 341, by artificers working under Philip II of Macedon and his Thessalian chief engineer Polyidus, meant the end of the Greek city-state as a military, and therefore as a political, power. In mainland Greece the city-state was replaced by the federal league, the most important being the Aetolian and Achaean. Only the island city of Rhodes, with its formidable navy, played an independent role. Mercenary troops were widely employed, especially as garrison troops, but the backbone of all these armies remained regular regiments levied from the citizenry. In the new kingdoms of the East drastic steps were taken to expand the existing systems of military settlement, and to replace the settlers with Greeks or Macedonians. Settlement was frequently compulsory. After his victory at Gaza, Ptolemy sent the soldiers captured in the battle to Egypt, ordering them to be distributed among the provinces. In return for his plot of land the military settler was subject to mobilization in time of war, and his sons had to undertake military training and a period of service before they could inherit the plot. A striking anecdote in Diodorus relates how one Herais, a woman of Abai near the Syrian border with Arabia, developed male genitals, changed her name to Diophantus, and was then conscripted into the cavalry of Alexander Balas. In 145 Diophantus participated in Alexander Balas' retreat to Abai following his defeat by Ptolemy VI and the pretender Demetrius at the River Oenoparas.

Whole regiments from Alexander's army were settled in this way. A regiment of Thessalians from Larissa founded another Larissa in Syria after serving with Seleucus I, and henceforward furnished the first *agema* of cavalry in the Seleucid army. The senior infantry regiment of Alexander's army, the

130

argyraspides, had a chequered regimental history. Upon the death of Antipater the new regent Polyperchon ordered the regiment to join the army of Eumenes of Cardia, who was ordered to march against Antigonus Monophthalmus. Eumenes won the battle, but Antigonus captured the baggage of the *argyraspides*, who agreed to hand over Eumenes and join Antigonus in return for their baggage. This was an age before guaranteed military pensions, and in 316 the youngest men in the regiment were 60, most were about 70, and some were older. Antigonus despatched the regiment to

The type of stone thrower used by Alexander the Great. The power was supplied by springs made from twisted sinew or hair.

A reconstruction of a late-Hellenistic catapult from pieces discovered at the Greek port at Ampurias in north-east Spain. These small catapults were generally called 'scorpions'.

Sibyrtius, the satrap of Arachosia, with orders to wear them out. The regiment must have deserted once again to Seleucus during his march eastwards during the years after 312, for the *argyraspides* ended their career in Seleucid service, and the regimental title was retained for over a century by the élite infantry regiment of the Seleucid army. The Companion cavalry regiment also entered Seleucid service, and in a similar way the élite cavalry regiment of the Seleucid army continued to be termed Companion.

The Decline of Cavalry

It was necessary to provide cavalry settlers with larger estates than those of infantrymen, and thus cavalry settlements were more expensive to maintain. In the 3rd century, as political conditions became more settled, and the local populations became more attached to their own royal dynasties, vast territories could no longer be seized in a single lightning cavalry raid. As a result, cavalry declined in both numbers and importance. King Philip V of Macedon had only 2,000 Macedonian cavalry to put into the field against the Romans, and his successor Perseus only 3,000. Thus Hellenistic armies found themselves heavily outnumbered in cavalry by the Romans. At Magnesia in 190 the Seleucid phalanx was left to fight an impossible struggle after the wings had collapsed; and the same fate overtook the army of the Achaean League at Leucopetra (Corinth) in 146. Cavalry tactics also declined. By the time Polybius – himself hipparch of the Achaean League in 170-169 – came to write of Alexander's cavalry at Issus, the Macedonian wedge formation had been forgotten, and in other passages he makes it clear that Hellenistic cavalry tactics had reverted to wheeling manoeuvres in square troops called *oulamoi*.

The Phalanx

Inevitably, greater reliance was placed on the phalanx. The troops forming the phalanx fell into two distinct types. There was the traditional hoplite, for many troops (especially Greek mercenaries) still retained hoplite equipment, together with their Macedonian equivalents, the *chalkaspides* ('Bronze Shields'); and the peltasts, a cross between hoplites and light infantry equipped with small bronze shields, daggers, helmets, and short pikes. Following contacts with the Italians and Galatians in the 280s and 270s, the Greeks and Macedonians began to adopt the large oval Celtic infantry shield, which the Greeks called a *thureos*, or 'door'. Troops called *thureophoroi* increasingly come into prominence.

The phalanx's principal drawback was its lack of flexibility. During an advance the line tended to lose its cohesion as the wings spread out, a problem experienced by Alexander at Gaugamela. This dislocation was particularly acute during an advance over rough terrain. This led to the development of what may be termed the 'articulated phalanx'. In this formation companies of pike-wielding phalangites were interspersed with 'joints' of lighter and more mobile infantry companies fighting in looser formation. The concept seems to have been employed first by Pyrrhus of Epirus in his Italian campaigns of 281-275, for Polybius tells us that he mixed up companies of phalangites with companies of Italians (presumably *thureophoroi*). Pyrrhus, a military writer and theorist, may well have invented the formation. It is unfortunate that the date when Rome adopted the maniple is unknown, for the two developments seem to be related. At the battle of Magnesia in 190 Antiochus the Great drew up the Seleucid phalanx in ten pike blocks, each 32 men deep by 50 wide, and each separated by two elephants.

Because the phalanx was an essentially linear formation, its flanks were extremely vulnerable, a problem exacerbated by the decline in Hellenistic cavalry. To counter an outflanking manoeuvre a second reserve line of phalangites was frequently drawn up some distance behind the first. This formation was termed a 'double phalanx'. At the battle of Sellasia in 222

Antigonus Doson drew up the Macedonian *chalkaspides* on the right flank, together with the Illyrian contingent, in an 'articulated phalanx', while on the left the Macedonian peltasts were drawn up in a 'double phalanx'. At Pydna in 168 the Macedonian army was again drawn up in a 'double phalanx'. In the front line the *chalkaspides* were drawn up on the right, the *leukaspides* (the vanguard regiment, or *agema*, of the peltasts) in the centre, then the mercenaries and Paionians, and finally the Thracians on the left. The peltasts were drawn up behind the *chalkaspides* in a second line. In the early stages of the battle the Macedonian phalanx carried all before it, but the Roman general Aemilius Paullus managed to snatch victory from the jaws of defeat by inserting his first legion between the two lines of the phalanx on the right flank. The Macedonian battle-line collapsed, and with it the supremacy of the phalanx.

Manpower Problems

Lack of manpower, rather than inferiority in military technique, sealed Macedon's fate. In 334, when Alexander crossed over into Asia, Macedon could mobilize some 24,000 phalangites. But by the time of the Cynoscephalae campaign in 197, Macedon could raise only 2,000 cavalry, 2,000 peltasts and 16,000 phalangites, and this by enrolling 16-year-olds and retired veterans. Subsequently Philip V strove to build up Macedon's strength for the final struggle with Rome. The Macedonians were required to beget and rear children, infanticide was suppressed, and large numbers of Thracians were settled in Macedon. King Perseus' army of 171 was the greatest led by any Macedonian king since Alexander had crossed into Asia, comprising 3,000 cavalry, 5,000 peltasts (including the *agema*), and 21,000 phalangites.

Even these numbers were inadequate to deal with Rome. Polybius calculated that in 225 the Roman Commonwealth's military manpower stood at 700,000 infantry and 70,000 cavalry. In the final struggle with Rome, Perseus and his generals consistently out-generalled their Roman opponents. For the Roman ruling classes, warfare was merely a means of acquiring booty to enrich their culturally impoverished society. Military positions were not filled on merit but on a rota basis with members of the next family in line stepping forward to enjoy the pickings. Finally, the war went so badly for the Romans that normal procedure had to be suspended temporarily and an experienced general, Aemilius Paulus, despatched to deal with the Macedonians.

Rome's military might was underwritten by its ability to conscript horde after uncomplaining horde of Italian peasant manpower. In 190 Rome had an army of 13 legions, plus allied troops, in the field – a total of some 182,400 men under arms. While the peasant served abroad for the duration of the war his land might be appropriated, or his family starve, but he never complained. The opportunities for rapine offered by the cities of the Greek world, adorned by centuries of cultural advancement, afforded some compensation. When one Roman army was cut down, another could be raised rapidly. Rome embodied 87 legions between 200 and 168. Macedon's limited reserves of manpower meant that she could not afford to lose a single battle. The Romans could afford to lose any number, as they did. In this manner the Greek world fell to Rome, and Greek culture never recovered.

After the Roman victory at Pydna, the Hellenistic monarchies in Syria and Egypt attempted to reform their armies along Roman lines. In 166 King Antiochus IV of Syria held a military parade at Daphnae which featured a 'legion' of 5,000 recruits in Roman equipment. Similar reforms in the Ptolemaic army are demonstrated by papyri dating from the reign of Ptolemy VI Philometor (181-145), indicating the introduction of Roman ranks, such as centurion, and consequently of Roman military organization, into the Egyptian army. Ultimately both kingdoms crumbled as the result of the manipulation of their internal divisions by their all-powerful neighbour in the West.

overleaf
*THE SIEGE OF
RHODES (305-304 BC)
Demetrius' main
achievements, earning him
his nickname Poliorcetes, 'the
Besieger', were in siege
warfare. In 305 he moved
against Ptolemy's ally, the
island-city of Rhodes.
Demetrius built a giant siege
tower, the Helepolis, and
cleared an approach path
750m wide for its advance,
which was coordinated with
that of two movable sheds or
'tortoises' shielding iron-clad
battering rams 55m long,
each worked by 1,000 men,
and eight further 'tortoises'
protecting the sappers. His
assaults brought down the
strongest fo the city's towers
and the wall adjacent to it,
but a Rhodian night attack
with fire missiles dislodged
some of the Helepolis' iron
plating and set fire to the siege
tower, which had to be
dragged back out of range to
save it from destruction. The
Rhodians meanwhile cut off
the fallen curtain wall by
building a temporary wall
behind it, but renewed
assaults brought down two
more curtain walls. At this
stage 1,500 of Ptolemy's
troops arrived to reinforce the
7,000 armed Rhodians.
1,500 of Demetrius' men
broke into the city in a night
attack, but were driven out
in a day of savage street-
fighting. Since Ptolemy was
able to reprovision the city,
Demetrius was obliged to
come to terms with the
Rhodians after a 15-month
siege.*

THE HELEPOLIS

Demetrius' Helepolis, the 'City-taker', was built by the engineer Epimachus of Athens. The base-platform, almost 25m square, was made from squared timbers held together by iron spikes. The space inside was divided by beams set 0.5m apart to provide standing room for some of the 3,400 men who moved the tower forward, the rest pushing from the rear. The whole structure was mounted on eight solid wheels, with rims 1m across and overlaid with iron plates. The tower could be moved in any direction by means of pivots. The corner-beams were almost 50m long, inclining inward, so that the first storey of the nine storey tower had a floor-area of 430 square metres and the top storey one of 90 square metres. The three exposed sides of the tower were covered with iron plates held by spikes. In front of each storey there were portholes, adapted in size and shape to the missiles fired through them. To protect the artillerymen inside, of whom there were over 200, these portholes were fitted with shutters which were lifted by a mechanical device. The shutters were made of hides stitched together and filled with wool, to yield to the impact of the stones from the Rhodian catapults. The Helepolis itself was armed on the lower storeys with stone-throwing catapults, capable of hurling rocks up to 85kg in weight. Lighter stone-throwing and javelin-firing catapults were mounted on the middle and higher storeys. To minimize confusion and the danger from fire, each storey was provided with a water-tank and two stairways, one for bringing up ammunition, the other for descent. The scale of these siege engines can be gauged from the tiny figures behind the 'tortoise' on the left of the picture.

THE EARLY ROMAN ARMY

PETER CONNOLLY

The origins of the Roman military system are lost in prehistory. It is not until Rome comes under Etruscan rule in the 6th century BC that we obtain our first glimpse of the army which was to dominate the Mediterranean for 600 years.

The Greek-style phalanx which the Etruscans had adopted during the 7th century, formed the core of the Etrusco-Roman army. It was supported by Latin/Roman contingents who fought on the wings with spears, axes and javelins in their freer native style. The use of native troops to fight alongside their own forces was probably typical of the Etruscan system. This system was later adopted by the Romans.

The ancient historians Livy and Dionysius of Halicarnassus give a relatively detailed description of the Etrusco-Roman army as it was reorganized by Servius Tullius in the middle of the 6th century. Servius' reorganization, which served both a political and a military purpose, ignored the racial make-up of the society. He divided the population into seven groups according to wealth; the wealth criterion was of crucial military importance, as the individual had to supply his own equipment.

Bronze Villanovan helmet made in two halves riveted together. This embossed helmet is typical of the Villanovan culture which flourished in north and central Italy during the 9th to 7th centuries BC. British Museum, London.

1 *The equites* were the wealthiest citizens grouped into 18 centuries. They formed the cavalry, supplying their own horses.
2 *The first class* (the next wealthiest) were formed into 80 centuries of spearmen fully armed with helmet, cuirass, greaves and round shield.
3 *The second class* were divided into 20 centuries of spearmen armed with helmet, greaves and Italian shield (*scutum*).
4 *The third class* were also divided into 20 centuries of spearmen but were armed only with helmet and Italian shield.
5 *The fourth class*, also 20 centuries, were armed only with spear and Italian shield.
6 *The fifth class*, also 20 centuries, were armed only with slings and javelins.
7 *Capite censi*, literally a 'head count' of all those with little or no property. They had no incentive to defend the state and were considered unfit to serve in the army. This group was to play an increasingly important role in the 3rd to 1st centuries BC as the state tried desperately to keep pace with the army's insatiable demand for manpower.

The 80 centuries of fully armed spearmen with round shields who formed the first class are clearly a Greek-style phalanx. The other four classes, armed in Italian style, are support troops fighting either on the wings or in front of the phalanx before the battle began.

The Latin League

At the end of the 6th century BC the Etruscans were driven out by the combined forces of the Latin towns and the Greeks who had colonized the coastline south of Latium. The victorious Latin towns formed an alliance against the Etruscans known as the Latin League. Rome was a founder member of this alliance. Initially the Etruscans posed the main threat to the League and the phalanx remained the basis of the Latin armies. However,

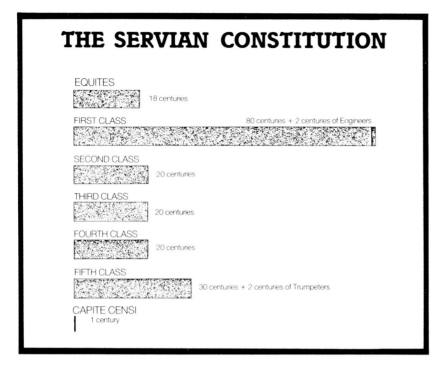

THE SERVIAN CONSTITUTION

EQUITES
18 centuries

FIRST CLASS
80 centuries + 2 centuries of Engineers

SECOND CLASS
20 centuries

THIRD CLASS
20 centuries

FOURTH CLASS
20 centuries

FIFTH CLASS
30 centuries + 2 centuries of Trumpeters

CAPITE CENSI
1 century

The structure of the army of Servius Tullius. The equites formed the cavalry. The eighty centuries of the first class formed a Greek style phalanx. The second to fifth classes were armed in native Italian fashion. The poorest citizens, capite censi, *who were grouped into a single century, were not liable for military service.*

there was a fundamental difference between Greece and Italy; the Etruscans, Latins and Greeks apart, Italy was divided into peoples and tribes rather than city-states. Set-piece battles, in which both sides formed up on mutually acceptable ground, seldom took place in Italy and the effectiveness of the phalanx was therefore limited.

As Etruscan power began to wane, the Latins increasingly turned their attention towards the hill peoples of the east, where the terrain was unsuitable for phalanx warfare. These hill peoples appear to have fought in loose formation, using javelins rather than spears, and the Latins must have been forced to adapt their methods to combat them. It is probable that as early as the middle of the 5th century the phalanx was already giving way to the more flexible system which was to characterize the Roman army.

At the beginning of the 4th century two significant events took place; the army began receiving pay and the phalanx was abandoned. The ancient sources connect both these events with the capture of the Etruscan city of Veii, which fell after a long siege in 396 BC. The first of these reforms could well be the logical result of a long siege which demanded that the soldiers, who would normally serve only in the summer months and so be free to sow and reap their crops, remain in arms all the year round. Pay represented compensation for the loss of their crops. The second is more difficult to understand as battle tactics have no relevance to siege warfare. In truth, it probably relates to an entirely separate event which occurred in the same area six years later – the disaster on the Allia.

Throughout the 5th century the Celts (the Romans called them Gauls) had been seeping through the Alps from Austria and settling in the Po Valley. They gradually took over the area, driving out the Etruscans and advancing down the Adriatic coast. In 390 one of the Celtic tribes, the Senones, crossed the Appennine Mountains and descended the valley of the Tiber. The Latin army sent to repel the invaders was cut to pieces on the banks of the Allia, just 17 km north of Rome, and the city itself was sacked. It was Rome's most humiliating defeat. The Latins were compelled to conduct an inquest and take the necessary precautions to prevent a repetition of the disaster. The Etruscans were no longer a serious threat to the Latins. The combined assault from the Celts in the north and the Latins in the south had broken their power. The

The warrior of Capestrano. This statue, found at Capestrano some 30km east of L'Aquila in the Appennine mountains, depicts a mountain warrior of the 6th century BC. He wears round breast and back plates and has a sword slung across his chest. Actual examples of these breast and back plates are 20-25cm in diameter, considerably larger than the one shown here. Museo Nazionale di Antichità degli Abruzzi e del Molise, Chieti.

main enemies of the Latins were now the Sabellian hill tribes and the Celts. The Latins were intelligent enough to adapt to the situation, and the Greek-style phalanx was abandoned.

The hoplite phalanx was essentially a defensive system designed to combat a frontal attack with spears and javelins. The Celts introduced a new form of fighting into Italy. They were much taller than the Italians and fought primarily with slashing swords. The direction of the Celtic attack was therefore from above or from the side but not from the front. The round hoplite shield proved to be of limited effect against such an attack, whereas the traditional

A Negau-type helmet found at Olympia in Greece. It was dedicated by Hiero, the Greek tyrant of Syracuse in Sicily, to celebrate his victory over the Etruscans at Cumae north of the Bay of Naples in 474 BC. This is a typical Italian helmet of the 5th and 4th centuries BC. British Museum, London.

An embossed bronze Villanovan shield with central handgrip from Bisenzio near Florence. This shield was made for ceremonial purposes and does not have the wooden backing essential for a battle shield.

Italian body shield, the *scutum*, with its curved resilient sides and spindle boss, was much more efficient. This shield, reinforced with a metal rim at the top and bottom, now became part of the standard equipment of the heavy infantry.

A new tactic also seems to have evolved. The well-armoured Italian-style spearmen of the *second class (hastati)* were re-armed with heavy javelins (*pila*) and placed out ahead of the heavy-armed spearmen of the *first class*. The job of the *hastati* was to break up the force of the Celtic charge and then retreat through gaps in the line of spearmen behind them. This is pure speculation as

TABLE OF EVENTS   753 – 121 BC

753	Traditional date of foundation of Rome.
616-510	Traditional dates of Etruscan kings of Rome.
578-535	Traditional date for reign of Servius Tullius.
510	Etruscans driven out.
493-431	Intermittent wars against hill tribes (Aequi and Volsci).
396	Capture of Etruscan city of Veii.
390	Battle of the Allia. Rome sacked by Gauls (Senones).
351	Etruscan cities of Tarquinii and Falerii defeated.
340-338	Latin War.
338	Rome takes over Latin League.
343-290	Samnite Wars.
295	Rome defeats confederation of Samnites, Umbrians and Gauls at Sentinum.
283	Senones defeated and driven out of Italy.
280-275	War with Pyrrhus.
264-241	First Punic War.
260	Rome launches first fleet.
225	Last Gallic invasion; Gauls defeated at Telemon.
218-201	Second Punic War.
218	Hannibal crosses Alps. Battle of the Trebbia.
217	Battle of Lake Trasimene.
216	Battle of Cannae; Rome's greatest defeat. Southern Italy defects to Carthaginians.
211	Capua recaptured by Romans. Siege of Syracuse in Sicily.
207	Hasdrubal, Hannibal's brother, defeated and killed.
206	Scipio defeats Carthaginians in Spain.
202	Scipio defeats Hannibal at Zama in North Africa.
215-205	First Macedonian War.
199-197	Second Macedonian War.
197	Battle of Cynoscephalae.
191	Gauls of Po Valley finally conquered.
188	Antiochus the Great, King of Syria, defeated at Magnesia.
171-168	Third Macedonian War.
168	Battle of Pydna.
149-146	Third Punic War.
146	Carthage destroyed.
133	Numantia destroyed.
121	Gauls of Rhone valley and Languedoc conquered; land route opened to Spain.

the sparse and unreliable literary sources of the period tell us nothing, but a change along these lines must have taken place.

The Roman historian Livy, writing more than three centuries after the event he is describing, gives us a brief glimpse of the Roman/Latin army in the middle of the 4th century, some 50 years after the changes outlined above must have taken place. Historians have made much of the contradictions in Livy's account, and have even tried to adapt it to fit the description given by the

THE UNITS OF THE ROMAN-LATIN ARMY DESCRIBED BY LIVY

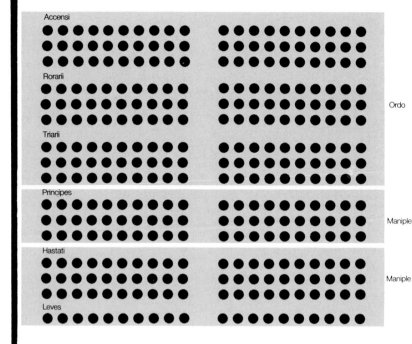

The double centuries of *accensi, rorarii* and *triarii* were grouped together to form one *ordo* (about 180 men). The *principes* and *hastati* each formed a maniple of about 60 men. There were 20 skirmishers *(leves)* attached to each maniple of *hastati*. Livy does not say how many centurions there were to each maniple of *hastati* and *principes*. Although Livy's account is confused and creates many problems, it would be totally wrong to suggest that he has made it up. Basically it must be correct.

Greek historian Polybius, who described the Roman army of his own day (*c.* 150 BC).

Livy, describing the Latin-Roman army in 340 when Rome took command of the Latin League, states that it consisted of three lines of heavy-armed infantry, the *triarii, principes* and *hastati,* supported by troops who appear to be progressively lighter armed, the *rorarii, accensi* and *leves,* the last being skirmishers. The *triarii* and *principes* appear to be the old Servian *first class.* The *hastati,* as their name suggests, were probably the old Italian-style spearmen of the *second class.* The *rorarii, accensi* and *leves* were the old *third, fourth* and *fifth class* respectively. These last three groups probably still fought on the wings and in front as they had in the old days.

The *triarii,* although armed with the Italian shield (*scutum*), still fight as a phalanx but are much reduced in numbers and have a purely defensive role. The *principes,* like the *hastati,* are now armed with heavy javelins and fight out ahead of the spearmen as a second advanced line.

The use of the *hastati* re-armed with javelins had clearly worked and the Romans must have decided to add a similarly armed second line (*principes*). After throwing their javelins the *hastati* drew their swords and charged in to close quarters, taking advantage of the confusion caused by the hail of javelins. If this failed to break the enemy, they retreated through the gaps between the *principes,* who then mounted a similar charge. Usually these two assaults were sufficient to defeat the enemy. However, if both lines were overcome, they would retreat through gaps in the *triarii,* who would then close ranks, level their spears and retreat to the safety of the camp. The *triarii* were the last line of defence, saving the army when the battle was lost. The Roman saying 'it has come to the *triarii*' implied a desperate situation.

In an era of varying fortune when the prospect of defeat must have been a constant nightmare, it is not surprising that the new army retained a strong defensive third line. At some point over the next 70 years the *rorarii* and *accensi* were absorbed into the *hastati* and *leves* respectively and half the *triarii* joined the *principes*, producing the army that was known to Polybius. This change may have come soon after Rome took over the Latin League, for the Latin allies of Rome formed the wings of the Roman army, making the *rorarii* and *accensi* redundant. The change must have taken place well before 256 because in this year Polybius describes the Roman fleet taking up the traditional Roman legionary formation of *triarii*, *principes* and *hastati*.

The Control of Italy

By 280 BC Rome was in total control of peninsular Italy. In a series of wars the Samnites, the Umbrians, the Etruscans and the Celts of the Adriatic coast had been brought to their knees and the stage was set for Rome's great wars against overseas enemies. Rome's flexible manipular system may have been developed during the long wars with the Samnites with their light-armed, fast moving armies, but unfortunately the literary sources tell us nothing of this.

With the exception of the Celts, who were driven out of Italy, the defeated peoples were allowed to govern themselves, with Rome controlling only their foreign policy. They became allies of Rome (*socii*) and were compelled to supply troops for the Roman army. They were also obliged to give up small portions of their land on which colonies were placed. In this early period these were usually small but strongly defended towns, a system adopted by the Etruscans, Latins and other peoples of Italy long before the Romans took over. These colonies were occupied by Latin or Roman citizens who maintained themselves by farming the local land. The function of some of these colonies was simply to keep the local population under control. Others guarded strategic points, such as the very early Latin colonies at Fidene, which controlled the Tiber crossing north of Rome; and Circeii, which overlooked the road leading into southern Latium. These strategic colonies, which were almost always placed on hill tops, formed a network of fortresses which could hinder enemy movements and, in war, allow Roman forces to operate deep in enemy-held territory. By the end of the 4th century the Romans had established colonies in Campania and Apulia. These were to prove immensely important when Hannibal occupied southern Italy.

Bas relief of a Roman galley with marines on the deck. Contrary to popular opinion these warships were not rowed by slaves. The crews were drawn from the poorest citizens of the fifth class. Plaster cast, Museo della Civiltà Romana, Rome.

From the earliest times colonies were established along the coast as a defence against seaborne attacks. The most famous of these was at Ostia at the mouth of the Tiber. It later became the port of Rome.

The colonial system had a secondary advantage; settlers were often selected from the mass of landless peasants (*capite censi*) who could not serve in

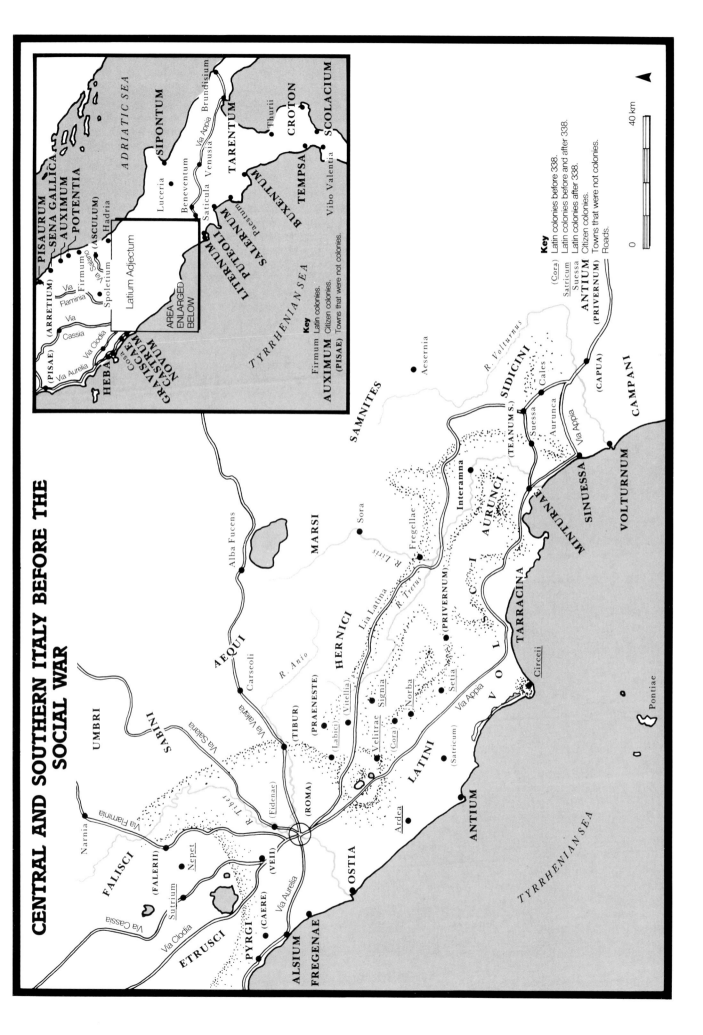

CENTRAL AND SOUTHERN ITALY BEFORE THE SOCIAL WAR

the army. On becoming colonists, they received a grant of land which immediately made them eligible for military service.

Overseas Enemies

In the hundred years which followed the subjugation of Italy, Rome fought a series of wars against enemies from overseas. The first of these was against Pyrrhus, king of Epirus, a brilliant tactician classed by Hannibal as second only to Alexander the Great. Pyrrhus crossed the Adriatic in 280 and landed in Italy with a Macedonian-style phalanx and 20 elephants. He inflicted a series of defeats on the Romans, but for all his tactical skill he was unable to win the war, suffering such grievous casualties that he was finally forced to withdraw. A Pyrrhic victory became the catchphrase for a victory so expensive that it was tantamount to a defeat.

Eleven years after the departure of Pyrrhus, Rome began the first of her two greatest wars. These were the wars with the maritime city of Carthage, the Punic Wars. The first war (264-241) was fought for the control of Sicily. For the first time Rome was compelled to build a fleet, sometimes with ludicrous but more often with tragic results. The ships were galleys, copied from a captured Carthaginian example. Not being sailors, the Romans tried to turn their sea battles into mass boarding operations so that they could utilize their superb infantry. They developed a huge boarding plank with a large spike on the end with which they tried to lock their ships to the enemy vessels.

This contraption, nicknamed 'the raven' (*corvus*) by the soldiers, proved remarkably successful at first but, with badly built ships, clumsy oarsmen and inexperienced captains, the Romans lost far more men to the elements than were ever killed by the Carthaginians. The *corvus* itself probably added to the instability of the ships, making them turn turtle. Fleet after fleet was wrecked off the stormy southern coast of Sicily. In one incident alone the Romans lost 220 warships and 800 supply vessels complete with their crews. But in time they learned to dispense with the *corvus* and acquired a degree of seamanship.

Control of the sea was the crucial factor in winning the war, but the Romans were never happy at sea. Contrary to popular belief, their sailors were not slaves. They were drawn from the poorest (*fifth*) class, were treated as soldiers and expected to fight when necessary. The never-ending demand for crews during the war must have forced the senate to lower the property qualification of the *fifth class* so that they could enrol sailors from the unpropertied poor (*capite censi*).

Battle fleets were maintained throughout the war with Hannibal (218-202) and down to the second defeat of Macedon in 168, but subsequently the warships were allowed to fall into disrepair, and the Romans relied on their Greek allies in the eastern Mediterranean to give them naval cover. Roman fleets did not appear in the Mediterranean again until the 1st century BC.

The Second Punic War brought Rome to the very brink of extinction. Hannibal tried to achieve what Pyrrhus had failed to do. He took the war to Italy, relying on an uprising of the subject peoples. It was a colossal gamble which nearly succeeded. In the summer of 218 he set out from the Carthaginian province in southern Spain, crossed the Pyrenees and the Alps to arrive in northern Italy with a mercenary army of 20,000 infantry, 6,000 cavalry and 37 elephants. The Celts of the Po valley, conquered only a few years earlier, flocked to his standard, doubling the size of his army.

The two chief magistrates of Rome, the consuls, with their combined armies opposed his advance near modern Piacenza and a battle was fought on the west bank of the river Trebbia. The Romans, in their customary manner, charged the Celts and Spaniards in the centre of the Carthaginian line. Hannibal had anticipated this tactic and had reinforced his wings with his elephants and African infantry. The Roman wings disintegrated under the impact, throwing their whole line into disarray. The legions in the centre extricated themselves by cutting their way through the Celts and Spaniards,

THE BATTLE OF CANNAE

STAGE 1

Hannibal's slingers and spearmen form a cover as he draws up his Celtic and Spanish swordsmen in a crescent. The spearmen withdraw and form up behind the cavalry.

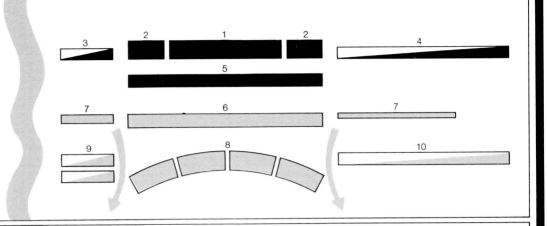

STAGE 2

The battle is opened by the light-armed troops. Then the heavy infantry engage and the legions drive back the Carthaginian centre, flattening the crescent.

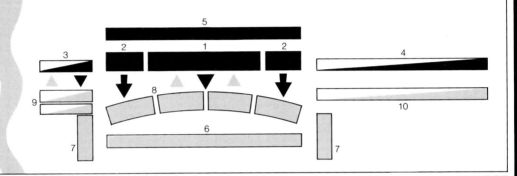

STAGE 3

In the centre the legions continue to push back the Spanish and Celtic infantry, whose line begins to cave in. On the Roman right along the river the Spanish and Celtic cavalry begin to drive the Roman horsemen back until a gap is opened up. Most of the Celtic and Spanish horsemen burst through the gap and fall on the rear of the allied cavalry, which breaks under the combined attack.

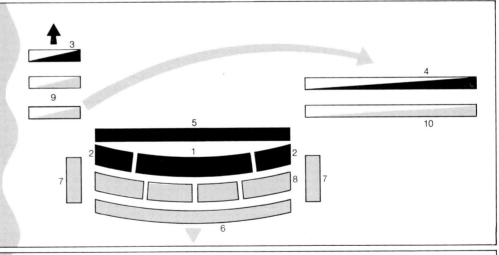

STAGE 4

In the centre the legions continue their drive until they are caught between the phalanxes. The Celtic and Spanish cavalry now charge legions in the rear.

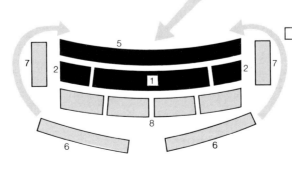

Key

1 Legions
2 Allied infantry
3 Roman cavalry
4 Allied cavalry
5 Velites
6 Carthaginian light-armed
7 Carthaginian spearmen
8 Celtic and Spanish infantry
9 Celtic and Spanish cavalry
10 Numidian cavalry

THE CORVUS

The Romans built their first fleet in 260 BC. It consisted of 200 quinqueremes copied from a captured Carthaginian vessel and 20 triremes. Not being sailors, they endeavoured to make use of their superior infantry even at sea. Their galleys were in fact little more than floating platforms propelled by oars. In order to board the enemy vessels they devised a combined boarding plank and grappling hook, nicknamed 'the raven' *(corvus)*. It consisted of a boarding plank about 11m long and over a metre wide with a metal spike at the far end. A rectangular hole was cut a third of the way along the plank which fitted round a pole about 7m high and 30cm thick. The pole was fixed into the bow of the ship so that the boarding plank could be swivelled round in any direction. A knee-high fence was erected on either side of the plank to protect the soldiers' lower legs. The plank was raised by a rope which passed through a pulley at the top of the pole and was tied to a ring on the spike. This is Polybius' description, but it is difficult to see how the plank could have operated unless it were made in two pieces hinged at the rectangular hole.

The corvus was raised before battle and, when the enemy charged, be it head-on or amidships, it was dropped so that its spike stuck into the deck of the enemy ship, locking the two vessels together. The marines then mounted the plank in pairs, the front two with their shields held in front whilst the others protected their flanks by resting their shields on the knee-high fence.

The system neutralized the Carthaginian tactical superiority for, as long as the Romans held their line in close order, it was impossible for the Carthaginians to attack them anywhere but at the front.

PETER
CONNOLLY

A bronze Montefortino-type helmet. This was the commonest type of helmet used in Italy during the 4th to 1st centuries BC. Hundreds of examples have been found coming from as far afield as Greece, Turkey, Spain and Germany, witnessing the expansion of the Roman domain. This type was developed from a Celtic helmet designed as a protection against slashing swords. British Museum, London.

denying Hannibal a total victory. Nevertheless, he had demonstrated his tactical brilliance with his sure handling of a wide variety of troops, in marked contrast to the Roman reliance on brute force.

In the spring Hannibal crossed the Appennine Mountains into Etruria where, on the northern shore of Lake Trasimene, he ambushed and wiped out a complete consular army. In spite of this second demonstration of generalship, the Etruscans refused to join him. Their spirit had long since been broken. Hannibal moved over to the Adriatic coast and descended on southern Italy. The Romans followed but cautiously refused battle.

Such discretion was not popular at Rome and the following year a massive eight-legion army (*c.* 80,000 men), under the joint command of the two consuls, was despatched to bring the war to an end. The Romans had learned nothing from their experience at the Trebbia. Their only response to the situation was to use an even larger sledgehammer.

The battle of Cannae, fought in the summer of 216 BC, was Hannibal's masterpiece. In the 20 months following the battle of the Trebbia he had turned his Celtic allies into a disciplined and reliable army. The two opposing forces formed up in the same way they had at the Trebbia but without elephants; all except one had died in the winter of 218-217. The Romans massed their centre intent on a breakthrough. Hannibal responded by forming up his Celtic and Spanish infantry in a crescent formation with the centre advanced towards the Roman line. He drew up his African spearmen behind the wings masked by his cavalry.

This time the Spaniards and Celts in the centre managed to hold, giving ground gradually while the Carthaginian cavalry stripped the Roman wings. The wings clear, the African spearmen charged the unprotected flanks, buckling the Roman line while the cavalry attacked the legions in the rear, cutting the Romans off from their camp. Unable to manoeuvre, the legionaries were slaughtered; 45-50,000 fell in the carnage. It was a black day.

Virtually the whole of southern Italy went over to the Carthaginians after the battle of Cannae. But the Romans gritted their teeth and determined to fight on. There would be no more battles. From now on it was to be a war of attrition. Gradually the Romans clawed back the lost territories, laying siege to the rebel cities knowing that Hannibal could not defend them all. Year by year they put more troops into the field, reaching a climax in 212 when 25 legions were brought into service.

In a desperate effort to retrieve the situation, Hannibal advanced on Rome but the Romans stayed within the walls, and with insufficient troops to invest the city he was obliged to withdraw. He must have known that he had lost the war. The final blow was delivered in 207 BC when his brother Hasdrubal was defeated and killed in northern Italy while trying to reach him with reinforcements. He retreated into the toe of Italy and remained there until he was recalled to defend Carthage against the young Scipio who had invaded north Africa. Hannibal had remained in Italy more than 15 years, never having lost a battle. At Zama in 202, Rome's greatest enemy was defeated. His old guard fought valiantly but they were no match for the new superstar, Scipio, who used the Carthaginian's own tactics against him.

Four factors had saved Rome: her enormous resources in manpower, which had enabled her to put nearly a quarter of a million men in the field in 212; her control of the sea, which stopped Hannibal getting reinforcements and supplies; the chain of colonies, which enabled her to wage war well behind enemy lines all over Italy; and, perhaps most important, her indomitable spirit, which would never admit defeat. This attitude was summed up in the reply given to Hannibal's ambassador after Cannae: 'Rome will not discuss terms of peace with a foreign enemy on Italian soil'.

The Hannibalic war was the watershed of Roman history. Within twelve years of overcoming Hannibal (202) Rome had defeated Philip V of Macedon (197) and Antiochus the Great of Syria (190) to become the most powerful state in the Mediterranean.

THE ROMAN ARMY IN
THE AGE OF POLYBIUS

PETER CONNOLLY

The defeat of the Macedonian phalanx by the Roman legions at Cynoscephalae in 197 was viewed by most Greeks with total disbelief, and many tried to explain it away. It had been an encounter battle fought over muddy broken ground in poor visibility, but the Macedonians had enjoyed the advantage of the sloping ground. It was inevitable that there would be a replay and 29 years later, at Pydna beneath Mount Olympus, the phalanx and the legion met again. The result was the same; the legions were victorious, and this time there were no excuses.

Hundreds of hostages were sent to Rome after the battle of Pydna. Among them was a young Achean noble named Polybius. At Rome he was lodged in the house of the Scipios, one of the leading families of the day, where he began to write a great historical work on the contemporary world. Polybius was in a unique position, for he understood the military systems of both Greece and Rome. He had been a cavalry commander and had seen active service against Rome in the Third Macedonian War. He travelled widely and was probably present at the siege of Carthage (146) and the siege of Numantia in Spain (133). Fortunately for those wishing to study the Roman army, he was addressing a Greek audience and thus felt obliged to explain the Roman military system, something which our other great source, Caesar, seldom does.

This chapter deals with Polybius' era (200-120 BC). Polybius' lengthy description of the Roman army follows his account of the great Roman defeat at Cannae in 216. It is therefore reasonable to assume that it was intended to portray the Roman army during the war with Hannibal. However, one must bear in mind that it was written 50 years after the end of that war, during which time the army must have continued to evolve. Allowance must be made for anachronisms. It is also important to remember that Polybius wrote in Greek and the terms he uses are sometimes those he regards as the Greek equivalent of the Latin term; for example, *taxiarch* for *centurion* and *ouragos* for *optio*.

Organization of The Consular Legions

Polybius states that under normal circumstances four legions were enrolled each year, two for each of the chief magistrates, the consuls. Between 200 and 120 BC there were never less than eight legions in the field. These extra legions commanded either by praetors, proconsuls (ex-consuls) or propraetors (ex-praetors). The word legion simply means a levy. When the Etruscans were driven out, the Romans appointed two chief magistrates (*praetors*) and split the army between them, creating two legions. Necessity gave rise to new legions.

The consular legions were numbered one to four. A legion normally consisted of 4,200 infantry and 300 cavalry. There was still a property qualification for service in the army, but there seems to be little doubt that the property requirement for the *fifth class* in the Servian system had been continually lowered over the years to allow the state to draw on the mass of poorer citizens to keep up with the expanding demands of the army. After the Battle of Cannae the Romans formed two legions of slaves. It is difficult to

AN AERIAL VIEW OF THE BATTLE OF CYNOSCEPHALAE, 197 BC

The Romans and Macedonians had been retreating westwards from Pherae in Thessaly using different routes which took them along either side of a range of low hills. Each was unaware of the exact position of the other. On the morning of the battle both sides remained in camp because of rain and mist. The Macedonian king, Philip V, sought to secure his position by occupying Cynoscephalae, a broad pass over the hills separating the two armies.

The Roman commander, Flamininus, sent out a scouting party which, in the mist, accidentally fell in with Philip's soldiers holding the pass and a skirmish began. Both sides sent back to their respective camps for reinforcements and gradually a full-scale battle developed. The Macedonians, occuping the pass, had the advantage of the ground but the Romans were nearer to their camp. The battle surged up and down the hillside as each commander sent in fresh troops. Finally, Flamininus ordered out his whole army and Philip was compelled to do the same.

The weather was clearing by the time that Philip, with his right wing, reached the top of the pass and he was able to see the Roman army deployed on the hillside below him. He ordered his right wing to form up in close order and charged the Roman left, driving it down the hillside. Flamininus, realizing that the situation demanded a desperate gamble, took command of the Roman left and, with his elephants in front, charged the Macedonian left, which had only partially deployed. The Macedonians were thrown into confusion and routed. Meanwhile, an enterprising tribune, seeing that the Roman right was now further up the hillside than the Macedonian right wing, led 20 maniples, probably the *triarii*, across the hillside (this is the moment shown in the illustration) and attacked the Macedonians in the rear, securing an overwhelming victory for the Romans. This victory underlined the superiority of the new flexible Roman system over the rigid Macedonian system.

PETER
CONNOLLY

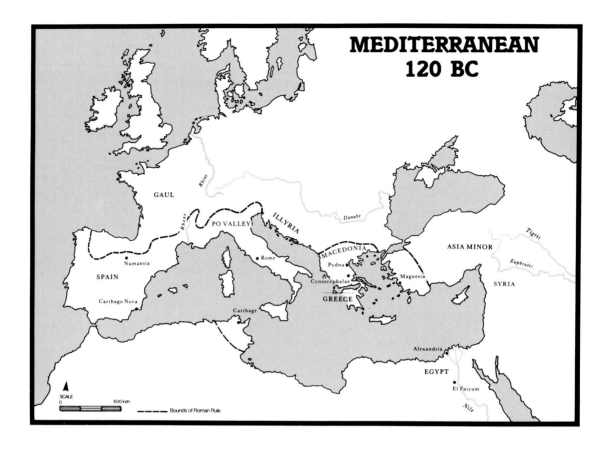

MEDITERRANEAN 120 BC

believe that this drastic measure was taken before exhausting the legitimate resources of the state.

The men chosen to form a legion were divided into five groups. The wealthiest 300 formed the cavalry. The poorest and youngest 1,200 men became the skirmishers, now called *velites*. The oldest 600 men made up the spearmen (*triarii*). The remainder were uniformly armed with heavy javelin (*pilum*) and sword but they were divided into two classes by age. The younger 1,200 formed the *hastati* and the older 1,200, who were in the prime of life, formed the *principes*. The legion was really a small army containing all types of troops: spearmen (*triarii*), heavily armoured javelin/swordsmen (*principes* and *hastati*), light-armed skirmishers (*velites*) and cavalry. The *triarii*, *principes* and *hastati* were each divided into ten units called maniples (*manipuli*). For organizational purposes, the *velites* were evenly distributed amongst the 30 maniples but they seldom, if ever, fought with them.

Polybius' description is a little confusing because he is describing the tactical structure of the legion and ignoring its organizational structure. The basic organizational unit in Polybius' time was not the maniple any more than it was the cohort in Caesar's time. At all times the basic organizational unit was the century. To understand Polybius' legion, it is essential to bear this in mind for Polybius never mentions the century (*centuria*) or the name centurion (*centurio*).

In battle order the *triarii*, *principes* and *hastati* were drawn up in three separate lines with the *hastati* at the front, the *principes* in the middle and the *triarii* at the rear. It is the author's contention that each of these was a double line, consisting of ten front (*prior*) and ten rear (*posterior*) centuries numbered one to ten in each case. Front and rear centuries with the same number were coupled to form maniples. The centurions of the front centuries were selected first and took the title '*prior*'; then the centurions of the rear centuries were selected, taking the title *posterior*. For example, the front centurion of the tenth maniple of the *hastati*, was called *decimus hastatus prior*. These titles still existed in the empire.

Polybius' statement that the senior (*prior*) centurions of all ten maniples in each line were selected first is probably only partly true, for the centurions commanding the first maniples of each of the three lines, known as the *primi ordines*, were senior to all the others. In Caesar's day, and probably in that of Polybius too, they were entitled to attend the general's council of war. The posterior centurions of the *primi ordines* must have been selected immediately after the prior centurions of the *primi ordines*, as their position and authority demanded that they were the second choice and not the 11th. The *primus hastatus prior* and the *primus princeps prior* were the senior centurions of the *hastati* and *principes* respectively. During the early empire they were known simply as *hastatus legionis* and *princeps legionis*. The highest-ranking centurion in the legion was the prior centurion of the first maniple of the *triarii*, the *primus pilus* (*pilus* is an alternative name for *triarius*). The *primus pilus* was a veteran chosen for his vast experience. He appears to have held the position on a yearly basis, even when the legion was in constant service. Spurius Ligustinus (see below) is known to have held the rank at least five times.

When both centurions of a maniple were present, the prior centurion commanded the whole maniple. Each centurion had a second-in-command (*optio*). It is almost certain that each century had a standard (*signum*) carried by a standard bearer (*signifer*). It seems unlikely that a maniple had its own standard or that the legion had one.

The *triarii*, *principes* and *hastati* all wore full armour: a breastplate, helmet and a single greave on the left leg were the minimum requirement. Those who could afford to do so wore a mail shirt. All used the curved oval *scutum*, a body shield with a horizontal handgrip. Made of fine-grained hard wood, it was about 1.2 m long, 0.75 m wide and weighed 8-9 kg. It was not designed to be wielded; the legionary fought from behind it, normally holding it with a straight arm and often resting it on the ground.

A sword and the remains of its scabbard found at Atienza some 100km north-east of Madrid in Spain. This type of sword found in Spanish graves of the 5th and 4th centuries BC is clearly the forerunner of the Roman gladius hispaniensis *(Spanish sword). Museo Arqueológico Nacional, Madrid.*

A Greek-type hoplite sword with iron scabbard found at Campovalano di Campli, 15km south-east of Ascoli in Italy. This type of sword was generally used in Italy prior to the introduction of the Spanish sword in the 4th or 3rd century BC.

Roman sword of the first half of the 1st century AD found at Rheingönheim in Germany. This is the famous long-pointed gladius hispaniensis, *an ideal weapon for thrusting.*

All the infantry were armed with a short double-edged sword (*gladius hispaniensis*) capable of cutting but designed primarily for thrusting. The wounds inflicted by this weapon horrified the Greeks, who had experience only of javelin, spear and arrow wounds. Livy, possibly quoting Polybius, refers to 'arms torn away, shoulders and all, heads separated from bodies with the necks completely severed, and stomachs ripped open'. This may be an exaggeration but certainly the last part is true. The name given to this sword betrays its Spanish origin but the literary sources do not reveal when or how it was adopted. It was certainly not introduced by Scipio Africanus, Polybius' hero, for if it had been the Greek historian would have mentioned it. It was probably introduced to Italy at a much earlier date, possibly as early as the 4th century BC, by Spanish mercenaries in the pay of either Greek colonists or the Etruscans.

Polybius states that the legionaries of the *hastati* and *principes* each carried two heavy javelins (*pila*). He adds that there were two types of *pila*, thick and slender, and implies that each legionary carried both.

Polybius' description of the sturdier *pilum* appears to be muddled and at odds with the archaeological evidence. The remains of several *pila* were found at Numantia in Spain, the site of a Roman siege in 133 BC. Only the metal parts of these weapons have survived. They have a long, thin iron shaft about 60 cm in length with an elongated, pyramid-shaped head. Some have a flat tang about 5 cm wide by which they were attached to the wooden shaft and others were socketed. These obviously represent Polybius' two types, the thick flat-tanged type and the slim socketed type. Polybius gives a complicated description of the tang extending half way down the wooden shaft and being secured with a multitude of rivets so that the wood and iron would not separate. This is probably a misunderstanding of his Latin source material, for it was essential that the weapon broke or buckled on impact so that the enemy could not throw it back.

The *triarii* were armed with long spears and formed the last-ditch defence, as they had in the 4th century. Their centuries were only 30 strong and even when the overall strength of the legion was increased, their numbers remained at this level. They were the last remnants of the strongly defensive legion. Sometimes they were not deployed on the battlefield but were left to guard the camp.

The *velites* were armed with a round shield (*parma*), about 0.9 m in diameter, and short javelins. Although very useful on campaign, where their flexibility enabled them to deal with small pockets of resistance, their use in a major battle was limited. Their role was to harasss the enemy with missile weapons before the battle began, beating up his advance and forming a screen covering the legions while they were being drawn up. They were withdrawn before the battle began and either remained behind the army or were sent to reinforce the cavalry on the wings.

The 300 cavalry were organized in ten troops (*turmae*), each *turma* being divided into three sections commanded by a *decurion*. The first *decurion* selected commanded the *turma* as a whole. The cavalry were armed with a round shield (*parma equestris*) and a sturdy spear with a metal point and butt so that the butt end could be used if the point broke off. It is possible that the cavalry also used the Spanish sword.

Each legion was commanded by six tribunes who were answerable to the general. Their job in battle, during this period and later, is far from clear. It is possible that two commanded each line.

Rome's allies, the nations conquered in previous wars, were obliged to supply infantry in numbers at least equal to the legionary levy and three times the Roman cavalry. The allies were almost certainly organized in cohorts, units of 400-500 men, rather than legions. The word legion is never used to describe an allied unit. It may have been normal for the allied towns or tribes to supply units composed of one maniple of each of the *hastati*, *principes* and *triarii* with their attendant *velites* and one or more *turmae* of cavalry. This was called a cohort (*cohors*).

The word cohort is first mentioned by Polybius when he is describing the campaigns of Scipio Africanus in Spain (206 BC). Livy also uses the word for the first time when describing the Spanish campaign but in a slightly earlier

opposite
Bas reliefs decorating the triumphal monument set up by the Roman general Aemilius Paullus at Delphi to celebrate his victory over the Macedonians at Pydna in 168 BC. The reliefs probably depict the skirmish between the opposing watering parties that led to the battle. Archaeological Museum, Delphi.

Top: a Macedonian soldier, with round shield, and a Roman legionary, with large oval shield, throwing his pilum, *and several cavalrymen.*

Centre: from left to right, a legionary fighting a Macedonian cavalryman, a legionary in a mail shirt and a Roman cavalryman also in a mail shirt.

Bottom: on the left, two Roman cavalrymen in mail shirts and two Macedonians. On the right are two more legionaries attacking a fallen Macedonian.

context (208). Livy mentions cohorts regularly during the years that follow the end of the Second Punic War. The first cohort to be mentioned by name is a cohort of the Marsi, a central Italian tribe, during the war against the Celts in northern Italy (196). The most illuminating reference to cohorts is in Livy's account of the events which precipitated the battle of Pydna (168). The account is of paramount importance as it is almost certainly drawn from Polybius, whom Livy claims to have followed for events in Greece. In this episode five cohorts are mentioned by name. Three of these, the Marrucini, Paeligni and Vestini, are drawn from tribal areas, all in central Italy and all long under terms of alliance with Rome. The other two are from Latin colonies at Firmum on the Adriatic coast and Cremona in the Po valley. Two allied *turmae* are also mentioned by name, which implies that the cohorts were there. These are both from Latin colonies and of particular interest is the fact that they are the partner colonies of the two just mentioned. Latin colonies were established in pairs. The two *turmae* are from Aesernia, the partner of Firmum (both founded in 264) and Placentia the partner of Cremona (both founded in 218).

Although not called a cohort by Livy, an earlier example of an allied cohort may be seen in the 500 Praenestines who in 216 BC were on their way to join the Roman army opposing Hannibal in Apulia. When they received news of the defeat at Cannae, they occupied the fortress of Casilinum (modern Capua). Here they withstood a Carthaginian siege lasting several months, surrendering only on the point of starvation. The Romans rewarded their bravery by granting them citizenship. The unit was commanded by a Praenestine *praetor*, Marcus Anicius.

This story is interesting for two reasons. First, it shows a unit of about 500 men drawn from one Latin town which had been made a Roman ally after the Latin War (*c.* 340). Secondly, it was commanded by a *praetor*, the original title for the chief magistrate of a Latin town. Rome's chief magistrates had also originally borne this name but at some time before 366 the title had been changed to consul. The old title survived in the name *praetorium* given to the site of the general's tent. The name *praetor* was reintroduced in 366 for a second-rank magistrate whose main job was supervising the administration of justice. By 197 the number had increased to six. Two of these were always in Spain, where Rome was forced to keep a permanent military presence.

It seems probable that the allies supplied cohorts, each consisting of a cross-section of those liable for military service under the command of local magistrates. Polybius states that the allies were divided into four wings (*alae*), two for each consular army of two legions. They were commanded by 12 prefects (*praefecti sociorum*), three for each *ala*. These were Romans and it is possible that they were matched by three senior officers of allied origin to bring them into line with the six tribunes of the legions. About 600 horsemen and 1,600 infantry were selected from the cream of the allies in each consular army to form the *extraordinarii*. These crack troops formed the vanguard on the march and supplied the consul's bodyguard. It is clear from Livy's account of the Ligurian war of 181 BC* that the infantry of the *extraordinarii* were divided into four cohorts.

The Army in the Field

Polybius' account is full of details of the Roman army on campaign, making it possible to reconstruct a picture of a 2nd-century consular army on the march, in camp and in battle.

At dawn the horn blower (*cornicen*) on duty outside the tent of the *primus pilus* sounded the end of the fourth watch announcing the beginning of a new

---

* Rome waged intermittent wars against the Ligurians in the later 3rd and early 2nd century for the control of the mountainous coastline around modern Genoa.

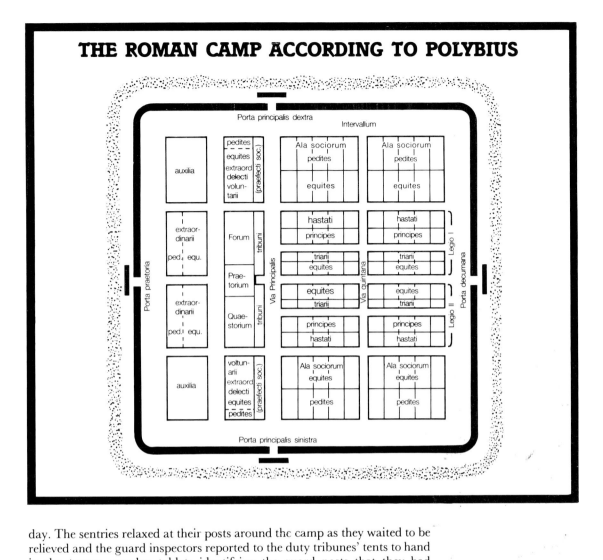

THE ROMAN CAMP ACCORDING TO POLYBIUS

Porta principalis dextra

Intervallum

auxilia

pedites
equites
extraord
delecti
volun-
tarii

(praefecti soc.)

Ala sociorum
pedites

Ala sociorum
pedites

equites

equites

extraor-
dinarii

ped. equ.

Forum

tribuni

hastati
principes

hastati
principes

Legio I

triarii
equites

triarii
equites

Porta praetoria

Via Principalis

Prae-
torium

Porta decumana

Via quintana

equites
triarii

equites
triarii

extraor-
dinarii

ped. equ.

Quae-
storium

tribuni

principes
hastati

principes
hastati

Legio II

auxilia

voltun-
arii
extraord
delecti
equites
pedites

(praefecti soc.)

Ala sociorum
equites

Ala sociorum
equites

pedites

pedites

Porta principalis sinistra

day. The sentries relaxed at their posts around the camp as they waited to be relieved and the guard inspectors reported to the duty tribunes' tents to hand in the *tesserae*, wooden tablets identifying the guard posts that they had inspected during the night. Soon the soldiers emerged from their tents, stretching and shivering in the chill morning air. They ate their breakfast amongst the armour and weapons in front of their tents as they waited for the second signal. When the horn sounded again, the duty maniples rushed off to take down the tents and pack the baggage of the senior officers, the consul, tribunes and prefects. They then dismantled their own tents and loaded their equipment on to the mules.

On the third blast of the horn the soldiers fell in, maniple by maniple in the *intervallum*, the 60 m space between the tents and the rampart. Legion I assembled beneath the rampart to the right of the rear gate (*porta decumana*). Legion II assembled in a similar position to the left of the rear gate. The allies formed up beneath the side ramparts, the right wing near the right side entrance (*porta principalis dextra*) and the left wing on the opposite side of the camp near the left entrance (*porta principalis sinistra*). Getting 20,000 men and their baggage out of camp was no easy task and would have been done in a systematic way, using all the gates. Even so, it would have taken several hours.

The *extraordinarii*, the cream of the allies, who were encamped around the general's tent, formed the vanguard and were the first to move out. They probably assembled at the front of the camp and would leave by the main gate (*porta praetoria*). In enemy territory the 600 horsemen of the *extraordinarii* would almost certainly have fanned out to form a protective screen ahead of the army, constantly on the lookout for ambushes and sending frequent messages back to the consul to keep him informed of the situation ahead.

Once the vanguard was on its way, the right wing of the allies moved out through the right side gate (*porta principalis dextra*) with its baggage train at the rear. It was followed by Legion I which left by the rear gate (*porta decumana*). Legion II was the next to leave, using the same gate. Each legion was followed by its own baggage train. The left wing of the allies, which formed the rearguard, moved out last using the left gate of the camp (*porta principalis sinistra*). Its baggage train was placed in front so that it could be more easily protected. The cavalry either rode behind its own legion/*ala* or on either side of the baggage train, keeping it in order and protecting it from attack. Roman cavalry horses were not shod and would have been obliged to keep off metalled roads.

Although the soldiers did not carry their food, cooking utensils, entrenching tools or personal belongings as they did 100 years later, each man wore his armour with his shield slung on a strap over his left shoulder and carried his weapons, either spear or javelins, and a bundle of palisade stakes.

A consular army of two legions plus its allied contingents and 2,400 cavalry stretched out for more than 20 km. Marching four abreast, as described by the Roman general Arrian, each legion must have extended about two kilometres. The Jewish historian Josephus describes the legions marching six abreast, but this would have been along wide Roman roads. Four abreast seems more likely in enemy territory where there were no Roman roads. Polybius recommends six feet (*c.* 1.8 m) per man so that they do not jostle each other. When marching in step, which both the Greeks and Romans must have done to perform complicated parade ground manoeuvres, it is possible to move in close order. But when marching in broken step carrying equipment, the soldiers had to march in open order, allowing about 2 m for each man to avoid jostling the man on either side or stumbling over the man in front should he trip or stop.

The baggage train, possibly as many as 2,000 mules per legion plus the siege weapons, must have more than doubled the length of the column. Further behind stretched an endless straggling line of camp followers: merchants of all kinds ready to meet the soldiers' every need and convert booty into hard cash; slave traders eager to buy the prisoners of war; slaves, girlfriends, and prostitutes. Before the last person had left the camp, the surveyors would already be looking for a site for the next one.

If an attack was threatened and the route was through open country, the army marched in battle order (*triplex acies*) with the *triarii, principes* and *hastati* in three parallel columns. This reduced the length of the army to 6-7 km. Each maniple was followed by its own baggage which presumably filled the gaps normally left between the maniples. If attacked, the baggage was moved behind the line and the gaps closed. Faced with an attack from the front, the army could easily wheel into line of battle. If the threat was from one flank the *hastati*, who formed the front line, formed up on that side. If an attack was then mounted from the other flank, the *hastati* would have to wheel round the front of the legion.

As the army neared the end of its march one of the tribunes and the centurions who formed the camp surveying unit were sent ahead to select a site for the camp. If contact had been made with the enemy, they looked for a site about 4 km from the enemy position close to a good water supply the enemy could not cut off or foul. The site had to be open, preferably on rising ground and with no cover which could be exploited by the enemy. The camp itself covered an area about 700 m square. A point which afforded maximum visibility was selected for the site of the consul's tent and a white flag was posted on the spot. A red flag was set up on the side nearest the water. Here the legions would camp. This was normally also the side nearest the enemy. The other key positions, the line of the roads and the ramparts, were similarly marked out so that by the time the army arrived each unit would know both where to leave its baggage and where to start work on the defences.

A marching camp was normally surrounded by a ditch three Roman feet (*c.* 0.9 m) deep. The earth was piled up on the inside, faced with turf and levelled off to form a low rampart. The two legions constructed the defences at the front and rear of the camp while the right and left wings of the allies built the right and left sides respectively. Each maniple was allotted a section about 25 m long. The centurions checked that the work of their maniples was done properly while a pair of tribunes or prefects supervised the overall work on each side of the camp.

Far stronger defences were needed when camping close to the enemy, and the work was likely to be hampered by attacks, particularly by enemy cavalry. Therefore as the army arrived all the cavalry, the light-armed troops and half the heavy infantry were deployed in defensive battle array in front of the projected line of the ditch facing the enemy. The baggage train was placed behind the line of the rampart and the remainder of the troops began to dig in. They dug a trench 12 Roman feet (3.6 m) wide and 9 feet (2.7 m) deep, piling up the earth on the inside to form a turf-faced rampart 4 feet (1.2 m) high.

On the march each soldier carried a bundle of sharpened stakes which were embedded in the top of the rampart to form a fence. The stakes were cut from sturdy branches and usually had two, three or at the most four lateral branches which were cut short and sharpened. They were planted close together in the rampart with the lateral branches intertwined so that it was hard to determine which branch belonged to which stake. This made it very difficult for more than one attacker to get hold of the same stake to pull it out and ensured that they would gash their hands in the attempt.

As work proceeded the infantry were gradually withdrawn from the battle line, maniple by maniple, starting with the *triarii* who were nearest the rampart. These troops were put to work digging the other sides of the camp. The cavalry were not withdrawn until the defences facing the enemy were complete.

Inside the Camp

Polybius' description of the inside of the camp is complicated and it is possible to interpret the details in more than one way. However, certain features are beyond dispute. Wherever possible the camp was laid out on a rectangular grid with two main roads intersecting at right angles near the centre of the camp. One of these roads, the 100 ft (30 m) wide *via principalis*, ran across the entire width of the camp, passing in front of the consul's tent (*praetorium*). The tents of the tribunes and prefects were pitched along this road on the same side as the *praetorium*. A second road (*via praetoria*), also 100 ft wide and running at right angles to the *via principalis*, was projected from the front of the *praetorium*. This was usually in the direction of the enemy. The two legions camped on either side of this road, Legion I on the right and Legion II on the left.

The legionary cavalry camped facing the road, each *turma* being allowed an area 100 ft (30 m) square in which to pitch their tents and tether their horses. The *triarii* encamped behind them, facing in the opposite direction, each maniple being allowed an area 100x50 Roman feet. A roadway 50 feet wide was left between the *triarii* and the *principes*, who pitched their tents opposite and facing them, each maniple being allotted a 100-foot square. The *hastati* were similarly encamped back to back with the *principes*. The allies pitched their tents in a similar way opposite the *hastati*, but would have required a much greater area for their cavalry.

The first maniples (*primi ordines*) were nearest the *via principalis* and the tenth maniples farthest away beneath the rampart. A space was left between the fifth and sixth maniples forming another road (*via quintana*).

This part of Polybius' description was confirmed early this century when a series of Late Republican camps were excavated at Renieblas in Spain. The excavations in Camp III, which is believed to be the camp Quintus Fulvius

Nobilior occupied in the winter of 153-152 BC, uncovered the remains of a large number of buildings including the foundations of a group of barrack blocks for half a legion or five allied cohorts encamped almost exactly as Polybius described. The barracks, being of stone, were built on a 130-foot (*c*. 40 m) grid, considerably larger than Polybius' 100-foot allowance for tents. The Greek historian completes his description of the interior arrangement of the camp by placing a market (*forum*) and supply depot (*quaestorium*) in the spaces on either side of the *praetorium*. The *extraordinarii* set up their tents behind these. A space 200 ft (60 m) wide was left between the tents and the rampart so that missiles thrown into the camp could not reach the tents. This space (*intervallum*) also served as a place for the army to assemble when preparing to leave camp.

Polybius adds that if the two consuls were operating together they camped back to back, forming a single oblong camp. This has led some commentators to suggest that Polybius was in fact describing half such a double camp and that in a single consular camp the troops would be more evenly distributed around the *praetorium*. There is much to recommend this view. The excavations in Camp III at Renieblas show a more even distribution of the troops but it must be pointed out that the position of the *praetorium* is unknown. Furthermore it is not a rectangular camp and is therefore atypical.

On the first night in camp everybody, including slaves, assembled before the tribunes where they individually swore the camp oath, vowing to steal nothing and to take anything they found to the tribunes. The soldiers then began setting up the tents. Those of the consul, tribunes and prefects were pitched first. Three maniples of the *hastati* or *principes* were allotted to each tribune on a three-day rota, one maniple taking on the duty each day. The duty maniples set up the tribunes' tents, levelled the area around them, fenced in their baggage and attended to their other needs. They also provided two guards, one for the front and one for the back of the tribune's tent. A guard consisted of four men who between them performed the duty round the clock. Eighteen of the *principes* and *hastati* maniples shared this duty. The other two were responsible for keeping the area in front of the tribunes' tents (*via principalis*) tidy, for it was here that the soldiers assembled during the day.

Each maniple of the *triarii* had to provide a guard (four men) for the cavalry *turma* behind it. They had to keep a general lookout and make sure the horses did not break loose or become caught up in their tethers. All the maniples took it in turn to stand guard round the consul's tent.

At sunset four men, one each from the tenth maniple of the *hastati*, *principes* and *triarii* and one from the tenth *turma* of the cavalry, reported to the duty tribune's tent to collect the password written on a wooden tablet. On returning to their quarters each man showed the password and then, in the presence of witnesses, passed it to the commander of the next maniple. So it passed up the line until it reached the first maniple whose centurion was bound to return it to the tribune before dark.

Besides the guards already mentioned who served round the clock, three overnight guards were posted at the stores depot (*quaestorium*) and two at the tents of each of the general's staff officers (*legati*). Guards from the *velites* were posted along the ramparts with ten at each gate. Each unit also appointed its own sentries for the night. These guards consisted of four men, one taking each of the four night watches. The centurions of the first maniple of the *triarii* were responsible for ensuring that the watches were sounded on the horn (*cornu*) at the correct times during the night. The men standing the first watch were escorted to the tribune's tent by their *optio* where they received a small tablet (*tessera*) identifying the position they had to guard.

Four men also reported to the tribune each evening. These were the cavalrymen whose duty it was to inspect the guards. The tribune divided the guard posts up amongst them in an arbitrary fashion so that the sentries could not know when they were to be visited. Each inspector was given one watch during which he had to inspect the posts on his list accompanied by two or three friends who acted as witnesses. During the night all the posts were visited. If awake, the sentry handed the *tessera* to the inspector; if asleep, the inspector passed on saying nothing. One can imagine the terror of the sentry who still had his *tessera* at daybreak, for it meant almost certain death if he had dozed off.

At dawn the guard patrols reported to the tribune and handed in the collected tablets. If a tablet was missing, the post was identified and the centurion of the maniple responsible was ordered to report to the tribune with the four sentries. The culprit, who was easily identified, stood immediate court-martial before the tribunes. If found guilty, the tribune touched him with a cudgel. He then had to run the gauntlet, being either beaten or stoned (*fustuarium*). Even if he managed to get out of the camp alive, he was doomed to live the rest of his life in exile. If it transpired that the guard inspector had failed to make his round properly, he suffered the same fate. Polybius adds that the night watches were most scrupulously kept.

Fustuarium was also inflicted on anyone giving false evidence and on soldiers who habitually committed the same offence. Minor offences were punished by fines or flogging. The worst offence a soldier could commit was desertion to the enemy. The surrender of these deserters was always demanded as part of the treaty arrangements after a successful campaign. They were often thrown to the wild beasts in the arena.

The tribunes, and presumably the prefects, were on duty in pairs. Dawn and dusk were their busiest times. At daybreak while one of the duty tribunes was receiving the reports of the guard patrols, the other had to attend the consul's dawn briefing where he received his orders for the day. He then returned to his tent where the centurions and decurions would be waiting. The chores for the day were allotted among the maniples, with the exception of the maniple which was on duty at the consul's tent. Having received their orders, the centurions returned to their maniples to select the men for the day's tasks.

A patrol consisting of a strong cavalry contingent, probably from the *extraordinarii*, sometimes reinforced by *velites* under the command of a senior tribune or the consul himself, would be sent out to inspect the enemy position. Sometimes the centurions of the *primi ordines* accompanied the consul. Once the area had been reconnoitred, the consul called a council of war to discuss the situation and the advisability of offering battle. The council of war was attended by the consul's staff officers, *legati*, (senators invited along on the campaign by the consul), the tribunes, prefects and the centurions of the *primi ordines*. This last class must have included the chief decurions of the cavalry.

The council of war was purely advisory. The final decision lay with the consul. If he decided to offer battle immediately, a red flag was hoisted outide his tent to inform the soldiers who would leave their chores, collect their weapons and assemble beneath the ramparts as they did when preparing to march.

The Army in Battle

The cavalry and the *velites* were sent out first to harass the enemy, encouraging him to accept the offer of battle, and to keep him at bay while the heavy infantry were being drawn up for battle. A strong force was tasked with holding the camp. If the consul felt certain of victory, this job was sometimes given the *triarii*. The legions would then move out through the rear gate (*porta decumana*), which normally faced the enemy, and the allies through the two side gates, putting them in the correct positions for the battle line.

If the consul seriously intended to offer battle, he moved the army forward until it was out of range of covering fire from the artillery in the Roman camp. If he was simply making a gesture, usually to raise the morale of the troops, he would line up just in front of the ramparts, under cover of his artillery and archers, a position from which it was easy to withdraw to the camp if the situation became threatening.

The infantry were drawn up with the *hastati* at the front, but well out of range of the enemy artillery. The *principes* formed the second line and the *triarii* the third. In all three lines the maniples were drawn up with a space equal to the width of a maniple between them. This was probably accomplished by withdrawing the *posterior* centuries and placing them behind the *prior* centuries, the space between the maniples being equal to the width of a century. This is the only reasonable explanation of Polybius' claim that at Cannae (216 BC) the maniples were 'many times deeper than they were wide'. This is not conceivable with the two centuries side by side. Such a description would demand that each century had a maximum width of three and a depth of twenty, whereas a six by ten formation for a century, with the *posterior* centuries behind the *prior* centuries, would give the same overall dimension and be totally acceptable. A space of about 200 m was probably left between each line, keeping the second and third lines out of missile range.

When the heavy infantry had been drawn up in its three lines and were ready to engage, the trumpets sounded to recall the *velites* who had been skirmishing between the two armies. The light-armed troops withdrew through the gaps left in the maniples and retired to the rear of the army. The posterior centuries of the *hastati* moved up to close the gaps in the line. The trumpets sounded again and they began to advance slowly on the enemy. When they had closed to about 100 m they raised their warcry and started to bang their long javelins against their shields. Then, at a range of about 50 m, they broke into a run, hurling their *pila* into the mass of the approaching enemy. The *pila* were launched at a range of about 30 m. In the confusion caused by the hail of heavy javelins they drew their swords and, with their left shoulders hard against the inside of the shields, charged into the enemy, trying to knock their opponents off balance. The enemy, forced to shield themselves against the barrage of *pila*, would have had little or no time to recover before sustaining the impact of the charge. The result was to throw them back and destroy the impetus of their own charge. Undoubtedly the Romans had also been showered with missiles as they advanced, but the *pilum* was uniquely effective. Its thin pyramid-shaped point and long metal shaft were capable of piercing a shield, with the weight of the wooden shaft driving it on until it reached the man sheltering behind it. Once it had penetrated a shield, the shape of the point made it very difficult to extract, rendering the shield unmanageable. If it stuck in a shield without going right through, or hit the ground, the weight of the wooden haft would normally cause the thin iron shaft to buckle, making it impossible for the enemy to throw it back with any serious effect.

This brings us back to the question of the two *pila*. It would have been impossible to throw two such heavy javelins one after the other during the charge. The *pilum* is a short-range weapon and there would not be time to throw two. It seems equally unlikely that the legionary held his second *pilum* inside his shield while fighting. The shield (*scutum*) is curved and has a horizontal handgrip following the curve, which makes it virtually impossible to hold a javelin in the left hand as the Greeks did. Other suggestions seem just as improbable. One can only conclude that Polybius knew that each soldier carried two *pila* on the march. *Pila* were not personal weapons, any more than were the palisade stakes carried by the legionaries. The second *pilum* was probably left stacked behind the lines, to be used only if the *hastati* or *principes* were required to enter the battle a second time.

The *hastati* bore the first shock of battle. Hand-to-hand fighting with a sword would be of very limited duration. The men of the rear ranks would, in time, move forward to play their part, pushing their way in alongside the man engaged and taking over at an opportune moment. If there was a lull in the fighting, as there often was, the *hastati* could fall back on the *principes*, open the gaps in their line and pass through the gaps in the *principes'* line. The *principes*, would then charge as the *hastati* had. The charge of the *principes*, who were the cream of the army, was normally sufficient to clinch the battle.

If the *hastati* were unable to disengage, the *principes* could deploy their centuries and filter through in the same way that individuals took over from the man in the front rank, and so relieve maniples which were under pressure. There was adequate room for this manoeuvre as a legionary was normally allowed six Roman feet (*c.* 1.75 m) in which to fight.

The *triarii* knelt on their right knees with their shields resting against their left shoulders to protect them from missiles. Their spear butts were stuck in the ground with the spears pointing obliquely forward like a palisade. This description is derived from Livy's account of the Roman army at the time of the Latin War (340 BC), but the function of the *triarii* had not changed and there is no reason to consider this formation anachronistic. If defeated, the *hastati* and *principes* retreated on the *triarii* and passed through their line. The *triarii* then closed their gaps and retreated to the camp, presenting a hedge of spears to the enemy, just as they had 200 years before.

This was the theory, but it could unravel in practice. At Cannae (216), where Rome suffered her greatest defeat, the consuls were over-confident. The defeats inflicted by Hannibal at the Trebbia (218) and Lake Trasimene (217) were attributed to the incompetence of the generals. At Cannae, the Romans fielded an army which massively outnumbered Hannibal's troops. With both consuls present, they scorned to consider the possibility of defeat. It was their singular misfortune to encounter one of history's great commanders. With supreme self-confidence, they appear to have left the *triarii* to guard the camp. When Hannibal's cavalry stripped the wings and attacked the rear of the Roman line, there were no *triarii* to hold them off. Well-armed spearmen could have held such cavalry at bay.

The defeat at Cannae underlines the weakness of the Roman system. At the Trebbia the legions had managed to break through the Carthaginian centre. This was the basic Roman tactic. It shattered the cohesion of the enemy army and in the past had always led to victory. Seldom was anything more imaginative tried. At Cannae the Romans massed their centre, determined to break through the Spaniards and Celts forming the centre of Hannibal's line. Not only was it using a sledgehammer to crack a nut, it was also a total misuse of swordsmen. It was the tactic of a pike phalanx. The fate of the Roman centre must have been much the same as that suffered by the medieval French infantry at Agincourt (1415), where they were so tightly packed that they could not manoeuvre. The Roman legionary needed 2 m of space in which to operate efficiently. This would have been impossible with rank upon rank pushing from behind. An additional factor was the 'tumbling effect' – a term coined by the military historian John Keegan – as the Romans, pushed on from behind, were forced to clamber over their own and the enemy dead, disrupting their ranks. Hannibal's men had no such problem as they were giving ground.

The disaster at Cannae reflected Roman miltary method at its most pig-headed. It took a genius to identify the reasons for defeat and remedy them. That genius was the young Publius Cornelius Scipio who was probably present at both the Trebbia and Cannae. At the age of 25 (210) he assumed command of the Roman forces in Spain and effected a complete tactical revolution. He knew that he had to find a way to use Roman troops, unquestionably the best in the world, in the same way that the Carthaginians used theirs. In the battles of Baecula (208) and Ilipa (206) he experimented to find a method of using Roman troops for a pincer movement. This was refined in North Africa where at the battle of the Great Plains (203) he successfully engulfed a Carthaginian army, using his *hastati* to hold the centre and deploying the *principes* and *triarii* on the wings after the battle had started. His crowning victory was at Zama (202) where he caught Hannibal and his Italian veterans in the same movement.

Rome had broken out of the straitjacket; things were never to be the same again. There were young men coming up who were weaned on the new tactics.

THE BATTLE OF ZAMA

STAGE 1

The Romans drew up their forces in the usual fashion with the legions in the centre flanked by the allies. The Italian horse were placed on the left wing opposite the Carthaginian cavalry and the Numidians on the right. The maniples were drawn up behind each other to leave gaps through the army. These were filled by the *velites*. Hannibal drew up his troops in three lines with the mercenaries in front, then the Liby-Phoenicians and Carthaginians, and finally his veterans at the rear. In front were elephants and light-armed troops.

1 Numidian cavalry
2 *Triarii*
3 *Principes*
4 *Hastati*
5 Italian Cavalry

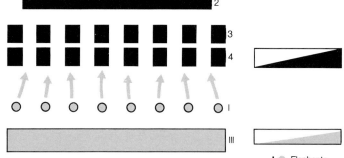

I ● Elephants
II Numidian cavalry
II Numidian cavalry
III Mercenaries
IV Carthaginians and Liby-Pheonicians
V Veterans
VI Carthaginian cavalry

STAGE 2

When the elephants charged they were attacked by the *velites* and drawn through the gaps in the line. The superior Roman cavalry drove off the Carthaginian horse and the legions advanced. The *hastati* broke the two front lines, driving them back on Hannibal's veterans. These levelled their spears to stop the fugitives from disrupting their formation, forcing them out on to the wings.

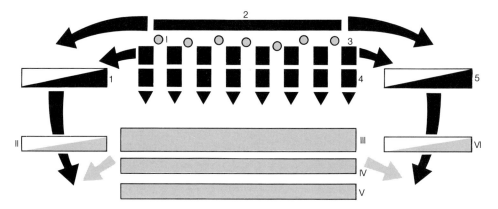

STAGE 3

Scipio now deployed his *triarii* and *principes* on the wings to outflank the Carthaginian forces. The veterans held on until taken in rear by the Roman cavalry.

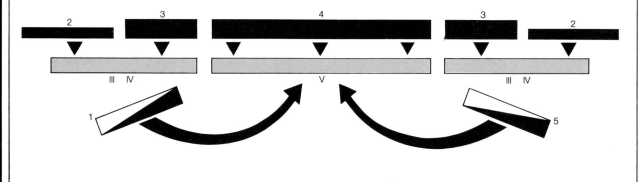

At the battle of Cremona (200) the praetor Lucius Furius held his centre with his allied forces and used his legions to engulf the wings of a Celtic army.

The cohort too was gradually taking over as the tactical unit, particularly for irregular warfare. Polybius' description of the cohort used by Scipio in Spain makes it quite clear that he is not just referring to allied units for he says 'the Romans call three maniples a cohort'. In 206 Scipio used such cohorts against Spanish hill tribes where there was no space to deploy a legion. As early as 200 the consul, Publius Sulpicius, employed cohorts under the command of tribunes, and therefore legionary, to try to dislodge the Macedonian forces of Philip V which had taken up a strongly defensive position in the hills. Although this example is found in Livy, who is not the most reliable source, it is probably derived from the lost account of Polybius. This use of cohorts is to be seen in the Balkans, Liguria and Spain, all mountainous areas. Cato's army in Spain (195) appears to be divided totally into cohorts. The *triarii*, *principes* and *hastati* were still used for pitched battles but they had become much more flexible.

The Army in Spain

In 218, at the very beginning of the war with Hannibal, the Romans had invaded Spain. They established a bridgehead at Emporiae (Ampurias) just south of the Pyrenees, with the aim of cutting Hannibal's supply route from southern Spain to Italy. This daring and imaginative move proved brilliantly successful and within a short time Rome had gained control of the entire north-eastern coast of Spain, bottling up the Carthaginian forces in the south. It was the beginning of Rome's longest military involvement, for although the Carthaginians were driven out of Spain by 206, Rome's long-drawn-out war with the tribes of the interior was not brought to an end until 133 and the pacification of the peninsula was not completed until the reign of Augustus in 19 BC, 200 years after the Romans first invaded.

After the defeat of Carthage, Macedon and Syria, the legions had been withdrawn and disbanded but in Spain, where the war seemed never-ending, the first permanent legions came into being, numbered five to eight. The Fifth, Seventh and Eighth are mentioned by Livy. Two praetors were sent to Spain each year with some 8,000 infantry and 500 cavalry to keep the four legions (*c.* 35,000 men) serving there up to strength. Allowing for losses, this suggests a six-year turn-round, which seems to be confirmed by Appian who, during the campaign of Pompeius in 140, refers to soldiers being replaced after six years.

Spain became the training ground of the Roman army and it was there that most innovations took place. But recruitment was difficult. Most men did not wish to spend several years away from farm and family and it appears that the property requirement for military service had to be constantly revised to obtain sufficient recruits. But what appeared a burden for some proved the salvation of others, as many of Rome's poorest citizens realized that a brave man could cut out a career for himself in a way that had never before been possible. It was the beginning of the era of the professional soldier.

Spurius Ligustinus

Livy records the career of such a man, Spurius Ligustinus, an impoverished farmer with a tiny plot of land. He was called up in 200 to fight in the Second Macedonian War. In his third year of service he was rewarded for his bravery with promotion to centurion in the tenth maniple of the *hastati*. He was discharged on his return to Italy after the defeat of Philip V, but in 195 he signed on for the army in Spain, where he was promoted to the *primi ordines* as *primus hastatus prior*. Four years later he joined the army which was to fight against Antiochus the Great in Asia Minor. Here he was promoted to *primus princeps prior*. He was discharged when this army returned to Italy and served for two years in consular armies in Italy which were disbanded at the end of

SCIPIO'S OUTFLANKING MANOEUVRE BEFORE THE BATTLE OF ILIPA

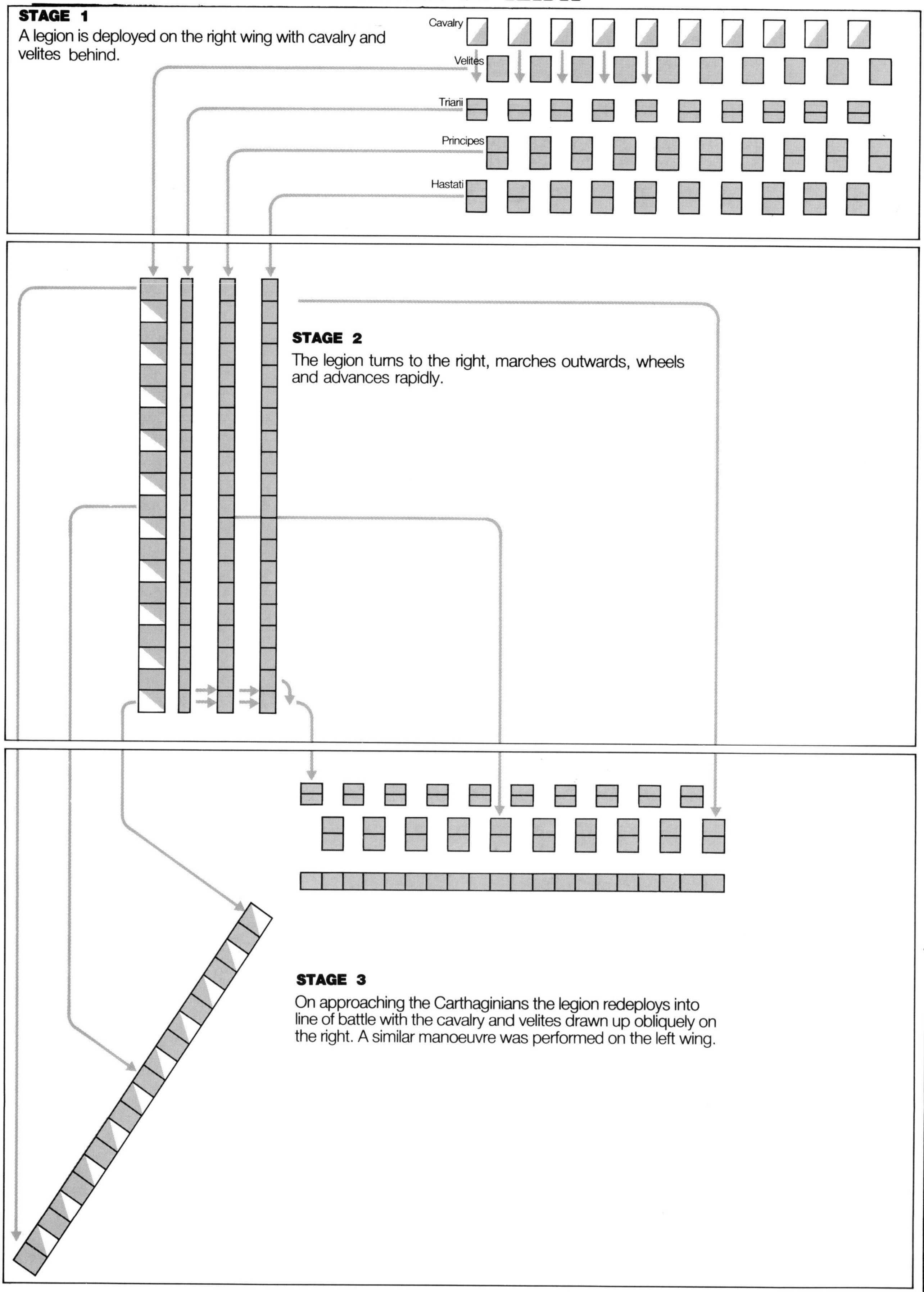

STAGE 1

A legion is deployed on the right wing with cavalry and velites behind.

Cavalry

Velites

Triarii

Principes

Hastati

STAGE 2

The legion turns to the right, marches outwards, wheels and advances rapidly.

STAGE 3

On approaching the Carthaginians the legion redeploys into line of battle with the cavalry and velites drawn up obliquely on the right. A similar manoeuvre was performed on the left wing.

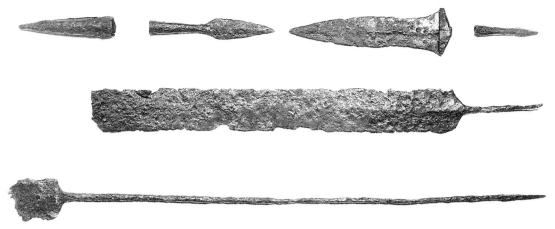

each year. He then returned to Spain, putting in two more terms there.

By 170 he had 22 years' service behind him – 16 years was the maximum a man could be forced to serve. In his latter years in Spain he had been *primus pilus* four times. He was decorated 34 times and had won six civic crowns, each awarded for saving the life of a Roman citizen. Although now over 50, he went on to be *primus pilus* again in Legion I, serving under the consul in the Third Macedonian War. Ligustinus' career is exceptional, but many impoverished farmers found their salvation in the army.

The long-service soldiers in Spain produced many problems that Rome had not encountered before. The recruitment of the landless poor was a problem in itself, for the Roman soldier traditionally fought not just for the state but for the preservation of his own lands. They also had nowhere to retire when they were no longer fit for service. This problem was underlined by Tiberius Gracchus when he returned from Spain after serving as *quaestor* there in 137 BC and tried to get land grants for the dispossessed poor. There was also the perennial problem of long-service troops in foreign lands – their associations with the local women. In 171 the Roman senate had to deal with the question of the troops' irregular marriages to Spanish women and the 4,000 children they had fathered.

Spain was the Roman El Dorado, a breeding ground for avarice and treachery, where governors lied, cheated and killed in their frantic search for gold and silver. Corruption became the norm. Treaties made by governors were casually disregarded or disavowed by the senate. The situation reached rock bottom in 137 BC when the governor Mancinus and his army were trapped and forced to agree to a treaty. The senate repudiated the agreement and handed Mancinus over to the Spaniards in chains.

For some years the war against the Celtiberians had been concentrated around the northern hill fort of Numantia, where the Roman forces had suffered a series of reverses caused mainly by the perfidy of the governors and the lack of morale amongst the troops. The senate finally acted in 134, sending Polybius' patron, Scipio Aemilianus, to Spain with the full authority of the state to bring the war to a satisfactory conclusion. Aemilianus had been a tribune in Spain in 149 and probably understood the situation well. He had commanded the Roman forces during the siege of Carthage in 146 when the city, once master of the Western Mediterranean, was destroyed and its people sold into slavery.

Aemilianus was a strict disciplinarian. On his arrival in Spain he threw all the traders and prostitutes out of the camp and introduced a Spartan regime. By the summer of 133 morale had been restored and he laid siege to Numantia. Starvation achieved what Roman arms had failed to do and the conqueror meted out the same treatment he had given to Carthage. The town was so thoroughly destroyed that even its site was forgotten.

At the beginning of the 20th century Numantia was rediscovered and the siege camps around the town excavated, revealing many details of Roman

Weaponry excavated in the Roman camps around and near Numantia. Top row from left: spear butt, spear head, dagger blade, catapult bolt head. Centre: part of a Celtic sword blade. Bottom: head of a pilum.
The dagger blade is 20cm long, the rest are in proportion. Römisch-Germanisches Zentralmuseum, Mainz.

opposite
Scipio was determined to convert his forces into a new-style, flexible army capable of performing Carthaginian tactics. Arriving in Spain in 210 BC, he found the legions there still demoralized after their defeat by the Carthaginians the previous year. But he was able to restore their confidence through a programme of intense training, and by 208 BC he was ready to test his new tactics in the field. At the battle of Baecula in 208 BC he managed to engulf the enemy's wings, but the vastly experienced Carthaginian commander, Hasdrubal, Hannibal's brother, managed to extricate his army and withdraw. Two years later he had far greater success with a similar tactic at Ilipa. Polybius' description of the Roman manoeuvres at the beginning of the battle has caused considerable debate and understandable scepticism, for they are more fitted to the parade ground than the battlefield.

weaponry and siege technique. A series of superimposed camps were also found 8 km away on a hill overlooking the village of Renieblas. These camps appear to be from a series of campaigns waged in the area between 153 and 80 BC. The internal buildings confirm many of the details in Polybius' description of the Roman camp.

The ability to reduce strongholds by siege was as important as victory in pitched battle. During Polybius' era the Romans were involved in many sieges varying from minor hill forts to major cities. The most famous are the sieges of Syracuse, Capua, Taranto, Carthage and Numantia. Polybius probably witnessed the last two, but unfortunately his account is lost. The Romans were unable to storm any of these places, and they appeared to have little faith in Greek mechanized siege warfare. At the siege of Syracuse in 213 they do not even appear to have had catapults.

If they were unable to storm the walls, the Romans preferred to blockade a town and wait for starvation or treachery to do their work. In this respect, although on a small scale, Numantia was a typical Roman siege. The siege lines around Numantia were very similar to those thrown up around Masada in Israel more than 200 years later. A series of camps were established at key points around Numantia at intervals of scarcely more than one-third of a mile. These were joined by a wall fronted with a ditch which cut the defenders off from outside help. The river was booby-trapped with spiked logs to stop boats and swimmers getting in or out. If a relief force had been expected, a second wall or rampart fronted by ditches would have been built facing outwards and the besieging army would have operated between the two walls.

The fall of Numantia marked the end of a great era of conquest and Rome entered an era of civil strife. But one short war took place which rounded off Rome's conquests in the West. Through all the years of fighting in Spain, Rome had been compelled to supply her forces by sea, but in 121 southern Gaul was invaded and the southern coastal strip (*Gallia Narbonensis*) annexed, opening a long-needed land route to Spain.

PRINCIPAL SOURCES

Livy (59 BC-AD 17)

A Roman historian; born at Padua in the Po valley. He wrote a history of Rome down to the time of Augustus, of which the last part, from 167 BC onwards, is lost. A useful source but with a poor grasp of military matters.

Dionysius of Halicarnassus (fl 30-8 BC)

Greek historian teaching at Rome who wrote a history of Rome down to the first Punic War. An indifferent historian but useful for giving the Greek word for military items, which sometimes clarifies matters.

Polybius (*c.* 203-*c.* 120 BC)

A Greek historian who was involved in the third Macedonian War, after which he was sent to Rome as a hostage and became a close friend of Scipio Aemilianus. He wrote a history of his own times which included a detailed description of the Roman army. Much of his work is lost, including all but fragments of the whole of the second half of the work. An invaluable source for our knowledge of the Roman army at this period.

Appian (*c.* AD 100- AD 170)

A Greek historian from Alexandria who moved to Rome *c.* AD 125. He wrote a history of Rome's wars which is useful for filling in the missing parts of Polybius, one of his main sources. However, it shows little knowledge of geography and is often oversimplified.

THE ROMAN ARMY OF
THE LATER REPUBLIC

LAWRENCE KEPPIE

By the later 2nd century BC, Rome had become the dominant power in the Mediterranean world. The ensuing century witnessed the army, now at the peak of its power as an offensive force, engaged against wild Celtic and Germanic tribes in the underdeveloped West, against sophisticated empires in the East, and finally against itself. Substantial areas were added to Roman domains. The army's tactics and weaponry were put to the test in unfamiliar terrains. The period is one of the best documented in the literary record; but inscriptions, which are so important later towards a picture of the army's institutions and of the origins, postings and promotion patterns of its members, are extremely few. In the absence of permanent military installations, archaeology makes only a limited contribution to our knowledge, with the exception of Caesar's campaigns in Gaul. This was to be a period of prolonged warfare, when Roman forces grew to unprecedented strength, and of revolt and civil unrest in Italy, which spilled over into the provinces.

Marius and the Roman Army

During the final two decades of the 2nd century BC, a troublesome foe appeared – Jugurtha, King of Numidia on the western flank of Rome's African province. A succession of Roman commanders proved incapable of restraining his ambitions, or were bribed to overlook them. The appointment of the consul of 109, the aristocrat Caecilius Metellus, brought a great improvement: Metellus stiffened discipline and morale in his forces, and opened hostilities in earnest. But the Roman public were anxious for immediate victory, and elected as consul for 107 Gaius Marius, who had been serving with distinction as a legate to Metellus, and who had returned home to stand as a candidate.

In a speech delivered before the people on the evening of his election as consul for 107, Marius complained loudly about the lack of professionalism among his high-born predecessors and promised competent leadership of the Roman army in the field. Marius is portrayed in our sources as an uncouth, unpleasant and intolerant countryman who had elbowed his way into the top echelons of Roman society. Despite his ringing speech (which calls to mind that delivered by General Montgomery to the staff of Eighth Army behind the Ruweisat Ridge in August 1942), Marius was initially no more successful than his predecessors in the mobile warfare of the hilly Numidian semi-desert, until the war ended abruptly in 105 with the capture of Jugurtha.

While he was still in Africa, Marius found himself elected consul for a second time for the year 104. This was against all precedent, which required a ten-year gap between tenures. While he was campaigning in Africa, Italy came under more serious threat from the north. Migrating German tribes (Cimbri and Teutones) had inflicted several reverses on Roman forces in southern Gaul, culminating in a massive defeat at Orange in 105 when at least 20,000 legionaries, and an equal or greater number of allies, fell. The invasion of Italy by these tribes, which awakened memories of earlier Gallic incursions, seemed imminent.

Marius went north in 104, and established his headquarters at Arles; but the tribes had moved westwards to the Pyrenees. Marius was now re-elected

TABLE OF EVENTS   118 – 30 BC

118	Jugurtha king in Numidia.
109	Caecilius Metellus consul, given command in Africa.
107	Gaius Marius consul.
106	Jugurtha captured.
105	Romans defeated at Arausio.
102	Teutones defeated.
101	Cimbri defeated.
91-88	Social War.
88	Sulla consul.
87-83	Sulla in Greece and Asia Minor.
82	Sulla dictator.
78	Death of Sulla.
80-72	Sertorius in Spain.
73-71	Revolt of Spartacus.
74-66	Lucullus in Asia.
66-62	Pompey in the East.
60	First Triumvirate.
59	Caesar consul.
58-49	Caesar in Gaul.
53	Crassus defeated at Carrhae.
52	Siege of Alesia; Vercingetorix surrenders.
49	Caesar crosses Rubicon.
48	Battle of Pharsalus.
44	Caesar assassinated, Ides of March.
43	Second Triumvirate.
42	Battle of Philippi.
41-40	Perusine War in Italy.
36	Sextus Pompeius defeated and killed.
31	Battle of Actium.
30	Suicide of Antony and Cleopatra.

consul for successive years, from 103 to 100. He thus gained time to retrain and re-equip his army. Good work had already been done by a predecessor Rutilius Rufus who introduced trainers from a gladiatorial school, some of them doubtless themselves Gauls, to improve the soldiers' weapons-handling. The tribes were finally brought to battle, the Teutones defeated at Aquae Sextiae (Aix-en-Provence) in 102 and the Cimbri at Vercellae in the Po Valley, in 101.

Marius' Reforms

Marius' name appears regularly in any account of Roman history as a major military reformer, a man by whose efforts the machinery of war, unchanged for centuries and more suited to local conflicts in Italy than to long drawn-out struggles far from home, was brought into line with current realities. Marius had both motive and opportunity to effect radical change, but it may be doubted if his personal contribution was as great as is sometimes claimed.

Two major reforms are nowadays ascribed to Marius. The first was his sweeping away of the old system by which men were conscripted for a fairly short span of six years and their replacement by volunteers who remained under arms for much longer periods. Thus was the army converted from a force of disciplined amateurs to one of professional fighters. Many of the ancient historians, and certainly many modern scholars, blame Marius for a subsequent change in attitude among the soldiery, which later threatened the very existence of the state as they knew it.

During his preparations for the campaign against Jugurtha, Marius had been authorized to hold a levy to raise extra troops to fill out the depleted ranks of the two legions already in Africa. This was normal practice; but it represented a political trap, as such levies were extremely unpopular with the smallholders and propertied classes which still formed the backbone of the legions. However, men attracted by the prospect of booty and Marius' military reputation did come forward as volunteers. In addition Marius called for volunteers from the *capite censi*, a class of citizenry who owned no property and were thus normally excluded from military service. The sources represent this as a revolutionary act, with far-reaching consequences, but it had been done before, on occasions of national emergency, for example during the war against Pyrrhus and at the time of Cannae. Here, as before, it seems no more than a one-off expedient. To maximize the numbers elegible for military service, the old property qualification for army service had been reduced (or retariffed) several times over the preceding century, and was now at a low level. It had already fallen below the point at which all those enlisting could afford to equip themselves for war. Some weapons were now provided, and in 122 the tribune Gaius Gracchus had a law passed through the popular assembly which for the first time required the state to provide a soldier's clothing. The sources do not claim that Marius abolished the property qualification; more likely it remained, at least for another generation.

The transition from amateur militia to a professional long-service army had been gathering pace throughout the previous century, and continued to do so. As the distance from Rome and the length of campaigns increased, generals looked to experienced men to provide continuity, and the percentage of such men in any legion undoubtedly grew. But the legal framework for raising an army did not change. The oath which the solders took bound them, as before, to serve their commander until released. Men conscripted at a formal levy (*dilectus*) were required to serve a minimum of six years, after which they could look for discharge, and agitate if they did not receive it. This combination of long-service near-professionals and short-service conscripts within the Roman army was not to be resolved until Augustus' far-reaching reforms of 13 BC.

Marius is also credited with a long-lasting tactical reform, by which he regrouped the soldiers of the legions into ten cohorts instead of 30 maniples. There is no specific reference to this regrouping in our sources, and it may be that the change was already of long standing by Marius' time. At most, the

Legionaries depicted on the 'Altar of Domitius Ahenobarbus', Rome, c.115 BC. The soldiers wear mail shirts, crested helmets, short swords and carry oval shields. Musée National du Louvre, Paris.

Roman cavalry locked in combat with Gallic warriors, on an Augustan period arch at Orange, southern France.

cohort system, well suited to an army garrisoning large areas in often difficult terrain, may now have been extended to the battlefield itself. It is clear that the new cohort consisted of one maniple each of the old *hastati*, *principes* and *triarii* (alternatively called *pilani*), together (probably) with some *velites*, a total of some 400 men. It was a convenient subdivision of the legion, capable of independent action. The idea seems likely to derive from the organization of the allied contingents which were provided annually to serve with the legions, and who would stand side by side in the battle line.

The old organization was not entirely swept away: under the Empire ground-plans of legionary fortresses (and auxiliary forts) show a preference for grouping barrack-blocks in facing pairs. Moreover, the centurions of each cohort under the Empire were named *pilus prior* and *posterior*, *princeps prior* and *posterior*, and *hastatus princeps* and *posterior*, reflecting their old status in the Republican battle line; old titles die hard. Indeed such titles, epigraphically reported down to the Late Empire, suggest that the first cohort was formed from those maniples of the *hastati*, *principes* and *triarii* which had originally stood on the extreme right of the old battle line, and so on in due sequence. Thus the maniples which had once stood at the extreme left of the line formed the tenth cohort. Specific evidence for the arrangement of cohorts in battle is lacking before the time of Caesar, but from his writings it is evident that they were distributed into three lines as distinct entities; the soldiers of individual cohorts were not themselves divided into three lines. The provision of arms and weapons from state factories, already normal by Marius' time, must have encouraged uniformity of equipment, militating against the old divisions. We last hear of the lightly-armed *velites* in Sallust's account of Metellus' campaign against Jugurtha. Henceforth soldiers seem to be equipped uniformly with the *pilum*, the oval *scutum*, and short *gladius*, and mail shirt. One small change in weaponry is ascribed to Marius by Plutarch: before Marius' time the *pilum* was attached to its wooden shaft by two iron pins. Marius had one of these pins replaced by a wooden nail, which would break on impact, making it impossible for the *pilum* to be thrown back, and more difficulat to dislodge from a shield.

According to the Elder Pliny (writing in the later 1st century AD), Marius made the eagle the chief standard of each legion, replacing other symbols such as wolves, boars, minotaurs and horses which had been used hitherto. This suggests a fresh focus of loyalty, which might be linked to organizational change. Festus (writing in the late 2nd century AD) notes that Marius made the legion 6,200 men strong, instead of the 4,000-man total which had previously been the norm. This may mean simply that in an emergency he filled out the few legions assigned to him beyond the normal complement, a procedure which Polybius also notices. The mainstream historical sources assume 5,000 or 6,000 men for a legion during the next 50 years; but they were often substantially understrength, being reduced by battle casualties and normal wastage to 3,000 or less.

Neither the training programmes ascribed to Marius, which included running under full kit, route marching and the carrying of one's own baggage, nor the army's strict, unrelenting discipline, constituted any originality of thinking. Rather they marked a return to the standards of earlier generations, which had been allowed to lapse, and were to lapse again. But henceforth the shambling gait of the heavily burdened legionary gained him the nickname 'Marius' mule' and the name of Marius has come down through the centuries as the archetypal Roman general.

No particular rewards had ever been envisaged for Roman legionaries, whose service under arms was regarded as a civic duty and responsibility, though donatives could be offered to a victorious army on the occasion of a Triumph. Occasionally, when colonies were being founded to consolidate Rome's control in Italy, men who had served in the army were accorded special allocations of land. However, even if the award of land was never accepted as a formal climax to service, those soldiers who had served long periods looked to the time when their service would end, and, with home ties increasingly loosened by long years under arms, they hoped to start a new life. The prospect of a sizeable plot of land, and an expectation of social advancement which it would bring, were important to the soldiers of the late republic, who made their wishes clear to their commanders. But the practice was resisted by the senate and all the landowning classes. Italy was already farmed intensively and the land fully developed; soldiers could only be accommodated at the expense of existing owners. Only in exceptional circumstances, as we shall see, were the soldiers successful in obtaining the land they so much desired.

The longer the period served, and the further the distance from Italy, the greater the bond that was formed between the soldiers and their commander. Eventually they came to resemble a private army. But the formal nature of the relationship had not changed: these were citizens in arms, under the leadership of an elected magistrate, in or more often after his year of office at Rome. By Marius' time, a recruit could see service from Spain to Turkey, in North Africa or Greece. But for the most part he had no say in the location of that service, be sure how long it would last, or know who his commander would be. Only time-served men who volunteered had any choice. By the end of the 2nd century BC there were usually six to eight legions under arms each year, some of them in more or less permanent garrisons, but their number fluctuated and the dispositions were altered according to current needs. If a campaign ended and a province no longer needed troops, the men were released into civilian life, not transferred elsewhere.

The Social War

The steady onward progess of Roman power and influence was jolted in the later 90s BC by the outbreak of civil war within Italy itself. Rome's Italian allies had shared the military burdens of expansion, but had been largely excluded from the social and financial rewards of empire. Down to this time they had continued to supply annually at least an equivalent force to the legions, and often more. Their discontent had been simmering for a considerable time. In 91 it boiled over into a revolt, known as the Social War. This was a campaign for civil rights, and equality of civic status and opportunity. Eventually, after a rude shock, the senate conceded virtually all the Italian demands; but there was hard fighting throughout Italy in 90-89.

The Social War had one immediate effect on army organization: the distinction between legions and the *alae sociorum* ceased to have any purpose. All Italians living south of the River Po were now full Roman citizens and could serve in legions. It is hard to say how great a practical difference this made, except that the old allied contingents had preserved a local identity and coherence. This was not carried forward, and legions might be recruited throughout peninsular Italy. The total number of legions in service automatically rose, and in the following decades there were seldom fewer than a dozen in service in any one year. The place of the allies as auxiliaries was

CROSSING THE RUBICON

The confrontation between Caesar and the Senate came to a head in the winter of 50-49. On 10 January Caesar decided to act. He ordered the XIII Legion, then at Ravenna, to march southwards to the boundary of his province which lay on the line of a minor river, the Rubicon. The river had acquired its special importance only by the administrative accident that it formed the northern limit of the territory of the Roman town of Ariminum (now Rimini), which was the first town lying within Italy itself at this time.

Caesar himself set out from Ravenna by night; to avoid the prying eyes of Pompey's agents, and after losing his way in the dark, caught up with his troops at the river, soon after dawn. He is said to have paused for thought before crossing.

By law he could not leave his province, or lead an army into Italy; so the crossing of the river was an unconstitutional act, for which he could be declared an outlaw. But with the famous phrase *alea iacta est* (a gambling metaphor), he led his men across. The die had been cast, i.e. it had been thrown into the air, and only the gods could say how it would fall.

Here the soldiers of the XIII Legion are crossing the river (on a small bridge, mentioned only in Suetonius' account). The bridge has a stone arch and a timber balustrade. The men have been marching for some hours from their start-line at Ravenna, and many are tired and thirsty. Their thoughts are on the marching still to come rather than constitutional

niceties. Most give the river scarcely a glance. The soldiers themselves are clad in mail, with their winter cloaks. Their shields are protected by leather covers – see the panel on the shield at bottom right, with the name of the legionary, the century in which he served and the numerals of the legion itself (bottom to top). They have their helmets slung over their shoulders, and their two *pila* strapped together, held in one hand; across their shoulders is a pole with their personal gear, in a leather satchel on a wicker frame. They march in files of six men. The marchers are followed by a water wagon pulled by mules.

PETER CONNOLLY

taken by provincial levies, of light infantry, slingers, archers and cavalry. Such troops had always been called upon, or hired, when the need arose. Now they became a more significant element in the army. The practice of drawing upon the equestrian order to provide cavalry had already been discontinued by the later 2nd century.

The impact of the Social War on individual soldiers is easier to surmise. It seems likely that rebel soldiers subsequently joined the legions to fight in overseas campaigns, leaving bitterness and shattered home life behind. (The aftermath of the American Civil War provides a 19th-century parallel.) When in 88 the consul Sulla, on the march with six legions to a war in Asia Minor, turned his forces round and marched on Rome itself, the Roman historians were appalled at the disloyalty of the troops to their capital city. Yet many of the soldiers were likely to have been disillusioned Italians, who felt no particular bond with Rome, but were thoroughly alarmed at the risk of losing the hoped-for booty of a campaign in the rich lands of the East.

The following years were to witness civil war in Italy when Sulla returned, then prolonged and difficult fighting (80-72 BC) against the rebel Quintus Sertorius who wrested Spain from legitimate Roman control and trained the tribes with Roman discipline. In Italy itself the slave army assembled by Spartacus outwitted many Roman armies (73-71 BC), until it was suppressed by the concerted might of Gnaeus Pompeius (Pompey), newly returned from victories in Spain, and Licinius Crassus. An interesting but somewhat forgotten achievement of Crassus was a wall and ditch 60 km long, constructed across the toe of Italy to bottle up Spartacus' forces.

Outside Italy the period witnessed Roman armies in action against the redoubtable Mithridates VI of Pontus, a kingdom on the north coast of Asia Minor, who swept through the Roman province of Asia, and overran Greece. This was the final round of conflict between the Romans and the successor kingdoms of Alexander's generals, whom Mithridates claimed to represent. Sulla (from 87), Licinius Lucullus (74-67) and Pompey (66-63) led Roman armies against him, with the legions ranged as in earlier generations against phalanx, swarms of cavalry and scythe-wheeled chariots. The legions were largely successful, but Mithridates was not finally driven from his kingdom until 63 when he retired to the Crimea and soon afterwards committed suicide.

Pompey returned to Italy in triumph in 62, to enter a turbulent political arena. In order to secure ratification of his *ad hoc* political decision-making in the East, and some concrete rewards for his soldiers, many of whom had been away from home for a decade or more, he entered into an informal alliance, the First Triumvirate, with the wealthy Crassus and the up-and-coming Gaius Julius Caesar, who as consul for 59 secured the measures necessary to satisfy his partners' objectives.

Disaster at Carrhae

After his consulship Caesar departed to a proconsulship in Gaul. His successes there prompted Crassus to mount an ill-advised and ultimately fatal military expedition against the Parthians, the chief remaining rival to the Romans in the Middle Eastern world, whose domains stretched from the Euphrates to the Indus in the ruins of the old Persian empire. As the campaign vividly reveals the deficiencies of the legion as a fighting machine in an unfamiliar environment, it seems reasonable to examine this episode in greater detail.

After serving as consul (with Pompey) in 55, Crassus departed for Syria, spoiling for a quite unnecessary and unprovoked confrontation. In 53, he rejected sensible advice to take the longer route through the Armenian mountains, terrain in which the Parthians could not bring their superiority in cavalry to bear. Instead, Crassus chose a more direct approach to the Parthian heartlands, crossing the Euphrates at Zeugma. As reported by Plutarch his field force now comprised seven legions, together with a similar number of light troops and nearly 4,000 cavalry. After advancing some 80 km eastwards, he learned that a Parthian force was nearby, and reformed the marching army into a large hollow square. Confronted soon afterwards by the massed Parthian cavalry and horse-archers under the inspired leadership of Surenas, the Romans stood firm, despite a great cacophony of sound from beating drums, the glinting of polished brass armour and clouds of dust and sand. What happened next is best reported in Plutarch's own words:

> 'The Parthians now went back a long way, and began to shoot their arrows from all sides at once. They did not need to aim at specific targets, for the Roman ranks were so densely crowded that it was impossible to miss the target even intentionally. They kept up a dense volley with their large, powerful bows, curved so as to give their arrows the maximum impetus. Straightaway the plight of the Romans was very awkward. If they remained in their ranks they were wounded one after the other; if they attempted to come to close quarters, they were unable to achieve anything, and still suffered casualties. For the Parthians shot as they fled, and do this most effectively, next to the Scythians. The Romans endured, so long as they had hopes that, once the Parthians had used up all their arrows, they would either break off the fight or engage at close quarters. But when they realised that large numbers of camels laden with arrows were at hand, and that those who had first ridden round them were getting more, then Crassus saw no end to it all and began to lose heart.'

Eventually it was decided to retreat under the cover of darkness, abandoning the wounded who were slaughtered at dawn. The main body reached the nearby caravan-city of Carrhae (Harran), which gave its name to the disaster (datable to early June 53), and after calling a short halt there, continued the retreat westwards under the cover of darkness. Some splinter groups reached Syria. Crassus was lured away from his few remaining escorts by the promise of a parley, and killed. Plutarch gives Roman casualties in the campaign as 20,000 killed and another 10,000 taken prisoner. Standards, including legionary eagles, were captured. The campaign showed how a poorly led Roman army in unfavourable conditions was helpless in the face of sound tactics. The bitter memory of the defeat lingered for a generation.

Bust of Julius Caesar. Museo Archeologico Nazionale, Naples.

The Age of Caesar

Crassus' military ambitions in the mid '50s were largely fuelled by the continuing, widely publicized victories won by his fellow 'triumvir' Julius Caesar. The latter's appointment as proconsul of the combined provinces of Illyricum, Cisalpine and Transalpine Gaul for five years from 58 onwards gave him unprecedented scope for his undoubted talents, and was to be the springboard for his later exploits. The progress of his campaigns from 58 until 49 BC (his command had been extended for a further five-year period) is known in great detail. Shortly afterwards Caesar wrote his own account (the *Commentaries on the Gallic War*), which because of the author's fame and intrinsic literary merit has survived to modern times. Caesar provides a quite remarkable picture of a Roman army of the mid-1st century BC in action, seen from the viewpoint of its commander. The strength of the Roman military system, and the effect of resolute leadership and solid training against numerically superior but poorly co-ordinated opposition are clearly seen, as is the army's expertise in engineering works.

The details of his conquests are well known: in a sequence of lightning campaigns he defeated a vast array of tribes from the Rhône Valley to the Channel. There was time to bridge the Rhine in 55 BC and to mount two expeditions to the offshore island of Britain, from which Caesar was lucky to return with his reputation unscathed. The later years (from 54 onwards) saw a determined revolt, led by the Arvernian nobleman Vercingetorix, culminating in a great confrontation round the town of Alesia. With the Gauls exhausted by

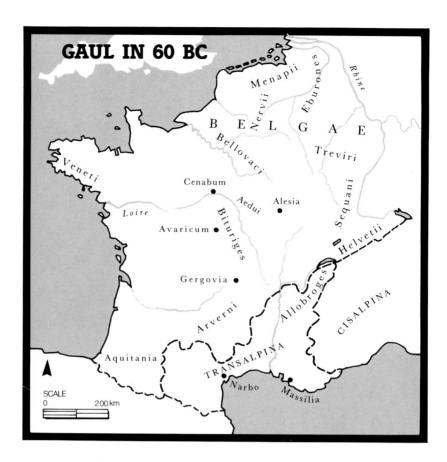

The tribes of Gaul, on the eve of Caesar's campaigns.

Caesar's perseverance, a huge new tract had been added to the Roman domains.

When Caesar arrived in his provinces he found four legions which had been serving there for some years. He was quick to enlarge his forces, which eventually reached a total of 11 legions. Many of the new recruits were from Cisalpina and Transalpina, and were probably not full Roman citizens by birth. In the crisis of 52 BC he raised a complete legion from native Gauls, the famous *V Alaudae* ('The Larks'). In addition there were some auxiliary regiments available: Numidian cavalry, Balearic slingers and Cretan archers. As his campaigns progressed, Caesar made increasing use of local auxiliaries, particularly cavalry, drawn from the aristocracy of the Gallic tribes. Later he was to deploy German cavalry, summoned by virtue of treaty obligations, against the Gauls themselves.

Caesar's army was typical of its time, with fine qualities instilled by training and discipline. But the soldiers were apprehensive about fighting Gauls, and even more alarmed by the prospect of the feared Germans. Some reputations did not withstand Caesarian scrutiny. Caesar, a master of human psychology, worked hard to imbue the legions with confidence in their leader and in themselves. Disaster was sometimes never far away: one of his legions, less resolutely led, was annihilated in the winter of 54-53, and in 53 Caesar himself suffered a serious reverse at Gergovia, though he is characteristically able to divert the blame.

Caesar rarely gives specific details about such mundane matters as camp layout and fortification, routine duties and the command structure and organization of his forces. All this would be familiar to his readers (though not to us), and did not need elaboration. There is much in Polybius' account which still holds good for Caesar's time. The overnight camp, as described by Caesar, was defended against attack by one or (more often) two ditches, with sloping or vertical sides, and by a rampart topped by timber breastwork and with timber-

178

framed towers at frequent intervals. On the march each legion normally moved independently, followed by its own baggage.

In battle the standard formation for the legion or group of legions was the traditional three lines. On one occasion only, in his later commentaries on the Civil War, does Caesar provide details of the disposition of cohorts. In 49 BC, drawing up his army against the Pompeians in Spain, he placed four cohorts in the front line, and three in each of the other two; but other dispositions could be adopted if the circumstances demanded. The cohorts of the third line were kept as a reserve, in the role of the old *triarii*. The backbone of the army were the centurions, promoted from the ranks, whom Caesar saw as the conduit of his views to the rank and file. The legion's chief centurion was drawn from their number, and held this post for one year only, thereafter reverting to his former rank. The tribunes, more aristocratic in origin and outlook, were less reliable; they held no executive commands. Caesar's use of his legates adds much to our understanding of their role. They were young senators, some without prior military experience; those who stayed loyal to Caesar enjoyed his patronage in the years that followed. The legates were employed in a variety of tasks, commanding small expeditions or building-parties, geographical areas or individual legions, or groups of legions. The post of 'legionary legate' grew out of this system, but was an Augustan development.

The legions each had their own artillery – stone-throwing *ballistae* and arrow-firing *scorpiones*, which might be brought up in support of a siege or used to defend a camp; only rarely was such artillery employed to support a legion in battle. Not enough is known to say whether each legion had a set number of artillery pieces; more probably they were built and augmented as necessary. The army in Gaul had no siege train, and did not need any of the sophisticated engines or devices developed in the Hellenistic age against the strongly defended cities of the eastern Mediterranean world.

Roman Engineering

Above all in the military field, the engineering achievements of the Romans excite our admiration. Apart from routine camp fortification, we learn of bridge building and siege techniques. For example, in 58 BC Caesar employed his one available legion to fortify the bank of the Rhône against the migrating Helvetii, 'for a distance of 18 miles, by means of a wall 16 feet high, with a ditch. When this was done, he placed forts at intervals and put garrisons into them'. The work was accomplished within two weeks. Some faint traces of these works were identified on the ground in the 19th century.

The siege of a stronghold of the Atuatuci (near Namur) in 57 reveals the army's capacity for swift construction work.

> 'When the Roman troops arrived, the Atuatuci made a series of sorties from their town and engaged in minor skirmishes; but when they found themselves enclosed by an earthwork 12 feet high, with a circuit of 12 miles and forts at frequent intervals, they stayed inside. After a line of mantlets and a siege-terrace had been constructed, and they saw a siege tower erected at some distance, the people on the wall at first laughed and ridiculed the idea of setting up such a huge apparatus so far away . . . But when they saw it was moving and drawing near the walls, they were alarmed at the strange, unfamiliar spectacle, and sent envoys to Caesar to ask for peace.'

It is interesting to see how quickly the Gauls learned the same techniques. In the winter of 54-53,

> 'the Nervii surrounded the camp [at Atuatuca] with a rampart nine feet high and a ditch 15 feet across. They had learnt these things by observing our methods in previous years, and were further instructed by prisoners from our army whom they kept secretly. But they had none of the proper tools for this sort of work and so laboured hard to cut up the

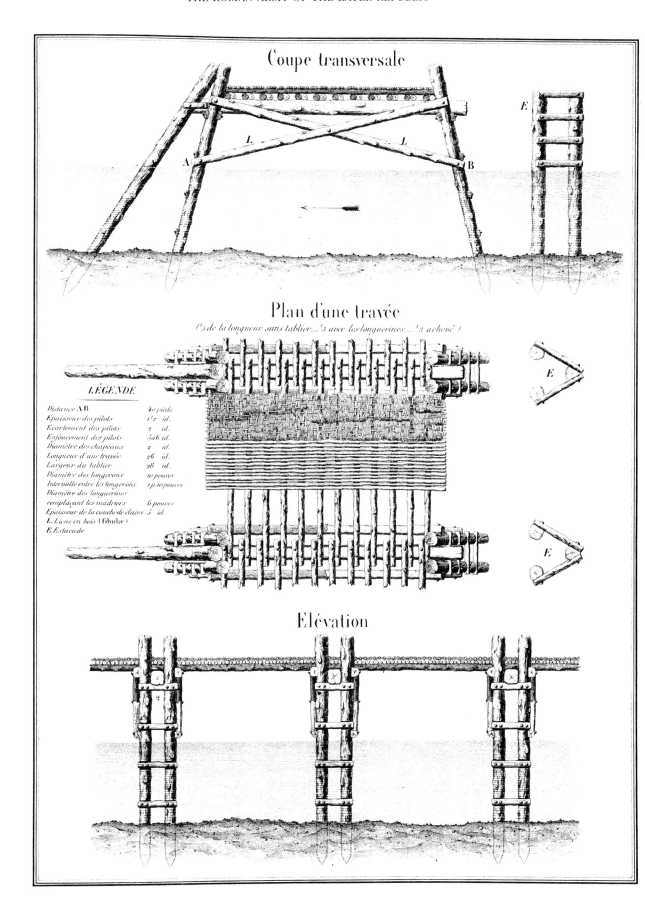

Coupe transversale

Plan d'une travée

('3 de la longueur sans tablier ___ '3 avec les longuerines ___ '3 achevé)

LÉGENDE

Distance AB	40 pieds
Epaisseur des pilots	1'2 id.
Ecartement des pilots	2 id.
Enfoncement des pilots	5à6 id.
Diamètre des chapeaux	2 id.
Longueur d'une travée	26 id.
Largeur du tablier	28 id.
Diamètre des longerons	10 pouces
Intervalle entre les longerons	1 p. 10 pouces
Diamètre des longuerines remplaçant les madriers	6 pouces
Epaisseur de la couche de claies	3 id.
L. Liens en bois (fibulæ)	
E. Estacade	

Elévation

sods with their swords, and to get out the earth with their hands or in their cloaks. From this some idea of their great number could be gained; in less than three hours they completed a fortification three miles in circumference, and in the next days began to erect towers as high as the camp rampart, to make grappling hooks and shelters, with the same prisoners providing the know-how.'

Caesar's clear accounts of the works undertaken add to their impressiveness. A classic account is his report of a bridge constructed across the Rhine in 55 BC in the neighbourhood of Coblenz:

'He [that is, Caesar, who always wrote in the third person] joined together pairs of 18 inch thick timber beams, set two feet apart, with their lower ends sharpened. Their lengths had been measured in advance to suit the varying depth of the river. These were fixed in the river with help of pulley gear, and made fast by being driven in with rammers. They were not set vertically but at an angle, so that they inclined towards the current. Opposite them, at a distance of 40 feet down river, were set two timbers joined in the same way, this time angled against the force and impetus of the current. Timber beams two feet wide were set horizontally across the gaps between each pair of piles, fitting neatly into the two foot wide space between the top ends of each pair of timber uprights. These horizontal beams rested on small fillets which kept the uprights the correct distance apart. They also kept the whole structure stable, and such was its strength that the stronger the current flowed, the tighter the constituent parts held together. Beams were now set lengthwise across these trestles, and on top of them at right angles were laid poles and wickerwork. More piles were driven into the river bed downstream, angled towards the main structure and tightly bound to it. Other piles were set a short distance upstream, so that if any treetrunks or boats were floated down by the tribesmen to break the bridge, their impetus would be broken by the barrier, and no harm done to the bridge. The work was completed and the army led across on the tenth day after the collecting of timber was begun.'

The Siege of Alesia

The siege of Alesia in 52 formed the climax to the war and is accorded extensive coverage by Caesar in his *Commentaries*. The Gallic town (Alise-Sainte-Reine, north-west of Dijon) occupied a lozenge-shaped plateau some 1,500 m long, between two rivers which separated it from hills rising on either side. When Vercingetorix retreated into the town and encamped his army on the adjacent slopes, Caesar immediately decided to enclose the town within a ring of fortification, some 18 km long. The army was distributed into a series of camps on the surrounding hills, and 23 smaller redoubts were built on the forward slopes, to limit the Gauls' freedom of movement, and protect the soldiers engaged on the construction of the siegeworks themselves. Caesar began by digging a 20-foot-wide and 20-foot-deep ditch across the flat ground west of the town, to act as a deterrent against sudden attacks from the town's defenders. Then

'he dug two ditches, each 15 feet wide and 15 feet deep, and filled the inner one, where it traversed low ground, with water diverted from a river. Behind the ditch he erected a rampart 12 feet high, adding to it a battlemented breastwork, with large forked branches projecting where the rampart and the breastwork joined, to slow down the enemy if they tried to get over. He placed towers at intervals of 80 feet along the entire circuit of fortification . . . Tree trunks or very stout boughs were cut, the branches lopped off, and their tops stripped of bark and sharpened; they were then fixed in construction trenches five feet deep. The timbers were set into these, with the lower ends fastened to one another to prevent

opposite
Caesar's bridge across the Rhine: plan and elevation based on his narrative. After Napoléon III, Histoire du Jules César, *1865-66.*

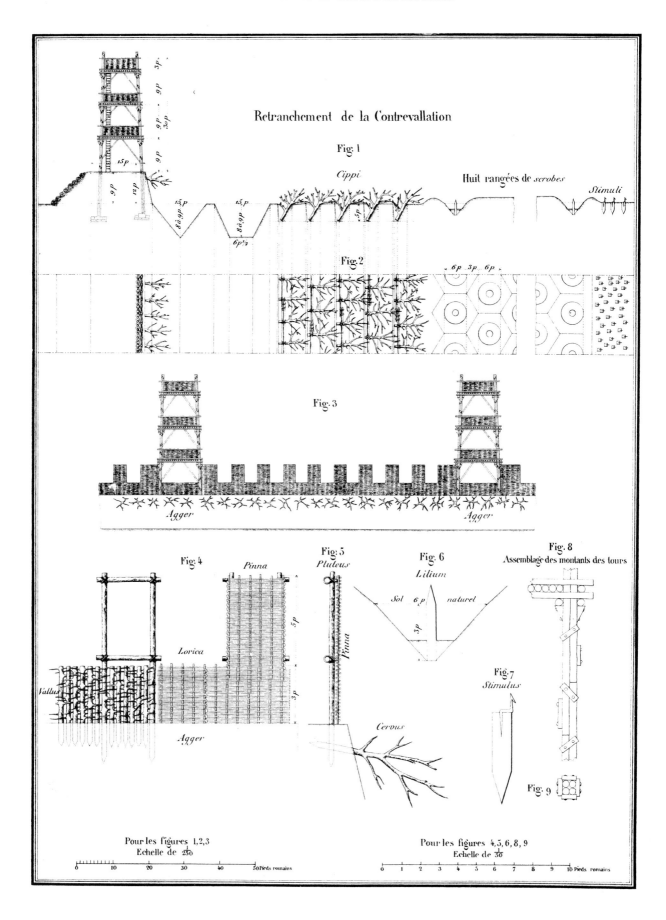

Retranchement de la Contrevallation

Fig. 1

Cippi

Huit rangées de *scrobes*

Stimuli

Fig. 2

Fig. 3

Agger

Agger

Fig. 4

Fig. 5
Pluteus

Fig. 6
Lilium

Fig. 8
Assemblage des montants des tours

Pinna

Lorica

Vallus

Agger

Pinna

Cervus

Sol   6 p   naturel

3p

Fig. 7
Stimulus

Fig. 9

Pour les figures 1, 2, 3
Echelle de 1/250

Pour les figures 4, 5, 6, 8, 9
Echelle de 1/50

them being pulled up, and the tops projecting. These were set in five rows in each trench, touching one another and interlaced. Any people who got in there were likely to impale themselves on the sharp points. The soldiers called them "boundary markers". In front of them, arranged in diagonal rows called quincunxes, pits three feet deep were dug, narrowing gradually towards the bottom; embedded into them were smoothed logs as thick as a man's thigh, with their tops ends sharpened and charred, so that only four inches projected above ground. To keep these logs firmly and securely in position earth was thrown into the pits and stamped down hard, to a depth of one foot, the rest of the pit being filled with twigs and brushwood to hide the trap. These were planted in sequences of eight rows three feet apart. The soldiers called them "lilies" from their resemblance to the flower. In front of these again were billets of wood a foot long with iron hooks fixed in them, sunk right into the ground, and scattered about everywhere. These the soldiers called "goads". When these works were completed, Caesar built similar fortifications facing the other way against the enemy outside.'

Clearly Caesar was worried about the likelihood of attack by other Gauls, which Vercingetorix was contriving to organize. Attacks were made on the lines of fortification from within and without but they were poorly co-ordinated, in spite of the Gauls' enormous numerical superiority. Amid desperate fighting Caesar kept his nerve, and Vercingetorix surrendered. Excavation of the fortifications in the 1860s, under the overall direction of Napoleon III, settled the identification of the site, and related Caesar's

opposite
Details of Caesar's siegeworks at Alesia, showing the 'boundary posts' (centre top), 'lilies' and 'goads' (bottom right). After Napoléon III, Histoire du Jules César, *1865-66.*

Plan of Alesia, showing location of Caesar's siegeworks (after Napoléon III).

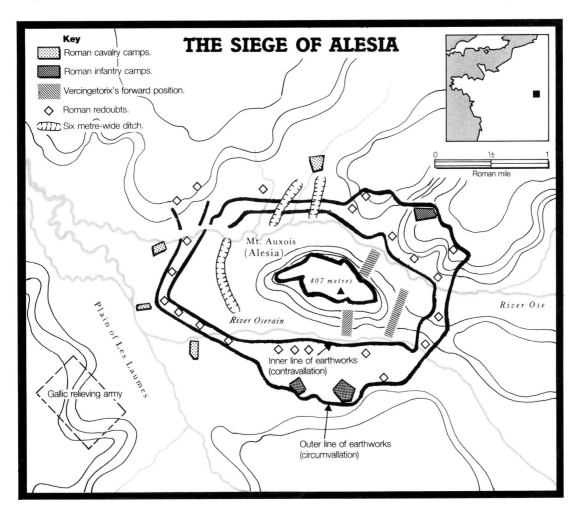

THE SIEGE OF ALESIA

Key
- Roman cavalry camps.
- Roman infantry camps.
- Vercingetorix's forward position.
- ◇ Roman redoubts.
- Six metre-wide ditch.

Mt. Auxois (Alesia)

407 metres

River Ose

Plain of Les Laumes

River Oserain

Gallic relieving army

Inner line of earthworks (contravallation)

Outer line of earthworks (circumvallation)

0 ½ 1
Roman mile

account to the details of local topography. The inner line of fortification was located on low ground. The outer line, in contrast, ran along the crests of the surrounding hills and linked together a total of eight camps; a few of the smaller redoubts were pinpointed and the sites of others estimated. Large quantities of Roman and Gallic weaponry were dug out of the ditches below Mont Réa on the north-west side of the town, but the details have remained unpublished. More recently, the ditch systems have been observed from the air, providing further confirmation of Caesar's account. Such double lines of fortification had been used by Roman armies before (for example, at Capua during the war against Hannibal). It is clear that the Roman army was familiar with linear fortifications long before it began to construct the familiar frontier works of the Empire.

The unparalleled length of Caesar's tenure in Gaul and his continuing success established a unique bond between the commander and his soldiers, which was soon to be tested in earnest. In January 49 Caesar crossed the tiny Rubicon, a river which was the formal boundary between his province and peninsular Italy, and flung his by now superbly trained and strongly motivated legions against the legitimate forces of the senate.

Roman against Roman

Thus far we have examined the progress of Roman arms against external foes, in both Western and Eastern lands. But the final decades of the Roman Republic witnessed several rounds of civil war, when legion faced legion; the same tactics, weaponry and expertise were available to both sides. Training, motivation and morale were to be crucial factors in the coming years. Caesar's veteran legions, which had served him so well in Gaul, were to be crucial to his continuing success.

The number of legions in service rose dramatically within a few months to about 50, and remained at a high level throughout the wars that now followed. Old soldiers re-enlisted, encouraged by hopes of promoted posts and financial reward; great numbers of raw recruits were conscripted at short notice. Rash promises were made of rewards after victory; on occasion these had to be kept. Those protagonists stranded far from the traditional Italian recruiting grounds formed local levies into 'legions' which they armed and trained in the Roman fashion. Such formations never enjoyed much success against regular legions, but the idea that the empire's population could be armed and equipped in a Roman manner to assume part of its military burden was implanted for the future. Vast numbers of auxiliaries were summoned by treaty obligations, and sent far from home. Client kingdoms on the fringes of the Roman domain became embroiled in the conflicts, to their detriment or advantage, as the floodtide ebbed and flowed across the Mediterranean world. There was to be heroism and self-sacrifice, terrorism and atrocities. This was civil war on an empire-wide scale, with armies transported by sea or marching huge distances between theatres of operations.

below, from left to right
Silver denarius issued by Caesar in 48-47 BC, to commemorate his Gallic conquests. The reverse shows a trophy of captured arms, including an axe and shield, and a war-trumpet.

Silver denarius issued by Q. Nasidius in 44-43 BC, while serving as an admiral with Pompey's son Sextus Pompeius. The reverse shows a war galley.

Silver denarius issued in 49 BC. The reverse shows a legionary eagle flanked by other standards, and names the consuls L. Cornelius Lentulus and C. Claudius Marcellus.

Silver denarius issued by Antony in 36 BC. The reverse shows an Armenian tiara, alluding to Antony's current campaign.

Silver denarius issued by Antony to his troops in 32-31 BC. The reverse shows a legionary eagle flanked by standards, and names one of his legions, legio XIX.

British Museum, London.

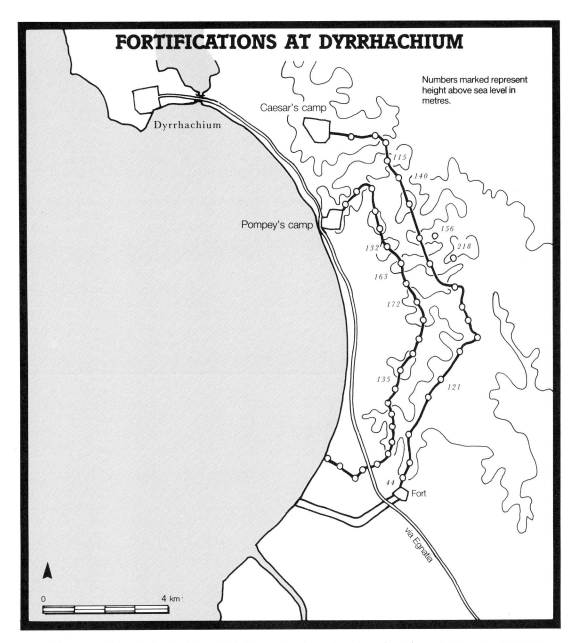

FORTIFICATIONS AT DYRRHACHIUM

Numbers marked represent height above sea level in metres.

Dyrrhachium

Caesar's camp

Pompey's camp

115
140
156
132
218
163
172
135
121
44

Fort

Via Egnatia

0   4 km

All the qualities of leadership which Caesar had displayed against the Gallic tribes were now directed against his fellow senators. By doubling his soldiers' pay to 225 *denarii* per year, which became the standard amount under the Early Empire, he secured their loyalty at a vital moment. Pompey, to whom leadership of the state's forces had been entrusted, made a strategic withdrawal to Brindisi, pursued by Caesar, but was able to cross over to Greece unhindered. His aim was to marshal Roman forces in the Eastern provinces, and the troops of client kings under obligation to him from previous wars, for a counter-invasion.

After quickly snuffing out elements in Spain which remained loyal to Pompey, and reducing Marseilles after a full-blown siege, Caesar crossed the Adriatic with 12 legions, including his most experienced troops, and attempted to encircle and entrap Pompey at his base, Dyrrhachium (now Albanian Durrës). Caesar himself is again a narrator of events in his authoritative *Civil War*, packed with precise detail and acute observation of the military scene. Caesar's troops, having been flung by their commander into the campaign

In the spring of 48 BC Caesar attempted to hem in Pompey's forces at Dyrrhachium by building a continuous fortification with redoubts at regular intervals. But Pompey built a similar, inner line to keep out his forces. Fierce fighting developed, which ended in Pompey's favour. Some traces of these siegeworks have been identified on the ground. (After G. Veith.)

FIGHTING IN THE ALPS

Although most of the Mediterranean lands had been
conquered by the time that Augustus became sole ruler of
the Roman world in 31 BC, there were still pockets of
resistance. One of the Emperor's many 'mopping up
operations' was the subjugation of the Alpine tribes.

This picture shows legionaries fighting their way up a
steep hillside against fierce opposition from Celtic warriors
issuing from a hilltop fortress. The legionaries wear mail
shirts and are equipped with the oval *scutum* and heavy *pilum*.
Some have thrown their *pila*, and advance with *gladius* at
the ready. They are led by a centurion, in scale armour,
wearing greaves on his legs and with a horsehair plume in
his helmet. In the middle distance is a military standard.
Most of the legionaries are still wearing the Montefortino-
type helmet, but either in Caesar's time, or very shortly
after, they began to adopt the iron Celtic helmet which later
became the standard legionary helmet.

The defending Celts are in brightly coloured checked
tunics and trousers. They carry oval shields and long
slashing swords. Their leader has an iron helmet,
elaborately decorated shield and mail shirt. Another warrior
in a helmet is about to engage a legionary (bottom right);
his shield is decorated with torcs. Their followers' hair is
whitened with lime; they advance in a headlong rush. In
the background, on level ground in front of their hilltop fort,
more warriors are assembling. A trumpeter blows on the
war-trumpet, or carynx. Behind is a standard-bearer,
carrying an image of a wild boar, much favoured by the
Celts, and shown on the Augustan arch at Orange.

The fort-ramparts are of stone and are defended by the
older men. Many such defences must have been stormed
by the Roman army during the Augustan campaigns
commemorated on the Tropaeum Augusti (now La Tarbie)
above Monte Carlo. Erected in 6 BC, it lists the 46 tribes
subjugated.

without adequate provisioning or back-up, suffered great privations. Eventually he was forced to break off the engagement, and withdrew inland across the mountains of Epirus into Thessaly. Pompey, having toyed with the idea of seizing Italy, tamely followed.

In June 48 the two armies came face to face near the town of Pharsalus, south of modern Larissa. What followed is one of the great set-piece battles of the age. Both armies rested one wing on the river Enipeus, and were drawn up in the traditional three lines. Pompey's powerful cavalry was grouped on his left flank, where alone it could have scope for movement, and might hope to outflank Caesar's line. Caesar had placed his favourite Tenth Legion on the extreme right, flanked by his few cavalry, among whom were dispersed some light-armed infantry. To counter Pompey's cavalry, he had made up a special force of six cohorts, drawn from the third line of each legion. These were placed a little way to the rear of the main forces and ordered to await a signal to advance. After battle was joined, when Pompey's cavalry seemed likely to sweep round Caesar's flank, the reserve cohorts moved forwards and, as instructed, used their javelins as a hedge of spears against the inexperienced riders, and drove them off. Next they attacked Pompey's legions in the flank. Caesar now moved his own third line up, and Pompey's legions broke and ran.

Pompey fled to Egypt by sea. As he was about to land at Alexandria, he was stabbed to death by a former centurion who had come to meet him. Caesar arrived soon after, to become embroiled over the winter of 48-47 in a local dispute between the young pharaoh Ptolemy XIII and his elder sister Cleopatra. He returned to Rome in 47, by way of Asia Minor, where he had swept aside the ambitious kinglet Pharnaces. As *dictator* Caesar set in motion numerous social, legal and constitutional reforms, and began the process of settling his old soldiers in colonies, in Italy itself and southern Gaul. But Pompey's sons made determined efforts to continue the struggle, first in Africa and then in Spain. Caesar had to inspire his by now weary troops to further efforts. Far from retiring from active campaigning, he now set himself a further military goal, the avenging of his old partner Crassus in a campaign against the Parthians. On the eve of his departure, the Ides of March 44, he was assassinated at Rome, at a meeting of the senate in Pompey's Theatre.

As a military commander Caesar has had few equals, for his daring strategy, his originality of mind, and decisiveness in action. He was a master of improvization, often acting on impulse and instinct, which could place his soldiers in difficult situations. But he was equally adept at extricating them from the consequences of his impetuosity. Caesar is sometimes hailed as a military reformer. Certainly, the long-service permanent legions of the Empire are largely descended from formations identifiable as fighting for Caesar, but it was his death and the subsequent civil strife which lengthened out the legions' lifespan and gave them permanent identity into the Empire, not any plans developed by Caesar. No positive programme of reform or review of the army's activities emerges from a study of his career.

Caesar's Legacy

Caesar's murderers had hoped that, with the principal demon removed, political life as they had known and enjoyed it would continue much as before. But others were waiting to profit by the new circumstances. The reins of power were seized by the consul Marcus Antonius (better known today as Mark Antony), who combined with Caesar's great-nephew and designated heir, Octavian, and with the proconsul Aemilius Lepidus, in an alliance known to us as the Second Triumvirate, against Caesar's assassins, the 'Liberators', led by Brutus and Cassius. Caesar's veteran soldiers, settling to a new life on their farmsteads, were persuaded (or bribed) to re-enlist, and became the mainstay of the Triumviral army.

Leaving Lepidus to control Italy, Antony and Octavian crossed the Adriatic to Dyrrhachium and from there marched eastwards along the main

Roman highway, the Via Egnatia, until they encountered their opponents' forces sitting astride the road at the town of Philippi, some 120 km north-east of Thessaloniki. Both armies contained some 19 legions. The army of the Liberators was superior in cavalry, and contained some Syrian horse-archers, but they were never able to deploy them. Both sides entrenched, building stone dykes, palisades and towers. At first Brutus and Cassius declined battle, and the resourceful Antony attempted an outflanking movement, which Appian describes:

> 'Arraying his forces each day for battle with all the standards showing, so that it might seem his entire army was drawn up, he had a part of his force work night and day to cut a narrow passage in the marsh, cutting down reeds, throwing up a causeway with stone revetments, driving in stakes and bridging over the deeper parts, in complete and utter silence. The thick reeds which were still growing round this passageway prevented the enemy from seeing his work. After working thus for ten days, he sent a strong column of troops by night suddenly, who occupied the strongpoints within his lines and at the same time fortified several small garrison posts.'

Cassius built a counter-fortification, and intercepted Antony's troops. This led to a general battle, in which Octavian's wing was beaten by Brutus, and Cassius' by Antony. Cassius over-hastily took his own life. There was now a long lull (three weeks rather than Shakespeare's two hours), during which the Caesarians continued to change the angle of attack, deploying their forces in a potentially dangerous manoeuvre along the edge of the marsh. Brutus extended his lines eastwards to avoid being outflanked. Finally, Brutus agreed

Battlefield of Philippi, north-eastern Greece, where Brutus and Cassius were defeated by Octavian and Antony in November 42 BC.

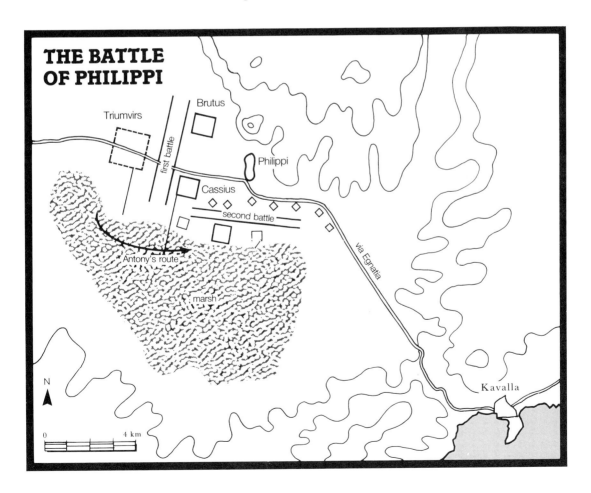

THE BATTLE OF PHILIPPI

Triumvirs

Brutus

first battle

Philippi

Cassius

second battle

Antony's route

via Egnatia

marsh

N

Kavalla

0   4 km

Marble relief from Praeneste (now Palestrina). It shows a warship with the crocodile emblem of Egypt at the prow, a tower built on the deck, and a group of armed legionaries. It belongs about 30 BC, and may depict the battle at Actium. Musei Pontificie, Vatican.

to a battle, against his better judgement. His troops were forced back and their lines broke up. Victory was complete.

The Triumvirs now reorganized their army, releasing the old Caesarian veterans who had rejoined, and those of their own levies who had been conscripted in 49-48 BC. More recent entrants were retained under arms, together with 14,000 men of similar status from the defeated armies, and merged into 11 legions, which for the most part retained the names and numerals of older Caesarian formations, such as the V *Alaudae* ('The Larks'), VI *Ferrata* ('Ironclad') and XII *Fulminata* ('Thunderbolt'). This was an important step towards the creation of the Roman imperial army. The reputation and long service of Caesar's legions were sufficient to secure their retention in the scheme of things, though Caesar himself was dead and all but a few of the original members now released. However, this new army was to be immediately divided, with the greater part being retained by Antony, as the core of an expedition, in Caesar's footsteps, against the Parthians. Octavian returned to Italy, and saw through the settlement of the released soldiers (probably about 40,000 men) on the land of 18 prosperous towns throughout the peninsula, in the teeth of local opposition and hostility. Octavian had to fight Antony's brother Lucius Antonius who soon shut himself up in the Umbrian hilltop town of Perusia (Perugia), which Octavian besieged with a double line of fortifications. Weakened by starvation over the winter of 41-40, Lucius' army surrendered.

Meanwhile Antony was to prove hardly more successful than Crassus against the Parthians. He penetrated into northern Mesopotamia, but in a long nightmarish march homewards through the Armenian mountains lost a high proportion of his forces. Octavian had been building up an army loyal to himself and eliminating rivals and opponents, including Pompey's son Sextus Pompeius in 36. Soon he was to gain useful military plaudits in Dalmatia, while Antony became increasingly infatuated with the resourceful Cleopatra.

190

Finally, in 32 the senate was persuaded to declare war on Cleopatra – in reality a move against Antony, who would not desert her. Once again it was civil war between East and West; again it was to be decided by a single battle, though this time at sea, at Actium off the west coast of Greece, with substantial land-based armies (of some 16-19 legions on each side) looking on. Octavian was present with his fleet but prudently delegated command to his competent lieutenant Vipsanius Agrippa. Antony was able to break through Agrippa's battle line, but only to flee with Cleopatra to Egypt where both soon committed suicide. In a gesture which recognized the shape of the new army, Octavian incorporated several of Antony's legions into his own army, though their manpower was doubtless substantially altered. As Caesar's heir, Octavian thus reunited his old army under a single command. Soon, as Augustus, he was to remodel the constitution and carry Rome into a new age.

PRINCIPAL SOURCES

Caesar

Senator who was consul in 59 BC, and crossed Rubicon in 49; dictator until his assassination on the Ides of March. Author of commentaries on the Gallic War (58-49 BC) and the Civil War (49-48); unknown followers continued the narrative down to 45 BC. Offers his own version of events to justify actions at Rome; many valuable details on military campaigns and institutions.

Appian

A native of Alexandria, who wrote under Antoninus Pius (AD 138-161). His works include a *Civil War*, about political and military events in the closing decades of the Republic, and accounts of Roman conquest of the Mediterranean lands; reliable and unsensational.

Plutarch

A native of Chaeronea in Greece, who wrote under Trajan (AD 98-117). Best known for his series of 'Parallel Lives' of Greek and Roman politicians and generals, including Caesar, Marius, Sulla, Lucullus, Crassus, Brutus and Antony.

THE EMPIRE

DR BRIAN DOBSON

AUGUSTUS' NEW ARMY: THE LEGIONS

The army of the Empire established by Augustus drew heavily on the nomenclature and traditions of the Late Republic. But it was new. Augustus decided to maintain his legions, adding some of Antony's; no more legions were to be disbanded, except when disgraced or wiped out. When new legions were raised for specific campaigns, they remained in being, although this was a rare occurrence. Throughout our period, which ends in AD 200, no emperor raised more than two legions, and even legions destroyed were not immediately replaced, notably the three legions destroyed in the great disaster in the Teutoburg forest, in Germany, in AD 9. The 28 legions on which Augustus settled soon after 31 BC was a shrewd estimate, particularly as at that time he had no intention of standing on the defensive but rather had plans for the expansion of the Empire. For the next 200 years the number of legions varied between 25 and 30. At the end of the period, 19 of Augustus' 28 legions were still in being, to which must be added two legions which had been reformed and renamed after they had disgraced themselves. Thus the legions were proud formations, drawing on a long historical tradition.

Length of Service

Of even greater importance than the retention of the numbers and often the names of the legions was the decision to change the period of service. It had become normal for a man to serve six years in the army, but now there was a return to the traditional 16 years, with a further four years served by a veteran with the legion, during which he was excused some duties. This decision, together with the abandonment of the practice of raising and disbanding legions for special campaigns, meant that the only ex-soldiers were old soldiers. There was no trained reserve of men below 40, nothing to parallel the former general spread of military training and experience through the populace, or the large number of 'veterans' with only 6-10 years' service of the Late Republic. In theory there was still a general obligation to undertake military service but in practice it fell on a small number of men for a long period of years. This was further emphasized when the period of service was extended to 20 years, with probably a further five as veterans retained with the legions. The reason for this was almost certainly the financial pressure of providing grants of money or land for the discharged men. Augustus had accepted that this must be part of the new arrangements; the failure to accept this responsibility had been one of the fatal weaknesses of the Republic. But the burden was considerable, and failure to discharge men on time and pay them their gratuities was one of the causes of the mutinies which followed the death of Augustus in AD 14. The distinction between service with full duties and the restricted duties of the retained veterans seems to have faded, and service was for 25 or 26 years, discharges only being made every two years.

Organization and Recruitment

The legion was unchanged from that of Caesar in being based on ten cohorts of six centuries each, the establishment strength of the century being apparently

TABLE OF EMPERORS AND EVENTS
31 BC – AD 211

31	Battle of Actium.
31 BC-AD 14	AUGUSTUS.
26-19 BC	Campaigns in Spain.
15 BC	Final campaign in Alps.
12-7 BC	Campaigns in Germany.
13-9 BC	Campaigns in Illyricum.
AD 4-6	Campaign against Maroboduus of Bohemia interrupted by –
AD 6-9	Revolt in Illyricum.
AD 9	Loss of three legions in Germany; Rhine-Elbe abandoned.
AD 14-37	TIBERIUS.
AD 14	Mutiny among armies in Pannonia and Germany.
14-16	Germanicus campaigns in Germany.
34-36	War with Parthia.
37-41	GAIUS (CALIGULA).
41-54	CLAUDIUS.
42	Scribonianus' revolt in Dalmatia.
43	Invasion of Britain.
48	Rebellion of the Iceni in Britain.
53	Parthians occupy Armenia.
54-68	NERO.
58-63	Corbulo campaigns in Armenia.
60-61	Boudica rebellion in Britain.
66-70	Jewish War.
74	Fall of Masada.
69-79	VESPASIAN.
69-70	Suppression of revolt of the Civilis and Batavians.
71-84	Conquest of Britain resumed.
79-81	TITUS.
81-96	DOMITIAN.
83	Campaign against the Chatti.
85	Decebalus, King of Dacia, defeats legate of Moesia.
86-89	Dacian War.
89	Revolt of governor of Upper Germany Saturninus.
92	Campaign against the Suebi, Sarmatae and Marcomanni.
96-98	NERVA.
97-98	War in Germany against the Suebi.
98-117	TRAJAN.
101-102	First Dacian War.
105-106	Second Dacian War.
112	Trajan's Column dedicated.
114-117	Parthian War.
117-138	HADRIAN.
122	Hadrian's Wall begun.
132-135	Jewish revolt and Bar-Kochba War.
138-161	ANTONINUS PIUS.
139-142	Campaign in Britain leading to building of Antonine Wall.
161-180	MARCUS AURELIUS with
161-169	LUCIUS VERUS.
176-180	COMMODUS.
162-166	Parthian war nominally under Verus.
166-175	First German War against Marcomanni, Quadi and Sarmatae.
170	Invasion of Italy by Marcomanni and Quadi.
175	Revolt of Avidius Cassius in Syria.
178-180	Second German War; offensive ended by death of Marcus.
180-192	COMMODUS as sole ruler.
180-184	War in Britain.
193-197	Civil War.
193-211	SEPTIMIUS SEVERUS.
198-211	with CARACALLA.
209-211	with GETA.
197-199	War in Parthia.
208-211	Campaigns in Britain.

80 men. A cavalry element, of 120 men, was however added once more. At a later stage, probably in the second half of the 1st century AD, the first cohort was reorganized on different lines, apparently with five double centuries. The reason for this is not known.

The officer structure was also changed. The staff officer (a legate) of the governor or general temporarily posted to command a legion or group of legions now became a permanent commander, still known as a legate, appointed directly by the emperor. The six tribunes remained, but one of them

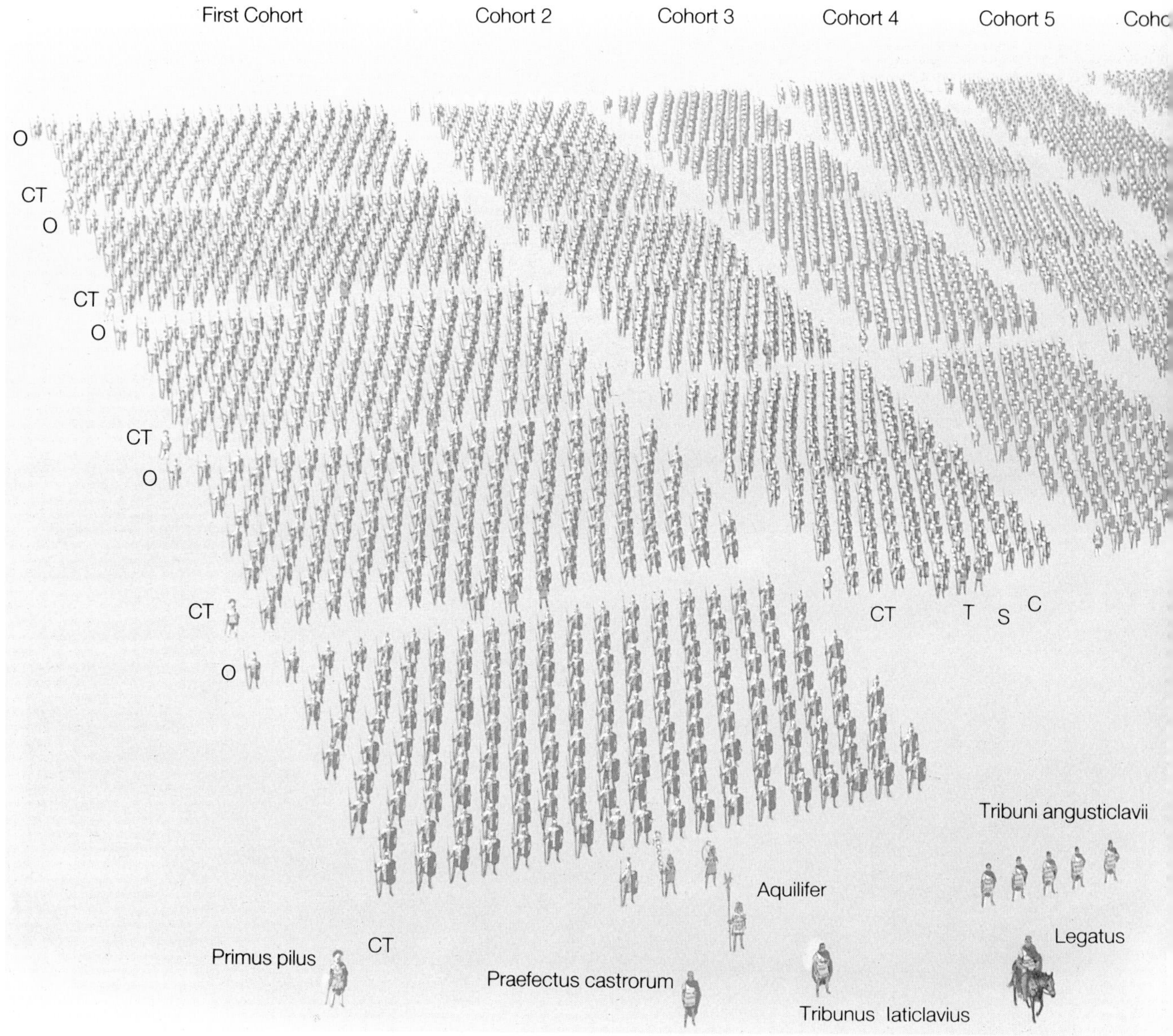

O
CT
O
CT
O
CT
O
CT T S C
O

Tribuni angusticlavii

Aquilifer

Legatus

Primus pilus CT

Praefectus castrorum

Tribunus laticlavius

The legion as reorganized with a first cohort of five double-centuries of 160 men and nine cohorts of five centuries of 80 men. 120 horsemen were attached to the legion.
C = cornicen CT = centurion O = signifier T = tesserarius

was a *tribunus laticlavius*, a man who wore the broad stripe on his tunic marking him out as a candidate to enter the senate. It is generally supposed that he was the senior tribune. As before, there was no cohort commander, the presumption being that the senior centurion would take command unless a tribune took charge. A new officer was the prefect of the camp, generally a former senior centurion. As his name suggests, he took charge of the running of the camp and the base, with prime responsibility for the equipment and its transport. The centurions remained the backbone of the legion, and the most senior centurion, the *primus pilus*, increased in importance. These most senior centurions soon monopolized the newly created posts of prefect of the camp in the legions and tribunes (commanding officers) of the cohorts in Rome, the fire brigade (*vigiles*), the Urban cohorts and the Praetorian cohorts.

The legions in Egypt were organized on different lines. The governor of Egypt was a prefect, an equestrian, not a senator, and the legions were supervised (but not necessarily commanded in battle) by a special officer, the *praefectus castrorum Aegypti*, instead of by legates. This man also had been a senior centurion. There was no *tribunus laticlavius*, just six tribunes of equal status.

The legionaries were long-service soldiers. Only wounds, ill-health or dishonourable discharge brought an early end to their service. In theory they

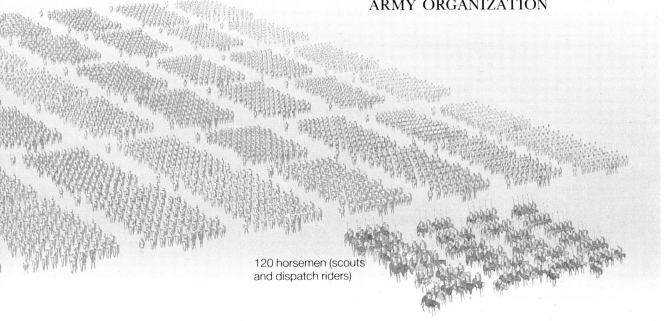

120 horsemen (scouts
and dispatch riders)

were Roman citizens, and were so in practice in the West. But in the East, where there were fewer citizens, men were often granted citizenship on recruitment. They could be conscripted or volunteer, and voluntary recruitment became the norm, at the latest by the 2nd century AD. There was a preference for volunteers. No longer was there the possibility of relatively short service under commanders who might secure their men a large share in booty, and the legions were to find permanent stations a long way from Rome and Italy. Service in the legions became steadily less attractive to Italians, who could now enlist in the cohorts in Rome. The burden of recruitment was increasingly borne by the provinces, particularly those in which the legions were stationed. With the growth of the number of recruits who were sons of soldiers, service became almost hereditary.

Arms and Armour

The legionaries remained heavy infantry, with standardized equipment: helmet, body armour and large shield for protection; and as weapons of attack

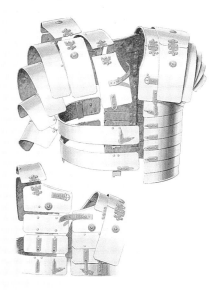

left
Front view of the rectangular scutum (shield) from Dura Europos in Syria. The linen and hide covering has been pulled back to show the construction from laminated strips of wood.

far left
A reconstruction of the Corbridge hook-type lorica segmentata. The main shoulder unit and chest unit are held together with hinges. All the shoulder, chest and upper back pieces on each side are riveted to leather straps. The two halves are then buckled together. The girdle plates are similarly riveted to leather straps on each side and then laced together, front and back. The girdle plates are joined to the shoulder unit with hooks.

195

the javelin (*pilum*) and the sword, the latter being the primary weapon. The effectiveness of the helmet was increased by the enlarging of the neck guard and by additional cheek pieces, reinforcing strips across the front and ear guards. Until the middle of the 1st century the body armour was the mail shirt, weighing some 12-15 kg. In the West it then began to be replaced by the *lorica segmentata*, a convenient term invented by modern scholars, and neatly expressed by Peter Connolly as 'the first articulated plate armour'. It is best understood from the accompanying illustrations. On Trajan's Column it is worn exclusively by legionaries and never by auxiliaries, but this seems to be an artistic simplification. The *lorica segmentata* was not as long as the mail shirt, though some protection was afforded to the lower abdomen by an apron of metal discs attached to straps. Greaves were sometimes worn. In front of helmet and body armour was the shield, shorter and rectangular in shape from early in the 1st century AD. This was made up of layers of strips of wood, with the rim reinforced by a bronze strip, and an iron or bronze central boss protecting the handgrip. The shield was encased in leather. It was 6mm thick, perhaps increasing to 10mm in the centre, and may have weighed 5.5kg or, with the proposed thickening in the centre, 7.5kg.

The javelin (*pilum*) has already been described. There is a possibility that when the heavy type was lightened during this period a new heavy javelin was introduced with a round lead weight where wood met iron. The sword with dagger shape and long tapering point was replaced in the late 1st century AD by a weapon with straight parallel sides and a shorter point; its blade length was 44-55cm compared with the 50-56cm of the earlier type. The dagger seems to disappear from legionary equipment around the end of the 1st century AD.

As a fighting instrument the legion underwent little or no change, with the addition of a small cavalry contingent. At the same time it gained a new permanence and continuity as a unit made up of long-serving soldiers which required a permanent base.

AUGUSTUS' NEW ARMY: THE AUXILIA

The table shows how all major Roman army units were made up of infantry centuries and cavalry troops. The basic infantry cohort was six centuries, the larger ten. Cavalry operated in multiples of four troops.

The *auxilia* were new, though as usual continuity in nomenclature often masks real change. There had been and continued to be soldiers taken into Rome's service from a variety of sources and on differing terms and periods of engagement. These might be men provided by compulsion from the defeated or overawed, by friendly allied tribes or kings, or simply men hired as

TABLE OF UNIT ORGANIZATION

	Troops (32 men)	Cavalry	Centuries (80 men)	Infantry	Total
legion cohorts II-X	—		6	480	480
legion cohort I	—	—	5 double	800	800
legionary cavalry	—	120	—	—	120
auxiliary infantry cohort	—	—	6	480	480
auxiliary mixed cohort	4	128	6	480	608
auxiliary infantry cohort (milliary)	—		10	800	800
auxiliary mixed cohort (milliary)	8	256	10	800	1056
cavalry regiment	16	512	—	—	512
cavalry regiment (milliary	24	768	—	—	768

A scene from Trajan's Column. In the foreground an auxiliary soldier is being bandaged by an orderly while a legionary is being helped to the first-aid station. Members of the imperial guard in the background wait to join in the battle raging immediately on our right (just off picture).

mercenaries. They might provide supporting arms for the legionary heavy infantry, cavalry being the most obvious example, but there was also a need for light infantry, archers and slingers. More manpower was always useful, though the Romans were careful to avoid the massive and uncontrollable numbers of other armies.

Organization

All these elements can be identified from time to time, for example, the troops of friendly kings who fought for Vespasian in Judea, or the Moors who were brought over for Trajan's Dacian wars. But from the time of Augustus there appear alongside them a number of regiments, cavalry *(alae)* and infantry (cohorts), which display signs of permanence and identity. Evidence of their organization does not become plentiful till the Flavian period, AD 69-96, but there are references to 70 cohorts and 14 *alae* in the army charged with putting down the Illyrian revolt in AD 6-9; and 26 cohorts and 8 cavalry regiments in Germany a few years later. Tacitus says that under Tiberius there were approximately as many auxiliaries as legionaries. There are problems, particularly with some units in the Rhineland, in determining whether cohorts are tribal levies or regular cohorts, especially with commanding officers drawn from tribal leaders and a strong link between cohort and tribe. However, these difficulties disappear after AD 69, when the links between tribes and the cohorts raised from them were finally broken. But there is incontrovertible evidence for the existence of regiments organized on an increasingly regular basis from the time of Augustus. Significantly, like the legionaries, the men in these regiments served many years; 25 years eventually became the normal maximum length of service.

The Mixed Units

In addition to pure infantry regiments (cohorts) and cavalry regiments (*alae*) there was a third variety, the mixed regiment (*cohors equitata*). Caesar had been impressed by and employed the Germans who fought as infantry mixed with cavalry. But the Roman model was not the same, as the Germans operated on a one-to-one ratio, while the Romans used a ratio of 4:1. Such a unit is attested in the army of Augustus. The basic organization appears to be related to that of the legionary cohort, as the accompanying table shows: the mixed cohort had added 120 cavalry, the same as the number of cavalry attached to the legion.

The Cavalry Regiment

The cavalry regiment had the same number of men, 480, organized in 16 troops (*turmae*) of 30 men. The number is sometimes quoted as 512, counting separately the two junior officers in each troop, the *duplicarius* (double-pay man) and *sesquiplicarius* (1½ times pay man), to make a troop of 32. The original troop had been divided into three files of ten, each with its own commander, and this is reflected in the name decurion for the commander of the whole troop (a decurion is literally a commander of ten men). The *turma* also had an extra officer, the *curator*, whose responsibility presumably lay with the horses.

The Milliary Units

These arrangements are further complicated by the introduction – under the Flavians or possibly in the 60s in the East – of a larger type of unit in each of the categories, infantry cohort, mixed cohort, cavalry regiment. In each case the term *milliaria*, literally a thousand strong, was used to distinguish the larger unit, and it is tempting to link it with the increase in the size of the first cohort in the legion. The infantry and mixed cohorts now have ten centuries, comparable with the five double centuries of the legionary first cohort; the cavalry element in the milliary mixed cohort is doubled; the *ala milliaria* now has 24 *turmae*. The resulting totals are shown, it being assumed that the century and *turma* keep the same establishment strengths of 80 and 32 respectively.

Number of Units

It is more difficult to calculate the number of such units than it is for the legions; they are more numerous and more easily destroyed. However, they observe the same rule that once formed they continue in being; they do not represent the sort of wartime forces which can be raised and then demobilized. It has been calculated that by the middle of the 2nd century AD there were 257 cohorts, of which 130 were mixed; 40 milliary cohorts, of which 22 were mixed; 82 ordinary cavalry regiments; and perhaps eight milliary regiments. This gives a force of some 227,000 men to add to the 157,000 legionaries as the standing peace-time army of the Roman state, a grand total of 384,000, of whom 71,000 were mounted.

Numeri

These are generally reckoned with the *auxilia*. *Numerus* means simply a unit, and it is best to think of *numeri* as units that were not cohorts nor *alae*, rather than as a specific type of unit. Little is known about them.

ANIMAL MANAGEMENT

Animal management in the field, especially as regards the basic question of feeding, raised huge problems in ancient warfare, upon which sources are by no means plentiful. Not surprisingly, Assyria provides one of the earliest references. Sennacherib shipped grain and hay to the Persian Gulf before his assault on Elam. Roman sources, however, offer further details on fodder, grains and containment of beasts.

According to Polybius, in a marching camp the horses were tethered in long lines, with what in modern British practice is termed a stable guard to prevent entanglement or other trouble. Much later, in the 370s AD, when cavalry had greatly increased, Vegetius tells us in *De Re Militarii* that in camps horses are pastured and guarded by four horsemen and four infantry from each century. Archaeology has provided evidence of fort stables, with manure, grain and shed teeth being found. British examples are Brough on Noe, Nod Hill and The Lunt, the last Roman fort in Warwickshire. Presumably only those animals on 'alert' would be stabled inside the camp, due to lack of space.

The question of forage for all animals raises a wide range of questions. Grazing was provided on the legionary *Prata* (army grazing grounds) attached to permanent camps. In Spain, the IV Legion Macedonica had grazing lands adjacent to Juliobriges, near Santander, and the IV Cohort of Gauls had grazing adjacent to Bidienienses. Polybius gives rations which

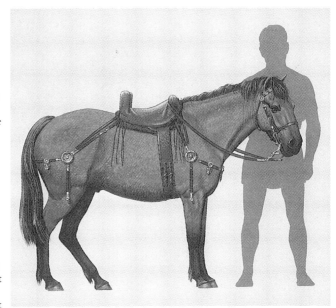

work out at 1.6kg per horse, and a papyrus from Oxyrhynchus attests to a similar weight in the 6th century. English cavalry horses, at an average height of 15½ hands, and therefore much heavier than Roman, at about 14½-15, received 5.4–6.3kg of oats or equivalent (eg barley) a day, with about 5.4kg of hay and some greenstuff when available. The protein content of grains in the ancient world was much higher than it is today. A cavalry horses's life would be largely spent on low-energy output where flesh would not be burnt off. Hay was provided at need, but from 362 the existing practice of not issuing it until 1 August appears in the Theodosina Code. We know from Ammianus Marcellinus that hay was gathered in massive quantities. He recounts the collapse of a huge stack in Osrhoene which smothered 50 grooms. On campaigns most horses (and mules) would have

subsisted on the little that could be carried, and on what they could pick up on the march. Caesar, in his *Gallic Wars,* makes frequent references to the collection of both fodder and grain and to the difficulties in obtaining it.

Recruiting

The men recruited into the *alae* and cohorts were normally non-citizens, although there was no bar to citizens entering them, and some did. Their service finally settled down at 25 years, and they received Roman citizenship on discharge, but no gratuities. Recruitment was unrestricted, although generally from within the Empire. Compulsory levies might be carried out, but there was also a strong voluntary element. Recruiting was normally conducted in the province where the unit was stationed. All units have titles, and in many cases they indicate where units were first raised, but these are no guide to their later composition. In effect, local recruiting may be narrowed down to recruiting from the frontier district of each province, again with a strong contribution from soldiers' sons.

Arms and Armour

The auxiliary infantryman wears armour which is similar to that of the legionaries but of inferior quality. The helmet is usually a cheap version of that worn by the legionary, the body armour is mail, scale or, in some cases, *lorica segmentata*. The shield is a flat oval. The sword is similar, but the javelin is normally replaced by a short spear. Thus armed the auxiliary infantryman is equipped to fight like a legionary. This is confirmed by the literary accounts. It is not clear if there were auxiliary cohorts which had a light infantry function. There were regiments of archers, generally recruited in the East, where new recruits were sought from the original homelands. They wear mail shirts, and use the composite bow, made up of wood with sinew outside and horn inside.

The Ala cavalryman rode a large pony, standing some 14-15 hands (1.4-1.5m). He had no stirrups, but the four projecting horns of his saddle anchored him securely, allowing him to use a spear like a lance and giving him a free swing with the sword. He wore a helmet which covered his whole head, leaving only eyes, nose and mouth visible; cross bracing was added to the helmet in the 2nd century. He wore mail or scale body armour, a heavy first-century AD type of 16kg being replaced by a simpler form, shown on Trajan's Column, which weighed only about 9kg, and used a flat, oval, sometimes hexagonal shield. His long sword (*spatha*) had a blade length of 60-70cm. Alongside the standard cavalry regiment there were special heavy regiments, the *cataphracti*, with both man and horse fully covered by armour. Hadrian formed the first regular unit of *cataphracti*, armed with a heavy lance *(contus)*. At the other end of the scale there was light Moorish cavalry, completely unarmoured, riding without a saddle or (it would appear) a bridle, and mounted archers using the composite bow. The cavalryman of the mixed cohorts had inferior quality

Trajan's Column. Roman auxiliary cavalrymen pursue enemy Sarmatian cavalry, who wear scale armour and have armour on their horses (the artist has not properly understood the latter).

arms and armour, related to the different rate of pay, but otherwise was similarly equipped to the *ala* trooper.

Officers

With the exception of a few legionaries transferred to junior officer posts in the cavalry, the majority of centurions and decurions were promoted from the ranks. Only the commanding officers of these units came from outside them.

AUGUSTUS' NEW ARMY: OTHER UNITS

There were a number of units which were neither legions nor *auxilia*. The most important were the units in Rome and the fleets. In Rome itself (not all of them originally) were stationed nine infantry cohorts (500 strong) of Roman citizens, the Praetorian Guard, *cohortes praetoriae*. These were essentially to protect the emperor from Caesar's fate. The *cohors praetoria* had been the general's bodyguard, normally made up of seasoned soldiers. These cohorts were not to represent the cream of the legions but to be a force directly recruited from Italy. Not surprisingly relations were not good between the legions and this force, privileged with 16 years' service, higher pay and higher gratuities on leaving service. The shorter service of the guard made it possible to continue the practice of holding men back from discharge (*evocatio*) to use them further as specialists and in some cases to become centurions; longer service in the legions meant that the device was little used there. Although the guard sometimes went to war with the emperor, there is no evidence that it had any special role in the Roman army, as has sometimes been suggested. Potential trouble in Rome itself was controlled by a further four cohorts, the urban cohorts, and the menace of fire was dealt with by instituting a fire brigade, the *cohortes vigilum*, seven cohorts to cover the 14 regions of the city. Two urban cohorts served outside Italy, at Carthage and Lyon respectively.

Naval warfare had occasionally been a feature of the civil wars. Between 31 BC and AD 200, with the exception of periods of civil war, there was no war at sea. Two fleets were stationed in Italy, at Ravenna and Misenum, each with perhaps some 50 ships (triremes) and 10,000 men. Other smaller fleets were stationed in the Black Sea, one each for the middle and lower Danube, the Rhine, and the seas around Britain, and two off Egypt and Syria in the Eastern Mediterranean, with detachments off Mauretania. Their principal responsibility was for convoy and protection against pirates, but from time to time the northern fleets in particular might be involved in campaigning, in a subordinate role.

Of specialist arms, the artillery available had not changed since the later Republic. The only innovation was the mounting of the small arrow-shooting catapult on a cart, which gave it mobility for use on the battlefield. The operation of catapults does not seem to have been entrusted to artillery specialists. The likely allocation was one arrow-shooter for each legionary century and a big siege catapult for each legionary cohort, though it is not know whether one *contubernium* (tent-group of eight men) in each century had the arrow-shooter as their permanent responsibility, as seems to have been the case in later times. There were engineer officers and men (*architecti*) whose responsibilities included the building and maintenance of the catapults. The building of roads, bridges, forts and the construction of siege-works fell to the ordinary soldiers and their officers. There is a strong suggestion that at first this was essentially the responsibility of the legions alone, but by the 2nd century the auxiliaries developed similar skills. Medical care was provided by bandagers and first-aid orderlies (*capsarii* and *medici*). There were also doctors (also called *medici*). Like the *architecti*, there seem to have been men of differing ranks with the same title.

A ROMAN CAVALRY REGIMENT (ALA QUINGENARIA) ADVANCING AND DEPLOYING INTO LINE OF BATTLE

At the front of the regiment rides the commanding officer, the prefect, with the flag-bearer of the unit (the *vexillarius*), a trumpeter and a bodyguard. Behind come 16 troops (*turmae*), each led by a standard-bearer (*signifer*). Each troop rides in three files of ten, the right-hand file led by the troop-commander (*decurio*), the other two led by the *duplicarius* and *sesquiplicarius* respectively. Two of the troops riding behind are beginning to swing out to lengthen the battle-line.

Musical instruments were used to sound the charge and recall, though there is some uncertainty about the types. Two types of standard are shown, as the precise form is not known. The precise deployment of the *ala* in battle would vary. Normally the regiment would be on one of the wings or as in Arrian's battle actually behind the infantry, awaiting the moment of release, at the enemy's flanks, at his rear, at demoralised and retreating infantry, at opposing cavalry. What emerges clearly from the picture is the size of the standard Roman cavalry regiment, a formidable weapon when used correctly. Comprising over 500 men equipped with helmets and body armour and riding large ponies, it could act in a light or medium cavalry role.

THE OFFICERS: RECRUITMENT
AND CAREERS

Senators

The provinces (apart from Egypt and a few minor ones) continued to be governed by senators. The crucial difference was that the emperor had his own province (in the sense of sphere of command), which came to include virtually all the provinces which contained legions. These he controlled through personally appointed senators, who were his legates and fulfilled the twin roles of civil governor and commander of the units in their provinces. Senators of lesser status were appointed by the emperor as his legates to command legions (except in Egypt), this post now becoming a permanent one. Provinces and legions tended to be held for three-year periods, though this is an average, not a rule. Young men who were candidates for the senate wore the broad stripe, and one of the six legionary tribunates (except in Egypt) was reserved for a broad-striper, the *tribunus laticlavius*.

These men gained their military experience in three stages, separated by or combined with administrative responsibilities. In their early teens or late twenties they served as tribunes, on a legionary commander's staff, generally for two or three years. These posts were in the gift of the governor. Then came seven to ten years of minor magistracies and leisure before the post of legionary commander was attained. There followed at least one more appointment, perhaps as governor of a province without legions, or with only one legion, before they achieved the consulate. The provinces held after the consulate might hold two to four legions, and men reached them often in their early to middle 40s. In the Empire men often reached high office at a relatively young age.

There was relatively little opportunity to demonstrate military ability in the early years, and political reliability was very important for the major commands. Almost half of the Roman senate would be required to serve as legionary commanders, so a relatively high degree of basic competence was demanded. Towards the end of the period, under Marcus Aurelius, the length of military service after the consulate for outstanding generals is tending to increase. They now might hold three or more major commands after the consulate and then move on to the emperor's personal staff.

Equestrians

This is the second major group. During the Republic, it was the major supplier of tribunes and prefects, although they had no organized career structure. The multiplication of auxiliary commands led to the establishment of a recognized hierarchy of posts: prefect of a normal-sized (quingenary) cohort; tribune in a legion or tribune of the larger size of cohort (milliarty); prefect of an *ala* (cavalry regiment). Under Hadrian the command of the larger-sized cavalry regiment (milliary) became a fourth stage. These commands were held one after another, each lasting some three to four years on average, by men who often had been senior magistrates in their own towns and were still in their early thirties. Commands of cohorts and legionary tribunates were in the gift of the provincial governor; it seems likely that when the officer changed provinces, which he would do at latest when he received his cavalry command, the emperor would be directly involved in the promotion, but he could of course intervene earlier. There was a filtering process. In the mid-2nd century there were only 141 vacancies as legionary tribune for approximately 270 commanders of the 500-strong infantry or mixed auxiliary regiments, enabling governors to avoid appointing men who had proved to be incompetent. The best of the 270, some 30 to 40, would have been appointed by the emperor to command the 1,000-strong infantry and mixed cohorts. Beyond lay 82 commands of cavalry regiments and finally eight commands of the larger size cavalry regiments.

Some equestrians sought and obtained commissions as legionary centurions, in effect securing jobs for life. There were also large rewards on retirement, particularly if senior posts were reached. In contrast, the equestrian officer had to secure each appointment, received nothing beyond his salary, and after 9-12 years retired home or switched to a career which was largely administrative and financial, that of the procurators. The senior centurions also might move on to the procuratorships, generally after service as tribunes in Rome. There were a few senior posts with military duties – for example, prefects of the'river and sea fleets – and some minor governorships which involved commanding auxiliary troops. But as strictly there was no purely military command above unit commander, there was no opportunity to specialize. There were some great prefectures, those of the fire brigade, of the corn supply, of Egypt, and of the Praetorian Guard, which Augustus confined to equestrians, but no exclusively military career led to them. However, increasing military pressure on the Danube frontier towards the end of the period, again Marcus Aurelius is a convenient point to take, brought some equestrian officers into the commands reserved for senators by transfer into the senate.

Men from the Ranks

The third main source of officers was from the ranks of the legions and from the guard. They were chiefly used to fill the ranks of the legionary centurionate. The centurion must not be thought of as a non-commissioned officer, but as a true officer, the equivalent of a captain in a modern army. Most of them seem to have come from the ranks, although there was a significant element of directly commissioned equestrians. On average the legionaries would have served some 14 years. Men from the Praetorian Guard became eligible for the centurionate when they had completed their 16 years' service and become *evocati*. They exclusively supplied the centurions of the *vigiles*, and many of the urban and praetorian centurionates alongside some directly-commissioned centurions transferred from the legionary centurionate, and also some legionary centurions. The legionaries supplied only legionary centurions, but these represent some 90 per cent of the posts available. They would be reached between the ages of 30 and 40, and were often held well beyond the maximum service for ordinary soldiers, into the 60s and 70s.

As noted above, auxiliary centurions and decurions were drawn mainly from their own ranks, and had little or no prospect of further promotion.

STRATEGY AND TACTICS

Augustus' army relied largely on time-honoured methods to achieve success. In battle it faced for the most part barbarian tribes; the only surviving empire, that of the Parthians, lacked siege techniques, and could therefore mount only raids. The Romans had a relative degree of success against them in war and diplomacy, without either side gaining permanent accessions of territory from the other till the time of Severus.

Battle

Success was gained first of all by the pitched battle, which Rome could generally reckon to win. The superior training and discipline of the legions was the key to victory, although increasing emphasis was placed on the auxiliaries, with the legions held in reserve. Rome's advantage lay not in superior technology but in the resources which permitted her to maintain a professional long-service army fully equipped with arms and armour. With the exception of

Parthia, her opponents relied on the small permanent bodies of military companions maintained by their chiefs and aristocrats and the tribal levy; their equipment depended on their own resources and their willingness to submit to the burden of helmet and body armour. In these circumstances little subtlety in battle tactics was required. The great disaster of the period, the loss of three legions in AD 9 under Varus, can be attributed to the Roman commander's belief that Germany was pacified. This led Varus to neglect march discipline, and his army shambled into the trap prepared for it by the German guides, serving as Roman officers and considered friendly but in fact deeply hostile. Its significance lay in the psychological shock it dealt the aged Augustus, not in the exposure of some fundamental weakness in the Roman army.

To be effective the battle must inflict disproportionately heavy losses on the enemy – there must be a killing ground. The heaviest casualties are often inflicted in pursuit, and for this the cavalry was invaluable. Scouting was also a primary role. Cavalry could not break infantry which remained steady and in formation, unless it was presented with opportunities to attack in flank and rear.

Although in general Roman battlefield tactics were not complex, there is evidence that in different parts of the Empire Roman fighting methods were adapted to meet those of the principal enemy. A notable example is suggested by the Adamklissi reliefs, from Trajan's great victory monument in Romania. The enemies used a two-handed battle scythe, and to counter this the legionaries wore special protective armour on the exposed sword arm. Trajan's Column in Rome from the same period, with its stylized Romans and Dacians, gives no hint of this innovation.

The Roman governor Arrian gives a tantalizing account of war against the Alans which suggests a carefully composed fighting force and battle line. Arrian was governor of Cappadocia (eastern Turkey) in AD 135, under Hadrian. He faced the Alani, one of the Sarmatian peoples, who were primarily cavalrymen (see plan, page 208). They did not all wear full armour for horse and man, as their relations do on Trajan's Column, but they used the long heavy two-handed spear, the *contus*. They relied on an initial charge, but if that was repulsed might rally and counter-attack, particularly on the flanks. Arrian drew up his two legions to meet them not in the traditional open order but in tight-packed ranks eight deep, with a ninth line of archers behind. The first four ranks seem to have carried the *pilum*, the second four a lighter weapon. On each flank an auxiliary infantry cohort stood on a hill, with the irregular troops, and archers behind. The artillery was deployed on the hills on the flanks and behind Arrian's centre. The mounted scouts, horse archers, and heavy cavalry, who had formed the vanguard on the march, now fell back before the advancing Alani. The horse archers formed a tenth rank in the centre; the cavalry, with their lances and spears, heavy and light, swords and axes, formed behind the centre and flanks. As the Alani approached, the legionary front ranks levelled their weapons, forming a hedge of spears, the first three ranks pressed closely together. From the ranks behind came a hail of missiles. Driven off, the Alans were then subjected to a controlled pursuit, with the cavalry behind the centre available to move to the wings to block any outflanking manoeuvre. Although the story is cut short, we know Arrian frightened off the Alani. The picture of the legions in this account, a generation after Trajan's Column, suggests a reversion to a mainly defensive role.

Siege Warfare

When forcing the enemy to give battle, the Roman expertise in siege warfare gave them a crucial advantage. Effective resistance to this was only likely to be mounted in the East, where technical knowledge matched that of the Romans, and the siege of Jerusalem in AD 70 exemplifies the problems of besiegers and besieged. The failure of Trajan before the city of Hatra, repeated by Severus,

Trajan's Column. Mail armour is clearly seen on the auxiliary in centre foreground. Behind, Eastern archers in scale armour use composite bows of sinew, wood, and horn.

opposite
Bronze parade helmet, worn for special exhibitions of cavalry sports. Found on the face of a corpse in a tomb near Nola. 1st or 2nd century AD. British Museum, London.

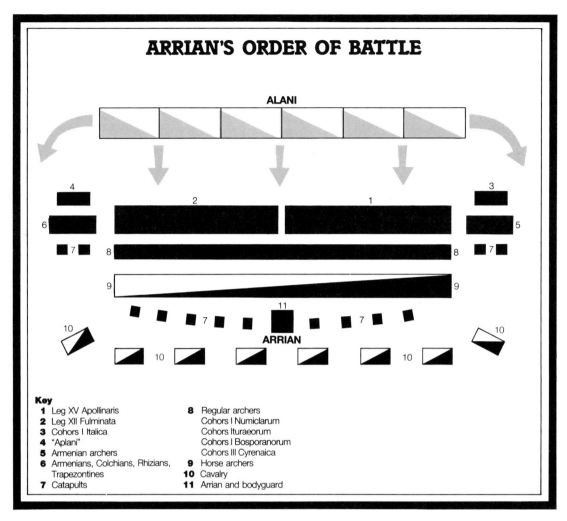

ARRIAN'S ORDER OF BATTLE

ALANI

ARRIAN

Key

1 Leg XV Apollinaris
2 Leg XII Fulminata
3 Cohors I Italica
4 "Aplani"
5 Armenian archers
6 Armenians, Colchians, Rhizians, Trapezontines
7 Catapults

8 Regular archers
    Cohors I Numiclarum
    Cohors Ituraeorum
    Cohors I Bosporanorum
    Cohors III Cyrenaica
9 Horse archers
10 Cavalry
11 Arrian and bodyguard

emphasizes that sieges can be lost. Nevertheless, Rome usually won her sieges, and no refuge was counted impregnable to the Roman army. Inaccessible was also a word not acknowledged by Rome, and the determined pressing home of the siege of Masada by the building of the great siege ramp underlined this point.

Vastatio – Kill, Burn, Destroy

If the enemy declines battle and does not take refuge in a known place, trusting in its impregnability or inaccessibility, if indeed there is no place that must be retained at all costs, then he can withdraw beyond the reach of the army and rely on guerrilla warfare. However, guerrilla warfare conducted in the absence of outside support or a secure base is not easy, and Rome's ruthless use of systematic ravaging (*vastatio*) made it even more costly. Crops were carried off or burnt, animals driven off or slaughtered, human beings were massacred or enslaved, buildings burnt. The Roman historian Tacitus speaks in a chilling phrase of the alternative employment of frightfulness and offers of peace to break the will to resist. Moreover, it is not true that mountainous regions posed insuperable problems for the legions, as any study of Roman military activity makes clear. The Alps, Spain, the Balkans, Armenia, Palestine, were all places where the difficulties of the terrain were overcome.

Rebellion

There is a recurring pattern to Roman conquest: a relatively rapid initial

Trajan's Column. Roman auxiliary soldiers are penned behind their fort walls by a Dacian attack.

Trajan's Column. A mixture of Roman troops engage Dacians: a slinger from hand on the left, a sling-user next to him with a store of stones in his cloak, semi-naked irregulars and regular auxiliary infantry.

Trajan's Column. Dacians hold a council of war inside their own fortifications.

PREPARE TO RECEIVE CAVALRY: LEGIONS AGAINST ALANS, AD 135

The painting illustrates vividly a change in tactics, whether it be a general change, a particular adaptation to meet the threat of the Alani, or standard operating procedure against cavalry. The charge of heavy cavalry is met by the legions forming a hedge of missiles, javelins from the rear ranks, and arrows from the archers and bolts and stones from the catapults, behind and on the flanks. To meet the charge, the front rank level their javelins *(pila)* at the horses' chests, and ranks two and three close up to brace the first rank against the shock. The horses will not charge on to the levelled points; as long as the legionaries do not flinch the line holds. There is no opportunity for the counter-attack by the Roman cavalry from the flanks and the rear. The legions remain crucial to the battle, but have sacrificed flexibility. Even in advance after the fleeing enemy they act as a mobile wall, moving at steady pace, to shelter behind if the enemy rally. They have come full circle and are acting once more as a phalanx.

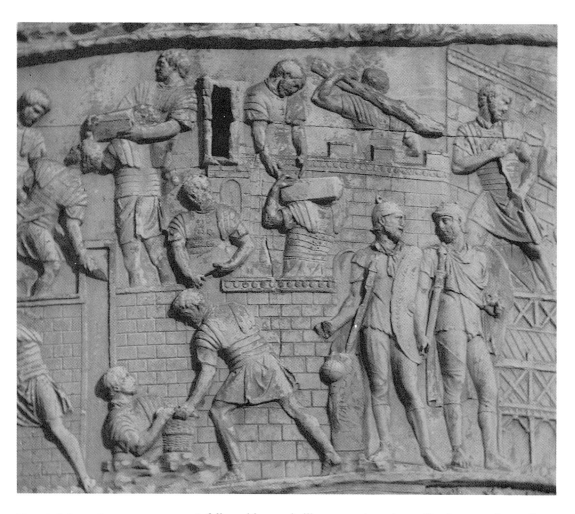

Trajan's Column. Roman legionaries are seen busy building a fort. Baskets are being emptied as ditches are dug, turves are being carried on shoulders, and timber is being brought in, while auxiliaries stand guard.

conquest, followed by a rebellion, sometimes immediately, sometimes after a lapse of time. The rebellions often led to the bloodiest struggles. The massacre of three legions in AD 9 was a rebellion, inasmuch as it was brought about by trusted native officers in territory which was considered pacified. So had been the great Illyrian revolt of AD 6-9, such was the Boudican revolt in Britain in AD 60 and the Jewish revolt of AD 66-70. The fighting in 69-70 on the Rhine was part-mutiny, part-rebellion. The second Dacian war (105-7) was a rebellion against the terms imposed after the first. There is an element of desperation on the one side, of shock followed by a ruthless determination to prevail on the other. Desperate resistance might be met by virtual annihilation. This was a fate meted out by Augustus to an Alpine tribe, the Salassi, the last 44,000 of whom were sold as slaves.

THE ARMY'S BASES

Conquest was generally secured by the demanding of hostages rather than the physical occupation of territory, which would have drained the strength of the army on campaign. Different problems revolved around the accommodation of the Roman army. In the summer on campaign the traditional marching-camp was employed, and in winter the more elaborate winter-quarters, with huts replacing tents. Here two factors came into play. For 25 years the soldiers had no other home but their barracks, and if they were returning each autumn to the same winter quarters, already happening on the Rhine at the end of Augustus' reign, these quarters might develop more permanent features. Building in stone completed the development but did not begin it. The second

212

feature is the existence of auxiliaries as permanent units, nearly 400 of them. There appears at first to have been a tendency to group them around the legionary bases, but this seems to have been abandoned in favour of a general network of auxiliaries housed in their own forts, about a day's march apart, linked by a road system. This may have been designed as much to facilitate the supply of these units, the prime source being the area immediately around a fort, as to hold down the conquered peoples. Forts were not generally pushed into unconquered territory, unless to hold important points during campaigning, and were otherwise sited at generally convenient places rather than those dictated by special local military considerations. They did not hold permanent garrisons; they provided accommodation for troops during the winter and at other times when they were not campaigning.

An important influence on the location of these forts was the development of linear frontiers, along which they were strung, following the line of a great river or an artificial barrier, so that the network becomes a single strand.

The Legionary Base

This is often termed a fortress, but the term is misleading – the legionary base has similar defences to the auxiliary fort, not stronger ones. These consisted of

Panel from the Tropaeum Traiani, Adamklissi. A legionary in mail armour with his right arm also protected by armour fights an enemy who is using a two-handed battle scythe, the falx. Muzeul de Arheologie, Adamklissi.

213

THE SIEGE OF MASADA

The palace complex created by Herod the Great, girded by massive walls, lies on the plateau in the centre of the picture, surrounded by the desolate landscape of the Dead Sea lands (the sea is on the right). Around it are seen the siege camps of the Roman legion X *Fretensis* and the auxiliary units operating with it, and the wall with its guard-towers built to prevent the escape of the desperate band of nearly 1,000 Jews who had taken refuge in the palace-fortress. Huge water-tanks and stores of food meant that they could not be driven by thirst or starvation to surrender. The Romans therefore could not rely on blockade, so they turned to their engineering skills. On the left of the picture a great ramp has been constructed, of earth and rubble held together by a timber framework. At the top a siege tower has been built to command the wall and prepare for the onslaught of the ram on the wall. Flames shoot high; the crisis of the siege has been reached.

Masada had been seized from a Roman garrison early in the Jewish rebellion of AD 66-70. It had been left to the last in the clearing-up operations, and fell on April 15, AD 74. The Roman commander Flavius Silva, under pressure as not only food but all drinking-water had to be brought in for his forces, had chosen the site for his ramp, 140m below Masada. On it, according to Josephus, he built a platform 90m high, surmounted by a stone pier 23m high, on which finally was built a tower 30m high. It was iron-plated against fire, and catapults within it cleared the defenders from the battlements. A ram brought down the wall, but behind it the Jews had built an earth rampart, contained in timber, which resisted the ram. Against this torches were then directed; for a moment the flames were driven back by the wind, but then the rampart caught fire. As the Romans prepared for the final onslaught the Jewish leader Eleazar exhorted his people to mass suicide. Two women and five children survived in hiding to greet the Romans next day. Rome had displayed her determination to seek out the last rebel and admit no site to be inaccessible or impregnable in face of the siege engineering skills and determination of her soldiers; the Jews had returned the answer of despair, respected by the Romans, who lived by a similar code.

earth ramparts or stone walls, surrounded by one or more ditches. It clearly has its roots in the camp, more particularly the winter camp. The points of difference are to be found not so much in the defences but in the internal arrangements. The base, unlike the camp, no longer contains the whole army, or a division of it, although it occasionally includes more than a single unit. The commanding officer's tent had once doubled as accommodation and as headquarters. These two functions are now separated: the commanding officer's house, while keeping the name of *praetorium*, became a sumptuous residence; the headquarters building became a new creation whose elements included a platform for the commanding officer and a shrine for the standards. Tent or hut lines become barrack buildings, regular storehouses or granaries appear, a hospital, workshops, and accommodation for riding horses, baggage animals, and carts.

The Auxiliary Fort

The legion, with its 5,000 men and many tradesmen, required more elaborate accommodation than the auxiliary unit. The auxiliary unit fort represented a scaled-down version of the legionary base, though with the same essential arrangements. Both devote most of their space to accommodation for the soldiers, and are primarily protected accommodation rather than defended strongpoints.

FRONTIERS

The early placing of the legions, in AD 14, is a significant indication of the way in which they were intended to function. The legions on the Rhine are disposed in two striking-groups of four, poised to invade free Germany or to turn back towards France if trouble threatened there. The legions in Spain were preoccupied with the extinguishing of internal resistance; they would be reduced in number, falling to one after AD 69. The legions lie back from the Danube, concerned with the recently won territory; Dalmatia still holds two legions, soon to be removed. In Syria the four legions are disposed ready to strike east against Parthia; they are the only legions in the whole of the East till Egypt is reached where the legions are concentrated in the delta, more concerned with the turbulent inhabitants of Alexandria than the people on the southern frontier. They were also well placed to join with the Syrian legions or repel the threat that might come from the north. The whole of North Africa, apart from Egypt and Cyrenaica, lay under the guardianship of one legion. Many provinces had no legions in them or even near them.

The situation in the early 3rd century was reached through a number of factors. Political distrust of the large provincial armies led to their reduction to a maximum of two legions per province. There was a shift in threat which downgraded the Rhine in relation to the Danube, where the establishment of Dacia and then the threat on the upper Danube increased the number of legions, long since drawn on to the river line, as frontier and line of communication. Where there was no great river, the legions stayed back. In the East a line of legions replaced the Syrian strike force, extending from Turkey to Jordan, with a salient in Mesopotamia. Yet still one legion kept the peace in North Africa west of Egypt and Cyrenaica. The most important feature of this overall deployment is not immediately apparent; the opportunities for shifting whole legions around the empire for campaigning, or from one province to another, have vanished. No legion has changed its base for some time, some not for centuries.

This tendency to take root is even more marked for the auxiliary regiments. They can still be moved within provinces, but on the riverine frontiers and the Rhine-Danube frontier, with most of the units committed to the line itself, the withdrawal of a unit would leave a noticeable hole. These

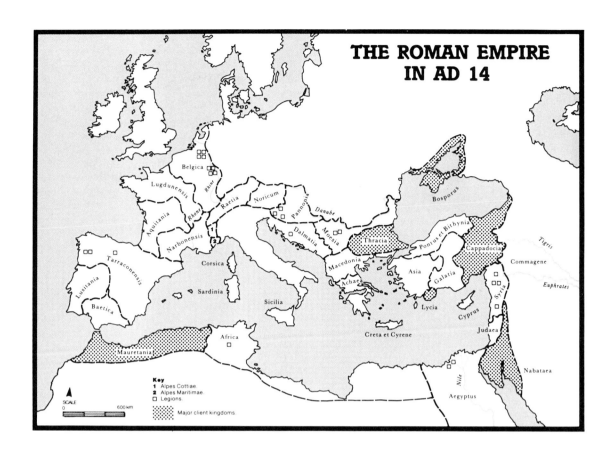

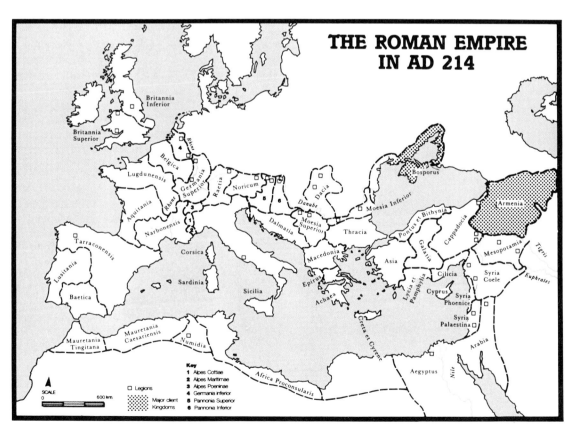

provinces were able to find room on their frontiers for all the units stationed in them. Britain was a notable exception. This meant that on most frontiers there were no troops stationed behind the lines. The deserts and mountain frontiers of East and North Africa posed different problems.

The frontiers had evolved slowly. There is no one uniform pattern, and no emperor was bound by a predecessor's policy, if policy is not too strong a word. The Empire always had boundaries, and these came to be treated as permanent frontiers at different times. The realization that Rome would not fulfil her destiny to rule the world came slowly. Augustus only turned to a notion of keeping the Empire within its boundaries at the end of his life after the twin disasters in Illyricum in AD 6 and in Germany. His immediate successor Tiberius was inclined to accept this view, not so his successors. Claudius shows how policy might vary. He expanded into Britain for his own glory, but restrained a general from moving across the lower Rhine. And in the Rhine mouth area and on the upper Danube he strung forts out along river lines for the first time. Just as the time when a frontier became permanent varied from province to province, so the system of control established on it was adapted to local conditions. Artificial barriers were required only where there were no great rivers, mountains, or deserts, and were slow to appear. They were part of more elaborate systems than those on the rivers, for they required the barrier to mark the line represented elsewhere by a natural physical obstacle; they required lateral communications without the natural advantage that the great rivers provided, being themselves lines of communications and supply; and the provision for watching them, involving chains of observation towers, was generally more elaborate than that provided on the rivers, which were also patrolled by fleets.

Britain was unusual in not being part of a continuous line, and thus had its own special frontier. Its geography also made it impossible to place all the units on the frontier lines. In its fully developed form, the frontier was marked by a barrier stretching 120km – Hadrian's wall.

This stone wall was perhaps some 5m high, fronted with a broad berm and a ditch 8m wide and 3m deep. It was defended by 80 small mile-castles about 1,500m apart and some 160 turrets. Two turrets were placed between each mile-castle about 500m apart. Many towers were eliminated as a result of experience and as a consequence of the decision to incorporate forts on the line, which provided increased patrolling. There were gateways at 1,500m intervals, though the majority of these seem in time to have been narrowed to passages for people on foot. There were forts approximately 11km apart, with a

A recently erected simulation of the west gate of the Roman fort at South Shields, on the eastern flank of Hadrian's Wall.

A tombstone depicts the deceased Roman auxiliary cavalryman, T. Flavius Bassus, riding down a barbarian, sometimes seen as representing death. Behind him stands his servant. Römisch-Germanisches Museum, Cologne.

few extra ones, and a road running close to the rear of the complex, the Military Way. The ditch behind, the Vallum, was dispensed with by the beginning of the 3rd century.

Another notable artificial frontier ran from upper Rhine to upper Danube, protecting an important line of communication. This was simply a wooden fence some 3m high, with a chain of towers, supported by fortlets and forts. There were guarded openings, where there were natural routes crossing the frontier, not at regular intervals. Later this was supplemented in Upper Germany by a bank and ditch, in Raetia replaced by a narrow stone wall, emphasizing that different provinces had different solutions.

Otherwise, with the single exception of Dacia, the frontier in Europe was Rhine and Danube. The East is more complex and less well explored; there were no artificial barriers, and roads were used to mark the line and forts guarded essential water supplies or major lines of communication. Egypt had its own system dominated by the control of the Nile valley. In North Africa there was the third great artificial barrier, or series of barriers, the *Fossatum Africae*, controlling access to the province of Numidia, a ditch 4-6m wide and 2.3m deep, with a dry-stone wall not more than 2.5m high.

Each of these frontiers is planned for the local conditions, but some generalizations are possible. The general effect is to commit the army to establishing close control of movement at the frontier line, whether it is artificial or natural. This was to eliminate unauthorized movement, particularly raiding, and in desert areas controlling seasonal transhumance, and would have been effective against low-intensity attacks. A major attack on one sector would cause problems, however, because of the difficulty of concentrating into a field army forces which were strung out along a frontier. This was compounded by the lack of reserves, obtainable only by withdrawing troops from another sector of the frontier or from another province, leaving new gaps. The solution was to draw on detachments rather than whole units, particularly of legions. After Marcus Aurelius no legion changed station. There was no central reserve, and the frontier could only be reinforced by troops marching or sailing – a journey measured in months. The provision of a force at the emperor's immediate disposal without stripping the frontiers was an increasingly urgent necessity.

SIGNALLING AND COMMUNICATIONS

This is a convenient place to discuss these problems for this army of nearly half-a-million men spread over frontiers of a total length well in excess of 10,000 kilometres. On the battlefield signalling was by the standards, those carried by the individual centuries, and by the musical instruments, trumpets and horns (*tubae* and *cornua*). The musicians would call the attention of the troops engaged in combat to the signals to be transmitted by the standards. Horns and other instruments (*bucinae*) signalled the changes of watch in camp. Towers were widely used on the frontiers and sometimes on lines of communication. They would be primarily for observation, as their close spacing suggests, but would be capable of transmitting messages based on their observations or picked up from other towers. Torch, fire and smoke signals may have been used, though the evidence available does not suggest that there was an effective semaphore system for sending detailed messages, which were carried by horsemen or on foot. The possibility of long-distance signals depends crucially on local conditions of visibility. There would be critical delays in the transmission of vital messages, which threw great responsibility on the men on the spot. Roman armies in the field were often effectively out of touch with their bases.

SUMMARY

Between the reign of Augustus and AD 200 the Roman army had become an organized body of almost half-a-million men, divided into legions, and the auxiliary cavalry and infantry regiments. The latter by the middle of the 2nd century had come to outnumber the legions, perhaps by as many as 227,000 to 156,000. The difference between legionaries and auxiliary troops had narrowed, with both types of unit fighting in a similar way, and with the auxiliaries including an increasing number of citizens.

They had a record of comparative success in the period up to AD 160. Augustus' considerable expansion of the Empire, adding Egypt, completing the conquest of Spain, clearing the Alps, and advancing to the Elbe and the Danube, had been marred only by the disasters of the rebellion of AD 6, forcing the abandonment of further conquest beyond the Danube, and of AD 9, carrying with it the abandonment of further conquest of Germany. Claudius had added the beginnings of conquest of Britain, though it was to progress in spurts and was never to be completed. Domitian's attack on the Chatti in Germany led to no great results, the Roman empire being content to occupy the area between upper Rhine and upper Danube against little or no resistance. Dacia was won by Trajan in AD 106, although his campaigns against Parthia brought no lasting gains. The client kingdoms of Mauretania, Thrace and Arabia had been absorbed. Rebellions in various parts of the Empire, notably in Illyricum in AD 6-9, Britain in 60-61, Judaea in 66-70 and again in the 130s, had been successfully put down. Rome had enjoyed the better of the exchanges with Parthia, with little alteration in the frontier. Now its units were spread around its frontiers, with little or no possibility of transferring forces without creating gaps.

Successive emperors had accepted that in sector after sector of the long frontiers there was no possibility of advance. Hadrian may be seen as standing at the end of this process, which had begun as early as the closing years of Augustus, though not as a binding decree. However, there was a cumulative effect, and it seems that Hadrian's reign is to some extent a turning point. He was followed by the unadventurous Pius, who paradoxically pushed forward the frontier in Britain and in Germany, though in the latter case no more than 30km.

Marcus Aurelius, successor to Pius, faced a Parthian war and then trouble on the upper Danube, relatively tranquil till then, which culminated in a breakthrough which penetrated into northern Italy. The situation was restored, and conquest beyond the Danube considered, but this was dropped with the death of Marcus, the main change being the movement of two newly created legions into bases on the middle Danube. The problems are clearly stated: dealing with breakthroughs which went beyond the line of frontier forts; and restoring mobility, the latter in part already being achieved by the use of detachments. A related need as the Empire felt itself under threat was to retain successful officers in longer and more exclusively military careers. All carried with them implications for the future which will be discussed in the next chapter.

PRINCIPAL SOURCES

Inscriptions, including careers of officers and men and records of units, diplomas (certificates of privileges granted, generally on discharge, often with lists of units), other documents, archaeological sites, structures and finds.

Trajan's Column, set up in Rome in AD 113, a pillar 30m high with a winding scroll depicting scenes from Trajan's two Dacian wars.

Adamklissi, set up in modern Romania under Trajan, a great circular monument with sculptures around its base showing scenes of fighting contemporary with the Dacian wars.

Tacitus (born c. AD 55)

A Roman senator, he wrote a biography of his father-in-law, Agricola, in AD 98. Agricola was governor of Britain AD 77-83/84, and an account of Britain and of previous governors is included. It is a valuable source, but should not be treated as straight history. Tacitus also wrote the *Histories* to cover the period 69-96, of which only the first two years have survived, and the *Annals* for the period AD 14-68. He is regarded as a most reliable source, when certain prejudices are taken into account.

Josephus

A Jew who fought against the Romans in the Jewish War of AD 66-70. On being taken prisoner, he changed sides and his account of the Jewish War reflects this. His description of the Roman army in action remains valuable.

Arrian

Governor of Cappadocia (eastern Turkey) under Hadrian in the 130s. His description of his order of march and of battle against the Alani is a first-hand account by the Roman commander-in-chief, and the latest detailed one during this period of the Roman army in action.

Pseudo-Hyginus

An unknown, writing at a date which has been variously estimated at late 1st, late 2nd, 3rd or 4th century, though the details must relate to the army before the great changes of the 3rd and 4th centuries. His work *De metatione castrorum* (on the laying-out of camps) describes how much room is allocated to the various units of the Roman army and then a camp for a particular size of army. It is much relied on for details of the composition of units and the arrangement of forts and legionary bases as well as camps.

Vegetius

De re militari, a work written in the late 4th century, but containing material apparently referring to earlier periods. It describes recruitment, training, organization, tactics, etc. It is difficult to avoid using it, but it requires caution and is urgently in need of a proper evaluation.

THE LATE-ROMAN EMPIRE

DR ROGER TOMLIN

'Be like the cliff against which waves beat for ever', the emperor Marcus Aurelius (161-80) told himself. This would-be student of philosophy, who glumly equated warfare with a spider catching flies, was forced to campaign year after year against tribes which crossed the Danube. Now and for ever, the Empire was on the defensive, like a burglar turned householder who invokes the rights of property. Its legions, long poised for further advance, were now committed to defence of the hardening frontiers; Marcus Aurelius had to raise two more to hold the upper Danube. He was also promoting equestrian officers to command legions, men like the cavalryman Valerius Maximianus, whom he publicly commended for killing a German chieftain in single combat.

After the murder of Marcus' unworthy son Commodus, the Danubian legions made Septimius Severus emperor (193-211). This superstitious African lacked military experience but understood the army. He increased its pay and privileges, including the right to marry, and took personal command of distant campaigns. Most important of all, perhaps, he increased the legionary army by one-tenth, raising three *Parthica* legions, commanded not by senatorial legates but by experienced officers who had twice been the senior centurion of a legion. Two of these legions garrisoned his new province of Mesopotamia, the empire's last significant conquest, but the other (the Second) was stationed outside Rome. Here the old Praetorian Guard was disbanded and replaced by ten cohorts of double strength recruited from legionaries. These élite forces, equivalent to three veteran legions (the largest provincial garrison was only two legions), were the ancestors of the late-Roman mobile army. They formed a strategic reserve, with which the emperor could reinforce the frontier armies – or curb them if they rebelled.

The Empire on the Defensive

Septimius Severus died, crippled by gout, at his headquarters in northern Britain. On his deathbed he is said to have advised his sons to 'enrich the troops and despise everyone else'. For all his energy, and the extra five legions, the Roman army lost the initiative to its new enemies. In Germany the tribes coalesced into two confederacies: the Franks on the lower Rhine; and the Alamanns beyond the palisade which linked the middle Rhine and upper Danube. East German peoples like the Goths and Vandals migrated southward, pressing other tribes against the Danube frontier and threatening Dacia and the Balkans. In the east a Persian dynasty displaced the Parthians and set about regaining Roman Mesopotamia and Syria.

Excavations at Dura Europus, the headquarters of the *Dux Ripae* who supervised a sector of the Euphrates frontier, his title foreshadowing the *dux* ('duke') who commanded 4th-century frontier armies, have revealed minute details of a 3rd-century cohort, the 20th *Palmyreni*. Tattered papyrus pages survive from its meticulous records of personnel, and even a calendar of deliberately old-fashioned religious observances. But static garrisons had to be reinforced for open warfare. Caracalla (211-17), Alexander Severus (222-35) and Gordian III (238-44) all took the Second *Parthica* to the east. Scores of tombstones recently discovered at its field headquarters in Syria give a glimpse of the inner cohesion of this formidable unit. The legionaries were mostly Thracians, Romans only by courtesy, recruited on the lower Danube; the unlucky ones were buried by their wives and comrades, their sons and brothers. Aurelius Mucianus, for example, who was training to be a *lanciarius*, was buried by a colleague. With his five lances clutched in his right hand, his oval shield, his lack of armour and left-slung sword, he looks quite unlike the old-style legionary.

Despite such men, the Empire was in peril of being dismembered. The emperor Decius (249-51) was ambushed and killed by the Goths. The Persians destroyed Dura and captured Valerian (253-60). In the disastrous reign of his son Gallienus (253-68), Syria itself was only saved by the initiative of a Roman protectorate, the caravan city of Palmyra. The Western provinces proclaimed their own 'Gallic' emperor. Gallienus himself sometimes controlled no more than Africa, Italy and its approaches, yet he improvised the weapon with which his 'Illyrian' successors achieved a military renaissance.

This weapon was an enlarged field army and officer corps. A medieval source credits Gallienus with being the first to form cavalry units, 'the Roman army having previously been largely infantry'. This is an exaggeration, since independent cavalry forces had contributed to the victories of Trajan and Severus, but we now hear of a cavalry army under its own commander; and gold coins were struck at Milan to honour, and no doubt repay, the 'loyalty of the Cavalry'. These *equites* included tribal contingents: Moorish horsemen, light cavalry of legendary ferocity; the élite of the Danubian garrisons; mounted archers from the east, mounted legionaries (*stablesiani*) and independent legionary cavalry (*promoti*); and the old imperial guard, the *equites singulares Augusti*, seconded from all the frontier armies. In effect, Gallienus' new cavalry army was an enlargement of this guard, compensating for his military weakness with its mobility. Mobile infantry he found in the usual way, by supplementing the Praetorian Guard and the Second *Parthica* with detachments (*vexillationes*) from the frontier armies, like 'the British and German legions with their *auxilia*' recorded near Belgrade. In the prevailing circumstances these detachments became independent units. Base silver coins struck by Gallienus in 259-60 honoured the Praetorian Guard, the Second *Parthica*, and legions on the Rhine and Danube with the civil-war title *pia fidelis* ('dutiful and loyal'). These coins, however, are not found on the frontiers, which Gallienus did not then control, but in northern Italy and its approaches; clearly they rewarded detachments which remained loyal after their parent legions had rebelled.

In this chaos of invasion and usurpation later (legend claimed there had been 30 usurpers in the reign of Gallienus), the embattled emperor conjured up mobile forces with which to counter-attack. 'Senatorial' sources are hostile to him because he ended the tradition which reserved the highest commands to members of the aristocracy. Instead, he promoted professional soldiers – men like the Thracian general (*dux*) Traianus Mucianus, who enlisted in a cohort, transferred to the Second *Parthica* and then to the Praetorian Guard as a cavalryman, rising to command a series of cavalry units and legionary detachments. Like other officers in the mobile army, he held the title '*protector* of the emperor'. This word *protector* is occasionally found earlier, of soldiers seconded to generals' bodyguards, but now develops into an important institution of the late-Roman army. However, this mark of distinction for the officer corps did not save Gallienus from a conspiracy among them, prompted by the defection of his cavalry commander Aureolus, and involving Mucianus' patron, the commander of the Praetorian Guard, and the future emperors Claudius (268-70) and Aurelian (270-75). These two, and their fellow-'Illyrian' Probus (276-82), were the leaders of a virtual junta of officers from the Danubian provinces where much of the army was recruited. In 15 years of campaigning from one end of the empire to the other, they restored its unity by defeating the Goths and other invaders, annexing Palmyra, and terminating

overleaf
The Roman Empire c. *AD 300*
The Roman empire lost outlying territories in Germany, Dacia (across the lower Danube), Egypt and Mauretania, but otherwise its frontiers were restored by Diocletian. The legions were shadows of what they had been in the 2nd century, but their location is still an index of Roman strategy: priority to the Danube frontier, and then the eastern frontier, with Diocletian's capital Nicomedia (for which Constantine would substitute Constantinople) mid-way between them.

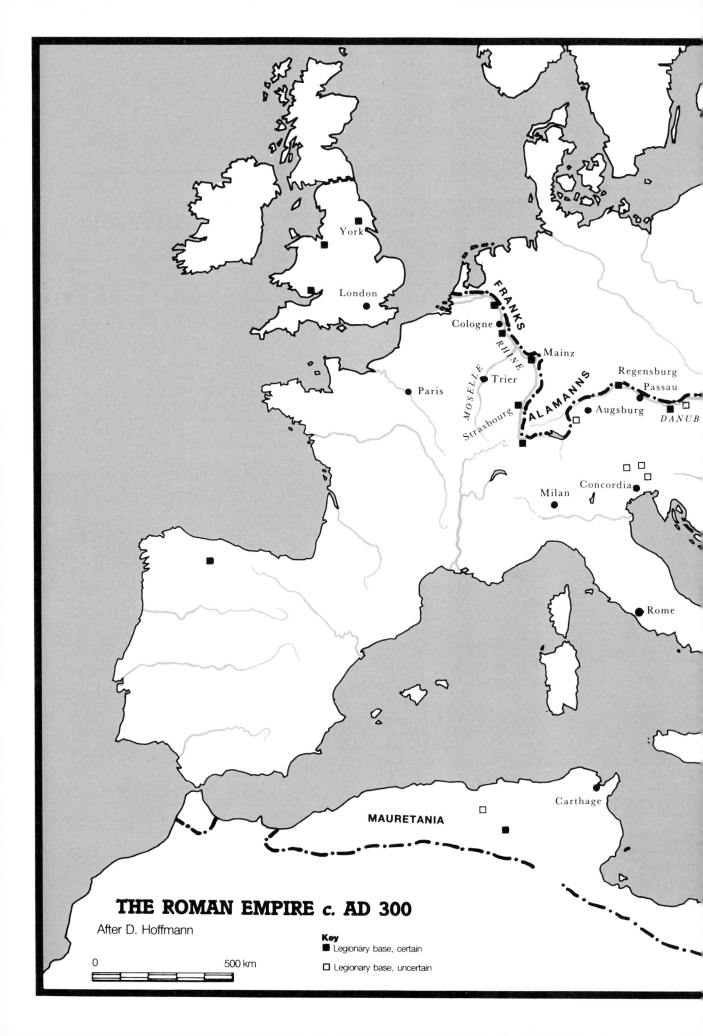

York

London

FRANKS

Cologne

RHINE

Mainz

MOSELLE

Trier

Paris

Regensburg

Passau

ALAMANNS

Augsburg

Strasbourg

DANUB

Milan

Concordia

Rome

Carthage

MAURETANIA

THE ROMAN EMPIRE *c.* AD 300

After D. Hoffmann

0   500 km

Key

■ Legionary base, certain

□ Legionary base, uncertain

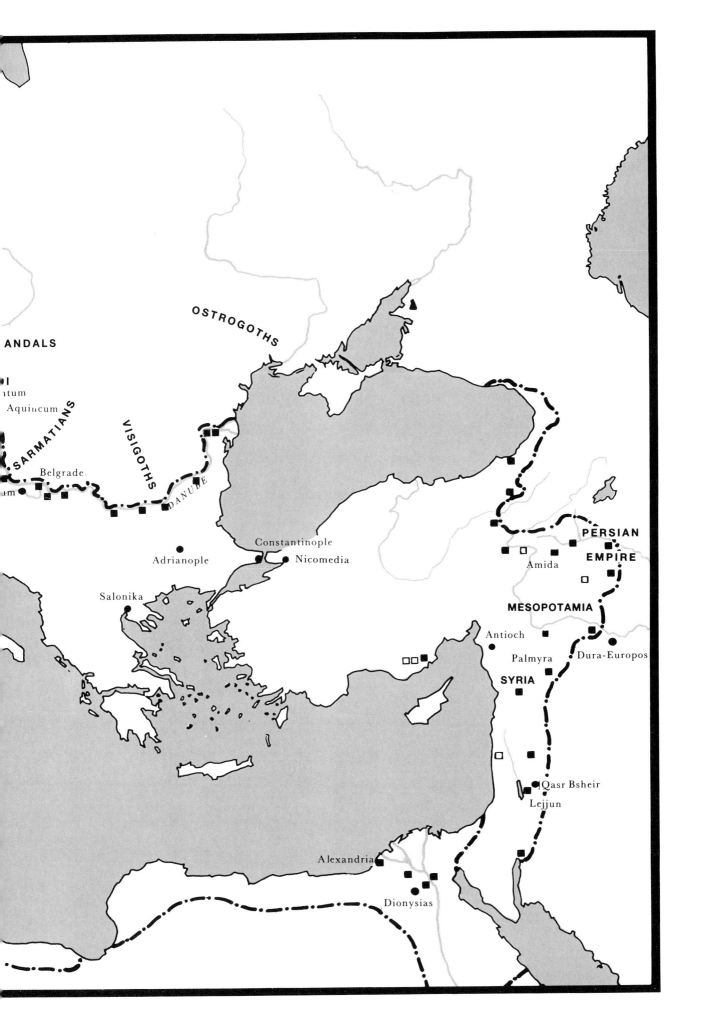

VANDALS

ANDALS

...ntum
Aquincum

SARMATIANS

VISIGOTHS

Belgrade

...um

DANUBE

OSTROGOTHS

Constantinople

Adrianople   Nicomedia

Salonika

PERSIAN
EMPIRE

Amida

MESOPOTAMIA

Antioch

Palmyra   Dura-Europos

SYRIA

Qasr Bsheir

Lejjun

Alexandria

Dionysias

the 'Gallic' empire. Roman prestige in the east was restored when Carus (282-3) sacked the Persian capital Ctesiphon. But Aurelian, after defeating a German invasion of Italy, began to build the walls which still surround Rome, an admission that even the heart of the Empire was no longer secure from sudden attack.

The Reforms of Diocletian

Military and political stability was finally restored by Diocletian (284-305), an administrative genius who made half a century's improvisation into a system. He divided the supreme command with three fellow-'Illyrians', Maximian, Constantius and Galerius. An African historian with no great sympathy for soldiers commented later: 'They may have lacked education, but they knew the miseries of life in the countryside and in the army, and made more than adequate emperors'. A famous statue-group now in Venice embodies their mutual loyalty and determination in purple stone: the four emperors stand in battle dress, one hand on another's shoulder, the other hand grasping an eagle-headed longsword. They watched each other's back against usurpation, and shortened the empire's reaction time to outside attack. Their most brilliant achievement was Galerius' counter-offensive against the Persians in 298. After an initial defeat in Mesopotamia, for which he was publicly humiliated by Diocletian, so later legend claimed, Galerius caught the Persian army by surprise in Armenia. The Persian king barely escaped alive, and his harem fell into Roman hands. Scenes from the campaign, ranging from Galerius addressing his mail-clad cavalry, to Persian elephants and Roman camels loaded with spoil, were carved on his triumphal arch which survives at Salonika. The restless energy which suppressed revolts and restored the old frontiers is also echoed by the record of his travels inscribed by one of Diocletian's veterans on his wife's tombstone: Aurelius Gaius, a legionary cavalryman who rose to be a lieutenant (*optio*) in the imperial entourage, never visited Rome or Italy, but crossed the Rhine and Danube time and again, and

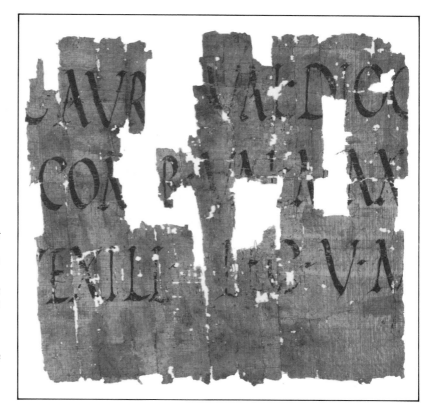

Papyrus fragment from Egypt, bearing the names of Diocletian and Maximian in 'monumental' letters, and 'Vexillation of Leg. V. Macedonica'. A record of a mobilized detachment of this Danubian legion in Egypt, intended for a public notice or for carving an inscription on stone. Egypt Exploration Society, housed at the Ashmolean Museum, Oxford.

served in 'India' (upper Egypt) and almost every province from Mesopotamia to Mauretania. He was also a Christian.

Towards the end of his reign Diocletian, intensely traditionalist despite his innovations, purged Christians from the army. A Christian critic accuses him of 'quadrupling' the army, an exaggeration prompted by his three colleagues and their field armies. The truth seems to be that most of Severus' 33 legions survived, a total almost doubled by Diocletian. The majority were posted in the traditional pairs to the provincial armies, under-strength, to judge by evidence like the fortress built for the new legion Fourth *Martia* at Lejjūn in Jordan: only 4.6 hectares in area, it is one-fifth the size of an old-style legionary base. These frontier legions were outranked by cavalry detachments (*vexillationes*), so-called because they had been detached from the mobile army of Gallienus and his successors. Some old-style *alae* and cohorts also survived in these rejuvenated provincial armies, whose commander-in-chief was now usually a professional soldier, a *dux*, instead of the provincial governor. (The separation of military and civil careers was completed by Constantine.) However, Diocletian retained the nucleus of a mobile army. Two new legions, the famous *Ioviani* and *Herculiani*, originally Danubian legionaries armed with the characteristic late-Roman weighted dart (*martiobarbulus*) instead of the old javelin (*pilum*), served in the imperial entourage, the *comitatus* which 'accompanied' the emperor. Soldiers now speak of serving 'in the *comitatus*', the word from which *comitatenses* ('mobile troops') derives. There were other élite legions, like the *Solenses* and *Martenses*, named after the other two patron gods, and the *Lanciarii* (with whom Aurelius Gaius served), in origin picked Praetorians and legionaries armed with lances like Aurelius Mucianus. The most senior of the 4th-century cavalry units were also organized at this time, the new guards (*scholae*) and the crack 'brigade' of *Comites* and *Promoti*, which was probably drawn from the *equites singulares Augusti* and the Praetorian cavalry. But the permanent field forces of Diocletian and his colleagues were small by later standards, and were supplemented as required from the frontier armies. Thus Galerius drew on the Danubian garrisons for his defeat of the Persians, while in Egypt a papyrus of 295 records the issue of fodder not only to the *Comites* in Diocletian's field force but also to as many as ten pairs of legionary detachments.

Diocletian also reformed the army's logistics, in which it was infinitely superior to its enemies. Imperial arms factories (*fabricae*) were organized; they made catapults, bows and arrows, longswords, spears, corselets, scale armour, shields and helmets. The late-Roman helmet, two or more iron plates crudely

Scene from the Arch of Galerius at Salonika. The Emperor addresses troops in scale armour and late-Roman helmets, before setting out to defeat Persia. Flags and snake standards fly overhead.

riveted together under a protective ridge, suggests that mass-production ousted craftsmanship. This state intervention was prompted by the collapse of the currency, and with it the old system of taxation. After half a century in which the army had requisitioned what it needed, at a 'fair' price or none at all, Diocletian ingeniously resolved the problem by levying foodstuffs, raw materials, and manufactured goods like clothing, in the form of taxes calculated as a percentage of the Empire's estimated production. In Egypt he urged a sullen population to obey a system devised for its benefit, without waiting to be compelled. In Egypt, however, at least according to Ammianus Marcellinus, the retired officer whose *History* is the prime source of information about 4th-century warfare, a tax defaulter was ashamed of himself if he did not have scars to prove it. The papyri contain vivid glimpses of the army's provisioning, including two fragments from the files of an Egyptian deputy governor. The first consists of copies of letters sent out by him in September 298, many of them relating to 'the auspiciously impending visit of Our Lord the Emperor Diocletian'. Local officials are threatened and cajoled into providing foodstuffs, 'so that by all means the most noble soldiers may receive their supplies without complaint' (19 September 298). The *ala Hiberorum*, for example, receives two months' rations of barley and wheat; the totals are given, and suggest that this cavalry unit numbered only 116 men and their horses. The second fragment consists of letters received from the procurator of the Lower Thebaid, many of them authorizing cash payments to units in early 300: thus on 30 January the procurator wrote to the deputy governor (who received his letter on 9 February), ordering him to pay the same *ala* 73,500 *denarii* (pay) and 23,600 *denarii* (in lieu of rations) due on 1 January for the last four months of 299. The mills ground slow but exceedingly fine; the deputy governor even acknowledges a requisition for hides to repair a cavalry fort's gates, and informs the bearer that it has been 'nibbled by mice and mutilated'.

The Dynamic Constantine

Diocletian abdicated in 305 and retired to a fortified palace on the Adriatic. Perhaps his greatest achievement was to have dominated his colleagues, but this balance was soon upset by an usurper in Britain, Constantius' son Constantine, who in 306 emerged from what he later called 'the lands of the setting sun' to become sole emperor in 324 after a series of civil wars and murders. He was a dynamic general who inherited the crack 'Gallic' army, a weapon he first tempered in successful campaigns on the Rhine. Captured German chieftains were thrown to the beasts in the amphitheatre. Then in 312 Constantine eliminated the first of his rivals, Maximian's son Maxentius, who had held Italy even against Galerius. Striking unexpectedly with only a quarter of his available forces – no doubt his 'mobile' units and detachments from frontier garrisons – Constantine quickly overran northern Italy. He then advanced on Rome, where Maxentius had cut the Tiber bridges and lurked behind Aurelian's walls. Disaffection among his subjects forced Maxentius to risk battle. He crossed the Tiber on a pontoon bridge, but his army was thrown back in confusion by Constantine's charge, and he was drowned when the bridge collapsed. Constantine gave the credit to his new patron, the God of the Christians, whose worship he now promoted. More prosaically, he monopolized a new infantry unit, the *auxilium*, which was to provide the shock troops of the late-Roman army. The first such 'brigade' was the *Cornuti* or 'horned men', apparently the soldiers wearing horned helmets to be seen on the Arch of Constantine, and the *Bracchiati* or 'armlet wearers'. Later we find them in Ammianus' pages with another élite 'brigade', the *Iovii* and *Victores*, raising a Germanic war cry before they charge. Maxentius' Rome-based troops, with their lack of battle experience, were no match for them. These savage *auxilia*, the Foreign Legion of the late-Roman army, seem to have been raised and recruited from Rhine-Germans, whether they were volunteers, prisoners-of-war, or young men from the *laeti* settlements of submissive

Qasr Bsheir, Jordan. Gate of the fort castra Praetorii Mobeni *with its inscribed lintel still in place, recording its construction in AD 292-305 by the governor of Arabia.*

Qasr Bsheir, Jordan. The well-preserved Diocletianic fort, c. 56m square, showing the high curtain wall and projecting towers typical of Late-Roman fortifications.

THE BATTLE OF THE MILVIAN BRIDGE, 28 OCTOBER, 312

Constantine's Blitzkrieg culminated in the defeat of his rival Maxentius just north of Rome. His advanced units, Moorish archers and German cavalry, pursued the stricken army to the banks of the Tiber, where the Milvian Bridge had been cut and replaced by a bridge of boats. This bridge collapsed under the weight, and Maxentius himself was drowned. The scene was depicted on the Arch of Constantine at Rome. Constantine's cavalry wear scale armour and typical late-Roman helmets. The horned motif on their shields may mark the *Cornuti* ('horned men'), Germans in Roman service. They carry the first signs of Constantine's dramatic change of faith. Over the figure of Victory has been painted the Christian monogram XP, the Greek initials of 'Christ', as suggested to Constantine in a dream the night before. Constantine himself later claimed to have seen a Cross of light, and then to have dreamed the *labarum*, an adaptation of the *vexillum* flag, in which he replaced a pagan motif with the Christian monogram. Whatever the exact details of his conversion, this victory convinced him of the power of the Christian God.

PETER
CONNOLLY

Germans established by Diocletian and his colleagues on derelict land in Gaul. Like the hard-pressed householder it resembled, the empire was now enlisting burglars in the police force.

Constantine also raised new legions, but more important sources of mobile infantry were the existing frontier legions and other garrisons. Legionary detachments were withdrawn for good, some of them under their old name like the Fifth *Macedonica*, the longest-lived of all legions (it was still part of Justinian's army in the 6th century), others under numerical names like the Eleventh (*Undecimani*) or names adopted from a previous station. The élite *Divitenses*, for example, had been a detachment of Second *Italica* stationed at the Cologne bridgehead of Divitia; they were 'brigaded' with the former garrison of Tongres, the *Tungrecani*. New cavalry units were added to the nucleus of the *scholae* and the *Comites* and *Promoti*, Germans like the *equites Cornuti*, and detachment from the frontier armies. The names of the latter recall Gallienus' cavalry army, their original source, with units like the Sixth *Stablesiani*, whose name is found on a silver-plated helmet lost *c.* 320 in a Dutch swamp with its wearer. However, the old *equites singulares Augusti* and the Praetorian Guard were disbanded by Constantine, no doubt because they had supported Maxentius, but also because they had been both superseded and defeated by the new mobile army.

The converse of these *comitatenses* were the *limitanei*, so called because they garrisoned forts and fortified towns in the frontier zone (*limes*). They were the old-style legions, *alae* and cohorts, and new-style *equites* (sometimes reduced to *cunei* on the Danube) and infantry mostly called *milites* or *auxiliares*. The evidence is still being accumulated, but they seem to have been much smaller than their counterparts in the early empire. Many of Diocletian's new forts in the east, for example, were quite small. The *castra* of Qasr Bsheir in Jordan, a fort so well preserved that its building inscription (293-305) is still in place, measures only 0.3 hectares and has stabling for precisely 69 horses or camels.

The 4th-Century Order of Battle

For administrative purposes, these garrisons were all grouped into armies covering one or two provinces, each commanded by a *dux*. The order of battle in the 4th century can be recovered from the enigmatic *Notitia Dignitatum*, an illustrated list of high offices compiled *c.* 395, which survives in several much later copies. Unfortunately its interpretation presents many problems, since it contains material of varying dates. Its purpose is also disputed, but an attractive idea is that it was an aide-mémoire for the office staff of the Western high command, which levied fees for issuing officers with their commissions. Among the entries is *ala V Praelectorum, Dionisiada*, the command of a cavalry unit at Dionysias in the Egyptian Fayûm. This was a typically massive Diocletianic fort with projecting towers and walls 4m thick. Since any external threat was remote, its strength suggests a defensive mentality and a ruthless application of general principles. The commandant in the 340s, Flavius Abinnaeus, is better known to us than most of his contemporaries, as by a happy chance his papers have survived. The first is a draft petition to the eastern emperor, Constantine's son Constantius II (337-61), in which Abinnaeus complains that when he presented his 'sacred letter' of appointment, he was told that similar letters had already been presented by other men. Theirs had been obtained illicitly, whereas Abinnaeus had been appointed after an audience with the emperor. Fortunately he was confirmed in his appointment.

The letters he received often reveal the 'police' duties of *limitanei*. 'Your valiance, my lord, is wont to restrain the robberies and usurpations committed in the localities by the more influential men', writes one petitioner. (Abinnaeus, a soldier of some 40 years' experience, who also owned farm stock and houses, is clearly one of the ubiquitous 'patrons' of late-Roman society.)

opposite
The Duke of Raetia, from his headquarters of Augsburg, was responsible for a salient which linked the Rhine and Danube frontiers. His units lay between the German Alamanni and the Alpine passes which led to Italy. Raetia became an important military command when Marcus Aurelius based a legion at Regensburg, but by the 4th century it had been broken into detachments along the frontier and lines of communication, supported by inferior units of infantry and cavalry. By now the most important units were the three modern cavalry detachments in the Augsburg triangle, one of which had been moved forward from its base in the interior.

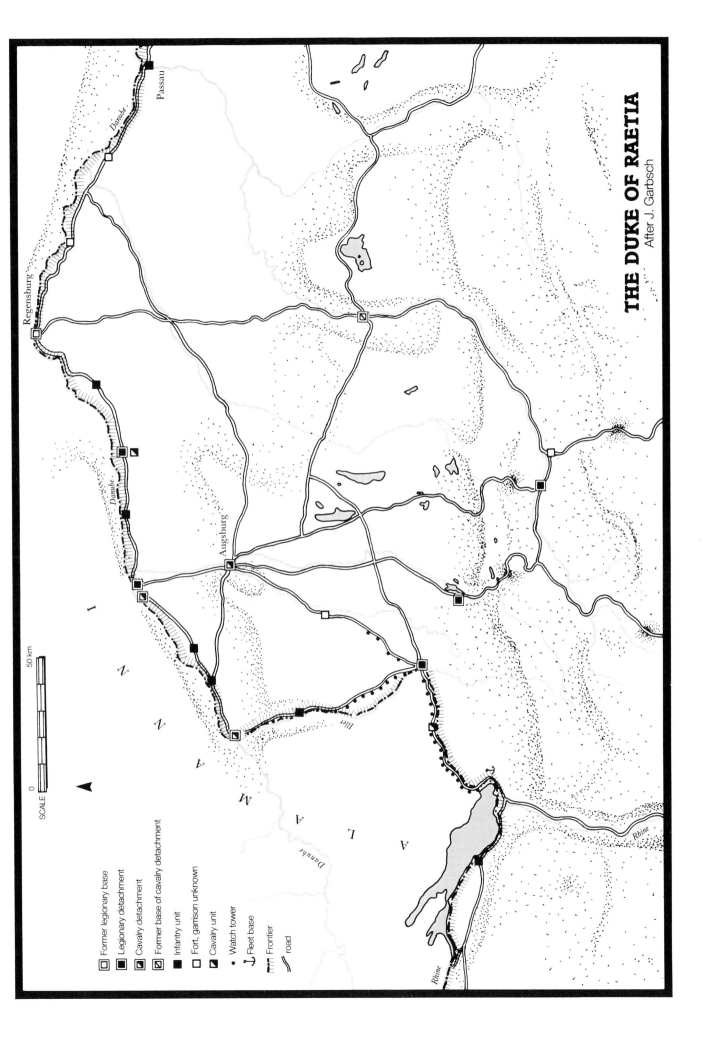

THE DUKE OF RAETIA

After J. Garbsch

SCALE

0   50 km

Passau

Danube

Regensburg

Danube

Augsburg

Iller

Rhine

Rhine

□ Former legionary base
■ Legionary detachment
◩ Cavalry detachment
◩ Former base of cavalry detachment
■ Infantry unit
□ Fort, garrison unknown
◪ Cavalry unit
• Watch tower
⌐ Fleet base
▥ Frontier
⌁ road

The Notitia Dignitatum, *illustration to the western Master of the Offices, whose control of the Guards* (scholae) *and arms factories* (fabricae) *is symbolized by spears, shields, helmets, mail shirts, etc. His letter of appointment is displayed in the background. Bayerische Staatsbibliothek, Munich.*

He receives appeals from the victims of burglaries and from people who have had sheep or pigs stolen. One of his own soldiers is alleged to have been drunken and violent; another to have led a gangs which stole the wool off the back of 11 sheep and drove off six pigs. A clergyman asks for a loan of the nets kept at headquarters, to catch gazelles which have been eating the crops. These intriguing documents illustrate the integration of a garrison with local society, not the old-fashioned idea that *limitanei* were only hereditary peasant militias. This is amply refuted by evidence like Ammianus' eye-witness account of the siege of Amida (359).

Ammianus, an officer on the staff of Constantius II's Master of Infantry, was trapped in this fortified town on the Tigris by a sudden Persian invasion. In 359 the Persians were attempting a new strategy, suggested by a Roman

defector, of bypassing the frontier fortress of Nisibis and advancing up the Tigris to fall upon Syria from the north-east. The Romans were deceived; but unfortunately for the Persian strategy – and for Amida – a Roman gunner aimed his *ballista* at a client king and shot his son who rode by his side. The Persian army was bound by its code of honour to avenge his death, and did so – at the cost of 30,000 dead and 74 days' delay, which saved Syria. Amida was strongly held, by its regular garrison the Fifth *Parthica*, four other legions which had taken refuge behind its massive walls, and a pair of *auxilia* which had been drafted from Gaul for supporting a local usurper. The latter played no real part in the siege, their sorties being as destructive to themselves as to the Persians, but the five legions fought tenaciously and skilfully, and might have saved Amida but for bad luck. The great siege illustrates traditional techniques still

The Notitia Dignitatum, *illustration of a typical ducate (frontier command), that of the Count of Isauria. He supervised the forts which cordoned off the wolf-infested Taurus mountains, the refuge of notorious brigands. His letter of appointment is displayed in the background. Bayerische Staatsbibliothek, Munich.*

THE WESTERN *COMITATUS* c. AD 395

The military hierarchy of the western Roman empire according to the *Notitia Dignitatum*.

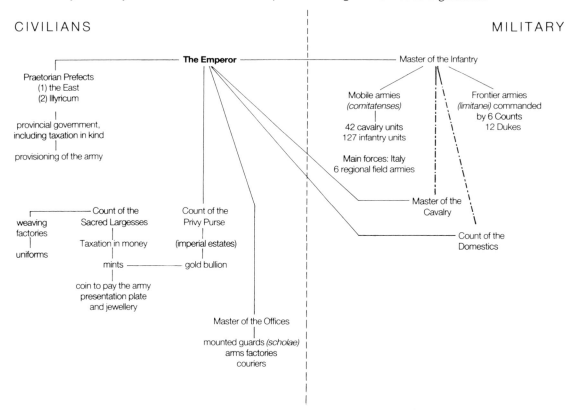

THE EASTERN *COMITATUS* c. AD 395

The military hierarchy of the eastern Roman empire according to the *Notitia Dignitatum*.

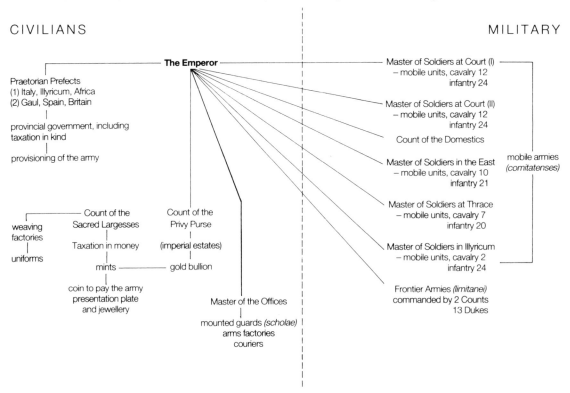

being practised in the late Empire. At first the Persians tried to storm the walls with the help of elephants, 'hideous with their wrinkled bodies, most gruesome of sights'. They began to raise siege mounds and iron-plated towers with a *ballista* on top. Then a Roman deserter betrayed an underground passage which led down to the Tigris from one of the towers. A force of 70 Persian archers crept into the tower by night through the passage; next day they opened fire, covering an attempt to storm the walls, but they were shot down by *ballista* fire. The Romans achieved another success when bombardment by their 'scorpions', the late-Roman ancestor of the mangonel, which lobbed large stones, brought down the Persian siege towers. But disaster struck when they raised a mound inside their walls to counter a Persian siege mound. It collapsed, bridging the gap between the wall and the Persian mound. The Persians threw in all their troops and stormed into Amida. Street fighting continued all day, but Ammianus prudently lay low until nightfall, when he slipped out of an unguarded postern and 'returned beyond all hope' to his native city of Antioch.

The essential difference between *limitanei* and *comitatenses* was that the latter, though they might have families, did not have fixed stations. If they were not on active service, they were billeted in towns, where they were entitled to one-third of available accommodation, an arrangement which caused friction with their civilian 'hosts'. *Comitatenses*, as their name implied, were ideally at the emperor's immediate disposal. A commentary on the 119th Psalm takes the route march as a metaphor of the text, 'Teach me, O Lord, the way of thy statutes; and I shall keep it to the end'. The men marched to a prescribed itinerary, with food and lodging arranged in advance, and regular rest-days, 'until they reach the imperial capital of the moment, where the weary armies find rest'. Constantine reorganized the high command by transferring the Praetorian Prefect's military authority to a Master of Cavalry and a Master of Infantry attached to his court, the Prefect remaining responsible for recruitment and supply. In practice the command of *comitatenses* could not be so centralized. We soon find regional armies, the most important being those of Gaul, the Danubian provinces, and the East (at Antioch), each of them commanded by its own Master of Cavalry. Smaller mobile forces were detached as required, usually under the command of a *comes* ('Count'), like the four units sent to Britain in 367 when the frontiers collapsed. In two brisk campaigns, of which we know very little, they restored Roman authority for the last time, and were withdrawn once more to the central reserve. Africa seems always to have had its own mobile army, strong in cavalry as one would expect, and by the time of the *Notitia* there were others in Britain, Spain and Thrace. Theodosius I (379-95) grouped the eastern forces into five armies, two of them at his immediate disposal, and all of them commanded by a Master of Soldiers. He thus avoided what happened in the West from the 380s, where a single commander-in chief, notably Stilicho during 395-408, dominated the government.

Soldiers of the Late-Roman Army

By using the *Notitia* lists and other sources, we can make some rough guesses about the strength of the late-Roman army. Valentinian I (364-75) at his accession may have divided about 150 mobile units with his brother Valens (364-78), the eastern emperor, if we ignore the African army. By the end of the 4th century, this total seems to have doubled; about one-third were cavalry. Unfortunately these are paper figures. The Spanish army, for example, numbers 16 units; yet we hear nothing of it when German invaders poured into Spain in 409. Worse still, we know very little about unit strengths. We have scraps of evidence, like Ammianus' note that two Danubian cavalry units in Mesopotamia in 359 totalled 700 men. He twice mentions detachments of 300 men from unspecified mobile units, once 500 from 'legions'. By contrast, we hear elsewhere of a detachment of Huns in Libya in the early 5th century which numbered only 40 men. The Diocletianic *ala* of 116 men has been mentioned already: the same document suggests that there were only 164 men in the *cohors XI/Chamavorum*. It may be that 4th-century mobile infantry units were of 'battalion' size, between 500 and 1,000 men strong, and that cavalry units were much less than 500 men strong. Frontier units, however, were probably far smaller. New forts tend to be small by earlier standards, and old forts were often reduced in size or show signs of reduced occupation. The legions certainly were shadows of their former selves. Third *Italica* in Raetia, for example, garrisoned four forts and its old fortress, as well as providing a 'legion' for the nearest mobile army. Julian (355-63) congratulated himself on taking 1,000 Germans prisoner in 'two battles and a siege'. In the siege, which lasted two months, 600 Franks were starved out of their refuge in two derelict forts and sent to Julian's cousin Constantius II for service in the eastern army. This implies that quite small numbers were important. We know that Julian's army in 357 numbered only 13,000 men; in 363, with the whole empire to draw on, and no other commitments, his two armies for the invasion of Persia totalled only 65,000 men. These are figures for first-rate troops and represent a fraction only of the paper strength; we get some idea of this from two 6th-century figures of unknown value, one for Diocletian's army at an unknown date of 389,704, and an estimate for 'the Old Empire' of 645,000.

Paper strengths were just that, and no more, when it came to fighting; but multiplied by pay and rations, they represent the cost of the army to the civil population. Late-Roman soldiers did not have to pay for their uniforms, arms and equipment, and were issued with rations which increased as they rose in rank. Payment in kind was supplemented by a regular salary paid in the copious bronze small change, and by donatives paid in silver and gold at five-yearly intervals. Officers also received imperial gifts, inscribed silver plate, gold and silver 'medallions', gold and silver belt-fittings and brooches. These terms were generous in a empire where most of the population lived at subsistence level, yet there was a severe shortage of recruits. Diocletian enforced the tradition that sons followed their fathers into the army, and in addition levied recruits from landowners as a kind of tax. Valentinian reduced the height qualification from 5ft 10in (Roman) to 5ft 7in; he found some men liable to military service were mutilating themselves, while others were being harboured by his own soldiers under the guise of 'relatives' or 'servants'. Among Abinnaeus' correspondence is a clergyman's plea for his brother-in-law, the son of a deceased soldier and the sole support of his widowed mother, who has been conscripted. The clergyman begs Abinnaeus to release him, or at least 'safeguard him from going abroad with the draft for the *comitatus*, and may God reward you for your charity'. It was the charity of Christians which made a convert of the future monk Pachomius, when he was a young conscript on his way to the *comitatus* in 324; he and his fellows were locked up every night for fear they deserted. Not surprisingly, therefore, the army also recruited non-Romans, mostly Germans. Some were prisoners-of-war like Julian's 600 Franks, but many were volunteers attracted, like the invaders, by a higher standard of living. They might even rise to high rank; one of Valens' generals was an Alamann king who had been kidnapped at a dinner party by order of Julian. The great Stilicho himself was the son of a Vandal cavalry officer. Frankish-born officers at the court of Constantius II in 355 protested that they were 'men devoted to the empire', and it is noteworthy that we almost never hear of treachery by German-born soldiers. They seem to have been successfully assimilated until the defeat of Adrianople (378), when a desperate shortage of fighting men forced the Roman government to enlist tribal contingents (*federati*) under their own chieftains. These did not have the same feeling of 'belonging', and after 395 became increasingly aware of their political and military power, which they used to extort subsidies and land from their reluctant hosts.

A recruit rose slowly, by seniority within his unit. A Christian writer uses the non-commissioned ranks of a cavalry regiment as a metaphor of the gulf

Apamea, Syria. Tombstone of Aurelius Mucianus, trainee lanciarius of the Second Parthica Legion, which was based here during the eastern expeditions of Caracalla, Alexander Severus, and Gordian III. This 3rd-century legionary, with his oval shield, five lances and left-slung sword, looks quite unlike the legionaries of Trajan's Column.

between a demon and an angel: recruit, trooper (*eques*), *circitor*, *biarchus*, *centenarius*, *ducenarius*, *senator*, *primicerius*, ranks unknown to the army of the early empire, all junior to *tribunus* (commanding officer). The largest collection of late-Roman soldiers' epitaphs is found in a cemetery at Concordia in northeast Italy: among some 30 NCOs and privates from the mobile army are a *biarchus* of 20 years' service, a *centenarius* (22), two *ducenarii* (20 and 23), two *senatores* aged 40 and 60, and the drill-master of the *Batavi seniores*, who died after 35 years' service. Abinnaeus himself was a *ducenarius* of 33 years' service in a cavalry detachment before a special mission took him to court, where he 'adored the Sacred Purple'. By kissing the hem of Constantius' garment, he automatically became a *protector domesticus*: the *protectores* from the reign of Diocletian were a kind of staff college in which senior NCOs prepared for regimental commands. After three years Abinnaeus became the prefect of an *ala*, when he found his rivals had used influence to take a short cut. Thus in 363 the senior member (*primicerius*) of the *protectores* was the 32-year-old future

The tombstone of the protector *Viatorinus*, deputy-commander of the Divitenses who garrisoned the bridgehead-fort of Divitia (Deutz); after 30 years' service, he was killed near the fort by a Frank. His unit was transferred to the mobile army by Constantine. Römisch-Germanisches Museum, Cologne.

Dura-Europos, Syria. Reconstructed wall-painting of the battle of Eben-ezer (I Sam. 4) from the synagogue. The Israelites and Philistines are represented as 3rd-century soldiers on the Euphrates frontier: scale-armoured infantry and mounted lancers. Dura Europos Collection, Yale University Art Gallery, New Haven, Connecticut.

emperor Jovian. It can be no coincidence that his father was a senior general, the *comes domesticorum*. The historian Ammianus, who was a *protector* in his early 20s, must also have had connections. By contrast, Flavius Memorius, the *comes* of the Tangiers army, had served 28 years in the *Ioviani* before he became a *protector*. The future emperor Valentinian, however, was already commanding a mobile detachment of cavalry at the age of 36, and the future emperor Theodosius was a *dux* at the age of about 28. Both were the sons of generals; Valentinian's father Gratianus, like Memorius, is one of the few private soldiers to achieve the rank of *comes*.

Gratianus also achieved a country estate, but most recruits, if they survived at least 20 years' service, received much less than a legionary of the early empire. Veterans were encouraged to cultivate derelict land, for which they received a small grant. They also received some tax concessions, including a limited exemption from the five-yearly tax on commerce which was used to pay the donatives of their old comrades-in-arms. Some veterans, however, were men of substance. One of them promised to reimburse Abinnaeus for any money he might have to spend to secure the promotion of his son within the local *ala*. Another, described as a 'landowner', requested him to arrest some local officials, so as to make them produce persons guilty of house-breaking. A veteran's daughter, another 'landowner', asked him to take action against a debtor who had beaten her up with the help of the village policeman when she demanded the money he owed her.

Constantine, in a speech to a restive gathering of his 'fellow veterans', promised them undisturbed leisure after their labours. Intelligent emperors advertised their closeness to their men. Galerius reconnoitred the Persian army with an escort of only two horsemen. Stories were told of both Constantius II and Theodosius begging a crust of bread in a moment of crisis. Julian, the 'sport' of Constantine's dynasty, who repudiated his uncle's Christianity, none the less swallowed porridge 'even a common soldier would have despised'. The dour Valentinian insisted on personally reconnoitring an Alamann position; in the ambush which ensued, he lost his splendid helmet and the man who was carrying it. He personally supervised the construction of small outposts, and leading a flying column somewhere near modern

Frankfurt, slept in the open under a blanket. His son Gratian, however, lost touch with the army by a passion for hunting and favouritism for a new unit; his men abandoned him for Magnus Maximus (383-8), the general in Britain whose first coins, minted in London to reward his supporters, pointedly imitated the coin portrait of Valentinian. The survival of the sons of Theodosius, Arcadius (395-408) and Honorius (395-423), is hard to explain, since they reigned as figureheads without military ability or interest. A critic compares Arcadius in the eunuch-haunted depths of his palace with a deep-sea mollusc.

The army was the ultimate, though not the sole, source of political power and public security. This was symbolized in the accession ceremonies. Valentinian, for example, after being chosen in conclave by the generals and ministers of state, was presented to the army. He was clothed in purple, crowned, and acclaimed as *Augustus*. Lifted on a shield, he was about to speak when the army interrupted him with a demand for a joint-emperor. Valentinian reprimanded them, delivered his prepared speech, and left for his palace, 'hedged in by eagles and standards, already an object of fear'. Ammianus also gives a splendid picture of Constantius II, a conscientious but ungifted general with the reputation of winning civil wars and losing foreign wars, making his state entry into Rome. He rode by himself in a golden carriage glittering with jewels, with purple silk snake standards hissing in the breeze overhead. Scale-armoured infantry and *clibanarii*, cavalry that looked like moving statues, marched either side. Amidst a storm of applause Constantius gazed stonily in front of him, moving his head only to bow as the carriage passed under an arch.

The 4th-Century Army on Campaign

Many years before, Aurelian had overawed a German delegation by receiving it on a platform with his army drawn up in a crescent on either side; his generals rode their horses, and behind them were the imperial standards, 'golden eagles, portraits of the emperor, the names of regiments picked out in gilt letters, all of them on silver-plated lances'. The 4th-century army on campaign tried to live up to earlier standards. Ammianus makes rhetorical complaints about its indiscipline – Valentinian's flying column gave itself away by looting and raising fires – but on the whole these are belied by his narrative. The *comitatenses*, given good leadership, fought tenaciously and usually with success against odds. What we hear of the maintenance of discipline may not be typical. The antiquarian-minded Julian distributed wreaths (of the wrong kind) after storming a Persian city, and also 'decimated' a cavalry unit; this punishment he may have misunderstood, since he selected ten victims, not a tenth. Valentinian revived another ancient punishment, according to an unreliable source, by making the *Batavi* encamp outside the fortifications. His general Theodosius, father of the emperor, treated disloyal African units very harshly: cavalry officers had their hands lopped off; the survivors of a legion were clubbed to death 'in the ancient fashion'; and deserters were burnt alive or lost their hands. Ammianus, who normally condemns cruelty when he finds it, seems embarrassed at having to defend this 'salutary vigour' and quotes a criticism of these 'savage innovations'. Contemporary legislation, it is true, is full of such threats, but trained *comitatenses* were too valuable to be treated with indiscriminate brutality. Reading Ammianus, one is struck by their *esprit de corps* and the survival of old skills. They still entrenched themselves in marching camps with palisades and built permanent forts in stone. They were expected to carry 20 days' rations. They bridged the Rhine, Danube and Euphrates by pontoon bridges, and handled small boats skilfully enough to make night-landings in Alamannia or to hunt down Sarmatians in the Danube marshes. Julian mustered 500 men 'who from early childhood were taught in their native lands to cross the greatest of all rivers', like the Batavians of the early empire; after they had

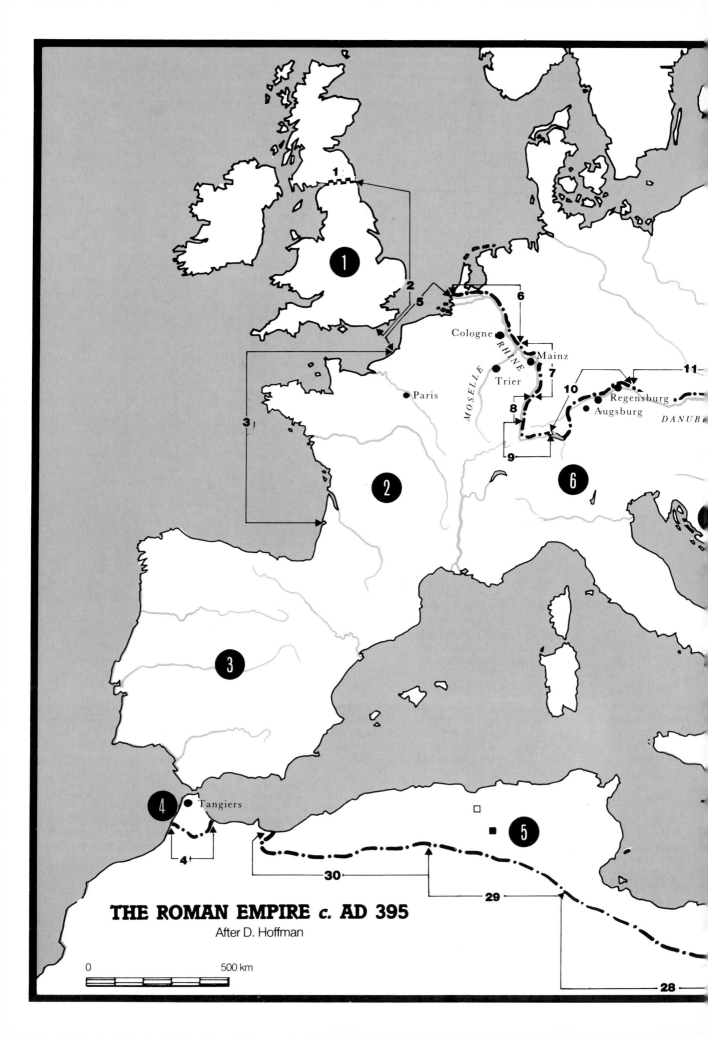

THE ROMAN EMPIRE *c.* AD 395

After D. Hoffman

Cologne

Mainz

Trier

Paris

MOSELLE

RHINE

Regensburg

Augsburg

DANUBE

Tangiers

0   500 km

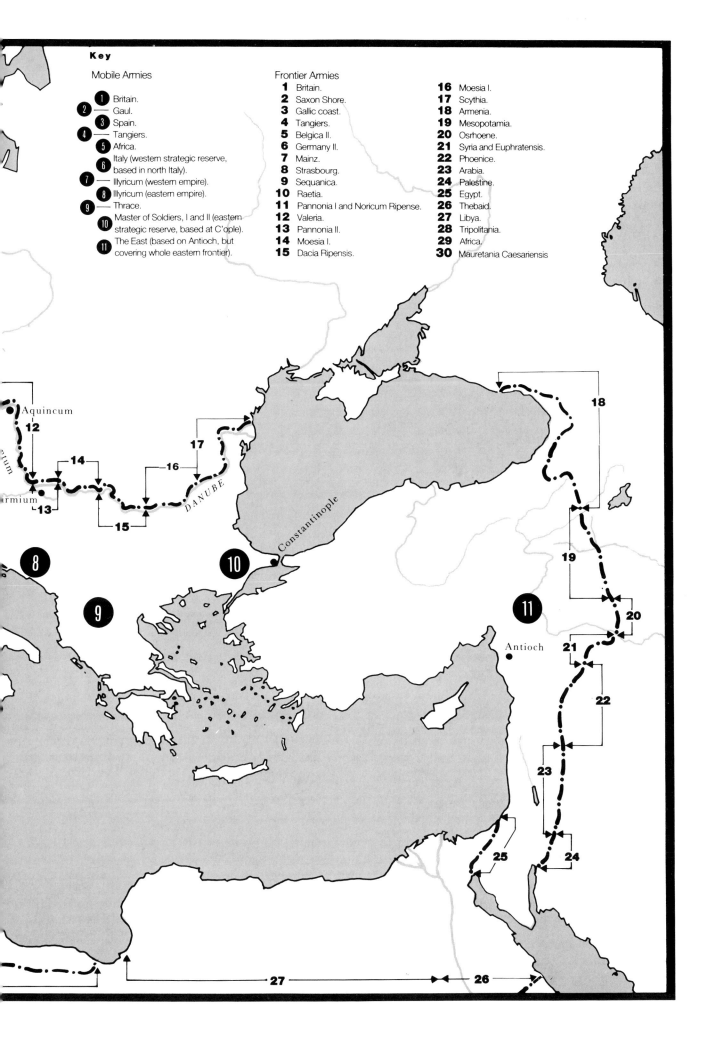

Key

Mobile Armies

1 Britain.
2 Gaul.
3 Spain.
4 Tangiers.
5 Africa.
6 Italy (western strategic reserve, based in north Italy).
7 Illyricum (western empire).
8 Illyricum (eastern empire).
9 Thrace.
10 Master of Soldiers, I and II (eastern strategic reserve, based at C'ople).
11 The East (based on Antioch, but covering whole eastern frontier).

Frontier Armies

1 Britain.
2 Saxon Shore.
3 Gallic coast.
4 Tangiers.
5 Belgica II.
6 Germany II.
7 Mainz.
8 Strasbourg.
9 Sequanica.
10 Raetia.
11 Pannonia I and Noricum Ripense.
12 Valeria.
13 Pannonia II.
14 Moesia I.
15 Dacia Ripensis.
16 Moesia I.
17 Scythia.
18 Armenia.
19 Mesopotamia.
20 Osrhoene.
21 Syria and Euphratensis.
22 Phoenice.
23 Arabia.
24 Palestine.
25 Egypt.
26 Thebaid.
27 Libya.
28 Tripolitania.
29 Africa.
30 Mauretania Caesariensis

secured a bridgehead across the Tigris, the rest of the army followed on rafts, or by using the local method of inflated animal skins.

The *comitatenses* were thus at least comparable with the auxiliaries of the early empire, the soldiers who defeated the Caledonians at Mons Graupius in 83. In 357 Julian, with his army of only 13,000 men, confronted an Alamann host of 35,000 near Strasbourg, but his men and their generals were confident of winning. The Roman cavalry was massed on the right wing, opposed by Alamann cavalry stiffened by light infantry, a tactic which Caesar had learnt from their ancestors the Suebi. When the armies met, an officer of the armoured cavalry (*catafracti*) was wounded, and the Roman cavalry fell back upon the infantry in disorder. (After the battle Julian is said to have humiliated the unit concerned by parading it in female clothing.) The Alamann infantry now made a series of charges culminating in one by 'a fiery band of tribal nobility including kings', which cut its way to the First legion. But the *Primani* stood their ground like the infantry 'wall' recommended by the late-Roman military theorist Vegetius, and the Alamanns faltered and gave way, suffering heavy loss in their retreat to the Rhine. This Roman victory carried something ominous: the poor showing of the cavalry. When Julian led his army against the Persians to the gates of Ctesiphon (363), before turning away in frustration, he twice punished cavalry units which had broken when caught by surprise, the first by 'decimation', the second by reducing it to infantry, 'which is more laborious and lower in rank'. Shortly afterwards the infantry actually complained of yet another unit, which had given way as the infantry was penetrating the Persian line. It was made to march with the camp followers, and four other cavalry commanders were cashiered.

The failure of the Persian expedition was only in part due to the cavalry's failure to support the infantry. Julian had made elaborate preparations, including a fleet of more than 1,000 craft which accompanied him down the Euphrates carrying provisions, and a siege train which enabled him to reduce a series of fortified towns on the way. The Persians meanwhile had been wrong-footed, a feint by Julian having convinced them that he was coming down the Tigris, and the Roman army reached Ctesiphon intact. Yet Julian decided not to assault the Persian capital as Carus had done, even though he had brought a siege train for the purpose. Instead he burnt his boats (literally), and tried to penetrate further east. These decisions were so extraordinary that legends were soon invented to explain them. It is true that it would have been hard for the fleet to return up-river against the current, but its cargo proved indispensable, for the Persians now adopted scorched-earth tactics, which was precisely the method adopted by the Romans in northern Mesopotamia to deny fodder to invading Persian armies. Julian was forced to retreat up the Tigris, harassed by the main Persian army (which had now appeared), until a lance-thrust from an Arab irregular cavalryman in the Persian service put an end to him. In the retreat the Roman infantry gained an ascendancy over the Persians, but it was starving. Julian's successor had to make a humiliating peace to extricate his battered army. Julian cannot be acquitted of strategic miscalculations and lack of anticipation. He was an amateur general of genius, but in those last days did he recall his campaign against the Franks in 358? He came near to disaster then, when the army ran out of biscuit, and found that it was too early in the year for them to be able to live off the country. Julian's failure in attack, however, was eclipsed 15 years later by a still more serious failure in defence.

The battle of Adrianople (9 August 378), the Black Day of the late-Roman army, has been seen as a victory of cavalry over infantry and a revolution in warfare. Limited offensives had failed to contain the Goths who had overrun the Balkans, so the eastern emperor Valens decided to mobilize his full force and assume active command. Unfortunately he decided to fight before his nephew Gratian arrived with the Western army, perhaps because he was jealous of him, or because faulty intelligence had underestimated Gothic numbers. As at Strasbourg, the Roman army made a long march in the heat of the day and arrived, hungry and thirsty, within sight of the Gothic wagon circle. There was a delay while the Goths renewed negotiations, if only to gain time for the return of their cavalry which was out foraging. Meanwhile the Roman army advanced in column, its right wing almost engaged, the left wing still coming up as fast as it could. A truce was being negotiated, when some Roman cavalry, presumably on the right wing, made an insubordinate attack which collapsed. Fighting became general, and at this moment the Gothic cavalry arrived. Ammianus unfortunately does not say where its first blow fell, only that the Roman left wing had now reached the wagons, when 'it was deserted by the rest of the cavalry, overwhelmed by weight of numbers like a collapsing rampart, and thrown back, leaving the infantry exposed'. Thus outflanked, the Roman infantry 'looked round and saw no means of escape', its formation was broken in a bloody mêlée, and the survivors were pursued until darkness fell. Two-thirds of the army was killed. Ammianus observes that the losses were equalled only by Cannae (216 BC). Here, too, the Roman cavalry had been driven from the field and the legions enveloped and crushed. The principal cause of disaster at Adrianople seems to have been the decision to assault the wagon circle – effectively a field fortification – while the enemy's powerful cavalry was uncommitted. This 'decision' was forced upon Valens by the undisciplined and incompetent cavalry on his right wing. The left wing, advancing hastily, was caught unprepared by a devastating charge on its flank or even from behind, leaving the infantry, already deployed in a crescent round the wagon circle and fighting hand-to-hand, fatally trapped. We know that there were post-mortems after the disaster, and that cowardice or lack of training were held responsible. This would seem to be a fair comment – on the Roman cavalry which lost the battle.

Collapse in the West

The trained infantry lost at Adrianople could not be replaced. The new emperor, Theodosius, was forced to settle the Goths in the Danubian provinces under their own chieftains. It was a fatal decision, but he had no choice. When he died in 395, they were soon on the move again – westward, against an empire already weakened by civil wars. For a time Stilicho, one of Theodosius' generals and the guardian of his son Honorius, kept them in check, but he was lethally discredited by the collapse of the Rhine frontier at the end of 406, when east German peoples, followed by the Alamanns and Franks, flooded into Gaul and Spain. Britain was cut off, for ever. Surviving Gallic garrisons were incorporated into the mobile army, a desperate expedient, since they were now of poor quality. The Visigoths invaded Italy; when their demands were ignored by Honorius, they sacked Rome (410). Effective power was in the hands of the Western commanders-in-chief, notably Constantius, Aetius and Ricimer, who tried to retain Italy and a few footholds by playing one invader off against another, but the last real hope of recovery disappeared in 429, when the Vandals crossed the Straits of Gibraltar to pursue an orgy of conquest across the last intact Western provinces. Carthage fell in 439, and Roman Africa became a Germanic kingdom. In 444 Valentinan II, the grandson of Theodosius, admitted economic and military bankruptcy. The taxpayers were exhausted, and could no longer provide the Western army with food and clothing: 'Unless the soldiers should be supported by trading, which is unworthy and shameful for an armed man, they can scarcely be vindicated from the peril of hunger or from the destruction of cold . . . [yet] if we require these expenses from the landowner, in addition to the expenses which he furnishes, such an exaction of taxes would extinguish his last tenuous resources'. Aetius' defeat of the Huns in Gaul (451) was only achieved with the help of the Visigoths, and did not save Italy from invasion the following year. Although Aetius was discredited, he was too powerful to be deposed, so Valentinian murdered him with his own hands. A few months later (455), the emperor himself was assassinated in revenge, and in the

COMPARATIVE PLANS OF SOME LATE-ROMAN FORTIFICATIONS

right
Albano legionary fortress *(after Benario)*
Albano, SW of Rome: the surviving circuit walls of the legionary fortress, the only one in Italy, built by Septimius Severus in the early 3rd century for his new 'mobile' legion, the Second *Parthica*.

below
Scarborough coastal tower *(after Rowntree)*
Scarborough: one of a series of towers built on headlands of the North Yorkshire coast in the 4th century, each of them protected by a walled and ditched enclosure. They kept watch for seaborne raiders.

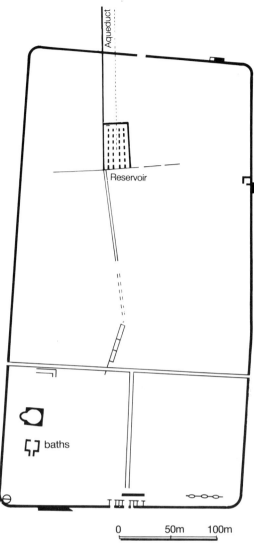

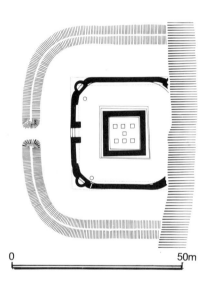

0   50m

0   50m   100m

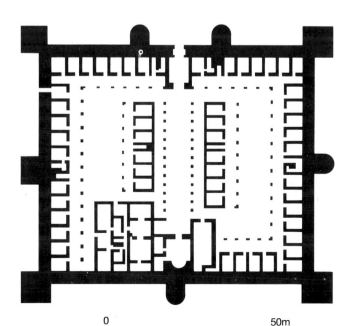

left
Dionysias fort *(after Schwartz and Wild)*
Dionysias in the Egyptian Fayûm: a fort with the massive walls and enfilading towers typical of late-Roman fortification, built in the late 3rd century, where Flavius Abinnaeus was commandant in the 340s.

right
The palace of Diocletian at Split *(after Marasović)*
Diocletian retired in 305 to a fortified palace on the Adriatic, which with its curtain wall and enfilading angle towers resembles the forts and fortresses being built on the frontiers.

0   50m

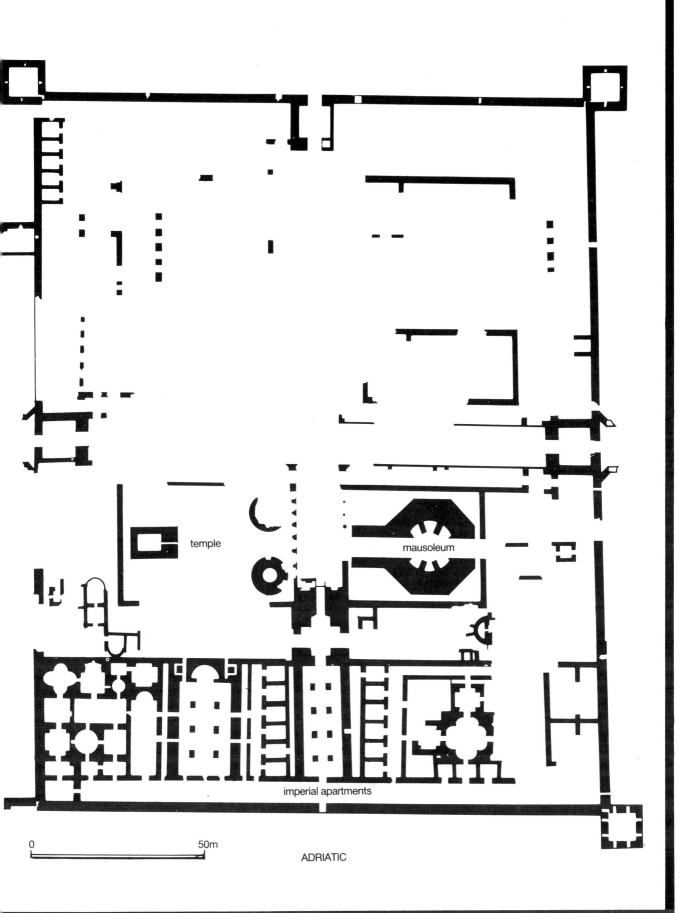

temple

mausoleum

imperial apartments

0   50m

ADRIATIC

ensuing confusion the Vandals descended on Rome and sacked it once more.

The Eastern empire survived the 5th-century crisis. It was economically stronger and, with the exception of its territory in Europe, was virtually untroubled by invasion. It even intervened from time to time in the West, but without lasting effect. The Western empire, however, was bleeding to death as it lost the territory which alone could support a regular army and was forced to rely increasingly on palsied diplomacy and German *federati*. Not long before the now-barbarian army of Italy deposed the last Western emperor (476), we catch a glimpse of the last *limitanei* on the upper Danube. The Ninth Cohort of Batavians, the garrison of Passau (to which it gave its name), sent some men to Italy to draw back-pay for the unit. No more was heard of them, until their bodies came floating down the river. When Abinnaeus' old fort was evacuated, the last troops even closed the gate behind them; but the Batavians simply melted into the civilian population. 'While the Roman empire still stood', our source comments, 'soldiers were maintained with public pay in many towns for the defence of the frontier, but when that custom lapsed the military units were abolished with the frontier'.

Conclusion

A pagan critic of Constantine accuses him of reversing the strategy of Diocletian, which had made the frontiers impregnable: most of the army was withdrawn from the frontiers and stationed in cities which did not need a garrison, a burden for the cities concerned, and demoralizing for the men themselves. This is a wilful misunderstanding of the strategy of the late-Roman Empire. It was impossible to hold the frontier line everywhere against all attack, since external enemies retained the initiative and could always concentrate superior forces locally. Instead, the screen of garrisons in the frontier zone would, at least in theory, check minor incursions and hinder major invasions by holding fortified towns and supply-bases and strongpoints of all kinds along the lines of communication. This would protect the civil population (tax-payers, if nothing else), deny food to the enemy, and gain time to concentrate mobile forces for counter-attack. The invaders would either be forced to disperse over the countryside to forage, where they could be hunted down piecemeal by small mobile detachments; or if they massed together, they could be brought to battle, when the Roman mobile army, better armed and disciplined and regularly provisioned, had a good chance of winning against numerical odds. Once defeated in the field, invaders could be pursued into their homeland, and reprisals would follow until they made peace. For the emperor himself, this strategy had an important side-effect: he could retain personal control of the empire's best troops and insure himself against usurpers.

The strategy also had its weaknesses. Much depended, as always in Roman imperial history, upon the emperor's ability and the loyalty it commanded. Slowness of communications – no army, however 'mobile', could move faster than the 15-20 miles its infantry could march in a day – led to the multiplication of mobile armies. This shortened the Empire's reaction-time, but divided its strength and increased the risk of an usurpation. Like Tiberius (14-37), the late-Roman emperor was holding a wolf by the ears. Despite the premium on mobility, the Romans still failed, as they had always done, to achieve a decisive superiority over their enemies in cavalry. Inactive troops, whether they were *limitanei* or *comitatenses* in reserve, were always liable to deteriorate. For a complex of reasons, such as the number and variety of its enemies, the aspects of its social system that we loosely call 'corruption', and the burden on a pre-industrial economy of filling so many 'idle mouths', the late-Roman Empire lacked the reserves to recover from a major defeat, as the Republic had done after Cannae. But even if we overlook the survival of East Rome, we must credit Diocletian, Constantine and Valentinian with achieving a military equilibrium that might once have seemed beyond hope.

PRINCIPAL SOURCES

Archaeology

Many late-Roman forts have been excavated, providing evidence of reduced unit size and changing methods of defence, indeed of emphasis on defence, and also (but less abundantly than for the early Empire) evidence of how soldiers lived, and of their arms and equipment. Late-Roman soldiers are depicted on many surviving objects, including mosaics, carved stone and ivory, silver plate and other domestic items.

Inscriptions and papyri

These, too, are less abundant than for the early Empire, but still valuable. Some inscriptions record building work, but many are gravestones and coffins of dead soldiers. Papyri are 'papers' preserved in the dry soil of Egypt, letters, legal documents, administrative documents and records.

The Theodosian Code (AD 438)

This great collection of extracts from imperial legislation since AD 312, arranged by subject, was compiled by order of the emperor Theodosius II. One of its 16 books is devoted to the administration of the army.

The Notitia Dignitatum (c. AD 395)

This illustrated 'list of high offices' dates from the division of the Empire between a Western and an Eastern emperor in AD 395, but is known to us from indirect but apparently accurate copies made in the 15th century. The chapters devoted to the army's various generals list the units they commanded and, where applicable, the units' stations, providing a detailed 'order of battle'. It is preserved with an illustrated treatise of c. AD 368-9, by an unknown author, which recommends various new weapons and military reforms.

Ammianus Marcellinus (c. AD 330- c. 395)

A Greek-speaking officer who served in the Roman army during the 350s and early 360s, who in retirement at Rome 30 years later wrote a history in Latin which continued Tacitus down to 378. The surviving books (for 353-78) are the major source of our knowledge of the secular history of the period; the military narrative is detailed and well-informed.

Other writings

A mass of literature, much of it Christian, survives from the late-Roman period; it contains many incidental allusions to military affairs, which can be pieced together into a mosaic, with many pieces missing. It includes church historians and minor Greek and Latin historians who can be used to supplement and extend Ammianus Marcellinus. Military success is emphasized in 'panegyrics', speeches in praise of emperors, including the poems Claudian wrote for Stilicho and the emperor Julian's own writings. The military theorist Vegetius, who vainly advocated a revival of the classical legion, probably wrote his account of its training and organization between AD 383-92.

BIBLIOGRAPHY

The Beginnings of Warfare

Breasted, J. H., *Ancient Records of Egypt*. University of Chicago Press, Chicago, 1906.
Luckenbill, D. D., *Ancient Records of Assyria and Babylonia*. University of Chicago Press, Chicago, 1926; reprinted Greenwood Press, New York, 1968.
Yadin, Y., *The Art of Warfare in Biblical Lands*. Thames & Hudson, London, 1963.

The Assyrians

Madhloom, T., *The Chronology of Neo-Assyrian Art*. Athlone Press, London, 1970.
Madhloom, T., 'Assyrian Siege-engines', *Sumer* 21, pp. 9-15. Baghdad, 1965.
Reade, J. E., 'The Neo-Assyrian Court and Army: Evidence from the Sculptures', *Iraq* 34, pp.87-112. London, 1972.
Salonen, A., *Die Waffen der alten Mesopotamier* (Studia Orientalia 33). Helsinki, 1965.
Wiseman, D. J. (ed.), 'Warfare in the Ancient Near East', *Iraq* 25/2. London, 1963.
Yadin, Y., *The Art of Warfare in Biblical Lands*. Thames & Hudson, London, 1963.

Hoplite Warfare

Adcock, F. E., *The Greek and Macedonian Art of War*. Berkeley & Los Angeles, 1957.
Anderson, J. K., *Military Theory and Practice in the Age of Xenophon*. Berkeley & Los Angeles, 1970.
Connolly, P., *Greece and Rome at War*. London, 1981.
Holladay, A. J., 'Hoplites and Heresies', *Journal of Hellenic Studies*, 102, pp.94-7, 1982.
Lazenby, J. F., *The Spartan Army*. Warminster, 1985.
Pritchett, W. K., *The Greek State at War* I-IV. Berkeley & Los Angeles, 1971-1983.
Salmon, J. 'Political hoplites?', *Journal of Hellenic Studies* 97, pp.85-92, 1977.
Sekunda, N., *The Ancient Greeks*. London, 1986.
Snodgrass, A. M., *Arms and Armour of the Greeks*. London, 1967.
Whatley, N., 'On the possibility of reconstructing Marathon and other ancient battles', *Journal of Hellenic Studies* 84, pp.119-34, 1964.

For translations of Herodotus, *The Histories,* Thucydides, *History of the Peloponnesian War,* Xenophon, *A History of My Times,* and many of Plutarch's *Lives,* see Penguin Classics. The essay on *'The Constitution of the Lacedaimonians',* attributed to Xenophon, is included in the volume *'Plutarch on Sparta'.*

The Persians

Balcer, J. M., *Sparta by The Bitter Sea: Imperial Reaction in Western Anatolia*. Scholars Press, 1984.
Burn, A. R., *Persia and the Greeks: the Defence of the West c.546-478 BC.* (Second Edition, with a postscript by D. M. Lewis.) Stanford University Press, 1984.
The Cambridge History of Iran, Volume 2: The Median and Achaemenian Periods, edited by Ilya Gershevitch. Cambridge University Press, 1985.
Cook, J. M., *The Persian Empire*. J. M. Dent & Sons Ltd, 1983.
Lewis, D. M, *Sparta and Persia*. E. J. Brill, Leiden, 1977.
Olmstead, A. T., *History of the Persian Empire*. University of Chicago Press, 1948, still available in reprint and paperback, Phoenix Books.

Alexander The Great:

Devine, A. M., 'Embolon: A Study in Tactical Terminology'. *Phoenix* 37, pp.201-217, 1983.
Devine, A. M., 'Demythologizing the Battle of the Granicus'. *Phoenix* 40, pp.265-278, 1986.
Devine, A. M., 'The Strategies of Alexander the Great and Darius III in the Issus Campaign (333 BC)', *Ancient World* 12, pp.25-38, 1985.
Devine, A. M., 'Grand Tactics at the Battle of Issus', *Ancient World* 12, pp.39-59, 1985.
Devine, A. M., 'The Battle of Gaugamela: A Tactical and Source-Critical Study', *Ancient World* 13, pp.87-116, 1986.
Devine, A. M., 'The Battle of the Hydaspes: A Tactical and Source-Critical Study', *Ancient World* 16, pp.91-113, 1987.
Engels, D. W., *Alexander the Great and the Logistics of the Macedonian Army*. Berkeley and Los Angeles, 1978.
Fuller, J. F. C., *The Generalship of Alexander the Great*. London, 1958.
Griffith, G. T., *The Mercenaries of the Hellenistic World*. Cambridge, 1935; Chicago, 1984.
Hammond, N. G. L., *Alexander the Great: King, Commander and Statesman*. London, 1981.
Hammond, N. G. L. and Griffith, G. T., *A History of Macedonia*, volume 2. Oxford, 1979.
Marsden, E. W., *The Campaign of Gaugamela*. Liverpool, 1964.
Markle, M. M., 'The Macedonian Sarissa, Spear, and Related Armor', *American Journal of Archaeology* 81, pp.323-339, 1977.
Markle, M. M., 'Weapons from the Cemetery at Vergina and Alexander's Army', in *Megas Alexandros*, pp.243-267 and plates I-VIII, Thessaloniki, 1980.
Romane, P., 'Alexander's Siege of Tyre', *Ancient World* 16, pp.79-90, 1987.
Tarn, W.W., *Alexander the Great*. Cambridge, 1948; Chicago, 1985.

Hellenistic Warfare

Devine, A. M., 'Diodorus' Account of the Battle of Paraitacene', *Ancient World* 12, pp.75-86, 1985.
Devine, A. M., 'Diodorus' Account of the Battle of Gabiene', *Ancient World* 12, pp.87-96, 1985.
Devine, A. M., 'Diodorus' Account of the Battle of Gaza', *Acta Classica* 27, pp.31-40, 1984.

The Early Roman Army
The Roman Army in the Age of Polybius

Connolly, P., *Greece and Rome at War*. Macdonald, 1981.
Gabba, E., *Republican Rome, the Army and the Allies*. Blackwell, 1976.
Keppie, L., *The Making of the Roman Army*. Batsford, 1984.
Lazenby, J. F., *Hannibal's War*. Aris and Phillips, 1978.
Salmon, E. T., *Roman Colonisation under the Republic*. Thames and Hudson, 1969; also *Samnium and the Samnites'*. Cambridge, 1967.
Scullard, H. H., *Scipio Africanus: Soldier and Politician*. Thames & Hudson, 1970.
Toynbee, A. J., *Hannibal's Legacy*. Oxford, 1965.
Walbank, F. W., *A Historical Commentary on Polybius*. Oxford 1957-1979.

The Late-Roman Army

Ancient Sources

Ammianus Marcellinus, trans. W. Hamilton.
Penguin Classics, 1986.
Abinnaeus Archive, The, ed. by H. I. Bell and others. Oxford,
1962.
De Rebus Bellicus, ed. by R. Ireland, M. W. C. Hassall. Oxford,
1979.
Notitia Dignitatum, Aspects of the, ed. by R. Goodburn, P.
Bartholomew. Oxford, 1976.
Papyri from Panopolis, ed. by T. C. Skeat. Dublin, 1964.
Theodosian Code, The, trans. C. Pharr. Princeton, 1952.

Secondary Literature

Ferrill, A., *The Fall of the Roman Empire: the Military Explanation*.
London, 1986.
Hoffman, D., *Das spätrömische Bewegungsheer*. Dusseldorf,
1969/70.
Johnson, S., *Late Roman Fortifications*. London, 1983.
Jones, A. H. M., *The Later Roman Empire*, pp.284-602. Oxford,
1964.
Luttwak, E. N., *The Grand Strategy of the Roman Empire*.
Baltimore/London, 1976.
MacMullen, R., *Soldier and Civilian in the Later Roman Empire*.
Harvard, 1963.
Williams, S., *Diocletian and the Roman Recovery*. London, 1985.

The Roman Army of the Later Republic

Brunt, P. A., 'The Army and the Land in the Roman
Revolution', *Journal of Roman Studies*, 52, pp.69-86, 1962.
Brunt, P. A., *Italian Manpower, 225 BC-AD 14*. Oxford, 1971.
Connolly, P., *Greece and Rome at War*. London, 1981.
Gabba, E., *Republican Rome: the Army and the Allies*. Oxford,
1976.
Harmand, J., *Une campagne cesarienne: Alesia*. Paris, 1967.
Harmand, J., *L'armee et le soldat a Rome de 107 a 50 avant notre ere*.
Paris, 1967.

Keppie, L., *The Making of the Roman Army, From Republic to Empire*.
London, 1984, 1987.
Napoleon III, *Histoire de Jules Cesar: II. Guerre des Gaules*. Paris,
1865-66.
Parker, H. M. D., *The Roman Legions*. Oxford, 1928.
Ritterling, E., article 'legio', in *Real-encyclopadie des classischen
Altertumswissenschaft*, xii, pp.1211-1829. Berlin, 1925.
Saddington, D. B., *The Development of the Roman Auxiliary Forces
from Caesar to Vespasian (49 BC-AD 79)*. Harare, 1982.
Smith, R. E., *Service in the Post-Marian Roman Army*. Manchester,
1958.
Warry, J., *Warfare in the Classical World*. London, 1980.

The Empire

Baatz, D., 'Recent finds of ancient artillery', *Britannia* 9, pp.1-17,
1978.
Birley, E., *The Roman Army. Papers 1929-1986*. Amsterdam,
1988.
Breeze, D. J. and Dobson, B., *Hadrian's Wall* 3rd edn. London,
1987.
Cheesman, G. L., *The Auxilia of the Roman Imperial Army*. Oxford,
1914.
Connolly, P., *Greece and Rome at War*. London, 1981.
Holder, P. A., *Studies in the Auxilia of the Roman Army from Augustus
to Trajan*. Oxford, 1980.
Johnson, A., *Roman Forts*. London, 1983.
Mann, J. C., *Legionary Recruitment and Veteran Settlement during the
Principate*. London, 1983.
Marsden, E. W., *Greek and Roman Artillery, Historical Development*.
Oxford, 1969.
Maxfield, V. A., 'The Frontiers – Mainland Europe', in *The
Roman World* (ed. J. Wacher), pp.139-193. London,
1987.
Parker, H. M. D., *The Roman Legions*. Oxford, 1928.
Robinson, H. R., *The Armour of Imperial Rome*. London, 1975.
Saddington, D. B., *The Development of the Roman Auxiliary Forces
from Augustus to Vespasian*. Harare, 1982.
Starr, C. G., *The Roman Imperial Navy* 2nd edn. Cambridge,
1960.
Webster, G., *The Roman Imperial Army* 3rd edn. London, 1985.

ACKNOWLEDGMENTS

Aerofilms, Boreham Wood 17 bottom
Ashmolean Museum, Oxford 82
Audio Visual Centre, University of Newcastle upon Tyne 58
Bayerische Staatsbibliothek, Munich 234, 235
F. Benitez 15
John Boardman, *Greek gems and finger rings*. Thames & Hudson,
London, 1970 92
A. H. Breasted, 'The battle of Kadesh', *University of Chicago
decennial publications*, first series, V, 1904 34
British Museum, London 37 bottom, 38, 42, 49, 69, 89, 96 left
Bulletin de correspondence hellénique, IV, 1880 78 top
H. Carter and P. E. Newberry, *The tomb of Thoutmôsis IV*, 1904
35 top, 35 bottom
Centre Belge de Recherches Archéologiques à Apamée – Marc
Balty 239 left
Peter Connolly 115 top, 115 centre, 115 bottom, 136, 148
J. C. Coulston, Newcastle upon Tyne 213
Deutsches Archäologisches Institut, Athens 227
C. M. Dixon, Canterbury 6, 57, 78 bottom, 107, 111 bottom,
142, 212, 219
Michel Durr 99
Egypt Exploration Society 28, 226
Werner Forman Archive, London 37 top, 48, 87
Photographie Giraudon, Paris 23
Shelagh Gregory 229 top, 229 bottom
Hirmer Verlag, Munich 20 top, 20 bottom, 26, 32 left, 32 right,
55 bottom, 60,, 75
Michael Holford, Loughton 22, 43, 50, 55 top, 59, 98, 139 top,
206

Istanbul Arkeoloji Müzeleri 130 bottom
Jericho Excavation Fund 17 top
John Lazenby 79
Mansell – Alinari 126 right, 177, 190, 197, 200, 207, 209 top,
209 centre, 209 bottom
Mansell – Anderson 111 top
Bildarchiv Foto Marburg 154 top, 154 centre, 154 bottom, 171
left, 171 right, 172
Münzen Kabinett, Staatliche Museen zu Berlin 130 top
Musées Nationaux, Paris 19, 96 right
Museo Arqueológico Nacional, Madrid 153 top
Novosti Press Agency, London 126 left
Georges Perrot and Charles Chipiez *History of Art in Persia*,
London, 1982 83
Römisch-Germanisches Museum, Cologue 239 right
Römisch-Germanisches Zentralmuseum, Mainz 167
Scala, Antella 106, 138
Trinity College Library, Cambridge 241
Tyne and Wear Museums Service 218
Trevor Watkins 16
Wellesley College Museum, Wellesley, Massachusetts 73
Yale University Art Gallery, New Haven, Connecticut 93,
240

The illustration on page 241 is reproduced by permission of
the Master and Fellows of Trinity College, Cambridge.

The photograph on page 218 of the reconstructed west gate of
the Arbeia Roman Fort, South Shields is reproduced by
permission of the Tyne and Wear Museums Service.

INDEX